327.73
R315 OS26R

DATE DUE

RETREAT FROM EMPIRE?
The First Nixon Administration

AMERICA AND THE WORLD
Volume II

Published in Collaboration with
The Washington Center of Foreign Policy Research
School of Advanced International Studies
The Johns Hopkins University

RETREAT FROM EMPIRE?

THE FIRST NIXON ADMINISTRATION

Robert E. Osgood

Robert W. Tucker

Francis E. Rourke

Herbert S. Dinerstein

Laurence W. Martin

David P. Calleo

Benjamin M. Rowland

George Liska

THE JOHNS HOPKINS UNIVERSITY PRESS

Baltimore and London

The Johns Hopkins University Press, Baltimore, Maryland 21218
The Johns Hopkins University Press Ltd., London

Library of Congress Catalog Number 72–12359
ISBN 0–8018–1493–6 (clothbound)
ISBN 0–8018–1499–5 (Paperbound)
Manufactured in the United States of America

Originally published, 1973
Johns Hopkins Paperbacks edition, 1973

Library of Congress Cataloging in Publication Data will be
found on the last printed page of this book.

CONTENTS

BIOGRAPHICAL NOTES

DAVID P. CALLEO, Professor of European Studies and Director of European Studies Programs at The Johns Hopkins School for Advanced International Studies, is also a Research Associate of the Washington Center of Foreign Policy Research and an Associate Fellow and Trustee of Johnathan Edwards College, Yale University. His publications include *Europe's Future: The Grand Alternative, Coleridge and the Idea of the Modern State, The Atlantic Fantasy,* and (with Benjamin Rowland) *America and the World Political Economy.*

HERBERT S. DINERSTEIN is Professor of Soviet Studies at The Johns Hopkins University School of Advanced International Studies and Research Associate of the Washington Center of Foreign Policy Research. Since receiving his doctorate in Russian history at Harvard University in 1943, he has published *Communism and the Russian Peasant, War and the Soviet Union, Intervention Against Communism: Fifty Years of Soviet Foreign Policy,* and articles in the professional journals. He is now engaged in a study of Soviet policy in Latin America.

GEORGE LISKA, Professor of Political Science at The Johns Hopkins University and its School of Advanced International Studies, is Research Associate of the Washington Center of Foreign Policy Research. Among his latest publications are *Nations in Alliance, Imperial America, Alliances and the Third World, War and Order,* and *States in Evolution* (forthcoming). Born in Czechoslovakia in 1922, Professor Liska came to this country in 1949, after briefly serving in his native country's Ministry for Foreign Affairs.

LAURENCE W. MARTIN is Director of War Studies at the University of London. From 1961–64 he was Research Associate of the Washington Center of Foreign Policy Research and Associate Professor of Political Science at The Johns Hopkins University School of Advanced International Studies. He is author of *Peace Without Victory*, co-author of *The Anglo-American Tradition in Foreign Affairs*, and editor of *Neutralism and Nonalignment: The New States in World Affairs*.

ROBERT E. OSGOOD is Director of the Washington Center of Foreign Policy Research and Professor of American Foreign Policy at The Johns Hopkins School for Advanced International Studies. In 1969/70, he served on the staff of the National Security Council. His books include *Limited War: The Challenge to American Strategy*, *NATO: The Entangling Alliance*, *Force, Order, and Justice* (with Robert W. Tucker), *Alliances and American Foreign Policy*, and *The Weary and the Wary: US and Japanese Security Policies in Transition*.

FRANCIS E. ROURKE is Professor of Political Science at The Johns Hopkins University. His major field of academic interest is administration and public policy. Publications by Professor Rourke which have a special relevance for foreign affairs are *Secrecy and Publicity: Dilemmas of Democracy*, *Bureaucratic Power in National Politics*, *Bureaucracy, Politics, and Public Policy*, and *Bureaucracy and American Foreign Policy*.

BENJAMIN ROWLAND, a graduate of Yale University, is currently an instructor at the Bologna Center of The Johns Hopkins School for Advanced International Studies. He will soon complete his work for the PhD in the International Affairs program of The School for Advanced International Studies. From 1965 to 1968 he served with the Peace Corps in Colombia and was an assistant director of the Peace Corps training program. He is a co-author (with David Calleo) of *America and the World Political Economy*.

ROBERT W. TUCKER is Professor of Political Science and Director of International Studies at The Johns Hopkins University. He is also a member of the faculty of The Johns Hopkins University School of Advanced International Studies and a Research Associate of the Washington Center of Foreign Policy Research. His previous publications include *The Just War*, *Force, Order, and Justice* (with Robert E. Osgood), *Nation or Empire?*, *The Radical Left and American Foreign Policy*, and *A New Isolationism*.

RETREAT FROM EMPIRE?
The First Nixon Administration

1

INTRODUCTION:
THE NIXON DOCTRINE AND STRATEGY

Robert E. Osgood

Continuity Amid Change

In the first volume of *America and the World*,[1] written at the end of President Johnson's Administration, we sought to establish the historical and analytical basis for answering the question: What will be the future pattern of American foreign policy? How new and how familiar is it likely to be? Writing at a time in which public and official disaffection with the Vietnam war seemed to portend drastic changes in America's foreign outlook, we wondered to what extent the reaction to the war would result in a reaction against the general foreign policy from which America's involvement sprang.

To answer that question we had to look beyond Vietnam. We had to view the war in Vietnam as an incident—to be sure, an exceedingly important one—in a much larger drama: the expansion of American power and involvements in the world since the onset of the cold war. This perspective called for the identification and assessment of determining factors and trends in the international and domestic environment of America's foreign relations in the course of two momentous decades. Only with this historical perspective could we have a sound basis for speculating about the future of America's foreign relations. Only this perspective could indicate whether America's world role had reached the limits of its expansion, whether it would begin to contract as drastically as it had expanded, or whether it would become stabilized through adjustment to a new international environment.

Compared to speculations about the future of American foreign policy that were current four years ago, our historical approach resulted

[1] Sponsored by the Washington Center of Foreign Policy Research, under a grant from the Ford Foundation, volume 1 of *America and the World* (Baltimore: The Johns Hopkins University Press, 1970) and this second volume constitute the first two publications in a continuing assessment of American foreign policy. It is expected that a new volume in the series will be published at the end of each presidential term.

1

in a greater emphasis on continuity amid change. There can be no doubt that in the four years of the first Nixon Administration significant changes have taken place in America's world outlook, in the pattern of international politics, and in American policy. The American rapprochement with China is evidence enough. Yet, looking at the basic structure of power in the world and at the objectives and strategy of American policy as a whole, we must say that our original emphasis on continuity amid change seems confirmed by developments. Again, our interpretation contrasts with more extreme appraisals in the United States and abroad. Indeed, it contrasts somewhat with the Nixon Administration's own claims to innovation. On the other hand, if one looks beyond this transitional period to a far more speculative future, it may be that a limited readjustment of American foreign policy has strengthened certain trends in the international environment which will change America's position in the world in ways that far exceed the expectations of the current policy-making community.

In this volume we address the same fundamental questions of continuity and change as in volume 1 of *America and the World,* but we do so with the advantage of the evidence of four years of a new administration's efforts to formulate and execute a revised foreign policy. Since 1968 the basic direction of America's foreign relations has been clarified by several developments:

1. The Vietnam war no longer dominates America's international outlook and policy. This is partly because American combat troops have been withdrawn but also because the war has been partially detached from America's relations with China and the Soviet Union, and, at the same time, prospectively brought within the context of tripolar U.S.-Sino-Soviet diplomatic maneuvers for the purposes of a settlement.

2. The Nixon Administration has explicitly defined the principal thrust of American foreign policy in what it calls an "era of negotiation." Its occasional rhetorical and conceptual flourishes, the unavoidable ambiguity of official statements of policy principles, and the claims of novelty and profundity that new administrations always make for their policies should not conceal the fact that this administration has been unusually articulate and substantive in presenting the outlines and rationale of its foreign policy, notably in the president's annual reports to Congress (*U.S. Foreign Policy for the 1970's*) and in Henry Kissinger's press briefings.

3. On the basis of this announced policy, there has been enough

time for the U.S. government to act, and for foreign governments to react, in order to resolve many of the ambiguities of written and spoken formulations and to indicate the scope of immediate changes in international politics.

These developments have clarified the essential features of what one might call America's post-Vietnam policy. Therefore, we are in a better position than four years ago not only to gauge the nature of American foreign policy for the next four years but also to make critical appraisals and to consider alternatives. Our basic task, however, is still analysis, not prescription.

Retrenchment Without Disengagement

From the vantage point of 1972, what appears to be the essence of American foreign policy as the Nixon Administration has formulated and executed it? Clearly, this policy goes beyond the Nixon Doctrine, which was essentially a rationale for retrenchment.[2] It encompasses a reasonably coherent conception of the patterns and modes of international politics and their relationship to America's position in the structure of international power, which could more properly be called the Nixon Strategy.

In its view of America's position in the world, the essential continuity of the administration's strategy with the past is evident. The United States, it affirms, must continue to define its broadest aim as the achievement of an international order congenial to American values, an aim that transcends specific tangible interests in various parts of the world. Moreover, it asserts that the United States' active

[2] President Nixon's characterization of his policy of retrenchment as a "doctrine" presumably arises from the desire to dramatize its contribution to American history by analogies to the Monroe Doctrine and the Truman Doctrine; but as a guiding principle of policy and action, it obviously suffers (or, possibly depending on one's view, enjoys) a lack of coherence by comparison. Official efforts to clarify the meaning of the Nixon Doctrine have stressed three guidelines, first delineated in the president's Guam press conference on November 3, 1969, which should govern America's relaxation of material and political involvement in behalf of other states: (1) "The United States will keep all of its treaty commitments." (2) "We shall provide a shield if a nuclear power threatens the freedom of a nation allied with us or of a nation whose survival we consider vital to our security." (3) "In cases involving other types of aggression we shall furnish military and economic assistance when requested in accordance with our treaty commitments. But we shall look to the nation directly threatened to assume the primary responsibility of providing the manpower for its defense." Richard M. Nixon, *U.S. Foreign Policy for the 1970's*, A Report to the Congress, February 25, 1971, pp. 12–14.

participation and leadership in world politics is the *sine qua non* of this international order.

In this international order, it affirms, America's major concern must be the relationship between the two superpowers and the relationships among them and the major Western European states, Japan, and China, because these are the states that have the greatest power to act and therefore the greatest responsibility for peace. The minimum rule of order governing their relations is that adversaries should refrain from changing the status quo by armed force. Adversaries will continue to project influence, pursue specific interests, and seek general political goals in competition with each other, but they must do so in ways that do not threaten a competitor's status and interests so drastically as to undermine its sense of autonomy and security. Above all, the superpowers, who alone have the capacity to destroy each other, must moderate their relations according to their common interest in avoiding war, crises in the shadow of war, and excessive arms competition.[3]

For the 1970s the Nixon Administration has defined this international order, not in terms of the post-war vision of a Big Three condominium vindicating the United Nations or of the Truman Doctrine and containment checking aggressive international communism, but rather in the more neutral and somewhat academic terms of a "stable structure of relationships." The emphasis in this concept of order is less on establishing a military balance and stabilizing mutual military deterrence—for these are regarded as achievements of the past that need to be consolidated—than on orchestrating through diplomatic means a global *modus vivendi,* based on rules of mutual restraint, between the United States and the Soviet Union. This *modus vivendi* is to be elaborated through a network of agreements and understandings held together by the linkage of mutual accommodations ("If you do not accommodate me on this issue, don't expect me to accommodate you on all these other issues").[4] With the consolidation of this

---

[3] President Nixon and his Special Assistant for National Security Affairs, Henry Kissinger, were especially concerned with the consolidation of such rules of order at their meeting with Soviet leaders in Moscow in the summer of 1972. See, for example, the agreement reached on "Basic Principles of Relations between the United States of America and the Union of Soviet Socialist Republics" (signed May 29, 1972) and Kissinger's press conferences in Moscow on May 29. *Presidential Documents,* Weekly Compilation, volume 8, pp. 943–44, 951–64.

[4] On this concept of a *modus vivendi,* see Kissinger's explicit endorsement of "linkage" as an instrument for developing a stable structure of relationships based on rules of mutual restraint in his remarks at Moscow on June 15, 1972. (News Release, Department of State, Bureau of Public Affairs, June 20, 1972, p. 31.)

network, the administration hopes, the role of military concerns—the problems of military deterrence, strategy, and crises, which preoccupied the United States and its European allies in the "era of confrontation"—will recede, and the role of the more complicated but less dangerous problems of managing multipolar diplomatic coexistence will largely replace them.

The U.S.-Soviet *modus vivendi* is to be achieved within a more complex balance of power and influence in which the People's Republic of China will play a key role. The tactical elaboration of this tripolar relationship constitutes the major innovation of the Nixon Strategy. The administration sees Soviet fear of China's political rivalry and ideological heresy, and China's fear of Soviet military confrontation in the north and encirclement in the south, moving the Soviet Union toward a genuine detente with the United States and its European allies, while bringing China into the international diplomatic arena as a counterpoise to Soviet ambitions. The resulting moderation of Soviet behavior, it is hoped, will be matched by the normalization of China's foreign relations, as both states realize their great stake in the new pattern of international politics. Moreover, Sino-Soviet antipathy, if it can be kept within peaceful bounds, is expected not only to constrain both countries but also to give them an incentive to improve their relations with the United States.

Meanwhile, according to this outlook, the major West European allies and Japan, through the more active projection of their political influence and economic power and through their increased contributions to their own defense, will impose additional constraints upon communist ambitions and influence. They will be active participants in a more fluid diplomacy that cuts across the old polarized relationships, as America's new relations with the adversaries foster a less rigid framework of diplomatic play. The more active and self-reliant participation of America's allies on the central diplomatic stage will help blunt the sharp edges of international antagonism, and it will give them a stake in consolidating the new international order. On the other hand, the basic structure of their relationship to the United States and the communist adversaries is not expected to change. They will assume greater responsibilities but within the existing security frameworks. They will carry more of the burden of their defense, but they will not seek military independence from the United States. They will assert their own policies and prescriptions more actively; but, reinvigorated by their self-reliance, they will remain America's faithful and cooperative allies.

In this emerging structure of relationships, the United States, in

President Nixon's outlook, must maintain its influence in behalf of a great range of interests throughout the world. Foremost among these are its treaty commitments. For its own sake and for others the United States must not become a "helpless, pitiful giant." It must remain the keystone of international order. Indispensable to this role is the strength of its alliances in Western Europe and Japan. Under the aegis of a less paternalistic American leadership their vitality will be restored.

President Nixon described this structure of relationships as a five-power balance, in which the poles of power all check each other evenly and none gains an unacceptable unilateral advantage at the expense of another.[5] But judging from the full record of the president's words, policies, and actions, this is a somewhat misleading description of what he really had in mind. As every student of international politics knows, the balance of power comes in many historical forms and can mean many different things. Clearly, the Nixon Administration's conception of the balance of power is far from the

[5] President Nixon's first adumbration of this concept in remarks before news media executives in Kansas City, Missouri, on July 6, 1971, described the emerging structure of power in economic terms. "What we see as we look ahead 5, 10, and perhaps 15 years, we see five great economic superpowers: the United States, Western Europe, the Soviet Union, mainland China, and, of course, Japan. . . . [t]hese are the five that will determine the economic future and, because economic power will be the key to other kinds of power, the future of the world in other ways in the last third of this century." *Department of State Bulletin* (July 26, 1971), p. 96. In an interview in *Time* on January 3, 1972, he added the notion of even balance: "We must remember the only time in the history of the world that we have had any extended period of peace is when there has been balance of power. It is when one nation becomes infinitely more powerful in relation to its potential competitor that the danger of war arises. So I believe in a world in which the United States is powerful. I think it will be a safer world and a better world if we have a strong, healthy United States, Europe, Soviet Union, China, Japan, each balancing the other, not playing one against the other, an even balance." Only Chou En-lai seems to have been impressed by the first statement at the time (he quoted it from memory on Henry Kissinger's first visit to China). But many took note of the second statement, which was criticized by several experts as anachronistic and unrealistic: See, for example, Zbigniew Brzezinski, "The Balance of Power Delusion," *Foreign Policy* 7 (Summer, 1972), pp. 54–59; Stanley Hoffmann, "Weighing the Balance of Power," *Foreign Affairs* 50 (July, 1972), pp. 618–43; Alastair Buchan, "A World Restored?" *Foreign Affairs* 50 (July, 1972), pp. 644–59; George W. Ball, "We Are Playing a Dangerous Game with Japan," *New York Times Magazine*, June 25, 1972, pp. 10ff. The first but less critical description of President Nixon's concept of a pentagonal world, based on both Nixon's statements and on his purported admiration of De Gaulle, was written by James Chace, "The Five-Power World of Richard Nixon," *New York Times Magazine*, February 20, 1972, pp. 14ff.

classical conception, which corresponded only imperfectly with reality in any case. In the latter conception several states of approximately equal power, unrestrained by enduring political or ideological affinities but moved by a common interest in maintaining the international system in equilibrium, continually maneuver for limited advantages in such a way as to restrain each other from upsetting the equilibrium.

Compared to the full-scale military balance of power represented in the classical multipolar model, the Nixon Administration's conception of the balance is still bipolar, although it allows for considerably more fluidity of relations and diffusion of power than prevailed at the height of the cold war. Like its predecessors in the cold war, the Nixon Administration regards the crux of international order as peaceful co-existence between the still antithetical political systems and world views of the United States and the Soviet Union. Now, however, it postulates the moderating factor as not so much the application of military containment in a zero-sum game as the elaboration of a network of agreements and understandings from which both sides stand to gain. The primary objective of this balance of power system is not to create some abstract design of pentagonal or tripolar equilibrium. Like his predecessors, President Nixon is preoccupied with containing and moderating the behavior of the Soviet Union. His development of a tripolar relationship through rapprochement with China is a means to this end. The other two poles are in the same camp with the United States and remain U.S. military dependents.

The Nixon Administration, in fact, while capitalizing on an incipient tripolar diplomatic relationship, is almost as opposed as preceding administrations to a full-scale pentagonal world. To be sure, it might view with equanimity the emergence of a European defense community, even if such a community were to construct a "European" nuclear force around an Anglo-French nucleus. But it is not encouraging this development, which remains quite hypothetical. As for a Japanese military role beyond defense of the homeland, let alone a Japanese nuclear force, the administration is definitely opposed to them and has said so.[6]

There is seeming incongruity in the administration's advocating self-reliance for its allies yet opposing military independence for the only allies that could substantially take care of their own security. Apart

[6] See Henry Kissinger's press conference in Japan on June 12, 1972. *Washington Post*, June 13, 1972, p. A18.

from national pride, the Nixon Administration is moved by two familiar and compelling reasons for perpetuating U.S. preponderance in managing the military, and especially the nuclear, counterpoise against the communist adversaries: (1) only the United States has the requisite experience and capability to control the central military balance; (2) the emergence of independent military forces in Europe and Japan would lead to independent nuclear forces, which would undermine international order and endanger peace.

To these reasons another one, less compelling at the height of the cold war, has been added: the emergence of one or two new major centers of military decision would endanger the era of negotiation. Such a development, it is widely thought, would upset the military equilibrium and the whole set of stabilized bilateral relationships that underlie detente. The Soviet Union and China would regard a new military power in their region as contravening the conditions of a new era of diplomatic accommodation and maneuver within mutual restraints among adversaries. They would not be alone in this view.

This consideration is particularly pertinent to the logic of retrenchment, for the administration's ability to reduce America's burden of involvement *without undermining its global commitments and influence or the confidence of its allies* depends critically upon reducing the level of international tensions and the expectation of war with adversaries. The essence of the Nixon Strategy lies in fostering the international conditions under which this objective may be attained.

The compulsion to retrench, to alleviate America's material and political burden in supporting its commitments and other interests, is the driving force of the Nixon Strategy. The simple fact is that President Nixon feels compelled to do what the Eisenhower Administration aspired to do after the Korean war and what any president would try to do after a period of expanding military involvement and expenditures culminating in war—particularly when the war has been peculiarly unpopular and unsuccessful. He strives to extricate the United States from the war with as little loss of prestige as possible, reduce military expenditures and military manpower levels, and prevent or limit American involvement in similar wars in the future.

Accordingly, since 1968 the United States has transferred a steadily increasing burden of the Vietnam war to the South Vietnamese, while withdrawing American ground forces and seeking a diplomatic resolution of the conflict on progressively less demanding terms. Military retrenchment has cut most deeply into U.S. ground combat forces, partly in response to the fact that manpower costs consume about 60 percent of the defense budget. Consequently, general purpose forces have been cut to the level of 1964, before American troops became actively involved in Vietnam.

Consistent with the retrenchment of general purpose forces, the Nixon Administration has formulated more selective criteria for armed intervention overseas. The United States, according to this formulation, will protect allies or countries whose survival is considered vital to American security against aggression by nuclear powers (read, the Soviet Union and the People's Republic of China). But in other cases it will expect the country directly threatened to assume the primary responsibility for defending itself, while the United States confines itself to furnishing military and economic assistance in accordance with treaty commitments. Even in behalf of allies U.S. armed forces will not be expected to cope with insurgency. In the case of an overt conventional attack upon allies and others, the American government will determine its response according to the nature of its specific interests, its commitments, and the efforts of the victims of aggression to defend themselves rather than according to any generalized commitment to oppose armed aggression.

These measures of retrenchment constitute a significant adjustment to the realities of American power and interests as they are generally perceived under the sobering influence of the Vietnam agony. The adjustment, nonetheless, is intended to take place within a familiar distribution of power and relationships among the major states. It envisions the maintenance of America's dominant role in containing the Soviet Union—but at a lower level of effort, a diminished prospect of armed intervention, and with greater material assistance from allies. For the time being, moreover, military retrenchment applies almost entirely to the capabilities and objectives of ground forces that might intervene on the Asian mainland. In Western Europe President Nixon, in the face of Senatorial pressure for substantial withdrawals, has pledged to maintain American troops at about their present level for an indefinite period.

Thus, as far as America's role is concerned, the Nixon Strategy might be described as *military retrenchment without political disengagement*. For domestic as well as international political reasons the two facets are dependent on each other. The foundation of this strategy is a stabilized military balance with respect to the Soviet Union, since this is regarded as the basis for moderating Soviet behavior and consolidating detente. The consolidation of detente through a network of interdependent agreements and understandings, in turn, is seen as the condition that permits American retrenchment without jeopardizing the security or confidence of America's allies. At the same time, military retrenchment is expected to make America's global engagement acceptable at home—the indispensable condition for any successful policy.

In resolving to move from an "era of confrontation" to an "era of negotiation," President Nixon has reaffirmed the objective of containment which was avowed at the beginning of the cold war. In opening new diplomatic relations with China, negotiating a strategic arms limitation agreement with the Soviet Union, and projecting mutual balanced force agreements in Europe, he has acted upon this reaffirmation to an extent that was impossible before the Soviet achievement of strategic parity, the accentuation of the Sino-Soviet split to the point of border warfare and the massing of Soviet arms on the Chinese border, and the winding down of the Vietnam war. The Nixon Strategy, however, is neither a repetition of cold war containment nor the construction of a full-scale multipolar world. It is essentially a diplomatic strategy, looking toward a global *modus vivendi* with the Soviet Union. Its indispensable foundation is the maintenance of America's political engagement, particularly in behalf of its major allies, at a lower level of effort and a lower risk of armed involvement. This presupposes greater political and economic independence on the part of allies, but within the framework of America's continued preponderance in the management of their security, for which they will contribute an increased share of the collective defense burden.

The Revised Premises of Policy

If the Nixon Strategy, though marked by considerable diplomatic innovation, depends on structural continuity in political-military relationships, it nonetheless reflects a significant change of foreign outlook. This outlook embodies premises about the efficacy of American power, the intensity of the communist threat, and the nature of America's vital interests which constitute a revision of the familiar cold-war consensus no less far-reaching than the revision of diplomatic strategy.

The Nixon Administration has none of the exuberant confidence in the capacity of the United States to intervene against a wide spectrum of local attacks and insurgencies in the third world that moved the Kennedy Administration. Rather, it makes a special point of contrasting its limited view of the efficacy of America's military power in the third world with President Kennedy's views. Responding to the frustrations of the Vietnam war, it takes the position, in effect, that if a besieged country cannot save itself with American economic and military assistance, American troops cannot save it—at least, not at a tolerable cost.

In a more striking revision of the cold-war consensus the Nixon Administration has drastically downgraded the communist military threat in the third world—most significantly, the Chinese military threat. Accepting a view that had already gained currency in the intelligence community and among American Sinologists, the administration concluded that China is neither able nor willing to extend its influence beyond its borders by military means and that it will only resort to war when it sees the defense of the homeland threatened, as in the case of General MacArthur's drive toward the Yalu in the Korean war. The disruptions of the Cultural Revolution contributed to this revised estimate, but the most important factor was the accentuation of the Sino-Soviet split. President Nixon was quick to appreciate the resulting political constraints on China and the diplomatic opportunities for constraining Moscow through rapprochement with Peking.

Recognition of the implications of the Sino-Soviet split has diminished the prevailing estimate of the communist military threat in another respect too. It considerably qualifies the disposition, which became ingrained after the Korean war, to regard communist aggression or the threat of communist aggression anywhere as a prelude to a chain of aggressions or "falling dominoes," leading to World War III in a process analogous to the expansion of fascism before World War II. To be sure, the Nixon Administration, like its predecessors, is acutely conscious of the danger that the Soviet leaders may interpret an apparent lack of American resolve to back up national interests with force in one part of the world as an invitation to act with impunity against American interests in another part of the world, thereby producing a confrontation of the superpowers. In this respect, maintaining the credibility of American will to use force against the threat of falling dominoes remains a central concern. But the Sino-Soviet split has helped to erode the American tendency to assume almost automatically that threats of communist aggression, even those in which the Soviet Union is not implicated, are threats to the central balance of power.

The accentuation of the split, by complicating bilateral U.S.-Soviet relations with an incipient tripolar relationship, has been as important as any factor in weakening the conviction that peace is indivisible and that the world is one great arena of conflict between International Communism and the Free World. The official revision of this

outlook is particularly marked with respect to the third world. There
the fragmentation of the communist system, together with America's
discovery of the heterogeneity of this vast area and the limited capacity of the less-developed countries to play on the central stage of
international politics (especially if the superpowers confine their competition in behalf of clients) has destroyed the image of the third
world as a decisive arena of the cold war. Now the Nixon Administration sees the third world not as a single arena of decisive competition but rather as a fractured and disorganized but potentially
dangerous area in which U.S.-Soviet competition has to be limited by
rules of mutual restraint, lest both sides stumble into unintended
confrontation.

The Soviet Union, in this revised perspective, is launched on an
elemental effort, more instinct than design, to achieve global political
parity with the United States by projecting its power and influence
to areas (particularly the Middle East and the southern periphery of
China) that were formerly the exclusive domain of European empires and America's postwar hegemony. This effort could be dangerous if the Soviets should seek or achieve special spheres of influence
in which they enjoy an exclusive advantage or if their support of
headstrong clients should trigger them into moves that threaten sudden changes in local balances of power. But as long as the United
States maintains a credible, though not overbearing, presence in these
peripheral areas, it need not fear competition with the Soviets in the
increasingly wide-ranging game of access and influence. Indeed,
there is now a widespread assumption in the government that as Soviet influence and commitments spread, the Soviet Union will incur
some of the same kinds of troubles and constraints that the United
States experienced during the expansion of its influence and commitments. Under these circumstances, therefore, President Nixon hopes
to moderate superpower competition in the third world and decouple
local competition and conflicts from the main business of arranging
a network of agreements and understandings that will stabilize relations among the developed centers of the world. The principal operating rule of mutual self-restraint on which this superpower relationship in the third world is expected to rest is the same rule that
applies to the more structured relationship between the superpowers
in Europe: each will have areas of special access and influence, but
neither should prevent the other from seeking political and economic
access to its sphere; and neither should seek an exclusive sphere of
preponderance to the other's disadvantage.

This kind of *modus vivendi,* in the Nixon Administration's revised outlook on the third world, is facilitated by the discovery that even some of the poorest and weakest countries have shown unexpected resistance to communist subversion. The plight of South Vietnam is regarded as the result of unique circumstances, not as a forecast of new wars of national liberation. In contrast to the apprehensions generated by the Korean war, the prevailing view in the government is that the less developed countries (now generously called "developing" rather than "underdeveloped"), particularly in Asia, are growing more secure and self-reliant. Thus President Nixon's second annual Report to Congress (released on February 25, 1971) declared, "The Asia of today is vastly different from the Asia which required, over the past several decades, so activist an American role. Asian nations now generally have a strong and confident sense of their own national identity and future. They have generally established healthier relationships with each other and with the outside world. They have created institutions of proven vitality. Their armed forces are stronger."

One suspects that this new-found optimism about indigenous resistance to the communist threat springs from more than an analytical revision of the excessive fears of the past. Like the new policy emphasis on multilateral as opposed to bilateral economic assistance, it is partly inspired by the longing to lower the intensity of America's involvement in the third world. Another concomitant of this longing is the downgrading of America's conception of the interests for which it would be willing to fight or threaten to fight. Considering the elusive quality of national interests, it is understandable that the administration's revision of interests is more diffuse and ambiguous and less articulate than its downgrading of American power and the communist threat. But *psychologically*, if not logically, these three aspects are inseparable. In a world in which the United States has lost much confidence in its power to cope with communist aggression and is sick of the costs of Vietnam, there is bound to be a strong tendency to downgrade the communist threat. In a world in which the fear of communist aggression and falling dominoes has abated, a primary incentive for the expansion of America's conception of its interests in areas of relatively low intrinsic material or politico-cultural value to the United States is bound to erode. With the erosion of this inflated "security" incentive, the structure of American interests in the world tends to revert to its basically Europe-oriented status before the Korean war, with the addition of Japan because of its ascendant power rather than because of sentimental and political affinities.

The Nixon Administration's downgrading of American interests in the third world, although largely implicit in descriptions of the altered international environment and of America's more discriminating and limited role in shaping it, shows through clearly in official affirmations (particularly in the first years of the administration) that the United States must apply more exacting criteria of national interest to future commitments and involvements, and that the enthusiasm for asserting American power in behalf of the security and independence of others, proclaimed by President Kennedy in his oft-quoted inaugural address, must now be considered excessive and outdated.[7] President Nixon evidently shares the general opinion that American interests in Southeast Asia became inflated far beyond objective security needs because American power and prestige became so heavily involved. In the future, he therefore affirms (in both the first and second annual reports), Americans must recognize that "we are not involved in the world because we have commitments; we have commitments because we are involved. Our interests must shape our commitments, rather than the other way around."

Will the Nixon Strategy Last?

On the face of it, the Nixon Strategy and the revised outlook it reflects seem like a strikingly successful adjustment of American power and policies to the changing domestic and international environment that is developing in the wake of the nation's disillusionment with and disengagement from the war in Vietnam. But the full test of success must await far more evidence as to whether the principal premises behind this adjustment are realistic in the long run. One can divide speculation about this question into five parts: Will the Nixon Strategy be sustained or not by the outlook and conduct of the Soviet Union, the People's Republic of China, America's major allies, the less-developed countries, and the American public?

[7] In his inaugural address on January 20, 1961, President Kennedy said, "Let every nation know, whether it wishes us well or ill that we shall pay any price, bear any burden, meet any hardship, support any friend, oppose any foe to assure the survival and the success of liberty." *Department of State Bulletin*, volume 44, no. 1128, February 6, 1961, p. 175. These words do indeed represent the exuberant spirit of national self-assertion and missionary zeal that characterized especially the early part of the Kennedy Administration, but they should be compared with Kennedy's words at the University of Washington on November 16, 1961, in an address delivered in a mood chastened by involvement in Laos, the Bay of Pigs, and Berlin: "We must face the fact that the United States is neither omnipotent nor omniscient, that we are only six percent of the world's population, and we cannot right every wrong or reverse each adversity, and that therefore there cannot be an American solution for every world problem." *Department of State Bulletin*, volume 45, no. 1171, December 4, 1961, p. 916.

Soviet Union. The evidence so far indicates that the Soviet Union is willing to play the international game according to Nixon's rules. The game of global *modus vivendi* and mutually restrained access and influence is compatible with major Soviet aims: stabilizing the status quo in Europe in order to be free to cope with China and in the hope that a relaxation of tensions will weaken and divide NATO and speed America's withdrawal from Europe; inducing the United States to concede military and strategic parity while narrowing the gap between America's and Russia's global naval reach: extending Soviet influence among the less developed countries in behalf of unfulfilled imperial ambitions, global political parity with the United States, and the containment of China; and achieving all these objectives at a minimum competitive cost and a minimum risk of confrontation with the United States.

As in the past, the Kremlin's largely self-imposed problems of security may occasionally lead it to resort to behavior that seems threatening to the United States and its allies. Soviet leaders will have serious problems in preserving a safe East European *cordon sanitaire,* managing the conflicting interests and pressures that accompany geographically expanding influence, and containing Chinese influence. But these are not the kinds of problems that are likely to move Soviet leaders to revert to a pattern of confrontation with the Western powers. The source of their troubles will lie elsewhere.

If Soviet leaders reject the international game the Nixon Administration projects, it will be because (1) imprudence and miscalculation in supporting client states entangles the Soviet Union in unmanageable local conflicts, (2) the rivalry with China provokes Moscow into military suppression (an action that becomes increasingly irrational but not out of the question as China increases its nuclear capability and legitimizes its participation in the diplomatic arena), or (3) the Soviets heal their split with China. Although any of these developments is possible, none is probable; but they remind us how contingent the success of the Nixon Strategy is on the absence of such surprises.

People's Republic of China. The chances are that China's foreign relations will also be compatible with Nixon's Strategy for the next five to ten years. The strategy is consistent with China's aim to check the two primary threats to its vital interests, as Peking sees them: the Soviet Union and Japan. If Chinese actions undermine the Nixon Strategy, it will more likely be the result of rivalry and competition with Japan, which might upset the diplomatic equilibrium and drive Japan into full-scale military self-reliance, than the result of China's threatening American interests and commitments directly. But for the immediate future, at least, all signs point to Peking's being as anxious as Tokyo to achieve a Sino-Japanese rapprochement.

The Major Allies. A more serious potential threat to the international environment on which the Nixon Strategy is based lies in the outlook and policies of America's major allies. In several respects they may regard their role in the projected structure of relationships as less satisfactory in the long run than in this transitional period.

The Nixon Strategy presupposes that at a time of growing divergencies between the United States and its allies on economic and monetary relations the allies will continue to accept the preponderant role of the United States in managing security interests. Is this assumption realistic? Even in a period of detente, the extent of an ally's military autonomy must affect in some way the extent of its autonomy in economic and other policies. The allies may conclude that they are sacrificing too much of the latter for too little of the former.

Similarly, with respect to European political relations, he who manages the military balance vis-à-vis the principal adversary presumably determines not only the military posture of the alliance but also, to an important extent, the diplomatic strategy of dealing with the adversary. When the issues of confrontation and deterrence have given way to the issues of accommodation and diplomatic maneuver, the allies are bound to be concerned that their special interests may be neglected by their protector in his pursuit of a *modus vivendi* with the Soviet Union.

At the same time, the apparent decline of the Soviet military threat diminishes the incentive of allies to defer to America's judgment about the policy requirements of their own interests and the interests of the alliance. Furthermore, America's concession of strategic parity to the Soviet Union, combined with its military retrenchment while the Soviet global military presence and political reach increase, tends to undermine allied confidence in the efficacy of American protection. If the United States nonetheless presses its military, economic, and diplomatic policies upon the allies, as one must expect the leader of the alliance to do, and at the same time tries to induce them to increase their share of the common defense burden, as the long-run stabilization of America's leadership requires, allied governments may decide that the benefits of alliance are not worth the costs. They may then, collectively or individually, decide to rely upon their own accommodations with the adversaries, whether or not they try to back their diplomatic independence with military self-reliance.

On the other hand, as long as the United States maintains a not incredible or ineffective military presence in Europe and East Asia and is reasonably considerate in informing and consulting its allies about its dealings with the Soviet Union and China, there are powerful practical incentives for the allies to collaborate with the Nixon Strategy. Above all, the existing division of responsibility is convenient, in that it gives the allies a time-tested security framework, provided by American troops and nuclear weapons, which relieves them of a material and political burden they might otherwise find onerous and nevertheless inadequate. Unless they should become so confident of Soviet and Chinese self-restraint as to believe that their security requires neither the American shield and umbrella nor the enlargement of their own military role, they can regard the preponderant American role as a good bargain. It is not only a good bargain in terms of military security; it also underwrites the detente that enables them to pursue independent economic and political policies without worrying too much about security considerations. Their assumption of a substantially independent military role would burden their foreign relations with security concerns, and, particularly in the case of an enlarged Japanese military role, it might disrupt the whole diplomatic equilibrium underlying detente by creating a new center of military decision-making.

Under the present structure of security relationships the allies may continue to worry about the declining credibility of American nuclear and conventional protection. But the evidence so far indicates that their declining confidence in American protection will be offset by their diminished concern about a military threat. The apparent diminution of the military threat also tends to mitigate allied dissatisfaction with America's preponderance in security affairs, since under the conditions of detente military power becomes less important as a measure and instrument of real influence.

Finally, another factor tending to sustain the present structure of relationships between the United States and its major allies is some formidable political obstacles to the development of substantially independent military forces in Western Europe and Japan. In Europe the distinctive obstacle lies in the traditional political difficulty of several states of roughly equal power and status subordinating their divergent interests and their national independence to the requirements of a unified defense force, and the special difficulties of creating a joint nuclear force that includes some kind of German association. Perhaps only the renewed fear of an imminent Soviet military threat to Europe after America's primary responsibility for European security had been withdrawn could overcome these obstacles to military coalescence. But, in the absence of this unlikely development, it is doubtful that the fear of U.S.-Soviet collusion or even the prospect of American unilateral withdrawal will provide the incentive for military coalescence in a period of detente.

In Japan the distinctive obstacle to supplanting American military preponderance in the region lies in the intense antimilitary reaction of the Japanese to the trauma of defeat in World War II. It lies in their consciousness of the intense fear and disapproval with which other states would view the slightest indication that Japan might abrogate the constitutionally prescribed limits of military self-defense, which are interpreted to confine Japan's military role to protecting the homeland from attack. Furthermore, any enlargement of Japan's military security role would be viewed as a prelude to Japan's production of a nuclear force, which is a prospect that provokes immense fear and aversion in all nations that have important relations with Japan. As in the case of Western Europe, one can imagine the constraints upon Japan's military role collapsing under the combined influence of declining confidence in American protection and rising fear of an adversary's power, but this prospect will also be a persuasive argument for continuing American preponderance in regional security.

At this time, the incentives for America's allies to operate within the existing structure of relationships clearly outweigh their incentives to supplant American military preponderance, despite their differences with the United States over economic and monetary relations. Indeed, their fear that the United States may lack the will and lose the means of protecting them adequately, or that America's preoccupation with the tripolar relationship may jeopardize their special interests, has only moved them to make more strenuous efforts to keep the United States engaged in their behalf.

Unless this incipient era of negotiation leads to an era of multipolar confrontation, the only developments that seem likely to alter the basic distribution of regional power and responsibility between the United States and its major allies are a resurgence of the allies' will to join the first rank of powers or America's abandonment of her role as protector. There are no signs of the first development, although the wide-spread expectation that Japan will eventually go that route may yet be fulfilled. The second development is more likely. If the United States abandons its role, it will probably be by neglect rather than design; and it will result in the erosion of the present structure of relationships, not the construction of another.[8]

[8] In chapter 6, we examine whether the present structure of relationships between the United States and its allies is likely to endure or erode, and whether an orderly transfer of security responsibilities to the allies might therefore be a more desirable structure for the United States to pursue.

Third World. Even if the policies and actions of the Soviet Union, China, and America's major allies remain compatible with the kind of international environment envisioned in the Nixon Strategy, this environment could be upset by the policies and actions of those states outside the great developed centers of the world. Nixon's Strategy depends on events in the third world not upsetting the diplomatic equilibrium between the superpowers. But if this condition is fulfilled, it will not be because of the tranquillity of the third world, for the developing countries seem doomed to suffer a long period of national and subnational conflicts, many of which will erupt into violence. Rather it will be because the superpowers manage to avoid entanglements in these conflicts.

Here the undoubted desire of the superpowers to remain disentangled runs into conflict with their desire for influence and status. The expansion of Soviet influence in the Middle East and Asia, for example, increases the possibility that in some local conflict Soviet leaders may be tempted to feel compelled to support a "client" in such a way as to come into dangerous confrontation with the United States. It increases the likelihood that the United States, confronted with a client's loss of territory or power in a local conflict in which the Soviet Union is aligned with the adversary, may feel compelled to run the risk of intervention in order to show the Soviets as well as America's allies that the United States does not desert threatened clients and to dissuade the Soviets from stretching the rules of the game to their advantage. If such a client were supported by China, this might compound the risk of superpower miscalculations and increase the likelihood of at least their indirect involvement in the local conflict.[9]

On the other hand, there are signs that the expansion of Soviet influence imposes new constraints on Soviet conduct as Soviet leaders become more aware of the hazards of supporting demanding but un-

[9] Thus during the Bengali revolt against Pakistan in the spring of 1970, President Nixon, in order to support an ally that had assisted Kissinger's visit to Peking and was believed to be threatened by India in alignment with Russia, leaned toward Pakistan in calling for a ceasefire, threatened to cancel his trip to the Moscow summit, and sent the carrier *Enterprise* into the Bay of Bengal. The Soviet Union, in turn, evidently assured India that it would use its naval forces in the Indian Ocean to counter any U.S. military action and carry out a diversionary move against Sinkiang if necessary to counter any Chinese military moves against India. However, the fact that neither the superpowers nor China came close to armed intervention may support the contention that the present structure of international politics impedes the likelihood of American entanglement in local wars. For a balanced assessment of this episode, see William J. Barnds, "India, Pakistan, and American Realpolitik," *Christianity and Crisis* (June 12, 1972), pp. 143–49.

responsive and unsuccessful clients like Egypt and of the difficulties of supporting some clients without alienating others. Moreover, as the superpowers consolidate detente with a network of agreements and understandings, they tend to become more cautious about upsetting detente through competition in peripheral areas, and the developing countries find it more difficult to exploit their competition. In any event, even if the Soviet Union or China or, once again, the United States should become entangled in a local war, this would not necessarily upset the great-power equilibrium. After all, detente and the tripolar balance developed during the Vietnam war, which the superpowers largely decoupled from their direct relations with one another.

There is another way, however, in which the frustrations and grievances of third-world countries might disrupt the great-power international game—not by entangling them in local conflicts but rather by harassing and importuning them to deflect their energy and resources to the concerns of the needy states. In recent years groups of poor states have combined to present grievances and demands to the rich states on issues of trade and development, the sale of petroleum, the exploitation of ocean resources, and the protection of the environment. Perhaps the most impressive of these coalitions in terms of size and political impact is the "Group of Seventy-Seven," which grew out of the first United Nations Conference on Trade and Development in 1964 and subsequent UNCTAD sessions in 1968 and 1972. Although this coalition has forced the industrialized countries to pay attention to a wide range of demands on economic and monetary issues and to concert their own position in answering these demands, the limited power of the poor states to alter the behavior of the rich in a period of muted superpower competition is manifest in the lack of significant economic concessions their efforts have won. In bare power terms the fact of the matter is that the third-world countries need economic relations with the developed countries more than the developed countries need economic relations with them.

The failure of developing countries to gain concessions from the developed countries by organized appeals to world opinion may drive them increasingly to look for bargaining levers in their control of resources that the big industrial states want. The contagious success of Chile, Ecuador, and Peru in asserting a 200-mile territorial sea boundary in connection with their move to control fishing has led to a succession of 200-mile claims by less developed coastal countries, as the technology of sea and seabed exploitation (particularly for oil and gas on the continental shelf) advances rapidly and industrial needs mount. The success of eleven Middle Eastern oil producing countries, concerted as members of the Organization of Petroleum Exporting Countries, in compelling the big international oil companies to pay substantially increased revenues to them may lead the producers of other primary commodities to combine to get better commercial terms from the industrial consumer nations.

Along with the activities of these commercially and nationalistically motivated blocs, the less developed countries show a growing inclination to deny or constrict the use of resources and facilities by developed states for non-commercial purposes; witness the constraints on the great maritime states' commercial and military use of the Malacca and Gibraltar straits for a mixture of reasons, including pollution and politics. Other conflicts of interest between developing and developed states are inherent in the adverse environmental effects, from the standpoint of developed states, that arise from the efforts of poor states to develop their economies.

Evidently, the opportunities for clashes of interest and policy between the developing and the developed states are increasing; and the developing states, out of frustration and despair tinged with national pride and animus, are increasingly disposed to use whatever levers they can find to redress the balance of power and benefits between the rich and the poor countries. This may constitute a significant addition to the modes of international politics and discourse. But unless the efforts of the smaller and weaker states become so effective and so disadvantageous to the major industrial countries that these countries regularly resort to the use of force to protect what they conceive to be indispensable interests and rights, it is unlikely that international politics will be reoriented along a rich-poor or North-South axis. And even then the imbalance of force would scarcely permit such an axis to survive. Basically, the reason that any such transformation of international politics is unlikely is less the self-restraint and deference of the developed states than the fact that most developing states will continue to need cooperation with and assistance from developed states and will continue to respond to a variety of interests in which they are divided among themselves.

The American Public. Contrary to a common view that Vietnam has destroyed any national consensus on foreign policy, it begins to seem that the war has helped to consolidate a new consensus as well as alter the old. If so, the Nixon Administration is largely responsible. If the Nixon Strategy and its underlying premises of foreign policy in fact represent a revised consensus (at least among those regularly concerned with foreign affairs), no less firm and coherent than the cold war consensus, the reason is clear: the strategy promises to preserve the familiar structure of power, including America's leading role, that underlies the relatively safe and predictable international order that emerged in the course of the cold war—but it promises to do so at a bearable economic and political cost and a tolerable risk of armed involvement.

On the other hand, the apparent satisfaction of America's foreign policy elites with the Nixon Strategy—Vietnam somewhat excepted—may not stand the test of time. Thus many wonder whether the American people, lacking the fears and aspirations of the era of confrontation, may in time revert once more to their traditional posture of political and military withdrawal from an intractable world. Reversion to the isolationism of the 1930s is hard to imagine after all that has happened to America's international position and outlook under the impact of World War II and the cold war. But it would not take nearly this drastic a constriction of America's role to negate the kind of world envisioned in the revised consensus. For that world requires the active maintenance of America's influence and leadership on a global scale.

Is it realistic to assume that the nation will sustain this kind of role? Even if the policies and actions of the developed and less developed countries should be compatible with the international game Nixon and Kissinger envision, will the United States be willing to play?

In 1973 it is too early to answer these questions confidently, because the nation is still adjusting to the repercussions of the war in Vietnam. The test of whether the current general acceptance of, or acquiescence to, the Nixon Strategy is enduring or merely transitional has yet to come. It can only come when major international events and developments that cannot now be foreseen test the stability of the present structure of power and interests among states, and when enough time has passed to test America's response to these events and developments. It will take more than another four years to test whether the revised foreign policy consensus, like the familiar cold war consensus, will sustain over the long run a steady projection of American power in accordance with a fairly coherent strategy.

A plausible case can be made for the proposition that the international role projected for the United States by the Nixon Administration is at once too demanding and too uninspiring to be sustained.[10]

---

[10] See, for example, Stanley Hoffmann, "Will the Balance Balance at Home?" *Foreign Policy* 7 (Summer, 1972), pp. 60–86.

Heretofore, the active projection of American power seems to have required a more compelling rationale than is likely to emerge in an "era of negotiation." In World War I this rationale was the vindication of America's neutral rights on the high seas, defeating the enemy who had threatened the basis of America's hemispheric security, and making the world safe for democracy according to the gospel of Woodrow Wilson. In World War II it was nothing less than national survival and the defeat of fascist aggression. In the cold war it was containing communist military expansion and stopping chains of aggression that would lead to World War III. But what comparable incentives for an active global role can any president offer the nation now?

Nixon's strategy requires maintaining a still substantial, though diminished, level of nuclear and conventional capabilities, military and economic assistance programs, and all the rest of the wherewithal of a global foreign policy. It also requires a not incredible willingness to intervene with armed forces in behalf of allies and, where vital commitments are at stake, nonallies too. Can this kind of posture be maintained in the long run without the sublimated anti-communist security motive of the past? That motive has faded under the disaffection with Vietnam. It has been outmoded by President Nixon's elaboration of detente with the Soviet Union and rapprochement with China. Can anything supplant it?

It is one thing to maintain American troops in Europe in order to protect Europe from armed attack, as after the Soviet-supported North Korean invasion of South Korea, or to bolster West Germany's sense of security when Stalin and Khrushchev were intimidating Berlin. It is quite another thing to maintain these troops to support West Germany's *Ostpolitik* or East-West arms negotiations, especially when the allies are pursuing trade and monetary policies unfavorable to American interests. It is one thing to sign a security treaty with Japan and keep Japan under American nuclear and conventional protection when Japan is weak and disarmed and the Korean War is raging. It seems much less imperative to maintain exclusive responsibility for the security of Japan's regional environment when the United States is engaged in rapprochement with China and detente with Russia, and the North and South Koreans are talking about peaceful reunification, while Japan itself has become an economic superpower, has recovered Okinawa and gained autonomy over American-used bases in Japan, and is actively pursuing its own rapprochement with China.

To be sure, containing Germany and Japan was from the beginning one motive for America's alliance with them, but can discouraging one's allies from pursuing an independent defense posture remain a compelling motive for maintaining America's preponderance in protecting its allies when the threat to their security has declined so substantially, when they are asserting their independent economic and diplomatic interests, and when they are materially quite capable of substantially relieving the United States of the burden of defending them?

What are the compelling reasons for sustaining overseas intervention capabilities and sizeable economic and military assistance programs in the third world when Americans no longer fear that dominoes will automatically fall if communist aggression anywhere is unopposed, when the nation is determined to avoid another Vietnam war, when economic aid can no longer be represented as the key to a struggle for the hearts and minds of developing countries or even to economic development, and gaining influence with recipients comes to seem less important than preventing them from dragging the United States into their local conflicts—when the name of the game in the main arena of international politics is not just containment but detente, rapprochement, *modus vivendi,* and diplomatic maneuver?

Ever since the announcement of the Truman Doctrine American policy makers have assumed, in a kind of conditioned response to the logic of the Greek-Turkish aid program applied to the rest of the world, that American security is at stake in containing communist expansion in the third world. If in their disillusionment with the undiscriminating application of this premise to Vietnam they should now reach the concluson—which is the truth of the matter—that scarcely anything that can happen in the third world would jeopardize American security in the strict sense,[11] what, if anything, could inspire them to keep projecting American power, money, and weapons throughout this vast disorganized area of the world at the levels anticipated by the Nixon Administration? Humanitarian concerns? Political and ideological preferences? Some new world mission?

These questions suggest that one need not assume a reversion to prewar isolationism in order to foresee the steady erosion of Amer-

[11] Robert W. Tucker, *A New Isolationism: Threat or Promise?*, explains convincingly how secure the United States has become since World War II from foreign actions that could seriously jeopardize U.S. territorial and political integrity or economic welfare, although Americans have got into the habit of including a broad range of other values, such as the prevention of armed aggression overseas, under the rubric of "national security."

ica's overseas power and America's will to use armed force. If the president and the nation as a whole will not support an active foreign policy with money, manpower, weapons, and action, the revised consensus might nevertheless continue to carry the day (if only by default) while the nation's strength and will to give it life steadily dwindle.

To be sure, something of the cold war consensus will remain, and presidents may wish to revive it on occasion. There will probably remain enough of a lingering anti-communism or at least a reflexive opposition to Soviet aggrandizement to make it difficult for many Americans to view with equanimity the extension of Soviet power and influence (regardless of the rules of mutual access) in the Middle East, the horn of Africa, Southern Asia, Southeast Asia, and Latin America. Thus domestically hard-pressed presidents, occasionally reverting to previous habits, may dramatize the Soviet threat in order to gain material and political support for moves dictated by the more subtle and less appealing requirements of maintaining a superpower *modus vivendi* and a multipolar diplomatic equilibrium. Or, lacking the opportunity to dramatize the Soviet threat, the president might try to mobilize support around more exalted political and humanitarian motives and appeal to America's inveterate yearning for moral gratification. In response to these conflicting tendencies the United States might revert to the erratic pattern of oscillation between intervention and retrenchment that characterized its experience as a world power before World War II, while the foundations of American power and influence continued to crumble. In this eventuality, the revised foreign policy consensus itself, as well as the material and political bases of its support, would collapse.

This is a plausible line of conjecture, but it probably exaggerates the need of popular support for a policy of moderated global engagement, and it may also exaggerate the extent to which support of such engagement requires a dramatic and compelling rationale. If international politics really is going to be dominated by diplomatic maneuver and negotiation rather than crises and confrontations, the normal business of conducting foreign relations will concern a relatively small group, smaller than at the height of the cold war. The composition of this group will vary, depending on the domestic interests involved; but normally, the evidence of recent years indicates, the president will have a good deal of latitude in conducting foreign relations as he sees fit. According to this assessment, if the president wants to maintain something like the present level of defense expenditures and of military and economic assistance, he will be able to count on enough support from the foreign policy establishment, inside and outside the government, to be able to sustain the critical programs on a routine basis. The rationale for this support would be essentially the maintenance of American influence at a moderate cost and risk in a reasonably congenial but potentially dangerous international environment. This is not a dramatic goal, but it may be compelling enough if the United States acts like other great states in history.

The history of great states and empires shows that they try to hold on to extensive power and influence under much greater adversity than the United States has experienced. If influence needs any special justification, apart from pride and honor (America "must not become a second-rate power" or "let down its friends and allies"), it can be found in the simple practical proposition that the United States, having played the key and indispensable role in constructing a new international order after the ravages of fascist aggression and World War II, cannot now afford to give up its leading role. For a leading American role, in this view, remains essential to any kind of military or diplomatic equilibrium—all the more so in a changing international environment that is adjusting to the decline of the cold war. In maintaining its leadership, however, the United States, chastened by Vietnam, must demonstrate its maturity by adopting a more flexible and selective, a less exclusive and more even-tempered, role. In this way, it may be argued, America would finally come of age as a world power psychologically as well as materially prepared for the long haul.

If this is to be the conventional outlook of the foreign-policy elites, there is little doubt that any president, who above all is responsible for representing the nation on the world stage, will share it, respond to it, and cultivate it. Only when the question of threatening or actually using American armed force arises will the president have to find more specific and dramatic reasons than these. Whether this is a crucial exception to the general latitude he may enjoy depends, of course, on the kinds and frequency of occasions on which the president will feel compelled to resort to force. It depends on whether the end of one era of confrontation is the prelude to a long period of diplomatic maneuver and moderated great-power relations or whether it is merely the transition to another period of confrontation in a more complex structure of power and interests.

Even in the latter case, however, it can be argued that the United States has matured beyond the stage in which it needs to justify each prospective intervention as a crusade or the salvation of world order.

If the rules of the game call for more selective, restrained, and cool-headed intervention, the absence of a messianic or universalistic rationale should facilitate a more professional approach to the problems of maintaining a reasonably congenial international order. After all, the psychology of a nation consolidating and adjusting its power after a quarter century of expanding involvements should be different from the psychology of a nation asserting and establishing its power after a century of isolation. Given a modicum of success in the former endeavor, the United States may find the rationale that sustained the latter simplistic and overblown. It would be ironic and surprising but not extraordinary if the trauma of Vietnam, by purging the American outlook of its excesses, ended by establishing a more enduring rationale of global influence.

2

THE AMERICAN OUTLOOK: CHANGE AND CONTINUITY

Robert W. Tucker

1

In considering the American outlook in 1972, it is instructive to recall the expectations of four years ago. In 1968 nothing seemed more likely to many observers than the prospect of far-reaching change in the nation's foreign policy. The trauma of Vietnam had presumably led to a breakdown in the foreign policy consensus of the past generation. Could a new consensus be established on the ruins of the old, one that would sustain even a substantially modified version of the nation's post World War II role and interests? Or would a growing public disinclination to risk further overseas involvements lead to the abandonment of American commitments and to the emergence, in substance if not in name, of a new isolationism? Finally, would not the anticipated reaction to a role the nation had grown tired of sustaining necessarily extend as well to the principal institution—the American presidency—that had forged this role?

These questions have not disappeared in 1972. Yet it is clear that for the time being the fears—or hopes—of four years ago have not been realized. On the contrary, what is striking in this respect is the marked contrast between the expectations of yesterday and the realities of today. If the trauma of Vietnam has led to a breakdown in the consensus of the past generation, the breakdown is scarcely apparent in the intensity of debate over and the scope of opposition to the Nixon Administration's foreign policy. Even the great, and persisting, issue that ostensibly led to the destruction of the old consensus no longer provoked by 1972 the kind of disaffection it once provoked. It last did so in the spring of 1970, in response to President Nixon's decision to send American and South Vietnamese forces into Cambodia. In retrospect, that response appears as the climax of intense opposition to continued American involvement in the Vietnamese conflict. Significantly, the aerial and naval measures taken by the administration against North Vietnam two years later in the spring of 1972, though far transcending in importance the earlier decision to expand the war to Cambodia, failed to elicit a comparable reaction. (To be sure, this remarkable fact has to be seen not only against the background of the steady withdrawal of American ground forces from Vietnam and the consequent reduction of American casualties but also in the light of the apparently successful—and certainly diverting—exercises in summitry that dominated the foreign policy scene in 1972. Even so, the projection in 1968 of the measures taken against North Vietnam in 1972, measures taken without incurring notable domestic opposition, would have been dismissed as pure fantasy.)

Moreover, the disagreement that has persisted over when and how to end the involvement in Vietnam cannot be taken as in itself indicative of any broader and deeper disagreement over America's role and interests in the world. Among the more articulate and influential critics of the administration's Vietnam policy, opposition has largely reflected the conviction that the longer American involvement in the conflict is permitted to drag on, the greater will be its cumulative effects on an already weary and disillusioned public. To this extent, what remains of the debate over Vietnam is perhaps most clearly indicative of a difference over how a disastrous war should be ended so as to prove least injurious to the greater interests of policy. But this disagreement scarcely bears out the view that the old consensus has been disrupted beyond repair or, still less, that a revised version of the old consensus can no longer obtain the support of a majority of the foreign policy elites. The essential continuity in change that has distinguished the Nixon Administration's foreign policy has not met with significant opposition, let alone with rejection, by these elites. Vietnam apart, the differences that have arisen between this administration and its more influential critics have not been very sharply defined and have only infrequently dealt with basic issues of policy.

If the essential continuity of America's global role has been confirmed during the past four years, so has the predominance of the principal institution that has forged this role. Contrary to the common expectation that marked the outset of his tenure as president, Mr. Nixon has not only turned back challenges to the powers he inherited but has added still further to the already impressive powers passed on to him by his predecessors. On more than one occasion, he has done so in open defiance of his adversaries, Congressional and otherwise, apparently in the conviction that, whatever the present ambivalence in public mood, there would be no widespread disposition to support challenges to the president's predominant role in the conduct of foreign policy. To date, events appear to have vindicated this conviction.

Elsewhere in this volume,[1] the methods are examined whereby a resourceful and determined president, skillfully employing the unique advantages conferred by his office, has been able to retain and even to increase his authority over the nation's foreign relations. Here it is sufficient to note that, quite apart from the abilities of the present occupant, these advantages were seriously underestimated by those who foresaw, as a reaction to Vietnam, the success of legislative efforts to restrict the president's powers in foreign policy. Where Mr. Nixon has not defeated these efforts, he has, with few exceptions, evaded them. In the process, he has managed to diminish even further Congress's already modest potential effectively to question the conduct of foreign policy. For that potential depends of necessity upon sources of information that have been increasingly closed to the Congress and, of course, to the public. By concentrating power over major foreign policy decisions almost exclusively in the White House staff, Mr. Nixon has been able to achieve a degree of control over the decision-making process that eluded his predecessors. The secrecy so essential to presidential power and initiative in foreign policy has been carried to new extremes by the simple device of excluding the major executive departments from the inner sanctum where the key decisions are made. What the bureaucracy no longer knows it can no longer tell. At the same time, under the protective mantle of executive privilege, those who do know need no longer tell (and, given their relationship to the president, have no incentive to tell).

Nothing seems more ironic than the fact that, coming to office when and in the circumstances he did, President Nixon has not only been able to increase the secrecy with which foreign policy is made and carried out but even to endow secrecy with a new kind of legitimacy. Once it had been thought that if Vietnam had shown anything, it had illuminated the need for obtaining prior public consent to critical foreign policy decisions. On this view, much of the opposition to Vietnam was to be explained by the public's sense of exclusion from participation and involvement in the decisions that had led to the war and to its subsequent escalation. In the words of one who had occupied a position in the inner circle of the Johnson Administration, the war was opposed mainly because "a majority of people believed the war was undemocratic—waged in violation of the

[1] See chapter 3.

tradition of consent which is fundamental to the effective conduct of foreign policy in a free society."[2] Whatever else may be said of this administration's record on Vietnam, it can scarcely be credited with having democratized the war by contributing to a heightened sense of public participation and involvement in decisions bearing on the conflict. The principal decisions relating to the war have been taken by Mr. Nixon with no less secrecy—and, when circumstances have required, with no less deceptiveness—than those of his predecessor in office. That the manner in which these decisions have been taken apparently has not represented a political liability for Mr. Nixon points to the conclusion that it is easy to overestimate the public's expectations of applying the processes of democracy to the conduct of foreign policy.

2

How are we to account for the disparity between the expectations of yesterday and the realities of today? One response has been to insist that these realities will not prove enduring, that yesterday's expectations were not ill-founded but simply premature. On this view, the domestic price for the involvement in Vietnam has yet to be paid. The Nixon Administration may have succeeded in putting off the day of reckoning; it has not succeeded in ensuring against that inevitable day. Moreover, Vietnam and its ultimate consequences apart, there is the broader issue of public understanding of and support for American foreign policy in the years ahead. Whatever the intrinsic merits of the rationale that formed the basis of policy throughout the period from World War II to Vietnam, that rationale —in the main, anti-communism—was both readily grasped and broadly sanctioned by the general public. The Nixon policy reformulation, on the other hand, lacks a rationale that can strike a responsive public chord. This is one reason, among others, why it requires a public that, though acquiescent, remains relatively uninvolved. But such a relationship, it is argued, will not sustain an activist foreign policy that continues to be predicated upon the capacity and willingness to intervene when necessary to vindicate our global interests and commitments.

The view that today's realities will not prove enduring is considered in later pages of this essay. Here it suffices to note that, even if this view were to be accepted, we would still be left with the task of accounting for the fact that the transformation of American foreign

[2] Bill D. Moyers, "One Thing We Learned," *Foreign Affairs* (July, 1968), p. 661.

policy predicted in 1968 has not yet occurred. If the earthquake of Vietnam destroyed the foundations of post-war policy, there still remains the need to explain why the structure continues to stand. Is it plausible to account for the absence to date of the kind of change anticipated four years ago in terms of the immense powers of the president and, of course, the determination of the present occupant to use these powers to maintain an essential continuity of role and interest? No doubt, this explanation is a signal part of the truth. Indeed, there is much to be said for the view that so long as a president—any president—has the power in foreign affairs the American executive has come to possess, the tendency will remain strong to pursue an activist foreign policy (and this quite apart from the domestic political advantage to be found in pursuing an activist foreign policy). On this view, what comes very close to a symbiotic relationship holds between an all-powerful president and a particular kind of foreign policy. It is not simply that the one has largely given rise to the other, but that the one has become largely indispensable to the other. At root, it is this conviction that informs the efforts of at least some leading Congressional critics of executive power in foreign relations.

Yet the theme of institutional obstacles—above all, the immense powers of the presidency—may be carried only so far. Given a widespread public demand for change in the nation's foreign policy, these obstacles are not insurmountable. The argument that they are insurmountable takes for granted what needs to be proved. It simply assumes that a demand for change, however widespread, can be and, in practice, has been denied by institutional forces bent upon resisting such change. The evidence, such as it is, does not bear out this assumption. Even in the one instance where it seems most persuasive, the continuing American involvement in Vietnam, it is far from clear that the president has effectively denied the will of a majority. What opinion surveys do seem to indicate is that the president has effectively manipulated that will and that he has been able to do so because, in addition to its customary permissiveness and propensity to follow the president's lead in foreign policy, the public has remained ambivalent on Vietnam.

There is, of course, no ambivalence about the public's desire to end the nation's involvement in the war. From the outset of the Nixon Administration, a substantial majority has insisted either that the war be settled by negotiation or that, negotiation failing, U.S. involvement come to an end through unilateral withdrawal. Does this expression of the public's will mean, however, that a majority has also been willing to accept the possible consequence of a negotiated settlement or unilateral withdrawal? One must remain skeptical, if only for the reason that the support given to a negotiated settlement has also been given to the president's successive terms for negotiating an end to the war.[3] However else one may characterize these terms, they can scarcely be construed as conceding the one critical goal for which the war ostensibly has been fought—the denial of a communist accession to power in South Vietnam. Nor is the public misled on this point in giving its support to the president's various negotiating positions. A pronounced public skepticism on the prospects of reaching a negotiated settlement has testified to an awareness of the intractability of the central issue the adversaries must somehow resolve if negotiations are to prove successful.[4]

It is true that a majority has also supported unilateral withdrawal as an alternative to a negotiated settlement. At the same time, there has not been a solid and persistent majority in favor of unilateral withdrawal regardless of consequences. Quite apart from a near unanimity of opinion on tying withdrawal to the release of American prisoners of war, when confronted with the prospect of a communist government in South Vietnam as the price of withdrawal (or, for that matter, as the price of a negotiated settlement), the public has moved from rejection to acceptance and back again.[5] The only safe conclusion to be drawn is that the public has been torn by contradictory desires. Although a strong desire to end the nation's involvement in the war has been apparent, a reluctance to face up to the possible, and even likely, consequences of unilateral withdrawal has also been apparent.

It may be argued that in this situation of public uncertainty and indecision, the president has had considerable latitude to move in the direction of ending American involvement in Vietnam with the assurance that he could carry the public with him. Even if true, the argu-

[3] This discussion draws from the monthly reports of the *Gallup Opinion Index* as well as the *Harris Survey*, particularly for the period from September 1971 to September 1972. See also the very useful study *State of the Nation*, ed. William Watts and Lloyd A. Free (New York: Universe Books, Potomac Associates, 1972).

[4] See, for example, the *Harris Survey* of June 12, 1972, in which 88 percent of those questioned expressed doubt that a resolution of the Vietnam conflict would occur by election time, 79 percent wanted to withdraw all American forces from Vietnam, and 45 percent opposed a coalition government which included the communists (38 percent supported such a coalition). At the same time, a clear majority did support peace terms which included a stand-still cease-fire, the release of prisoners of war, and the establishment of a neutral regime in Saigon.

[5] See Watts and Free (eds.), *State of the Nation*, pp. 195–96, for evidence on this shifting response of the public to the prospect of a communist government in South Vietnam as the price of withdrawal.

ment does not bear out the view that Mr. Nixon has subverted the will of a majority. Instead, it asserts that the president has not used his power and position to re-form the majority will, a very different matter. Moreover, it is by no means clear that, if the president were to obtain peace at the price of conceding the goals for which the war was ostensibly fought, the longer term public reaction would be favorable when judged in terms of continued support for the larger aims of Mr. Nixon's foreign policy in Asia and elsewhere. Despite the adverse effects Vietnam has had, and continues to have, on the public's attitude toward foreign policy, a thinly disguised American defeat might precipitate a reaction against maintaining the larger structure of American interests and commitments by comparison with which the present reaction would seem quite modest. (To be sure, for those who wish the nation to abandon its present role this prospect poses no problems. But for those who view the prospect of a radical alteration in America's global role with dismay—as most of the influential critics of the administration's Vietnam policy do—the possible long-term consequences of defeat in Vietnam cannot be lightly dismissed. On this point, the president may prove to be much closer to the truth than his Vietnam critics.)

It is in the light of these considerations that it seems reasonable to conclude that the president has not so much defied the public's will with respect to the war as he has taken advantage of what he has rightly perceived as an ambivalence in that will. This ambivalence partly explains the widespread public support for Mr. Nixon's decisions in May 1972 to mine the harbors and to resume sustained heavy bombing of North Vietnam. The North Vietnamese offensive directly confronted the public with the stark prospect of defeat, one it has never clearly accepted. At the same time, the retaliatory measures taken by the president promised to ward off an ignominious end to the conflict at a relatively low cost in American blood and treasure.[6]

---

[6] Of course, public support for the president's actions taken against North Vietnam must also be explained by the public's view that these actions improved the prospects of an early termination of the war. Then, too, there is the almost uniform pattern of public approval of major escalatory measures taken by presidents in the course of the war. This tendency to support the president in the face of a challenge to American power and prestige is probably inseparable from the feelings of increased belligerency with which the public has responded to this and earlier communist offensives. These considerations, however, do not detract from the point that the public had never clearly faced and accepted the consequences of defeat in Vietnam. Indeed, the Democratic presidential candidate in 1972, by laying bare these consequences, appeared to increase the public's support for Mr. Nixon and his Vietnam policy.

Thus by changing the costs of the war while effectively exploiting the public's unwillingness to accept defeat, the president was able to marshall majority support for measures that carried the war as never before to North Vietnam. The lesson that is underscored by this latest chapter of the Vietnam agony has been apparent throughout the course of the conflict. In the absence of definitive results, public disaffection with the war has been largely a function of costs.[7] To the extent, then, that yesterday's expectations of far-reaching change in American foreign policy were based upon the shift that eventually occurred in public attitudes toward the war, the meaning of the shift was given a broader significance than it merited. In itself, the shift was not indicative of a deeper change in outlook toward the nation's proper role and interests in the world. There is no evidence that an important, let alone a decisive, factor in prompting a majority to believe that American involvement in Vietnam had been a mistake was the implausibility of the rationale given for the war, an implausibility that, once apprehended, would presumably lead the public to view with a new skepticism other American interests and commitments. Instead, the evidence points to the conclusion that a majority of those who finally came to view the intervention as a mistake and to favor withdrawal did so primarily on the grounds that we had not won the war and showed little prospect of doing so.[8]

This is not to deny that Vietnam affected the public's attitude toward foreign policy as perhaps no other event since the early post-

[7] In varying degree, this tendency is also characteristic of more select and elite groups. The point deserves emphasis since the charge of a pragmatism that verges on sheer moral obtuseness is often directed only against the public (and, of course, the government). As will be presently noted, however, the foreign policy elites' disaffection with the war also proved to be largely a function of cost *to this nation*. It is true that some morally sensitive critics have insisted that the costs of the war must be seen in their generality and not only in their particularity, that they must be calculated in terms of the lives of others as well as of our own. The record is clear, though, that it was American lives which above all prompted growing elite opposition to the war. This is true even of the most idealistic of the groups opposing the war, the leadership of the younger generation, given the correlation between the intensity of youthful dissent and the liability of youth to the draft.

[8] A Michigan Survey Research Center finding in 1968 illustrates the point: "[Among] those who viewed the war as a mistake almost as many favored escalation as were for withdrawal! All told ... a five-to-three majority regretted the original intervention, but at the same time those calling for 'a stronger stand even if it means invading North Vietnam' outnumbered those advocating complete withdrawal by about as large a margin." Philip E. Converse and Howard Schuman, " 'Silent Majorities' and the Vietnam War," *Scientific American* (June, 1970), p. 20.

war years, but that the deeper and more lasting effects of the war on the public remain as uncertain today as they were in 1968. The one—indeed the only—indisputable lesson that may be learned from Vietnam is that success, in a relatively brief period, is the great solvent of serious public disaffection over a foreign policy that entails serious costs in blood and treasure. But this lesson apart, and it is scarcely a novel one, the experience of Vietnam is less than revealing about the nature of the constraints policy makers will henceforth ignore only at their peril. Certainly, there was little in the Vietnam experience by 1968—just as there remains little in that experience today—affording grounds for the belief that the public had broken its deeply ingrained habit of deferring to presidential judgment and initiative. On the contrary, perhaps the most impressive aspect of the relationship between the public and its government in the course of the war has been the persistent permissiveness of the public, even after it had ample reason to distrust the wisdom of its leadership.

What was distinctive about the domestic reaction to Vietnam was not the lack of popular support for the war after 1968. A comparison between the Vietnam and Korean wars shows that public weariness and disenchantment with each conflict become equally manifest after a certain point.[9] Vietnam has been distinctive because of the opposition it aroused among the leadership of the younger generation, among the intellectuals, and, particularly, among those who comprised the foreign policy elites. At the same time, it was not so much the disaffection of the elite young or even of the intellectuals that proved to be critical, but the disaffection of the liberal and moderate elites who had long formed the core of the foreign policy consensus. It was the disaffection of the latter that gave the opposition to Vietnam a significance it otherwise would not have possessed.

Yet there was little reason for believing that the opposition to the war of a major portion of the foreign policy elites indicated as well a breakdown in the larger foreign policy consensus. In this respect, it is instructive to recall the manner in which elite opinion evolved in the course of the war. It was not only the public that responded to pragmatic considerations of cost and effectiveness in changing its attitude toward the war. So did the greater part of the disaffected among the elites who, in the initial stages of the war, supported the intervention or, though entertaining reservations about the wisdom of intervention, fell short of clear opposition or, though unreservedly opposed

---

[9] John E. Mueller, "Trends in Popular Support for the Wars in Korea and Vietnam," *American Political Science Review* (June, 1971), pp. 358–75.

from the start, saw in the war a misapplication of American power given the unfavorable circumstances in which that power was applied.

In the light of the history of the war, and of the correlation between its costly yet frustrating course and the swelling ranks of influential critics, it is reasonable to conclude that the majority of liberal and moderate critics came to oppose the intervention not so much because they did not share the outlook and interests that were bound, sooner or later, to issue in a Vietnam, but because they concluded that the war could not have a successful outcome or that, whatever the outcome, the costs had become entirely disproportionate to the interests at stake. This explains why liberal critics of the war have insisted on viewing the American role in Vietnam as a tragedy (in contrast to radical critics who have been equally insistent upon viewing this role as a crime). To the liberal and moderate critics of the war, our intentions were good and our objectives worthy. Given the political realities in Vietnam, however, we have fought a war in which success was all but precluded from the start. And to the extent success was ever a meaningful prospect, it was so only through means which, if they did not jeopardize the ends, were disproportionately costly. It is this disparity which, in the view taken by a host of conventional critics, not only defined the tragedy of Vietnam but, in the end, defined the immorality of the war.

To the extent that influential opposition to the war was based on cost and effectiveness, the broad consensus that formed the foundation of American foreign policy since World War II remained essentially intact. Of course, the debate and dissatisfaction precipitated by the war also transcended the war, even before 1968. But the significance of the debate over American policy generally was not easy to assess, if only because the ostensible adversaries appeared to share the same basic conception of America's role and interests in the world.

This essential agreement precluded characterizing the debate, at least insofar as its principal parties were concerned, as one between interventionists and non-interventionists. Liberal opposition to the war did not imply an anti-interventionist position in principle, even as applied to Asia, and scarcely could have done so in view of the interests liberals continued to find vital to the nation. This opposition did express the conviction that military intervention was a means that must henceforth be employed with much greater caution and selectivity, that it should seldom, if ever, be undertaken in predominantly internal revolutionary conflicts, since in such conflicts it is likely to prove ineffective and even counterproductive, and that it should never be undertaken simply out of an obsessive attachment to the status quo. The qualifications so stated, even if taken at face value, spelled out a position that still left the door open to future interventions.

The debate engendered by Vietnam did reveal differences in the conceptions of America's vital interests entertained by critics and supporters of American policy. At the same time, in retrospect, these differences often were exaggerated by liberal critics. If the latter had a rather more restricted view of the nation's role and vital interests, that view scarcely revealed the broad differences liberal critics were wont to claim. The prevailing liberal critique assumed that America would, and should, continue to occupy a leading, if not a preponderant, role in the international hierarchy. It reaffirmed the vital American interest in the preservation of a favorable balance of power in Europe and Asia, and thus in the need to maintain *some* kind of containment policy with respect to the Soviet Union and China. It did not dispute the need to preserve the essential structure of America's alliance relationships, particularly with Western Europe and Japan. The desirability of maintaining America's military hegemony over its principal allies was no more questioned than the undesirability of promoting the one development that held out the prospect of a substantial devolution of power—nuclear proliferation. Even with respect to the third world the departure marked by the liberal critique was relatively modest, and consisted as much in a changed estimate of the threat held out to the American interest in the underdeveloped nations as in a changed estimate of the interest itself.

The principal thrust of liberal criticism was simply that the world had changed since the early years of the cold war but that American policy had not changed with it. Early containment policy, on this view, had been a limited and effective response to the threat held out by the Soviet Union to the balance of power destroyed by the war. The success of that policy, which focused upon Europe, had been made possible by a combination of uniquely favorable circumstances: the unparalleled power and prestige with which America emerged from the war, the starkness and simplicity of the confrontation with the Soviet Union, the almost complete prostration of those who formed the objects of confrontation, and the near perfect conditions Western Europe afforded for carrying out a policy of containment. In these circumstances, the issues that were later to plague American policy could scarcely arise, or, to the degree they did arise, could not appear very significant. In particular, whether containment was to be directed against Soviet power or communism itself, or both, was not an issue of practical importance so long as communism remained an apparently monolithic movement. Clearly, it did not appear as an important issue in Western Europe, the control of which formed the principal occasion for, and stake of, the cold war in its initial years.

In the prevailing liberal critique, it was the very success of early containment policy that paved the way for a diplomacy culminating in the disaster of Vietnam. For this success, when taken together with the momentum generated by the cold war itself, helped reinvigorate an outlook that had never been abandoned. The quintessential expression of this outlook was, of course, the Truman Doctrine, with its unlimited and indiscriminate commitment, its sense of universal crisis, and its messianic hope of redeeming history. The gradual triumph of the Truman Doctrine in policy describes the essential course of American diplomacy over the following two decades. What began as a policy largely limited to Europe, directed primarily against the expansion of Soviet power, and designed to restore a balance of power, ended as a policy unlimited in geographic scope, directed against communism itself, and designed to preserve a global status quo bearing little, if any, relation to the balance of power. The failure of this policy was foreordained if only because it reflected a view of the world profoundly at odds with reality. Although the world of the 1960s bore only a limited resemblance to the world of the late 1940s, it was precisely in the radically altered circumstances of the 1960s that the aspirations expressed in the Truman Doctrine achieved their most excessive policy manifestation. Vietnam afforded the perfect example of a policy incapable of distinguishing between vital and less-than-vital interests, of a policy bound to result in the overcommitment of the nation's resources. It illustrated, as no other event could, the extent to which American policy had become synonymous with an indiscriminate counter-revolutionary stance that, quite apart from its gross overestimation of what American power can accomplish, ran the danger of betraying the American purpose both abroad and at home.

To the liberal critic, then, Vietnam appeared as a legacy of the cold war (particularly the Asian legacy), and of the excesses and rigidities in thought and action the cold war had encouraged. Above all, Vietnam and the larger policy that led to Vietnam revealed a failure of political intelligence. It is this emphasis on intellectual error that formed the inner core of liberal criticism of Vietnam and that separated it so clearly from radical criticism. In the far less influential radical critique that emerged in the course of the war, Vietnam laid bare the lengths to which American imperialism would knowingly and deliberately go to defeat a social revolution found to threaten our hegemonial position; in conventional liberal criticism, Vietnam revealed the disastrous consequences to which our ingrained misconceptions could lead when circumstances so combined to produce a kind of limiting case. Whereas radical criticism called for the abandonment in toto of America's postwar role and interest, liberal criticism called instead for the abandonment of an outlook that had led to the deformation of role and interest which culminated in Vietnam. The liberal critique did not signal a basic break from the post-war foreign policy consensus but an insistence upon readjusting that consensus to changing circumstances abroad and at home.

3

Given the nature of the prevailing critique of American foreign policy, the response of the Nixon Administration took much of the ground from under the larger debate occasioned by Vietnam. It did so by assimilating, though not without qualification, the major points of what by 1968 represented conventional criticism. Thus it became the settled orthodoxy of the new administration that the conditions marking the period of the classic cold war had been profoundly altered and that American policy must adjust to a new world. The liberal critique had emphasized the extent to which a once rigidly bipolar world had evolved into a multipolar world, politically and economically, if not militarily. The Nixon Administration placed an even greater emphasis on this evolution and on the changes it necessitated in relations with our major allies and our major adversaries. Toward the former, who had presumably regained much of their past vigor and self-assurance, a more equal and balanced relationship was now required. Toward the latter, who were deeply divided yet no longer took a position of unremitting belligerenge toward this nation, a more creative connection reflecting an at least partial accommodation was now possible (and, in view of the admitted loss of our strategic superiority vis-à-vis the Soviet Union, was even deemed essential).

The liberal critique had insisted that an increasingly pluralistic world, though far more complicated than the world of a generation ago, was nevertheless a safer world, since pluralism not only meant that communist expansion no longer carried the threat to American interests it once carried but that the prospects of communist expansion in the developing nations had markedly declined. The Nixon Administration cautiously endorsed this assessment by emphasizing the "new capacities" of the developing nations to provide for their own security as well as the "new sense of national autonomy" that was found to guide their decisions. The danger, taken with the utmost seriousness at the beginning of the 1960s, that a hostile power or combination of powers might succeed in shutting America off from the nations of the third world, was discounted.

In Asia, the achilles heel of American policy in the postwar period, the conventional critique had traced American policy errors culminating in Vietnam generally to a misunderstanding of the nature of the threat posed to American interests and of the appropriate means for countering this threat. In particular, Chinese power had been exaggerated, as had the ability and will to project this power, while the constraints placed upon China's freedom of action had been largely neglected. Intent upon reducing its presence in Asia, and confronted with new evidence that the split between the two great communist powers had progressed from its political-ideological stage to a potentially more ominous stage, the new administration cautiously moved toward accepting a view the preceding administration had resisted.

Above all, the Nixon Administration responded from the outset to the point that had been the common denominator of conventional criticism: the overextension of American power. To be sure, even as a statement of intent the Nixon Doctrine was scarcely a striking response to the critique of American globalism. Characteristically cautious and carefully qualified, it avowed that America "cannot—and will not—conceive *all* the plans, design *all* the programs, execute *all* the decisions and undertake *all* the defense of the free nations of the world." While promising to apply "rigorous yardsticks" to new commitments, and to view existing undertakings as a "dynamic process," the determination to retain existing commitments was reaffirmed. If interests were henceforth to determine commitments, rather than the other way around, there was little indication that existing commitments failed to reflect interests. Even if some commitments were ill-conceived in origin or outdated in terms of the interests they had once reflected, emphasis was placed on the importance of the method employed in altering them, lest instability result and credibility be placed in question. Thus the insistent cautionary note that "abrupt shifts are unsettling" and that change, though incremental, must not lead to a "reputation for unsteadiness." As applied to Vietnam, these qualifications were themselves sufficient to justify continued American involvement in the war, whatever the wisdom of the initial intervention. Moreover, these qualifications suggested that the anti-interventionism of the Nixon Doctrine was not only of modest proportion but that, in a number of respects, it was reminiscent of earlier statements of intent with respect to the American role in Asia. It is worth recalling that from Truman to Nixon successive administrations have looked to America's Asian allies to assume primary responsibility for their defense against non-nuclear aggression, and particularly to assume primary responsibility for defending themselves against internal subversion. In calling for allies to make a greater effort to provide the manpower for their own defense—a defense that would still be supplemented by American military and economic assistance—the Nixon Doctrine appeared to traverse well-worn ground.

Despite these considerations, the Nixon Doctrine was generally interpreted as a triumph of sorts for the liberal, and limitationist, critique. That it was on the whole well-received, notwithstanding its highly cautious and elaborately qualified character, suggests that the prevailing criticism of American globalism did not necessitate a striking—let alone a radical—response. The anti-interventionism of the majority of liberal and moderate critics had also been carefully circumscribed, and in many respects not markedly dissimilar from the qualifications of the Nixon Doctrine. Indeed, given the principal thrust of the liberal critique of American foreign policy—with its emphasis on style and outlook as much as on policy itself, with its disagreement over means as much as over the substance of interests, and with its relatively optimistic assessment of what was required to preserve American interests—the Nixon Doctrine appeared to strike almost exactly the right note. It decried an outlook and a style that had been marked by unlimited aspirations and that in the changed circumstances of the 1960s had led to the overestimation of what American power could accomplish. In emphasizing the inherent limits to any nation's wisdom, understanding, and energy, it called for a new modesty in thought and action. It no longer found in anti-communism the guiding principle of American efforts. Instead, its cool tone suggested that crusades of any kind were the very antithesis of the new style and outlook. At the same time it did not relinquish the substance of interest, but promised change in the methods by which interest would henceforth be served. Even in Asia, the area to which the Nixon Doctrine was initially and primarily addressed, the emphasis was on method. Although promising no more Vietnams, the Nixon Doctrine did not concede that the price would be a substantial sacrifice of American interests. In this last and critical respect, it implied what the liberal critique had implied, that America's role and interests could on the whole be maintained by other, certainly less painful methods.[10]

In responding to the liberal critique, the new administration also took advantage of the opportunities afforded by this critique to claim to have effected "profound changes," not only in outlook, but in the substance of policy as well. If these claims rather exceed the bounds of a custom indulged in by every administration, it is only fair to add that the temptation to excess was in no small measure due to the efforts of yesterday's critics. The very exaggerations of the liberal critique of American policy could not but lend a measure of credence to the more pretentious claims to change of the present administration. In this sense, liberal critics were all but hoisted on their own petard. Having as often as not simply caricatured American policy, and having eventually come almost to believe in their own caricature (or, at any rate, having persuaded others that it was an accurate portrayal), the juxtaposition of the liberal caricature with the Nixon Doctrine is startling. Instead of policy makers who remained insistently blind to the great changes that had occurred over a generation, we now had an administration that would make a fetish of explaining these changes. And instead of policy makers who were resolute in their pursuit of an anti-communist obsession divorced from considerations of interest, we now had an administration that would act only in terms of a cool calculation of interest. If the contrast, though misleading, was more than a little persuasive to many, the Nixon Administration could scarcely have been expected to have abstained from exploiting it.

This is not to say that the Nixon Doctrine precluded any change in the structure of American interests. The new administration acknowl-

[10] Still, it is essential to emphasize that the methods of the post-Kennedy liberal critique are not to be identified with the methods promised by the Nixon Doctrine. In the liberal critique, it was assumed that American interests, particularly in the third world, could be maintained without resort to armed intervention and that in those exceptional circumstances where they could not intervention would, in any event, prove counterproductive (above all, in predominantly revolutionary conflicts). The Nixon Doctrine, too, assumes that the need for direct intervention has markedly declined in the third world. At the same time, it acknowledges, if only by implication, that armed intervention may prove necessary, even in revolutionary conflicts, to vindicate American interests, and that where this is the case the emphasis would be on air and naval power rather than on ground forces. In this light, the "test case" of the Nixon Doctrine to date has not been Cambodia, as the president once insisted, but the air and naval measures initiated against North Vietnam in the late spring of 1972.

edged from the start that a changed world not only required change in the methods of policy but also permitted and even required a certain redefinition of interests. Thus in a pluralistic world, the domino theory must at least be modified, but so also must the interest one had in each and every domino. If there is no "test case" for wars of national liberation, the interest one has in intervening in any particular war of national liberation is subject to change. If the process of modernization is going to prove to be slow, and its course cannot be controlled by outsiders, there is no need to see in it a matter of vital concern. If China is no longer found capable of or intent upon overturning the Asian balance of power, the interest in containing China may be reinterpreted. These were among the commonplaces of the conventional critical view that change was required not only in the methods but in the interests of policy. They are also among the recognizable features of the present administration's philosophy and—to an as yet uncertain degree—policy.

Yet a modest redefinition of interests, and one that is largely contingent upon a cautiously optimistic view of the world in which these interests must be preserved, does not add up to a revolution in American foreign policy. Innovations in diplomatic method aside, the change in role and interests suggested by the Nixon Doctrine has been a distinctly limited one. Now as before, America would play a predominant role in the world, however that role might be redefined. Now as before, American power would remain the indispensable element in world order, or, to employ a more currently fashionable phrase, in a stable and lasting structure of peace. This order would no longer be defined primarily—if, indeed, at all—in ideological terms. In consequence, the requirements of order would increasingly be seen in the more traditional terms of a balance of power between states rather than, as before, in terms of the external balance as well as the internal order maintained by states. More generally, the detailed definition of the kind of world order sought by this nation would be relaxed, though the extent of this relaxation remained unclear in doctrine and, in any event, would have to be seriously tested in practice. Even so, these qualifications do not substantially affect the point that for this administration, as for its predecessors, the nation's security and well-being would continue to be broadly equated with a world in which America occupies a preponderant position in the international hierarchy and in which change could be effected only in certain ways while certain types of change would be precluded altogether.

It is this essential continuity of role and interests that explains the

persistence with which the Nixon Administration has sought to vindicate the American commitment in Vietnam. Why is it that the president has been so insistent upon vindicating this commitment if the
circumstances in which it was initially made have changed dramatically? Why has he persisted in an involvement that at the very least
has complicated his efforts to establish "a more creative connection"
with the major communist powers? Surely it will not do to answer
that the liquidation of any commitment, however unwise in conception and disastrous in execution, cannot be effected overnight, particularly one of the magnitude of Vietnam. If the point is unexcep-
tionable, it is also irrelevant after four years. Nor will it do to argue
that the war has continued, despite the ostensible invalidation of all
the reasons originally given for intervening, because of "pure organizational momentum" and the inability of a bureaucracy, on its own,
to undertake a drastic change of course.[11] Whatever else may be said
of this administration's conduct of foreign policy, it can scarcely be
charged with permitting high policy to be subject to bureaucratic
control. "The "dis-establishment of the bureaucracy" has been generally regarded as a distinctive achievement of the Nixon Administration. Yet the war has continued and the determination to avoid defeat apparently has remained unimpaired.

It is no more persuasive to attempt to account for the continuation
of the war by pointing to the constraints imposed by domestic politics. For those constraints, such as they are, have hardly impelled the
president to follow his chosen course. Although anti-communism has
by no means disappeared, its significance—both in sustaining public
support for foreign policy and in constraining the freedom of policy
makers—has markedly declined. Moreover, the point hardly needs
making that both in his rhetoric as well as in his policies Mr. Nixon,
long regarded as the ideologue par excellence of the cold war, has
made an important contribution to this decline. The argument that
the president has been constrained to persist in Vietnam because he
has feared appearing too soft on communism will no more bear serious examination than the argument, occasionally voiced by high officials in the early period of this administration, that vindication of the
American commitment in Vietnam was necessary in guarding against
the prospect of a dangerous reaction from the right. The president's
well-established anti-communist credentials ensured against his serious vulnerability to the charge (by whom could it have been made

[11] See John Kenneth Galbraith, "The Plain Lessons of a Bad Decade," *Foreign
Policy* (Winter, 1970–71), p. 41.

among his major political opponents?) of being soft on communism. As for the fear of provoking a dangerous reaction from the right by conceding on Vietnam, in view of Mr. Nixon's policy of evoking the patriotism of Middle America to support continued involvement in the war, the best that can be said of this argument is that it is self-serving.

Viewed from almost any plausible perspective, it is apparent that by persisting in Vietnam the president ran substantial risks to his political position at home. That these risks did not materialize by 1972 —indeed, that what once appeared as a serious electoral liability was ultimately converted into an asset—is of less interest here than the fact that Mr. Nixon was willing to run them. While it is impossible to say what the president might have done had the public responded differently to his handling of the war, it is possible to find in his unyielding stance a measure of his conviction that defeat in Vietnam, certainly defeat in the early years of Mr. Nixon's Administration,[12] would eventually jeopardize the domestic support needed for his larger policies. If time and again the President has insisted that defeat in Vietnam would set off a deep and sustained public reaction against further involvement abroad, a reaction that would make it impossible for America to continue playing a preponderant role in the world, there is no reason to doubt his sincerity. Nor is it apparent that he has been wrong in this insistence.

In this light, the "constraints" at home that explain Mr. Nixon's Vietnam policy are largely self-imposed and result from a determination not to compromise essential long-term public support for—or, at any rate, toleration of—a policy that changes in order to conserve. If the substance of the nation's global position is to be preserved, the by now familiar argument runs, the public's confidence in America's power and in the will of a president effectively to use that power when challenged must not be allowed to erode. The same imperatives of prestige and credibility hold true for adversaries and allies, all the more so, in fact, in a period of retrenchment. In this view, it is not decisive that the circumstances in which the commitment in Vietnam was made have changed—and, indeed, changed in response to developments that may be related only marginally to the perserverance with which the American commitment has been held. If a modest and orderly retreat of American power is to be undertaken without

---

[12] That is, defeat before the withdrawal of American ground forces, the sustained attempt at Vietnamization, and the compensation for ultimate failure to save South Vietnam by successes elsewhere. Even then, the dangers implicit in ultimate failure would persist, as the president has made clear.

sacrifice of, or jeopardy to, the larger structure of interests on which America's world position continues to rest, it is essential that it not be done, and not *appear* to be done, as a response to defeat in Vietnam.

The administration's response, then, to the alleged contradiction many critics have found between the refusal to accept a settlement tantamount to defeat in Vietnam and the desire to establish more normal and stable relationships with the communist powers has been that this contradiction is more apparent than real. No doubt, America's continued involvement in Vietnam has complicated efforts toward developing the new triangular relationship with the Soviet Union and China. But this relationship, it has been argued, would prove abortive and, if nevertheless persisted in, even dangerous, unless undertaken by an America whose prestige and credibility remained unimpaired. The acknowledgement of strategic equilibrium between the United States and the Soviet Union does not thereby ensure either that the Soviets will accept the desirability of maintaining political equilibrium, let alone of endowing this equilibrium with a measure of legitimacy, if it is entered into by an America that has shown itself unwilling or unable to fulfill its commitments. The acknowledgement that the communist government in China is not only legitimate but entitled to lay claim to interests it has long been denied cannot be attended by an American defeat in Asia that might well tempt a Chinese government to reconsider its gradual adjustment in conduct and aspiration to what has increasingly resembled a more conventional statecraft.

It is substantially in this manner that a change in the circumstances in which the commitment to Vietnam was made has not been seen by the Nixon Administration as invalidating the larger considerations that initially prompted the intervention and that, in any event, continue to rule out the acceptance of defeat. Now as yesterday, the preservation of the structure of order American policy has sought to create and maintain in the post-World War II period rests upon the preservation of a balance of power. Among nuclear powers, however, this balance must be understood primarily in political and psychological terms. It rests less on the structure of material power and relative material advantage than on deterrent threat. Yet there is no reliable way to maintain the credibility of the threat that continues to undergird the American position in the world save by manifesting determination to refuse defeat once there has been a recourse to force. In 1972, the integrity of the American commitment remained for the Nixon Administration, as it earlier remained for the Johnson

Administration, the heart of the matter in Vietnam. Indeed, concern over the integrity of the American commitment has appeared all the more marked in an administration whose outlook has taken on the air of a settled imperial power shorn of much of the former exuberance over, and confidence in, what it can accomplish, yet determined to preserve the substance of its interests. Given this dominant outlook, there is no need to speculate, in relation to Vietnam, on the reasons for this administration's insistence on maintaining its prestige and credibility.

Vietnam apart, the essential continuity in outlook and policy of the Nixon Administration is apparent in relations with major allies. A devotion to "partnership" and the need to create "more balanced" alliances is novel to this administration only to the extent that it has made such a fetish of its dedication to these ends. In fact, dedication to the same ends forms a recurrent theme of American policy over the past two decades. The Johnson Administration, in particular, spoke increasingly of the need to establish more equal relations with our major allies, thereby promoting true partners with whom we could share our great responsibilities. It is true that in stressing its commitment to partnership the Johnson Administration remained unwilling seriously to consider those measures indispensable to the creation of true partners. In the manner of its predecessor, and its successor, the Johnson Administration was unwilling to accept the consequences of a diffusion of power and a devolution of responsibility by encouraging allies to take measures by which these goals might alone eventually be realized. Although urged to bear a greater share of the cost of their defense, allies were not encouraged to seek military independence from the United States. Instead, partnership was interpreted to mean the perpetuation of America's military hegemony. This devotion to the idea of partnership without equality persists almost unimpaired today. The Nixon Administration, for all its commitment to promoting more balanced alliance relationships, has been quite as reluctant to alter America's dominant military position. The grand designs of the past have been set aside. They presupposed a degree of unity between America and her allies which never afforded much promise of materializing even under the far more favorable circumstances of yesterday. The determination to retain ultimate control over the security and military freedom of action of allies remains substantially unchanged.

It has been argued that the very act of renouncing grand designs for allies is itself a significant break from the alliance policy of an earlier period in that it is indicative of a new sense of self-restraint and a determination henceforth to act with greater discretion. In what has become a more fluid diplomatic system, one in which America's power to lead her allies has diminished, the Nixon Administration's attitude toward its ties with major allies is represented as at least a partial return to more conventional alliance relationships. Clearly, the alliance policy of this administration reflects a strong desire to reduce the costs of maintaining our alliances while giving us more freedom of maneuver and independence of action. It is equally clear, however, that the administration has shown little disposition to acknowledge that a substantial price may eventually have to be paid for the new policy. While allies are expected to contribute an increasing share of the cost for their defense—and to compromise, partly for the sake of allied solidarity, on issues of trade and monetary reform—they are also expected to do so within an alliance structure that remains, so far as the ultimate issues of security are concerned, unchanged. Yesterday, America's military preponderance over its major allies was necessitated by their intrinsic weakness and, of course, by the immoderate character of a rigidly bipolar system. Today, these allies may have recovered much of their former vitality and the international system is otherwise tending toward moderation. Even so, America's military preponderance is held to remain as necessary as ever if the emerging diplomatic equilibrium is not to be upset and an era of negotiation is not to deteriorate, once again, into one of confrontation.

If the Nixon Administration has not abandoned the interest in keeping Western Europe and Japan in the role of military dependents, neither has it abandoned the primary goal of American policy since the late 1940s: the containment of communism. The point would hardly be worth making were it not for the fact that many, confusing words with acts and tactical methods with strategic aims, have seen in the successive elaborations of the Nixon Doctrine the at least partial abandonment of a policy of containing the major communist powers. Even more have found in the Nixon policy reformulation the abandonment of an outlook and policy that opposed the emergence to power of communist regimes in the developing states, presumably out of an obsessive fear of communism.

In a curious way, the present administration has appeared to encourage these views if only by virtue of its deliberate de-emphasis of ideology and its evident penchant for explaining policy in the idiom of conventional diplomacy. Yet the contrast between the policies of this and preceding administrations cannot rest on these differences, however striking they may appear. A policy that emphasizes ideological motivation and that speaks in an idiom appropriate to such emphasis may be no less guided by self-interest than a policy that eschews ideology and speaks only of national interests and the need for equilibrium. Surely it is not simply, or even primarily, an abstract ideological commitment divorced from considerations of interest and power that explains the post-war policy of containing the Soviet Union and China. Nor can this explanation account for America's interventionary policy in the third world. If America did not cease to pursue an interventionist and counter-revolutionary policy once it was no longer plausible to equate the expansion of communism with the expansion of Russian (or Chinese) power, it was because of the apprehension that the abandonment of such a policy would open the way to developments inevitably leading to the loss of American influence in much of the third world. This apprehension may have been misplaced, but that is a very different matter from saying that it reflected an abstract ideological interest divorced from solid self-interest. On the contrary, whatever the idiom with which it was expressed, the interest this apprehension reflected evidently forms one of the perennial goals of all great powers.

Although the third world clearly has been demoted in the scale of concerns of the Nixon Administration, it remains unclear to what extent the demotion results from a redefinition of interests rather than from a redefinition of the threat to interests that remain essentially unchanged. It may be, and has been, argued that to the extent developments in the third world no longer permit the great powers to view their contest for influence there in preclusive, let alone irrevocable, terms, the interest itself must change. But quite apart from the fundamental, and unanswered, question this argument must raise, it is open to the objection that it assumes the American interest in the developing world has been no more than a function of its conflict with its major communist adversaries rather than, in part, a function of the desire to exercise influence for its own sake—a desire that, so long as it is entertained, must dictate an anti-communist stance. At any rate, the point remains that the present administration has not acknowledged an essential change in the definition of American interests in the third world. Although it does accept the view that the threat to those interests has diminished, the optimism reflected in this view is not without limits. To the extent that a policy of much greater restraint, bordering at times even on indifference, has been adopted in relation to the third world, it is still contingent upon the assumption that the consequences of such a policy will not lead to marked instability or to the substantial reduction of American influence. If the aspirations, and even more the fears, of yesterday have receded, they have by no means disappeared.

It is, of course, the policies pursued toward the Soviet Union and China that have marked the most spectacular developments of the past four years. The Nixon Doctrine held out the promise of evolving more creative and, on balance, more advantageous relationships with the major communist powers. Has the promise been at least partially fulfilled? Only the resolute partisan would insist that it has not. The detente with the Soviet Union has been consolidated to an extent few would have predicted even as late as 1970. Moreover, this consolidation has been undertaken without the concession of interests that were not already implicitly conceded. It was not the Nixon Administration but its predecessor that, in action if not in word, accepted the Soviet Union as an equal in strategic power. So, too, the Johnson Administration accepted the inevitability of expanding Soviet interests, particularly in the Mediterranean, consequent upon the rapid growth of Soviet naval power. The conclusion by the governments of West Germany, Poland, and the Soviet Union of treaties that comprise, in effect, a treaty of peace for Central Eruope, only legitimize a status quo that the American government had long accepted. With perhaps the exception of the Soviet position in the Asian subcontinent—a position that, at best, represents a dubious asset—Soviet interests and influence have nowhere expanded since 1968 to the relative disadvantage of the United States.

Nor is this all. In a period characterized as one of American retrenchment, the Nixon Administration has, if anything, improved its credibility in the eyes of its major adversary with respect to American willingness to use force when vital interests are threatened. European observers, prone to misinterpret the American scene and the domestic constraints imposed on the president, and persuaded that the voices of neo-isolationism represent the wave of the future, may increasingly doubt this will.[13] The Russians—and, for that matter, the Chinese—apparently do not. That is not surprising, given the obsessiveness with which the president has insisted that America's prestige and credibility must be maintained at any price, and given a pattern of behavior that has been quite consistent with this insistence. At the same time, the marked sensitivity shown toward Soviet challenges to established American positions has not impaired the effort to broaden detente. Although in refusing to react to the mining of the harbors of

[13] See, for example, Walter Laqueur, "From Globalism to Isolationism," *Commentary* 54, no. 3 (September, 1972), pp. 63–67.

North Vietnam in the spring of 1972 the Soviet Union suffered a humiliation in many ways comparable to that suffered a decade earlier in the Cuban missile crisis, the effect was not to hamper the improving relationship between the two superpowers.

It does not seriously detract from the achievements of the Nixon Administration in dealing with its major adversaries to note that these achievements were largely conditioned by the lengths to which the conflict between the Soviet Union and China had gone by late 1968. Without question, the decision of the Soviet leadership to turn a political-ideological rivalry into a political-military confrontation presented this administration with a golden opportunity its predecessor had not been afforded. In the absence of the threat posed to China by Soviet forces, the moderation of Chinese policy and the limited success of Washington's rapprochement with Peking is difficult to imagine. Similarly, in the absence of Soviet apprehensions over the possibilities of this rapprochement, Moscow's determination not to permit humiliation in the Gulf of Tonkin to jeopardize a broadening detente with the United States is difficult to imagine. Even so, the point remains that if the Nixon Administration did not create the conditions it has benefitted from, it effectively exploited these conditions once they became apparent. To what extent it has been able to exploit Sino-Soviet hostility to secure a more satisfactory settlement of the war in Vietnam remains uncertain at the time of writing. In a broader perspective, the issue is of limited importance. If a satisfactory settlement of the war provided an immediate motive for developing the triangular relationship, it was clearly not the only motivation nor, in all probability, the most important. Barring an altogether unexpected turn of events, the larger opportunities afforded by this relationship will remain when the war in Southeast Asia has become only a memory.

In the context of the broader themes discussed in these pages, what is significant about the "more creative connections" the Nixon Administration has sought to establish with the Soviet Union and China are the changes thereby effected in the policy of containment. If these changes do not abandon the broader aims the United States has pursued since World War II, they clearly do imply important innovations in the methods for achieving a strategy whose objectives have remained remarkably constant. Nor does it diminish the significance of these innovations in method to insist that they are, in large measure, the product of necessity and that, in the perspective of the time-honored conventions of diplomacy, they are scarcely new. For all this, they remain no less striking when juxtaposed with the methods of past administrations.

It is undoubtedly the case that the methods of containment altered in the period from Truman to Nixon. Even so, there remained a certain inner core of consistency in method that, as much as anything else, gave containment its distinctive cast. In essence a strategy of indirection, save when directly challenged, containment concentrated on alliance relationships and "awaited," as it were, a basic change in the external behavior of adversaries. Did this change that formed the ultimate promise of containment presuppose basic change in the nature of the Russian (and Chinese) regimes? From the outset, the question provoked divergent responses that were, in turn, partially reflected by the divergent views entertained over the means containment should emphasize. In a sense, these differences came to a head, and found extreme expression, in the debate occasioned by the intervention in Vietnam. In a more moderate form, however, the same differences were earlier apparent in the disparate views given to containment and its implementation by such men as George Kennan and Dean Acheson.

Yet these differences had a common denominator. Whether change in the behavior of adversaries would ultimately come from their domestic transformation or simply from their adjustment to an international environment they could no longer effectively exploit, the guiding idea persisted that it was only in the creation of such an environment that the promise of containment would eventually be realized. Men might, and did, differ over the characteristics of this environment and the priorities of effort it required. Here again, Vietnam illuminated these differences as no other event had while giving them their most extreme expression. But the liberal and moderate opposition to Vietnam did not challenge the prevailing view of a generation: that the Soviet Union and China would eventually be induced to alter their aims and to accept our vision of a stable and moderate international system, as a result of an environment that left them with no real alternative. Instead, the liberal critique argued that this alteration had in large part already occurred precisely because the desired environment had already been largely realized.

The Nixon reformulation of containment is novel to the degree that it is no longer content with a strategy of indirection, which had as its principal corollary an emphasis on allied solidarity as the principal and only reliable path for achieving a stable and congenial international environment. Although alliances remain essential, there is no longer the same disposition to pay the price previous administrations were able, and willing, to pay in order to reassure the querulous and to pacify the disaffected. Although the alliance system is still considered a vital ligament of a stable structure of peace, it is no longer seen as a substitute for dealing directly and continuously with adversaries. The need to retain cooperative relationships with allies is henceforth to be balanced against—and not sacrificed to—the need to hold out positive inducements to adversaries. The hope is that these inducements will progressively moderate the behavior of adversaries and, eventually, promote a common interest in maintaining an order which has a broader and more durable base than the fear of mutual destruction.

It is apparent that this reformulation of containment reflects a more modest estimate of what American power can accomplish (or prevent). With respect to allies, it betrays an awareness that this nation no longer possesses the ability to lead—or, less euphemistically, to impose solutions—by virtue of sheer magnitude of power. In any conflict of interests with allies, the latter still have more to lose than we do. But this power to impose greater injury than is suffered is a very different thing from the power we formerly enjoyed. With respect to adversaries as well, the Nixon reformulation of containment no longer reflects the sense of omnipotence that, perhaps more than any other factor, prompted the view that we did not have to deal with adversaries in order to achieve a stable and congenial international environment. The significance of this change has been partially obscured by the compensatory tough image the Nixon Administration has assiduously, and rather successfully, cultivated. In giving the impression of a willingness to go to the brink rather than to sacrifice American prestige and credibility, President Nixon has stolen a page from John Foster Dulles' book, though the more recent exercise has been carried out with far greater finesse and sophistication in less favorable circumstances. Whereas Dulles only evidenced faith in the stick when dealing with the Soviet Union and China, Nixon has seen to it that the carrot is never far removed from the stick. Although extremely sensitive to what it interprets as a challenge by adversaries, this administration has also been willing to hold out incentives its predecessors were not.

The question persists whether the changes in diplomatic method introduced by the Nixon Administration may eventually lead to a substantially transformed position for the nation. Clearly, such transformation was not the intent of those responsible for the new policies. On the contrary, the guiding assumption on which this administration has proceeded is that the nation can maintain its predominant position but at a lower and domestically tolerable price. At the same time, the grandiose aspirations of yesterday have of necessity been set aside. The desire for stability per se, which formerly competed with the urge to universalize liberal-capitalist values and institutions, emerges triumphant. In consequence, the vision that once formed a critical part of the rationale of American foreign policy has faded, leaving in its place the more mundane view that America must still remain the principal guarantor of a global order now openly and without equivocation identified with the status quo.

4

Although the Nixon policy reformulation has not gone unchallenged, even the most cursory survey of the American scene in 1972 reveals the dramatic decline since 1968 in the disaffection over American foreign policy. How are we to reconcile this decline with the claim that the Vietnam war led to the breakdown in the foreign policy consensus of the past generation? That there appears to be no plausible way of doing so must raise questions about the deeper significance of the debate occasioned by the war. In retrospect, what appears most striking about the debate is, as earlier noted, the extent to which ostensible adversaries shared the same basic conceptions of America's role and interests in the world. Without this broad consensus, and its persistence, it is impossible to account for the general favor with which the Nixon policies have been received by a majority among the foreign policy elites who broke over Vietnam. Given the persistence of this broad consensus among the foreign policy elites, it is not surprising that the charge of neo-isolationism the President has on more than one occasion indiscriminately thrown at his Vietnam critics has been found gratuitous.

This is not to suggest that, Vietnam apart, the differences that have arisen between the Nixon Administration and most of its critics have been without significance (though *how* significant they should be judged is a matter on which, as will presently be argued, one is entitled to remain skeptical). The question here, however, is whether these differences justify the conclusion that those who formed the influential and articulate core of the postwar consensus on foreign policy have now defected, that they and the administration entertain broadly disparate views of the nation's role and interests. Thus posed, the answer seems apparent.

These remarks evidently do not apply to the more extreme forms of dissent that arose in the course of the Vietnam war and persist today. They clearly do not apply to the radical left critique of American foreign policy, a critique that may be distinguished from other criticism not only by virtue of its consistent rejection of America's role and interests in the world but by virtue of the explanation given for a policy invariably described and condemned as imperialistic.[14] The essence of the radical critique is not simply that America is aggressive and imperialistic but that it is so out of an institutional necessity. It is the central assumption that American imperialism must ultimately be traced to the institutional structure of American capitalism that is the common denominator of radical criticism. It is the same assumption that most clearly separates radical criticism from all other criticism of American foreign policy.

Moreover, the radical demand that America abandon its world position—that the empire be dismantled—cannot be seen as an end in itself. It is because radical critics find an intimate and dependent relationship between American interests abroad and the maintenance of repressive institutions at home that they are so intent upon dismantling the empire. The unqualified rejection of American foreign policy is primarily intended as a means for the transformation of domestic society. If for no other reason than this, the isolationism of the radical left ought not to be confused with the isolationism of yesterday which found (or with the varying non-radical expressions of isolationism today which continue to find) in a particular form of foreign involvement a serious threat to the nation's political institutions and general well-being. In contrast to a more traditional isolationism, the isolationism of the radical left holds only so long as America retains her capitalist institutions and, in consequence, is a repressive force in the world. With the advent of socialism, the reason for isolationism would disappear, for a Socialist America would presumably be a liberating force in the world.

The influence of radical criticism may be traced, in part, to the decline of the cold war and, in still larger measure, to the coincidence of Vietnam with this decline. Once events created the occasion for skepticism over the motivations and aims of American foreign policy, the radical critique provided a response that seemed persuasive to many, especially among the younger generation. Not only did it appear to explain an otherwise inexplicable war, it related that war to an expansive strategy that has presumably dominated American diplomacy throughout the century, and most clearly in the period following World War II. In this manner, radical criticism came to exert

[14] For an extended consideration of the radical left critique, see Robert W. Tucker, *The Radical Left and American Foreign Policy* (Baltimore: The Johns Hopkins University Press, 1971).

in the middle to late 1960s an unexpected influence on a generation of students for whom the cold war appeared, at best, unnecessary and the problem of insecurity unreal. Yet the inner appeal of radical criticism was not so much to be found in its explanation of the recent past and present but in its promise for the future—a future in which a sinful nation may yet redeem itself and, by so doing, serve as an example to the world. In radical criticism, a provisional realism masks an idealism and belief in America's providential mission that run deep in the American grain.

Although the influence of radical criticism may be expected to persist, it is already apparent that this influence is declining with the passing of the war in Vietnam. Even if Vietnam is seen to be as much a precipitant as a cause of the disaffection that enabled radical criticism to gain its influence, the end of the war must deprive it of the one issue that gave it an apparent persuasiveness and saliency. Then, too, the further attenuation of this influence may be expected to result from the partial acceptance of the radical critique in quarters where only yesterday it had been altogether rejected. The evident strength, although not the distinguishing characteristic, of radical criticism must be found in its insistence upon the self-interested character of American foreign policy. The principal lesson radical criticism conveys—whatever the intention of radical critics—is that America has behaved much as other great states have behaved. The increased receptiveness to this view by conventional critics—indeed, the willingness of an administration openly to profess self-interest as its guiding motivation—has gone far in depriving the radical critique of what had once been its most effective argument. It is as though a partial victory of this critique has created the condition for its diminished influence.

At any rate, radical criticism never formed the significant core of dissent from the nation's foreign policy. Although in time the consequences of this influence could prove to be very important, for the present and immediate future it is the criticism of those who comprise the foreign policy elites to which attention must be directed. It is not the future establishment that determines the state of the debate today over American foreign policy, but the present establishment—those who have been among the articulate and, on the whole, sympathetic expositors of policy in years past. Having defected over Vietnam, and the excesses of policy that presumably led to Vietnam, have they otherwise returned to the fold of the Nixon policy reformulation, even while criticizing from within certain features of this reformulation?

Clearly, a minority has not returned and shows few signs of doing so, even when the war is brought to an end. There is, for example, little reason to expect that a Senator Fulbright can again be brought to support American foreign policy in anything resembling the manner he once supported it, at least short of a transformation in policy that is for the present and immediate future altogether improbable. The same must be said for a substantial portion of the nation's intellectuals who can be expected to continue a position of general opposition in the years ahead. The question that must be raised here with respect to this non-radical opposition is not one of influence—which can scarcely prove to be much more than peripheral—but of content and consistency. In the case of radical opposition this question does not arise, since the radical critique permits no ambiguity in its denial of any substantive world role and interests for the nation. It does arise, however, in the case of non-radical critics who continue to urge a fundamental reorientation of American policy. What is the nature of this reorientation?

Despite years of debate over and opposition to American policy, the answer is still by no means apparent. What is apparent is that an opposition which has in some respects broken from the foreign policy consensus—if only by virtue of its emphasis on the importance of domestic reform, its insistence that an unnecessary preoccupation with foreign policy has long impeded this reform, its mounting opposition to what it considers as consistently inflated defense budgets, and its belief that American influence in the world can best be realized not through the traditional means of statecraft but by the power of the example we set at home—in other respects remains curiously tied to that consensus. It remains tied to that consensus not simply because it dismisses with indignation the charge of isolationism, but because it continues to share a number of basic assumptions that undergird the consensus, whether old or revised, assumptions that so long as they are accepted must make very difficult a substantial change of role and interests.

Thus, so long as it is accepted that America's security remains dependent upon its alliances, if only its alliances with Western Europe and Japan, and that the further proliferation of nuclear weapons must be avoided, it is difficult to see how we are to consummate the fundamental reorientation of policy that is advocated. It will not do to reply that this reorientation can be effected by abandoning the anticommunism that provided so important a motivation of American policy in the period of the cold war. For this motivation may well be abandoned—at the very least, it may be markedly downgraded—and yet the essential structure of the American position may remain unchanged. The assumptions respecting the requirements of American security cannot simply be equated with an obsessive anti-communism, however much this obsession cemented the postwar consensus and prompted the excesses that culminated in a Vietnam. If there is to be a fundamental reorientation of American policy it can come, in all probability, only by virtue of a growing persuasion that the structure of American security has changed radically since World War II.

There is very little evidence, however, that those who have ostensibly ranged themselves generally in opposition to American foreign policy believe that such a change has occurred. With rare exception, they have refrained from questioning the continued need to retain the essential structure of U.S. alliance relationships. While apathetic, if not hostile, toward existing military arrangements with allies, they have evinced little enthusiasm for the abandonment of such arrangements if the consequence would be the military independence of allies. Since a withdrawal of the American military presence in Europe and Asia could be expected to result in further nuclear proliferation, a discreet silence is observed on this issue, a silence that reflects the conviction that proliferation must measurably increase the prospects of nuclear conflict and, given the assumed indivisibility of a nuclear peace, the threat to American security.

In sum, the difficulty in the position of those who persist in calling for a fundamental reorientation of American policy is that they have seldom made clear, and seem unable to make clear, save in the most general terms, the nature of this reorientation. Although the mistakes of the past have received thorough and effective airing, the possibilities of the future remain obscure. In large measure, they have remained obscure because the basic assumptions of American policy, past and present, are more deeply rooted in those who otherwise call for new departures than they themselves realize or care to admit. The persistent influence of these assumptions inhibits the serious consideration of radically novel, though viable, alternatives and leads instead to vague proposals that may serve to appease a sense of regret and guilt over the support afforded American policy in the past but that scarcely can be regarded as plausible alternatives for the future.[15]

[15] It is in this manner that Senator Fulbright may be understood when he rejects the "old internationalism" of the cold war, calls for a "new internationalism" which would reconsider "our most basic assumptions about international relations," and substitutes for the "illusory realism" of post-war American policy the "practical idealism" of the United Nations charter. William Fulbright, "Reflections: In Thrall to Fear," *The New Yorker* (January 8, 1972), pp. 59–62. Also *Congressional Record*, April 14, 1971, p. S-1787. In this context, it may not be

There remain those critics who by no stretch of the imagination can be seriously considered as having broken from the broad consensus on role and interest that has undergirded post-war policy. In the past, they have comprised the influential and articulate core of the foreign policy elites, and though largely ignored by this administration, they continue to do so even today. Their chief sin, in the eyes of the president, has been their opposition to the administration's continued involvement in Vietnam. Whatever their reasons for opposing this involvement and whatever the intensity of their opposition, that they have opposed Mr. Nixon's Vietnam policy has been sufficient to confirm the president's long-standing distrust of the foreign policy establishment.[16] These critics, for the most part liberal and moderate in outlook, have structured the principal debate today over foreign policy. Vietnam apart, of what does their criticism consist?

---

irrelevant to remind ourselves that the "practical idealism" of the charter, at least in its inception, was one that presupposed a world in which peace and order would be defined and enforced by the great powers. In the scheme of the charter, it is the great powers who are "above" the law: although peace requires their cooperation, enforcement measures cannot be taken against them. The charter's design of order is dependent on the condition that the great powers retain a basic identity of interests, that each has a vested interest in the status quo sufficient to serve as a basis for at least minimum cooperation in order maintenance. So conceived, there is not much difference between the "practical idealism" of the charter and the "practical idealism" of the Nixon Administration. These schemes of order, let it be noted, have no intrinsic relationship to justice. On the contrary, they presuppose that in the event of a conflict between the demands of justice and the requirements of order, it is the former that will have to be sacrificed.

[16] Mr. Nixon has seen fit to define the establishment on several occasions. In an interview with C. L. Sulzberger, the president spoke of the establishment as "the people who, after World War II, supported the Greek-Turkish aid program, the Marshall Plan, NATO. But today they are in disarray because of two things. They are terribly disillusioned about Vietnam, which is so hard a problem to understand. And they have an enormous concern with home problems of a sort and a degree that did not face us a generation earlier." (New York Times, March 10, 1971, p. 14). While staunch "former internationalists," they have, in the president's view, "developed neo-isolationist tendencies, at least in some degree." More recently, in an attack on "opinion leaders" who have failed to support his Vietnam policy, Mr. Nixon has referred to "the leaders of the media, the great editors and publishers and television commentators . . . the presidents of our universities and the professors . . . those who have the background to understand the importance of great decisions and the necessity to stand by the President of the United States when he makes a terribly difficult, potentially unpopular decision" (New York Times, October 17, 1972, pp. 1, 28). Even "some of our top businessmen" are included among the opinion leaders that have given the president "precious little support" in his Vietnam policy.

Although there are differences in emphasis, the general thrust of this criticism is clear enough. The Nixon Administration, the indictment runs, while effecting a number of needed changes in policy, has done so through methods that may not only cancel out its own achievements but, in the process, jeopardize the solid achievements of the past generation. Particularly in a period of change, the question of method may prove to be crucial. Yet notwithstanding its own strictures about the importance of method, this administration has acted with an insensitivity toward others, above all toward our major allies, that may well have serious and lasting consequences. In doing so, it has given the impression of opportunism and of a lack of clear commitment that may only succeed in getting the worst of all possible worlds. While the loyalty of allies may be undermined, however inadvertently, the behavior desired of adversaries, and for which allied relationships have been compromised, may not prove forthcoming or, in any event, lasting.

The more serious question arises whether the impression of opportunism is simply the result of ill-chosen tactics or whether it signifies the abandonment of a strategy based on alliances in favor of one that stresses independence of action and that increasingly views allied relationships in a competitive-cooperative context. Given the president's apparent enthusiasm for a pentagonal world comprised of the United States, the Soviet Union, China, Japan and Western Europe—"each balancing the other, not playing one against the other, an even balance"—and given the evident disparity between this view and the realities of world power relationships, the suspicion must arise that what is really meant is a world in which America no longer intends to view her alliances as a matter of first priority. On the theory that allies have nowhere else to go, they will instead be pressured to make new concessions to America, while this nation, intent on pursuing the advantages of the triangular relationship with Russia and China, does little to compensate or to reassure them.

Finally, the criticism is made that the purposes of the Nixon policy reformulation remain, in the last analysis, unclear—or, to the extent they are clear, that they add up to little save equilibrium and stability. It may be granted that the purposes informing post-war policy left much to be desired, even when taken at face value, and that they were often compromised in practice, whether as a result of the necessities—real or alleged—of the cold war or as a result of a self-interest that identified American preponderance in the world with the triumph of freedom and self-determination. The point remains that these purposes provided a standard against which others could, and did, insist that American behavior must be judged. More importantly, they made up a central part of the foundation on which public support for post-war policy rested. In giving short shrift to them, the Nixon Administration has had little to put in their place. To be sure, the administration's "structure of peace" is also qualified by the attributes of "progress" and "freedom," but the qualification invariably appears as an afterthought and a concession to those who are unable to comprehend what statecraft is all about. In the purposes it perfunctorily evokes, the Nixon Doctrine appears, at best, as little more than a pale reflection of the Truman Doctrine. In place of the admittedly defective vision of the Truman Doctrine, the Nixon Doctrine substitutes no vision at all beyond a celebration of the status quo and an insistence that America must remain the giant among nations.

In more ways than one, this criticism must appear curious, and even ironic, when juxtaposed with the prevailing critique of only yesterday. Then, the bane of American policy was too grandiose a vision (and, of course, a partially flawed vision), today it is faulted for having no vision at all. Whereas only yesterday the achilles heel of American policy lay in its obsessive concern with the fate of the developing world, today it is increasingly criticized for its apparent indifference to this world. And whereas only yesterday it was the rigidity of American policy that elicited the attention of critics, today it is the sudden and unilateral shifts in policy that elicit criticism. One is almost tempted to conclude, when considering this emergent critique of the Nixon Administration's foreign policy, that fate defeats men in nothing so much as the overfulfillment of their desires.

The criticism of method is clearly the easiest and, in many respects, the most effective of the charges brought against the Nixon diplomacy. It is an easy criticism to make not only because of the penchant this administration has shown on occasion for taking sudden and unilateral action but because the Nixon Doctrine rather pointedly reserves to this nation an independence of action with respect to allies that preceding administrations did not claim and, indeed, were usually at pains to disavow. It is an effective criticism among the foreign policy elites if only because it calls attention to a diplomatic style that is identified with a discredited isolationist past. In large measure, however, America's postwar devotion to multilateralism has masked throughout the substance of unilateral action. For the very strong, multilateralism is at once a luxury, in that it does not materially restrict their behavior, and an advantage, in that it gives their actions a legitimacy they might not otherwise possess. In the post-war years, America's vast power and the weakness of her allies allowed the appearance of multilateralism and the reality of unilateralism, since the very weakness of allies meant that the nation's commitments, and its alliance relationships generally, were, for all practical purposes, unilateral in character. With the passing of the unusual circumstances that marked the postwar period, it was only to be expected that the multilateral obsession would decline. This is not to deny that the diplomatic methods employed by this administration partly reflect the character of a president strongly given to secrecy and to the sudden move. Nor is it to ignore the determination with which the Nixon Administration has sought to obtain maximum domestic political benefits from its foreign policy initiatives, even though these benefits may prompt tactics offensive to allied sensibilities. It is only to insist that a growing disposition to curtail the multilateral fetish must also be seen as a function of the altered American position and would very probably have characterized the diplomacy of any administration coming to office in the circumstances of the past four years.

At any rate, the issue of tactics is not, as such, the principal concern of those critical of the departures marked by the Nixon diplomacy. Instead, it is the shift in priorities these tactics presumably reflect, a shift away from a strategy that centered on alliances to one that balances alliance interests against the interest in developing new and more advantageous relationships with adversaries. Without question, this shift is a major innovation—perhaps the major innovation—of the Nixon policy reformulation. Without question, this shift also explains the otherwise inexplicable presidential references to a pentagonal balance of power, an "even balance," that does not correspond to reality. There is no "even balance" in the world today nor is there any persuasive, or even plausible, evidence that the administration has ever entertained the intention of working toward such a balance—assuming it to be possible. On the contrary, the evidence points to the conclusion that the president's vision of an "even balance", as his goal of "more mature political partnerships," are euphemisms for a policy which seeks to lighten our alliance burdens without jeopardizing our influence and ultimate control over allies, above all in the political-strategic realm. Although allies are expected to shoulder more of the costs of alliance arrangements, they are not expected to challenge America's military hegemony. Nor is the expanded scope to be afforded allies for pursuing their own diplomatic initiatives expected to interfere with the larger "structure of peace" that America will primarily manage. Should the constraints imposed by alliance relationships impede the development of the administra-

CHANGE AND CONTINUITY 65

tion's larger policy, they will be resisted, though presumably not to the point of driving allies toward military independence or neutralism.

To argue that in a period of supposed retrenchment this is not only an ambitious policy but a strikingly audacious one is to state the obvious. Not content to hold on to the substance of America's existing interests, though at reduced effort and risk, it seeks to improve upon those interests through exploiting the opportunities afforded by Soviet-Chinese rivalry. While allies are to be deterred from challenging America's military hegemony over them, this nation will enjoy the freedom of maneuver and independence of action necessary to broaden a detente with its adversaries, a detente, moreover, in which America will hold the initiative by virtue of its role as "balancer" between the great communist powers. Critics of the administration's foreign policy do not oppose the latter effort and are scarcely in a position to do so. Their objection is simply that this effort ought not to be bought at the price of allied solidarity, a price they argue the administration has obscured even while paying.

Yet the same charge that is in effect brought against the administration may also be brought against most of its critics. In their separate ways, both want the best of all possible worlds. Admittedly, the administration's strategy requires a delicate balancing act that holds out no assurance of success. Allies may not accept the subordination of their interests, or what they perceive as the subordination of their interests. To the degree that the developing triangular relationship produces the moderated environment that no longer requires this subordination its very success may prove to be the condition for the rebellion of those who no longer find compelling reasons to accept America's military hegemony. Whether that rebellion takes a passive form, leading to neutralism and a partial accommodation to Soviet aspirations, or an active form, leading to military autonomy and a heightened nationalism, the result will be the loss of the American postwar role of protector of Western Europe and Japan. Even if this result does not exacerbate existing conflicts over monetary and trade issues, it will still mean a new world in which the American role is considerably diminished and the prospects presently held out by the triangular relationship placed in doubt.

The alternative strategy offered by critics seems scarcely more promising. Is it plausible to assume that alliances can be strengthened at the same time that the triangular game with Moscow and Peking is successfully pursued? It would not seem so. If not, the latter would have to be sacrificed to the former, and American policy would have to await, in the manner of yesterday, an adjustment in the behavior of adversaries. At the same time, in choosing to concentrate on alliance policy, though at the expense of detente, this alternative strategy must minimize the significance of the conflicts of interest that have arisen among allies, conflicts which make the vision of the Grand Alliance—with America as its chief orchestrator—more elusive today than ever, while neglecting the domestic pressures for retrenchment *and* detente. These conflicts of interest could be substantially diminished in the longer run only if America accepted a position with respect to allies of an equal among equals. There is no more disposition among most critics to accept such a status, however, than there is in the Nixon Administration, especially over the issue of security. On this issue, critics are as one with the administration in opposing a course of action leading to the military autonomy of allies since that course might, and probably would, lead to the eventual dissolution of the alliance structure. Even a more compromising position on matters of trade and monetary reform than the Nixon Administration has taken would still leave the principal issue of security unaltered, unless we are to assume that the tired prescriptions of greater candor, consultation, and coordination with allies would, if once taken seriously, lead to true partnerships.

Although these differences cannot be ignored, their significance should not be exaggerated. Neither side in this controversy wishes to sacrifice the prospects of detente, just as neither side wishes to encourage allies to take responsibility for their own security. For both sides, a devolution of power and responsibility, with the nuclear proliferation and loss of American influence devolution would entail, is considered inimical to American interests. In its emphasis on developing the triangular relationship, while maintaining what amounts to a holding operation with respect to allies, the Nixon Administration has responded, as it had to respond, to domestic pressures. Even so, the response to these pressures has been relatively modest when considered against the inauspicious circumstances in which this administration came to power. What is remarkable—the point cannot be made too often—is how little, not how much, America's alliance interests, as her interests generally, have changed in the past four years.

Does it matter that these interests now have a different rationale, that grandiose purposes have been replaced by rather antiseptic goals? Many think it matters a great deal in terms of insuring the requisite domestic support for foreign policy. But the issue of domestic support apart, and it will be considered shortly, are these valid grounds for criticizing a policy the purposes of which are openly defined as those of equilibrium and stability? Obviously such grounds exist if the position is taken that there are more compelling purposes than stability, that instability may be far preferable to an unjust status quo, and that, in any event, "equilibrium is not a purpose with which we can respond to the travail of our world."[17] If this position is clearly far removed from the outlook of the Nixon Administration, it is another matter to pretend that this administration, in jettisoning the idealism of the past, has introduced something new to American foreign policy. What is new is only the candor with which goals are now pursued that have increasingly defined the substance of American policy since the early years of the cold war.

5

If the analysis developed in preceding pages is sound, skepticism over the viability of the Nixon policy reformulation in terms of its domestic support cannot rest on the prevailing outlook of the present foreign policy elites. There is no persuasive evidence that these elites have broken in a fundamental way with the broad consensus that continues to define American foreign policy. Disagreements over method, even though sharp on occasion, are not to be confused with disagreements over the substance of the American role in the world. Criticism of the size of defense budgets, or of the need for particular weapons systems, is not to be seen as a rejection of the substantive interests that American power must continue to protect. A minority apart, the debate occasioned by the Nixon foreign policy—Vietnam excepted—has been very much an in-house debate carried on within implicitly well-defined limits.

At the same time, the relationships between this administration and the foreign policy elites have differed, and considerably so, from the relationships with these elites entertained by past administrations. Throughout the cold war, the elites provided a vital link between an administration and the public, in that they assumed a large share of the burden of explaining, and eliciting support for, an administration's policy; during the past four years they have been all but shunted aside by a president who has preferred to take his case, when the necessity has arisen, directly to the people.

---

[17] Henry A. Kissinger, "Central Issues of American Foreign Policy" in Kermit Gordon, ed., *Agenda For The Nation* (Washington, DC: The Brookings Institution, 1968), p. 612. Kissinger adds that "our conception of world order must have deeper purposes than stability but greater restraints on our behavior than would result if it were approached only in a fit of enthusiasm." The fits of enthusiasm are surely gone, though the deeper purposes than stability are no more apparent today in the Nixon policy than they were in Kissinger's essay.

In part, this bypassing of the elites may be accounted for on grounds of history and temperament. Never in his career has Mr. Nixon been known for his intimacy with the foreign policy establishment. His mistrust of the bureaucracy is well-documented. Toward the unofficial, but no less important, part of the establishment he also kept a considerable distance. In turn, the establishment never displayed any particular warmth toward Mr. Nixon. In an ideological age, he still seemed too ideological; for a generation of cold warriors, he nevertheless appeared too militant. Understandably, some residue of the past has persisted, despite the marked changes in roles that have since occurred.

Nor is the president particularly given to sharing power, least of all in foreign policy. Even if his past relationships with the establishment had been closer than they were, and even if the foreign policy elites had not opposed him on Vietnam, there is ample reason for believing that Mr. Nixon would still have been rather reluctant to continue the former pattern of relationships. The same must of course be said of his principal assistant in foreign policy, Henry Kissinger. The elites can effectively mediate between the summit and the plains only if they are certified to do so by those at the summit. This certification, however, is inevitably a form of power which acquires some independence, even though modest. Moreover, this certification, if it is to serve effectively the tasks for which it is intended, sets limits to the lengths secrecy can be carried. But secrecy is itself, as Mr. Nixon has so clearly demonstrated, one of the tap roots of presidential power in foreign relations. Thus, while the elites have by no means disappeared, one of their most important functions has come very close to disappearing in the past four years. What used to be the possession of a relatively substantial number has now become the effective possession of two. Beyond the president and his Assistant for National Security Affairs, there are today no certified communicators of American foreign policy.

The longer term effects of the relationships Mr. Nixon has developed toward the foreign policy elites are necessarily speculative. The view has been taken by some observers that, if persisted in, the present relationships—or rather the lack thereof—must result in elite discontinuity, and, indeed, perhaps even in the virtual disappearance of a group that has played so indispensable a role in America's postwar foreign policy.[18] In some measure, however, the current situation

---

[18] See for example, Stanley Hoffmann, "Will the Balance Balance at Home?" *Foreign Policy* 7 (Summer, 1972), pp. 67ff.

may be expected to change in a second Nixon Administration, if only because the president's by-passing of the elites, as well as his more than occasional attempt to discredit them in the eyes of the public, must be attributed to persistent elite criticism of the administration's Vietnam policy. That the Nixon Doctrine was, on the whole, well-received by the elites did not for the president offset the fact of their unremitting opposition to his course of action in Vietnam. Nor is this surprising, given the apparent depth of Mr. Nixon's conviction that the success of his larger policy—a policy with which his influential and articulate Vietnam critics were in general agreement—remained dependent upon the manner in which the war was finally settled. If there is no reason to question the sincerity of those who found in the president's continued involvement in Vietnam a threat to the greater and enduring interests of policy, there is also no reason to question the sincerity with which the president saw this continued involvement as essential for the ultimate success of his larger policy. During his first term in office, Vietnam remained the salient issue of American foreign policy. In view of the broad chasm separating Mr. Nixon and the elites on this issue, for this reason alone the possibilities of forging a closer and more traditional relationship were necessarily limited. Although it would be excessive to entertain the prospect of intimacy between this particular president and the present elites, with the ending of the American involvement in Vietnam there is at least the prospect of a modest improvement in what has become a distant and often hostile relationship.

At the same time, the question must be raised whether there will continue to be the same need of the elites in the immediate future that there was in the period of the cold war. A positive response must assume that there will be a continuing need to maintain the kind of public support for foreign policy that obtained during the cold war. Yet this assumption is surely questionable. Whereas the exigencies of the cold war did require a high degree of public support, Mr. Nixon's "era of negotiation" appears compatible with a high degree of public indifference. Indeed, nothing would seem so inimical to the logic of the Nixon policy reformulation as the kind of public enthusiasm the foreign policy elites helped to generate and maintain during the years of the cold war. This is perhaps one reason—apart from those given above—why Mr. Nixon has been less than anxious to reinstate an unofficial foreign policy establishment whose principal function is to mediate between government and public. A policy that depends upon retaining maximum mobility and freedom of maneuver requires only a permissive public—not an understanding one. Between apathy and zeal, the former is preferable to the latter.

These considerations apart, it is apparent that there will be a continued need for a bureaucratic elite. It is equally clear that this elite will have to be a highly qualified and professional one, given a world in which the simplicities—however strenuous—of the cold war have been succeeded by the complexities of an evolving multipolar system. Even so, it does not appear that the size of this elite will have to be anywhere near the size of the bureaucracy to which the cold war gave rise. To be sure, doubt persists over whether the younger generation can be expected to produce even a substantially reduced bureaucratic elite, given the disillusioning experience of Vietnam and a resulting apathy toward foreign affairs. But if this is a problem, it is one for the 1980s, not the 1970s. For the more immediate future, the relevant issue is whether talent is presently available for conducting the kind of policy the Nixon Administration has inaugurated. Despite the corrosive effects on bureaucratic morale that have resulted from the manner in which this administration has conducted high policy, there seems little warrant for the conclusion that a crisis of elite discontinuity is close at hand, if not already upon us. Without monumental effort, the second Nixon Administration could go far toward rehabilitating the bureaucracy and restoring its now admittedly low morale.

Skepticism over the domestic viability of the new policy does not of course focus exclusively, or even primarily, upon the attitude of the foreign policy elites. Even if the latter on the whole accept and support the Nixon policy reformulation, there remains the all important issue of its reception by the public. Will the public support, in the aftermath of Vietnam, a policy that, although considerably less demanding of its psychic and moral energies, will continue to require a substantial portion of the nation's material resources?[19] To those who believe the public is unlikely to support the new policy, whatever the momentary successes of that policy, there are the effects of Vietnam that have yet to run their full course. When they do, they will give rise to constraints on foreign policy that will prove difficult to reconcile with the requirements of the Nixon policy reformulation. Whereas the public mood runs strongly toward disinvolvement, the Nixon strategy is clearly one of continuing involvement (even though, one hopes, at a lower cost). The public today is more anti-inter-

[19] The most forceful criticism of the Nixon foreign policy from the point of view of its domestic viability has been made by Stanley Hoffmann, *ibid.*, pp. 60–87.

ventionist than at any time since the late 1930s. Yet the Nixon Doctrine remains predicated, as it must, upon the capacity and willingness to intervene when necessary. Moreover, the new policy requires for its success a much clearer isolation of external "necessities" from internal currents than did cold war policy. But the public is not only far more reluctant today than in the recent past to allow foreign policy to be formulated independently of the domestic mood, it is also seen as more determined that domestic problems and needs not be subordinated to the requirements of foreign and defense policies.

To the extent the public has nevertheless supported the Nixon Administration's policies, it has done so, on this view, because it has misunderstood their real meaning. The public continues to find a promise of disengagement that is not in fact there. When the true implications of the Nixon Doctrine are finally laid bare and its costs made apparent, the support it now enjoys may therefore be expected to decline markedly. Nor will it prove possible, when confronted with a resistant public, effectively to appeal to the motives and outlook that formed the basis of public support for American policy since World War II. Anti-communism, so critical in sustaining public support for policy in the past no longer provides the support it once did and cannot be counted upon to do so in the future. Vietnam stretched this all important element of the post-war consensus to a breaking point, and the Nixon Administration has done little either to rehabilitate it or to find an effective substitute. To the contrary, in its principal policy moves as well as in the explanation given for these moves, the Nixon Administration has further dissipated this once central public motivation.

This, in brief, is the general thrust of the argument that the Nixon policy reformulation may well prove unable to command the necessary public support. Does it reflect an accurate assessment not only of the recent changes in public mood but of the deeper and more lasting significance of these changes? Beyond this, does it project a plausible view of the kind and degree of public support for foreign policy an administration must enjoy today and in the immediate future to maintain the American role and interests? There is, of course, no question but that, quite apart from the decline of the cold war, Vietnam has been critical in bringing about a public outlook on issues of foreign and military policy which forms a marked contrast to the outlook of earlier years. It is above all Vietnam that explains the reversal of a long pattern of strong public support for placing the defense requirements of major security policies over domestic needs. Even more clearly, Vietnam has led to the marked drop in public support for employing American military forces, and particularly ground forces, in defense of nations—including America's allies—attacked by communist or communist-backed forces.

What is still not clear, however, is the deeper and more lasting significance of the apparent change in public mood that Vietnam has brought about. Does the public's present mood signal the emergence of new and important constraints on foreign policy, constraints that this and future administrations will ignore only at their peril? A reliable answer is difficult to give, if only because, as earlier noted, the one indisputable lesson to be learned from Vietnam—that success is the great solvent of serious public disaffection over foreign policy, and particularly over military intervention—is of narrow compass. By itself, it is less than revealing about the nature of the constraints policy makers will henceforth ignore at their peril, given the distinctive characteristics of the war in Vietnam.

Nor do these constraints appear very clear if viewed in the light of current public attitudes toward military intervention generally. There is no way of knowing at this juncture how stable and persistent the present anti-interventionist mood will prove to be. Of necessity, the relevant opinion surveys have been undertaken in a period of public disillusionment over Vietnam, a fact that cannot but affect the results. Although time may deepen this disillusionment, it may also moderate an anti-interventionist disposition; indeed, there are indications that this moderation may have already set in.[20] Much will depend upon how Vietnam is seen in retrospect, and this will depend, in large part, upon the ultimate outcome of the war. Now, as four years ago, it remains the case that if the outcome in Vietnam cannot issue in success—in the sense that no possible outcome can compensate for the tangible and intangible costs of the war—it still holds out a broad choice of failures. It will surely make a difference

[20] Compare, for example, the results of the *Time-Louis Harris Poll* published in *Time*, May 2, 1969, with the results of the polling done by the Gallup Organization in the summer of 1972 for Potomac Associates and published in Watts and Free, *State of the Nation*, pp. 200–201. In the earlier survey, only 27 percent favored sending U.S. troops to the support of Italy if attacked by outside communist military forces and 26 percent favored defending West Berlin against communist attack. In the later survey, 52 percent favored U.S. military defense of any major European ally attacked by Soviet Russia. Indeed, there appears to be a rather significant difference in the public willingness to intervene on behalf of allies if the results of the Gallup polling of 1971 for Potomac Associates are compared with the results of a year later. See Albert H. Cantril and Charles W. Roll, Jr., *Hopes and Fears of the American People* (New York: Universe Books and Potomac Associates, 1971), pp. 47–49.

whether that outcome is one that effectively leaves the political future of South Vietnam open rather than one that is no more than a transparent facade for a communist victory. Whereas in the latter eventuality the domestic effects are likely to prove far-reaching by strengthening a public disinclination to risk overseas involvements, in the former eventuality the domestic effects may prove more limited than commonly anticipated. Thus, the cease fire agreement concluded between the United States and North Vietnam in January 1973 is likely to have, if it holds up, a marked impact on how the war is seen in retrospect. The nation's memory of Vietnam may yet turn out to be considerably more favorable than its current assessment.

Then, too, since survey questions dealing with public attitudes toward intervention are hypothetical, the results can prove quite misleading. In an actual crisis, the public—whose permissiveness in foreign policy remains, despite Vietnam, very liberal—may be expected to be more supportive of involvement, particularly if the president were to make a strong case for intervention. In part, the strength of the case would of necessity depend upon the area of intended intervention. In part, however, it would depend upon the instruments or means of intervention. It does not seem unreasonable to assume that a measure of the present opposition to future intervention, above all in Asia, is an opposition to the use of American troops in a costly and seemingly inconclusive land war rather than an opposition to intervention itself. If this is true, a strategy that places substantially greater emphasis on aerial and naval power to back up present commitments, while otherwise relying on indigenous troops supported by American military aid, may evoke little serious opposition, short of its being put to the test. And even if put to the test, it may receive public sanction, or toleration, provided the use of American ground forces is avoided and, of course, provided the effectiveness of intervention can soon be made apparent. It would not be the greatest irony of Vietnam that the last, and most impressive, "lesson" the public may learn from the war will be the lesson of the final six months rather than the first six years.

Finally, and most importantly, it is impossible to assess the significance of the public's present attitudes toward the future use of American military power abroad without also assessing the extent to which this attitude is based on a changed perception of America's vital interests in addition to a changed perception of the possible threats to those interests. Does the public's current anti-interventionist mood reflect an awareness, however inarticulate, that the conditions of American security have changed, and considerably so, over the past quarter of a century? The question must be raised independently of the decline of anti-communism. (A decline of anti-communism, let it be emphasized, not its death. A more than residual anti-communism persists, however muted today, and could probably once again be evoked with effect, even by this administration.[21]) Although anti-communism has clearly been a—if not *the*—central element of the post-war consensus on foreign policy, it has not been the whole of that consensus. In its origins, it is well to recall, this consensus also expressed a conventional security interest. Indeed, the initial, and decisive, measures of post-war policy were seen as much in terms of a narrower conception of security—security interpreted in terms of a balance of power—as they were in terms of the broader purposes of the Truman Doctrine, which came to be equated in the public mind primarily with anti-communism. There is no reason why a "stable structure of peace," the requirements of which are still equated with American security, cannot elicit sufficient public support even though this structure is seen primarily in conventional balance-of-power terms. At least, there is no reason why it cannot do so if the public's perception of the conditions of American security remains relatively unchanged, as would appear to be the case. Even if there has been a modest change in this perception, it remains no less true today than in the past that "the determination of what constitutes vital American interests to be defended by military means if necessary is a decision which the public tends to leave to its policy-makers."[22]

These considerations suggest that it is, at the very least, premature to pronounce the death of the consensus that has underlined popular support for American policy since World War II. Much of the old consensus remains, as does the public permissiveness that attended it. To the extent this consensus has changed, the question persists: In what sense has it changed? Is it the consensus on the rationale of policy that has changed, or is it the consensus on the substance of policy itself? It will not do to argue that this is a distinction without a difference, thereby implying that a change of rationale must bring a change of policy. Nothing is more commonplace than the experience of unchanging interests supported by changing rationalizations.

[21] See Watts and Free, *State of the Nation*, p. 217, in which 46 percent of those questioned agreed with the proposition that: "The U.S. should take all necessary steps, including the use of armed force, to prevent the spread of communism to any other parts of the free world." This response is, admittedly, a marked decline from the response of earlier years, but it is scarcely negligible.

[22] Gabriel A. Almond, *The American People and Foreign Policy* (New York: Frederick A. Praeger, 1950), p. 105.

The history of statecraft is nothing so much as the history of nations that acquired interests for one set of reasons and subsequently held on to the same interests for quite different reasons. Why should this nation prove an exception to an experience that appears well-nigh universal?

What evidence there is does not point to a public mood in rebellion against preserving the substance of the American role and interests in the world. If it points to a mood that is increasingly concerned with domestic problems, this concern is not to be equated with a demand that the nation's international position be abandoned or that it even be seriously altered. There is clearly a strong disposition to reduce the costs of America's involvement abroad, particularly the psychic and emotional costs. Moreover, the broadening detente with the Soviet Union and China has led to a lessened preoccupation with the threat of communism and the prospect of war. When taken together with the impact of Vietnam, this has contributed, in turn, to a willingness—even a desire—to take a more modest view of America's interests.

Although these changes in public mood are not insignificant, they do not portend the kind of transformation that would seriously threaten the Nixon foreign policy. They do not indicate the absence of a public consensus on the substance of policy. They do indicate that this consensus no longer has the cohesiveness it once had and, even more clearly, that it no longer elicits the enthusiasm of an earlier period. The exuberant mood of yesterday is gone and with its disappearance has gone the old idealism that was, after all, the other side of the coin of anti-communism. But the new policy, as already observed, does not require the visions—or illusions—of yesterday and would likely find them more a liability than a blessing. The motivations and rationale that were needed to overturn the historic bases of American policy and to expand to our present position are not the motivations and rationale that are needed to keep, more or less, what we have. To accomplish the latter, a conservative and familiar melange of reasons—that in an uncertain world it would be dangerous to let go of what we have, that considerations of prestige and pride forbid us from doing so, etc.—will probably prove sufficient, and the Nixon Administration has not been deficient in providing them.

There is no persuasive reason, then, for believing that the public does not understand the Nixon foreign policy. At least, there is no persuasive reason for believing that the public does not understand this policy in the very proximate manner it normally understands any policy. There may be some misapprehension over the budgetary implications of the Nixon Doctrine, though even here the alleged degree of misunderstanding often seems to reflect aspiration more than fact. Besides, even if the public does set a price tag on the Nixon Doctrine that is lower than the doctrine implies, the president has demonstrated considerable skill either in obscuring the cost issue or, when this is impossible, in making the costs appear palatable. Thus for a defense budget that has increased in absolute terms, there are the attractions of arms control agreements, an all-volunteer army, and the promise to use the manpower of allies rather than American troops. If these attractions have been qualified, they have not been dispelled by the fact that arms control agreements have been attended by the insistence on developing new weapons systems, that an all-volunteer army has meant increased manpower costs, and that an emphasis upon using the forces of allies has resulted in a rise in military aid.

These considerations of the domestic viability of the Nixon policy reformulation have centered on the present and immediate future. They prompt the conclusion that, barring unexpected developments abroad, the short-term prospects for this policy look reasonably good. It is another matter to speculate on the longer term prospects. The marked uncertainty that necessarily attends any speculation on the more than immediate future is compounded here by the doubt that persists over the future outlook of the group whose views have been most sharply affected by Vietnam—the elite young. Whether Vietnam will remain a "crucial experience" for this group, as Munich was a crucial experience for a preceding generation, remains unclear.[23] It is always possible that time and circumstance will moderate an outlook that rejects further military involvement abroad, that finds American security no longer requiring such involvement, and that, in general, is strongly critical of the projection of American power in the world. With the end of the Vietnam war, the hostility to American foreign policy the war engendered may erode; there are some signs that this is already occurring. On the other hand, should the present hostility —or, at least, indifference—continue to characterize the outlook of the relatively small group that in other circumstances could be expected eventually to conduct the nation's foreign policy, the prospect arises that control over foreign policy will gravitate to a new group. The president has given more than an occasional indication that he is not averse to such a development.

---

[23] See Graham T. Allison, "Cool It: The Foreign Policy of Young America," *Foreign Policy* (Winter, 1970–71), pp. 144–60.

The attitude of the elite young apart, far-reaching change in American foreign policy might eventually stem from a growing consciousness on the part of the public that the stakes of foreign policy have changed, and considerably so, since the 1940s. If the public should once become persuaded that security, whether interpreted in a narrower or in a broader sense, no longer required the retention of the nation's present role and interests, the minimum domestic support, or acquiescence, any administration must have might erode. The result of this erosion need not signal a return to the isolationism of the past. Even if it did not, it might still lead to a radical alteration in the American position of the last three decades. There are no solid indications, however, that the consciousness which must form the precondition of such alteration has struck deep roots. Nor is there any assurance that if and when it does, the public will refuse to support a foreign policy that can no longer be rationalized in the terms of the past. After all, it is only the persistence of a belief in America's "exceptionalism" which prompts the common assumption that this nation will retain an imperial position only if it is persuaded that its security so requires. Once this belief is set aside, there is no reason to expect that America will abandon a position security may no longer require yet one that continues to respond to other motivations, not the least of which is the desire to retain the nation's influence in the world.

3

THE DOMESTIC SCENE:
THE PRESIDENT ASCENDENT

*Francis E. Rourke**

When Richard Nixon took office in 1968, the feeling was widespread that presidential power had grown far too dominant over the conduct of foreign affairs and that the time was ripe for a re-assertion of congressional and public influence over American activities abroad. This attitude was a major legacy of the war in Vietnam, that costly and frustrating military stalemate that seemed largely to result from questionable commitments made by American presidents beginning in the 1950s. One of the leading contenders for the Democratic presidential nomination in 1968, Senator Eugene McCarthy of Minnesota, attracted wide support with a campaign that openly promised to downgrade the importance of the presidency in the American political system.

Certainly, it seemed unlikely that any substantial aggrandizement of presidential power could occur. In Vietnam presidential wisdom had proved quite fallible, and executive power suddenly loomed as a source of danger rather than salvation for American society. If the outbreak of World War II in 1939 seemed to confirm executive wisdom and congressional ignorance during the foreign policy debate of the 1930s, Vietnam in the 1960s appeared to furnish equally dramatic proof of the need to limit presidential authority and to allow Congress and the public a greater voice in policy decisions. Now at last it seemed to be time to question the long-standing assumption that what is good for the president is necessarily good for the country.

Nixon's success in preserving presidential hegemony over foreign affairs in the face of the discouraging prospects that prevailed when he took office was a major triumph of his administration. By the end of his first term in office, his command over the development of national security policy in the United States was as complete as any president's in modern times. A variety of congressional efforts to curb the president's discretion in foreign affairs had been beaten back or so watered down that they were no longer recognizable as serious challenges to executive authority.

* Joseph Cantor assisted in preparing the section on Congress in this chapter.

Indeed, in April 1972 Nixon took steps to escalate the war in Vietnam that were even more daring in their assertion of presidential prerogatives than those President Johnson had undertaken in 1965. To be sure a war powers bill may eventually be enacted requiring the consent of Congress for any long-range American military involvement abroad. But given the techniques of persuasion open to American presidents, and their ability to mobilize public support for presidential leadership in foreign affairs, it seems wholly unlikely such measures will seriously limit a president determined to assert the powers of his office.

The manner in which Nixon accomplished this triumph showed a keen awareness of the realities of American politics as they affect the conduct of foreign policy. He bet—and in the long run his wager appeared to rest on an accurate assessment of public opinion in the United States—that Americans would support continued military involvement in South Vietnam if casualties could be reduced and the costs of the war in terms of human life could be shifted to the South Vietnamese. The steady withdrawal of American troops from South Vietnam between 1969 and 1972 was accompanied by a gradual attrition in the anti-war sentiment which had beset Lyndon Johnson during his last years in the White House.

Nixon's performance in office also showed an ability to capitalize on the assets of the presidential office in the conduct of diplomacy. Foremost among these attributes is the secrecy with which the chief executive can move—a secrecy that Alexander Hamilton long ago asserted was a major strength of the presidency. From the first days of the Nixon Administration, institutions of government, such as the executive departments, that could not be trusted to keep presidential secrets were down-graded. At the same time the Special Assistant for National Security Affairs was placed in a commanding position at the summit of American government largely because his activities could more easily be hidden from the public eye.

But while Nixon's record in office can be explained in part in terms of the political pressures that prevalied when he became president, or the opportunities afforded him by the office he held, it was also shaped in no small measure by his own personality and political style. With respect to secrecy, for example, one of his biographers describes Nixon as an extraordinarily private man, whose bitterness over the exposure of the "Nixon fund" in the 1952 presidential campaign came not least from the fact that it forced him to reveal intimate details about his economic circumstances. As Garry Wills puts it in *Nixon*

Agonistes: "The public self-revelation for which Nixon would be blamed in later years was . . . forced on him, against all his own inclinations, personal and political. By temperament and conditioning, Nixon is reserved, with Quaker insistence on the right to privacy."[1]

Thus, while he has lived most of his adult life in the bath of publicity that normally immerses party politics and election campaigns in the United States, Nixon as president exhibited a keen awareness of the value of secrecy for the actual task of governance once a politician has been elected to office. From De Gaulle, whom he long admired, Nixon appears to have learned that a certain remoteness in the ruler and the process by which he rules exerts an irresistible fascination for the public and creates an air of mystery about a regime whose activities in the full light of day seem quite prosaic.

The efforts Nixon made to preserve presidential hegemony over foreign affairs between 1969 and 1972 thus mirror his sensitivity to the forces that shape voter attitudes in the United States, his ability to exploit the advantages of the office he held, and the nuances of his own outlook toward political life. These efforts were designed to defend and expand the authority of the presidency and his own power in office in three main arenas of combat: in the marketplace of public opinion, in the halls of Congress, and within the corridors of his own executive establishment.

Each of these struggles will be discussed separately in the pages that follow. It should be noted, however, that they are tightly linked in the everyday operation of the American system of politics. Nixon's ability to maintain public support was a critical prerequisite for his success in fending off attacks on his policies in Congress, and criticism in Congress was always invigorated by any evidence of erosion in the level of Nixon's public support. Moreover, as Richard Neustadt long ago pointed out, executive officials closely monitor a president's standing with the public and are far more likely to defy or evade his commands when his standing with the public is low than when it is high.[2]

But while Nixon constantly manipulated these linkages within the American political system, the essential thrust of his presidency was to create a situation in which he could rule independently, with his discretion broad and his options open. Much of what he did seems

[1] Garry Wills, *Nixon Agonistes* (New York: Signet Books, 1971), p. 103.
[2] Richard E. Neustadt, *Presidential Power* (New York: John Wiley & Sons, Science Editions, 1962), pp. 86–107.

best described as an effort to create an autonomous presidency in foreign affairs—free of influence from Congress, the press, the elites outside of government, and even, to a significant extent, the ordinary executive apparatus. During his administration Nixon was often charged by his critics with trying to transform the White House into a monarchy. If so, the office he had in mind was far more powerful than that of any mere constitutional monarch who reigns but does not rule. Throughout his tenure in office Nixon constantly sought to keep a firm grip on the reality as well as the image of power.

Foreign Policy and the American Public

One of the first problems to which President Nixon addressed himself when he took office in 1969 was the task of reducing the level of domestic discontent over the war in Vietnam. As noted earlier, Nixon's major calculation at this point was that he could lower the level of public dissatisfaction with the war if he could reduce its costs as perceived by the American people. He also appears to have concluded that public opinion did not require him to end indirect military support activities for the South Vietnamese, if such activities did not result in large American casualties and if the public could be persuaded that they were necessary to prevent a communist takeover that would humiliate or dishonor the United States in international politics.

Out of this analysis of the relationship between American public opinion and the war in Vietnam emerged the Nixon policy of Vietnamization, designed to reduce American casualties by shifting responsibility for carrying on combat activities on the ground to the South Vietnamese. This policy enabled Nixon to assert that he was indeed winding down the war, a claim he could support by referring to the fact that American troop strength in Vietnam dropped from nearly 540,000 when he took office in 1969 to slightly more than 25,000 by the 1972 presidential election.

To be sure the president's critics could still point out that the war did not end for the South Vietnamese, and that after the escalation of hostilities in 1972 it became as destructive for them as it had ever been. It was also true that more than 100,000 men in American sea and air forces were still heavily engaged in the war from bases outside of Vietnam. During brief periods when the war became more visible to the American people—as, for example, during the invasion of Cambodia in 1970 and of Laos in 1971—the administration suffered temporary setbacks with public opinion. Nonetheless the decline of

American troop strength and casualties in Vietnam, coupled with the reduction in draft calls at home, did have the eventual effect of softening the impact of the war in domestic politics.

While reducing the visibility of Vietnam, the Nixon Administration never succeeded in eliminating it as a troublesome foreign policy problem on the domestic horizon. Vietnam figured prominently in the presidential campaign of 1972 and was certainly the issue most helpful to Senator George McGovern in winning the Democratic presidential nomination in that year. It was also a major factor driving the president toward his historic summit meetings with the Chinese and the Soviets in 1972, for while there were other matters to discuss at these conferences, nothing seemed to have higher importance on the president's own agenda than the prospect that the Soviets and the Chinese might be of some assistance in negotiating a satisfactory end to the war.

The fact of the matter is that Vietnam always presented the president with the possibility of unfavorable developments that could be turned to his political disadvantage in the United States. The policy of Vietnamization might succeed in producing some temporary alleviation of public discontent at home, but this often seemed to be only a remission of the malady it was designed to cure. Pictures of South Vietnamese troops trying to escape the battlefield during the ill-fated invasion of Laos in 1971 by clinging to the skids of American helicopters were severely damaging to Nixon's effort to lower the profile of the war in American politics, as was the flight of South Vietnamese soldiers from Quang-Tri during the North Vietnamese offensive in 1972. Such incidents stirred immediate fears in the White House of a collapse in Southeast Asia which would discredit the policy of Vietnamization and damage the president's standing with the American electorate.

So the administration's success in reducing public discontent with the War in Vietnam was a precarious triumph, always capable of being upset by unforeseen developments in an environment over which the president had only limited control. Much of the administration's energy in foreign affairs thus went into the task of handling the war in such a way as to minimize the possibility that opponents might exploit the issue to its disadvantage. This required a fusion between the processes of domestic and international politics, such as peace proposals submitted to the North Vietnamese that were actually directed to an American audience, and constant trips by Kissinger to Paris to engage in highly publicized "secret" negotiations which could dominate the headlines in American newspapers.

Nixon's strategy for dealing with domestic critics of the war and his policy of Vietnamization had several key aspects. For one thing the administration chose to distinguish between the "attentive" groups such as journalists, academicians, and other segments of the population who take an active interest in foreign affairs and the general public not ordinarily concerned with international politics. It concluded that the general public was far less opposed to the American involvement in Vietnam than the attentive foreign policy "elite" and that appeals to national pride and patriotism could rally mass support for the American effort in Vietnam if the burdensome costs of the war could be simultaneously reduced.

Hence, President Nixon sharply departed from the practice earlier presidents had followed during the cold war years. He went over the heads of the so-called elites upon which presidents had traditionally depended for the support of American activities abroad and sought to draw support for his policies from nationalist sentiment within the general public. The Middle America to which Nixon linked his administration was mobilized in order to compensate for the erosion of support for American policy in Vietnam among many of the groups that had long been key elements in the internationalist consensus in American politics.

At the height of the peace demonstrations in 1969 and 1970 the so-called "hard-hats" emerged as a bulwark of support for administration policy in Vietnam. These were blue-collar workers, particularly in the construction trades, whose participation in activities related to foreign policy had traditionally been minimal. Groups of such blue-collar workers attacked peace marchers and organized counter-demonstrations of their own in support of administration policy. They were even called to the White House to be thanked by the president for the support they had given him. In a speech delivered before the annual convention of the AFL-CIO in 1971, the president paid fulsome tribute to the hard-hat constituency that had rallied behind his Vietnam policy at the time of the Cambodian crisis, when those he labelled "intellectuals" had deserted him. "When the intellectuals were protesting, 150,000 workers marched down Wall Street to support me . . . I want you to know that I appreciate that."[3]

Subsequently, in speaking before an organization representing the families of American prisoners of war in Vietnam, the president attacked the "opinion leaders" in the press, the universities, and business who had failed to support his decision to bomb North Vietnam

[3] *Time*, Nov. 29, 1971, p. 29.

and mine its ports in the Spring of 1972. As Nixon put it: "Let me tell you that when that decision was made, there was precious little support from any of the so-called opinion leaders of this country."[4]

Closely related to the administration strategy of relying upon mass rather than elite support in the conduct of its Vietnam policy were the sharp attacks levelled at the media of communication from the vicinity of the White House. Nixon had inherited a substantial credibility gap from the Johnson Administration, which had often promised more than it could deliver and on frequent occasions released information regarding the course of the war which subsequent events proved to be highly inaccurate. What the Nixon regime sought to do was to convince the public that the media (especially television) were equally unreliable and guilty of as much distortion in presenting the facts as wide segments of the population believed the government to be. While this strategy could not erase public distrust of information released by the government, it could help create a credibility gap for the mass media which would diminish public acceptance of any challenge they might make to the accuracy of government claims.

Whether or not the public sees an event in foreign affairs is in no small measure determined by its prominence on the political horizon. Another major feature of the Nixon strategy in dealing with Vietnam was thus an attempt to make it less prominent by directing attention to other aspects and objectives of American foreign policy. Hence, the strenuous efforts of the president during the latter part of his administration to "normalize" relations with China were aimed in part at decreasing the salience of Vietnam in American politics. The negotiations and agreements concluded with the Soviets in 1972 on disarmament, trade, environmental control, and a variety of other subjects were also designed to shift public concern away from Vietnam and toward problems on which there was considerably less political division in the United States.

During the Nixon years as in earlier periods of the cold war, summit meetings with the leaders of communist states were a major avenue through which the president could portray himself to the American public as a peace-maker. Their value to Nixon in this respect was considerably heightened by the fact that the United States continued to be engaged during his administration in armed conflict in Southeast Asia. It seems fair to conclude that Nixon derived more domestic political advantage from his summit encounters with the

[4] New York *Times*, Oct. 17, 1972, pp. 1, 28.

Soviets and the Chinese in 1972 than any American president had gained from earlier sessions of this sort. Much of the profit came from the fact that these meetings enabled the president to push Vietnam out of the spotlight it had occupied since 1965 in domestic discussion of foreign policy in the United States.

Such a summary review of Nixon's strategy and success in dealing with public opinion does not adequately portray the fluctuations and vicissitudes of his relationship with public opinion during his first four years in office. Starting from a high point of 68 percent public approval in Gallup poll ratings which he reached in his first year in office, Nixon's popularity declined over the next two years to a low of 48 percent in mid-1971.[5] From this low standing it began to rise until it had a reached a high of 61 percent in May 1972.

Opinion on the president's handling of his most troublesome problem, Vietnam, also fluctuated widely over the course of his first administration. The highest level of support he received on this issue, 65 percent, came in January 1970. His support on Vietnam reached its lowest level, 20 percent, in February 1971. Moreover, an increasingly larger percentage of the American public came to believe that the United States had made a mistake in becoming involved in Vietnam in the first place. But as the president's own high standing in the polls suggest, public dissatisfaction with the war in Vietnam—which flared up again following the escalation of military activity in 1972—did not have a substantially adverse impact upon his own reelection prospects. As the 1972 presidential election approached, a much smaller percentage of the population identified Vietnam as the major issue facing the country than had been the case when he took office.

Perhaps nothing was more conforting to Nixon in his handling of Vietnam than the fact that this issue was as great a source of difficulty for his Democratic opponents as it was for him. For one thing, the president was always able to point out that the massive American involvement in Vietnam had begun under his Democratic predecessor and that he had in some sense "inherited the war."

Second, the war continued to be a divisive issue within the ranks of the Democratic party even after the departure of Lyndon Johnson from office. Witness the fact that George McGovern's adamant opposition to the war as the Democratic candidate for president in 1972 helped bring about major defections by traditional supporters of

[5] The poll data in this section are drawn from the monthly reports of the *Gallup Opinion Index* between 1969 and 1972.

the Democratic party, such as George Meany, the president of the AFL-CIO. The war was not, of course, the only factor causing splits within the Democratic party in 1972, but it was clear that it would be difficult to restore unity to the Democratic party as long as Vietnam remained a major issue in American politics.

Thus, from the perspective of the 1972 presidential election at least, it was to Nixon's political advantage to "wind down" but not necessarily to end the Vietnam war. Not only did continuation of the war divide his Democratic opponents, it also served as an issue around which he could rally nationalist sentiment behind the Republican flag during his own re-election effort. Critics of the war could be charged with giving "aid and comfort" to the enemy. Moreover, a complete end to the war might well shift voter attention from foreign to domestic issues, where all polls showed the Republicans considerably more vulnerable to attack. The war, therefore, never was the political liability for Nixon that many observers believed it to be.

One final aspect of Nixon's handling of public opinion in the area of foreign policy that should be noted is the high premium he placed on the importance of surprise. The announcements of Kissinger's first trip to China and of the president's own summit meetings with the leaders of both the People's Republic of China and the Soviet Union came quite unexpectedly. The ability of the president to spring such surprises was the product in large measure of his successful resort to secrecy in the conduct of foreign affairs. His determination to conceal his intentions before he was ready to disclose them was one of the major factors which led Nixon to exclude some of the principal executive organizations usually involved in foreign policy from the circle of discussion when major decisions were being made.[6]

This attachment to executive secrecy also led Nixon to restrict his communications with the press. The president did not schedule a single formal televised news conference from June 1971 to June 1972. In 1971 only nine ad hoc meetings were held with reporters, compared to the twenty-four to thirty-five such conferences presidents had conducted during each of the past twenty-five years. While newsmen were highly critical of this presidential inaccessibility, it was accepted with equanimity by the public.

Indeed this secrecy was actually of great help to Nixon in creating a public image of administration competence in foreign affairs. That he was acting on the basis of secret information in some of his major

[6] For a more complete discussion of Nixon's relationship to the executive bureaucracy in this respect see below, pp. 95–100.

foreign policy decisions seemed to be a source of reassurance for the public. A secret trip abroad by Kissinger always seemed to promise more during the Nixon Administration than a publicly announced visit by Secretary of State Rogers. Although Americans traditionally have believed that secrecy in government conceals corruption and incompetence, Nixon was able to win public acceptance of the notion that in foreign policy at least it signifies a masterful control of events that are far too complex for public understanding.

Secrecy was also extremely useful to Nixon as a means of immobilizing critics of his performance in foreign policy. With respect to problems for which the administration appeared to have no public solution—the Vietnam negotiations, for example—it was always able to intimate that substantial progress was being made in secret. The prospect that such secret plans might actually be afoot made Nixon's domestic opponents hesitate to attack his Vietnam policy. Their inhibitions in this respect were reinforced by the apparent willingness of the public to accept the legitimacy of the president's right to govern in secret in foreign affairs.

Nixon's closed style of conducting foreign affairs left him open to the charge of communicating more information to adversaries abroad about the foreign policy of the United States and the intentions of its president than he shared with the American public. Great care was taken to send Kissinger to Moscow and Peking, so that the rulers of these states would not misunderstand what America was up to when it mined the harbors of North Vietnam and attacked it from the air in 1972. No such equivalent efforts were undertaken to brief the American people, who would have been considerably better informed if Leonid Brezhnev and Chou En-lai had chosen to disclose what they had learned from Kissinger about these momentous decisions in American foreign policy.

The Containment of Congress

The period between 1969 and 1973 was one of deep concern in American politics over the balance of power between the president and Congress in the sphere of foreign affairs. There was strong and even bitter feeling within the legislature that the president had established a monopoly of power in this area of policy never intended by the constitution. Some part of this rancor may have been inspired by partisan considerations, since a Democratic Congress faced a Republican president for the first time since the 1950s. But legislative dissatisfaction with the exercise of executive power in foreign affairs went deep into the ranks of Republicans as well.

Opposition to the president was stronger in the Senate than in the House and more intense in the Senate Foreign Relations Committee than in the Senate as a whole. Nonetheless, antagonism toward presidential hegemony over foreign affairs was evident throughout Congress, and by 1972 it was even beginning to manifest itself in places like the House Foreign Affairs Committee and the Senate Armed Services Committee that had long been citadels of congressional support for presidential leadership in the conduct of diplomacy.

However, any summary appraisal of the Nixon Administration's experience between 1969 and 1973 must inevitably conclude that the president was able both to maintain his commanding position in foreign affairs and to fend off congressional attacks on his policies. Much of the president's success came from his ability to take dramatic and forceful action in international politics on his own initiative as chief executive—the withdrawal of American troops from Vietnam beginning in 1969, the invasion of Cambodia in 1970, the initiation of a trip to China in 1971, and the mining of Haiphong harbor and resumption of large-scale bombing of North Vietnam in 1972. Each of these presidential surprises presented Congress with a *fait accompli* that it could either support or denounce, but could not alter.

While thus relying in large part upon his own constitutional prerogatives as the nation's chief diplomat and commander-in-chief of its armed forces, Nixon was also able to assert his legislative leadership within Congress and to defeat or emasculate most congressional efforts to commit the United States to foreign policy positions to which he was opposed. The success he achieved with respect to Vietnam was particularly striking, since public discontent with the war remained at a high level throughout his first administration, and Congress was in a strong position to challenge his leadership.

Nevertheless, Nixon won far more battles on the Vietnam issue in Congress than he lost. Up until 1972 nearly every attempt to put both the House and Senate clearly on record as favoring a withdrawal of American troops from Vietnam on terms other than those favored by the president was defeated. A major exception was the so-called Mansfield Amendment enacted by Congress in 1971 as part of the defense procurement authorization bill. The Mansfield provision urged the president to establish a final date for the withdrawal of all U.S. forces from Indo-China, subject only to the requirement that U.S. prisoners of war be released and an accounting be made of those missing in action.

In signing the bill President Nixon plainly stated his conviction that the Mansfield Amendment did not concur with the policies of his administration and that he would not be subject to it. "It is without binding force or effect," he said in what will surely become a landmark statement of presidential independence of congressional efforts to control the conduct of foreign policy. "It does not reflect my judgment about the way in which this war should be brought to a conclusion. My signing of the bill that contains this section, therefore, will not change the policies I have pursued and that I shall continue to pursue toward this end."[7]

Nixon thus chose to interpret Congressional action in the Mansfield Amendment as merely an expression of legislative opinion rather than an attempt to bind him to any specific course of action. Over the years of his administration, there were many such expressions of the "sense of Congress," very often in support of the president's policies on the war rather than against them. There were, for example, resolutions of support for the president's peace terms and resolutions condemning the treatment of American prisoners of war by North Vietnam.

Moreover, many anti-Vietnam war resolutions passed by the Senate were later defeated in the House and eliminated or watered down in conference committees to conform to presidential policies. But opponents of presidential policy continued to introduce resolutions designed to bring about the withdrawal of American forces from Vietnam, even when there was little prospect they would win legislative approval, and Congressional committees periodically scheduled hearings on the war so that the president's critics could appear and testify on a platform from which they could command the attention of the media and a vast national audience. The Senate Foreign Relations Committee played a leading role in this respect and provided the principal legislative impetus for a number of efforts in the Senate to change American foreign policy. But a wide range of other committees and subcommittees were also involved, including a Senate Judiciary Subcommittee, chaired by Senator Edward Kennedy, which held highly publicized hearings on the plight of refugees in Indo-China.

None of these tactics succeeded in forcing the president to deviate from his chosen policy of Vietnamizing the war on the ground and maintaining a strong American participation in the air and on the sea. This is not, however, to say that they were altogether meaningless. The strategy of Nixon's Congressional opposition on Vietnam can perhaps best be described at that of a guerrilla army, facing in the form

---

[7] *Congressional Quarterly Almanac* (Washington, D.C., 1971), p. 305.

of the presidency a superior force it could not defeat in direct confrontation. It was thus confined to techniques of harassment, which
were certainly instrumental in holding the administration to the policy of negotiating an end to the war and withdrawing American
troops from Vietnam. At the very least, the opposition was able to
keep the war at the forefront of presidential and public attention.

Congressional efforts to influence the president in the conduct of
foreign affairs were by no means confined to Vietnam. In 1970, for
example, the Senate passed a resolution stating that no national commitment had been made to Spain, in spite of the treaty of friendship
that had just been concluded with that country, and in 1972 it urged
the president to recognize the new nation of Bangladesh. Perhaps the
greatest success Congress enjoyed in its confrontations with the president was in its attempts to prevent the emergence of "future Vietnams." It was, for example, able to set limits on the number of Americans who could be stationed in Laos and Cambodia, and it eliminated
provisions to supply jets to Taiwan from the 1970 foreign aid bill.

The most promising avenue open to the president's critics in Congress was the appropriation process upon which the Vietnam war
and other military activities abroad depended for financial support.
As noted already, the Mansfield Amendment was enacted as a rider
to a defense appropriations act. Virtually every major appropriations
bill involving military spending that came before Congress during the
first Nixon Administration became the center of a fierce dispute over
the war or other national security issues such as the high level of
defense spending.

In almost every case the Nixon Administration was successful in
defeating Congressional efforts to use the appropriations process as
a means of turning American foreign policy in new directions. The
struggle over foreign policy in these years was not a simple case of
legislative-executive conflict, for the House of Representatives proved
a bastion of presidential strength in this encounter. The attempts of
the Senate to compel an American withdrawal from Vietnam on
terms other than those favored by the president were repeatedly rejected by the House, which aligned itself with the president during
virtually every major confrontation between the White House and
Congress between 1969 and 1972.

The alliance thus forged between the House and the president was
a product in part of conflicting institutional interests between the two
branches of Congress. The House has tended to look upon efforts to
increase Congressional influence over foreign policy as beneficial primarily to the Senate. Under the constitution the House has consider-

ably less important a role in the conduct of foreign affairs than the upper chamber. Unlike the Senate, it has no voice in the ratification of treaties or the confirmation of ambassadors. Any success in augmenting the legislative role in foreign policy could thus appear to many House members as increasing the advantages Senators already enjoy over them in terms of prestige and visibility in the eyes of the general public.

In addition, the leadership in the House, Speaker Carl Albert and the Majority Leader Hale Boggs, firmly supported the president's position on major foreign policy questions. On the other hand, the majority leader in the Senate, Mike Mansfield, persistently sought to put his colleagues on record in opposition to the Vietnam War and in favor of reducing the number of American troops in Europe.

Over the course of the Nixon years there was some weakening in the tenacity of this House support for the White House. In 1972 the Democratic caucus in the House put its leadership under strong pressure by voting in favor of withdrawing American troops from Vietnam. The same shift occurred with respect to the House Foreign Affairs Committee, which supported administration policy in Vietnam up until July 1972, when it finally approved an end-the-war measure opposed by the president. Until this time, the House committee had never deviated from its support of Nixon's politics in Vietnam. But even with this erosion of support, the administration was still able to defeat a crucial end-the-war amendment on the foreign aid authorization bill in August 1972.

The most far-reaching attempt to increase the legislative role in foreign affairs was the action by the Senate in approving the so-called War Powers Bill in 1972, which was designed to curb what one Senator called "presidential wars." This bill specified certain emergency circumstances in which the president was authorized to commit the armed forces of the United States into combat abroad in the absence of a declaration of war by Congress. The approval of Congress was required for any such commitment to continue beyond 30 days. The administration fought vigorously against this bill, which it regarded as an unconstitutional infringement upon the president's discretion in the exercise of his national security responsibilities. In 1972 both the House and Senate also approved legislation requiring the president to submit to Congress within 60 days the text of any executive agreement with a foreign country.

Even in the face of this limited legislative success, it is hard to escape the conclusion that the congressional effort to play a major role in the foreign policy process between 1969 and 1972 was largely an exercise in futility. The administration won the crucial battles, and the opposition never gained the upper hand even on the issue of Vietnam. On other leading foreign policy questions the president's position of leadership was never in serious jeopardy from his legislative critics. The SALT agreements and other major aspects of the administration's foreign policy sailed easily through Congress.

But on Vietnam as well as on other issues the most important constraints under which the president operated did not come from Congress. The crucial decisions of his administration, such as the invasion of Cambodia in 1970 and of Laos in 1971, the resumption of the bombing of North Vietnam, and the mining of the North Vietnamese coastal waters in 1972, were shaped primarily by the imperatives of the political and military situation in South Vietnam as perceived by the president, and the potential impact of this situation upon domestic politics in the United States. In such case, the president made his decision in terms of opportunities and constraints that he saw in the international and domestic arena and then informed Congress of what he had decided. Sometimes, as in the case of the mining of the North Vietnamese coastal waters, the process of advising Congress occurred only minutes before the general public was itself informed by the president in a nation-wide address on radio and television. Even more remarkable perhaps, by the time the decision was announced to anyone outside the executive branch, it had already been carried out.

While this procedure was the source of much legislative unhappiness, Congress accepted this cavalier treatment with resignation. Direct challenges to presidential authority in foreign affairs have just not been considered good politics by most members of Congress. As noted in the previous volume of *America and the World*, "such challenges always have an element of *lèse majesté* about them, offensive to the dignity of the country as well as its chief executive. Moreover, since the president commands such a vast bureaucratic establishment in foreign affairs, it has been hard for his critics to convince the public that their sources of information are better than his."[8]

Nixon and the Executive Apparatus

During the 1960s it became common for former officials in the Kennedy and Johnson Administrations to suggest that presidential decisions in national security policy were largely shaped by the bureaucratic apparatus. Sometimes, the bureaucracy was said to exercise this power by defining the options available to deal with critical problems in foreign affairs. Witness, for example, the following description

[8] Francis E. Rourke, "The Domestic Scene," in Robert E. Osgood et. al., *America and the World* (Baltimore: Johns Hopkins University Press, 1970), p. 164.

of the way in which President Johnson was led in 1965 to begin the massive American involvement in Vietnam which was to haunt all American politics in the years that followed:

In the summer of 1964 the President instructed his chief advisers to prepare for him as wide a range of Vietnam options as possible for post-election consideration and decision. He explicitly asked that all options be laid out. What happened next was, in effect, Lyndon Johnson's slow-motion Bay of Pigs. For the advisers so effectively converged on one single option— juxtaposed against two other, phony options (in effect, blowing up the world, or scuttle-and-run)—that the President was confronted with unanimity for bombing the North from all his trusted counselors.[9]

Moreover, even when the decisions of Kennedy and Johnson did not seem to derive their initial inspiration from bureaucratic advice, it could still be argued that each president was a prisoner of his own bureaucracy, like the Russian czar who, in Max Weber's words, "was seldom able to accomplish permanently anything that displeased his bureaucracy and hurt the power interests of the bureaucrats."[10] It is inescapably true that a great many presidential decisions in foreign affairs cannot be executed except through the machinery of government, and that control over this process gives bureaucrats an opportunity to shape executive directives to their own specifications.

In many cases, the end product of bureaucratic activity scarcely resembles or may actually negate a president's original intentions. Bureaucratic sabotage is a favorite theme in the accounts former members of the Kennedy Administration have given of their experience in government. It was not until six weeks after President Kennedy's Vienna meeting with Khrushchev in 1961 that the State Department prepared what the president regarded as a wholly unsatisfactory response to the Russian leader's *aide memoire* on Berlin. Similarly, at the time of the Cuban missile crisis in October 1962, Kennedy discovered that the American missiles he had ordered removed from Turkey several months earlier were still in place, a highly vulnerable target for Soviet efforts to win American concessions in exchange for removing Russian missiles from Cuba. As Robert Kennedy was to lament years later:

The President believed he was President and that, his wishes having been made clear, they would be followed and the missiles removed. He therefore

[9] James C. Thomson, Jr., "How Could Vietnam Happen? An Autopsy," The *Atlantic* 221 (April, 1968), p. 52

[10] H. H. Gerth and C. Wright Mills, *From Max Weber: Essays in Sociology* (New York: Oxford University Press, 1946), p. 234.

dismissed the matter from his mind. Now he learned that his failure to follow up on this matter had permitted the same obsolete Turkish missiles to become hostages of the Soviet Union.[11]

Sometimes the failure of bureaucrats to adhere faithfully to presidential goals during the Kennedy and Johnson Administrations has been traced to ideological prejudice or commitment on their part. John Kenneth Galbraith, for example, attributes American involvement in Vietnam to the cold war mentality of executive organizations which presidents were not able to change.[12] More commonly, however, bureaucratic resistance to presidential directives has been attributed to the inertia which characterizes all large organizations. Once bureaucrats establish a set of routines necessary to pursue a particular course of action, these routines become very difficult to alter. Means are transformed into ends, especially when the career interests of bureaucrats are linked to their perpetuation. From this perspective, bureaucracies pursue obsolete policies not because they are passionately committed to them, but because they are accustomed to the routines associated with these goals and derive advantage from them.

Taming the Bureaucracy. The difficulties encountered by Presidents Kennedy and Johnson in maintaining their ascendancy within the executive branch in the sphere of foreign affairs throw into bold relief one of the most striking developments in the Nixon Administration: the subordination of the regular executive departments in the foreign policy process to presidential control and the emergence of the Special Assistant for National Security Affairs as the president's chief instrument for the realization of his major foreign policy objectives.

The assignment of a reduced role to the traditional bureaucratic apparatus in national security decision-making reflected a number of views to which Nixon had been strongly attached long before coming to office. For one thing, the loyalty of bureaucrats to a Republican administration had always been suspect in his eyes. Back in 1958 when he was serving as vice-president in the Eisenhower Administration, Nixon had charged the State Department with "undercutting" and "sabotage" of official policy when it released an analysis of mail from constituents showing heavy public opposition to an American commitment to defend the islands of Quemoy and Matsu off the Chi-

[11] Robert F. Kennedy, *Thirteen Days: A Memoir of the Cuban Missile Crisis* (New York: New American Library, Inc., 1969), p. 95.

[12] John Kenneth Galbraith, *How to Control the Military* (New York: Signet Books, 1969), pp. 16–17.

nese mainland.[13] From Nixon's perspective there was little reason to expect the bureaucracy to be any friendlier to him than it had been to his Republican predecessor.

Even more important, and not altogether unrelated to Nixon's misgivings regarding the loyalty of bureaucrats to his administration, was his conviction that the higher stages of diplomacy could only be conducted in secret. Unlike Woodrow Wilson, whom he so much admires, Nixon has always been a staunch advocate of secret diplomacy. Whatever attractions Wilson may have for him, they certainly do not include the doctrine of "open covenants, openly arrived at." As Nixon put it during the 1968 election campaign: "That is not the way diplomacy is conducted. The Vietnamese war, for instance, will be settled at secret high-level negotiations. The Johnson administration has boxed itself in where it can't undertake these. But a new administration could and would."[14]

This commitment to secret diplomacy made it inevitable that the executive departments would not figure largely in Nixon's conduct of foreign policy. All modern presidents have found that there are innumerable crevices in these large executive agencies through which information can leak to the outside world. President Johnson, for example, complained bitterly in his memoirs about the unauthorized release of information by executive officials at the time of the Tet offensive in 1968. This disclosure revealed that the American commander in Vietnam, General William Westmoreland, had asked for additional reinforcements for the half-million American troops then under siege by the North Vietnamese. Westmoreland's request provoked a public uproar and led eventually to the negotiations in Paris and a reduction of the American presence in Vietnam.

The tendency of departmental officials to leak confidential information is in part a reflection of the innumerable contacts such officials have with reporters and congressmen. The existence of these ties alone made it difficult for Nixon to trust departments with presidential secrets, since they enhanced the likelihood of an accidental leak of information the president did not wish to disclose. In conversations with a newsman, for example, an official can reveal far more than he intends, since a skilled reporter can draw shrewd conclusions not only from what an official says but from what he fails to say.

Far less innocent, however, is the very common practice of execu-

[13] See MacAlister Brown, "The Demise of State Department Public Opinion Polls: A Study in Legislative Oversight," *Midwest Journal of Political Science* 5 (February, 1961), p. 16.

[14] Wills, *Nixon Agonistes*, p. 31.

tive officials' deliberately leaking information to reporters or legisla-
tors, sometimes to advance the policy views or jurisdictional ambitions of their agency, but very often for the purpose of embarrassing
the president or frustrating his efforts to achieve his policy objective.
Events during his administration were ultimately to prove that Nixon
had reason for concern on this score. In 1972 he was put in an extremely awkward position when the minutes of certain National Security Council meetings were leaked to the press. These meetings
had been held to discuss the outbreak of armed conflict between India and Pakistan, and the minutes revealed that there was a substantial gap between the neutrality the Nixon Administration was pro-
fessing in public and the secret efforts it was making to assist the
Pakistanis, or at least to discourage the Indians.

Because he found the major executive departments unsuitable for
the conduct of high level diplomacy, Nixon turned instead to his own
White House apparatus and established the Office of the Special Assistant for National Security Affairs as the chief instrument for the
achievement of his foreign policy objectives. Nixon's appointee to this
office, Henry Kissinger, soon came to be recognized as the president's
chief deputy on all matters of salient importance in foreign affairs by
the public, by other participants in the foreign policy process, and
even by the heads of foreign governments. Through his position as
head of the National Security Council staff, Kissinger was able to establish firm command over the planning and development of foreign
policy.

A key factor in Nixon's decision to centralize so much power in
Kissinger's hands was the secretive way in which the office of his National Security Adviser could function. Alone among high foreign
policy officials Kissinger was protected by the doctrine of executive
privilege from having to appear or testify before Congress unless he
chose to do so. Such secrecy provided some insurance (although not
total protection) against unauthorized leaks of information. It is hard
to imagine how a great coup of the Nixon administration, Kissinger's
secret trip to China in 1971, could have been managed through the
ordinary bureaucratic apparatus without a leak occurring at some
point in the process.

An equally attractive aspect of Kissinger's apparatus from Nixon's
point of view is the fact that its primary identification is with the
president rather than, as is commonly the case with a regular executive department, a set of outside constituencies or its own organizational interests. Nixon's delegation of power to his National Security
Adviser was one manifestation of a general tendency on his part to

shift power from the old-line departments to his own White House staff.

The expansion in the size and power of the White House entourage is in fact one of the most marked characteristics of the Nixon Administration. A study published by a House committee in 1972 found a very substantial increase in the number of persons employed by the Executive Office of the President in general and by Kissinger's NSC staff in particular. "Under this administration," the committee report said, "the National Security Council has grown 50 percent and many observers believe that the upper-level bureaucracy of the State Department may be redundant, or badly overshadowed, insofar as policy-making functions are concerned."[15]

In strengthening the position of his own palace guard, Nixon was certainly following in the footsteps of his predecessors. From Roosevelt in 1932 to Johnson in 1968, all American presidents had come to lean heavily upon White House advisers to help formulate or carry out major presidential decisions. Because of his distrust of bureaucrats and a personal predilection for privacy, Nixon has carried this tendency further than some of his predecessors, but he certainly did not initiate it.

Nevertheless, the function of the National Security Adviser under Nixon does differ markedly from his role under previous presidents. In the first days after the establishment of the National Security Council in 1947, the task of the adviser and his staff had been mainly that of ensuring that all the principal agencies involved in foreign policy were given an opportunity to be heard on major issues facing the president in the international arena. The adviser acted as an intermediary between the president and the agencies carrying on activitive abroad, but he was not himself a principal source of advice in the foreign policy process. President Nixon brought to fulfillment a trend that had been clearly visible during the Kennedy and Johnson years. The Special Assistant for National Security Affairs was now given principal responsibility for advising the president as well as for monitoring the communications channeled to the chief executive from the regular executive establishment.[16]

In thus broadening the authority of his special assistant over foreign policy, President Nixon had the proclaimed objective of widening his

[15] U.S. House of Representatives, 92d Congress, 2d sess., Committee on Post Office and Civil Service, *A Report on the Growth of the Executive Office of the President* (Washington, D.C., 1972), p. 5.

[16] For analyses of these Nixon innovations in the organization of national security policy-making, see I. M. Destler, "Can One Man Do," and John P. Leacacos, "Kissinger's Apparat," *Foreign Policy* 5 (Winter 1971–72), pp. 3–27.

options on the problems that came before him. His fear was that the national security organizations in the executive branch would negotiage and compromise differences on issues and present the president with a united front in support or opposition to a projected course of action. In such situations, the White House might well be reduced to the role of ratifying rather than initiating foreign policy decisions. As he put it in a mid-term report to Congress on the scope and objectives of his foreign policy: "I refuse to be confronted with a bureaucratic consensus that leaves me no options but acceptance or rejection, and that gives me no way of knowing what alternatives exist."[17]

It is also possible to explain Nixon's decision to centralize control over foreign affairs in Kissinger's office in terms of the kind of policy he intended to pursue. The decision-making system he created was much more suitable than the traditional departmental structure for conducting the direct negotiations he wanted to undertake with China and the Soviet Union in order to exploit divisions in the communist world and establish a new balance of power in international politics. These were new departures, if not radical innovations, in American foreign policy, and the regular departments were not regarded by either Nixon or Kissinger as suitable instruments for launching novel ventures. The role the old-line departments best fulfill, performing the routines necessary to carry out the policies of the past, was not especially useful for an administration bent on moving in new directions. In the words of Stanley Hoffman, "the new strategy, geared to the subtleties and shifts of the balance of power, requires a centralized and lofty machinery: the National Security Council system."[18]

In a highly original analysis of the Cuban missile crisis, Graham Allison argues that the positions executive organizations take on issues of foreign policy mirror not so much their conception of the national interest as their own organizational interests.[19] According to Allison, national security organizations seek policies that will protect or expand their own jurisdiction, and their behavior in crisis situations is often governed by these self-serving concerns. Since American

[17] As quoted in Alexander L. George, "The Case for Multiple Advocacy in Making Foreign Policy," *The American Political Science Review* 66 (September, 1972), p. 754. George is quite critical of the structure Nixon devised for the conduct of foreign policy.

[18] Stanley Hoffmann, "Will the Balance Balance at Home?" *Foreign Policy* 7 (Summer, 1972), p. 63.

[19] Graham T. Allison, *Essence of Decision: Explaining the Cuban Missile Crisis* (Boston: Little, Brown and Co., 1971).

foreign policy has increasingly depended upon the activities of large organizations since World War II, it has inevitably been shaped by bureaucratic as well as national imperatives. Looking at the administration of foreign affairs from this perspective, it can be said that Nixon's shift of power to Kissinger's office is a means of liberating policy from bondage to the organizational interests that come into play when the president uses the large executive departments for the achievement of his objectives in foreign affairs. However, as will be discussed later, the Nixon arrangement does not free foreign policy from the possibility of bondage to presidential interests.

Presidential Ascendancy. The commanding position Nixon achieved within the executive apparatus decisively refutes the belief that foreign policy must inevitably be dominated by the administrative organizations responsible for carrying it out, a belief to which the label "bureaucratic determinism" has sometimes been attached. Contrary to what supporters of the Kennedy and Johnson administrations have sometimes tended to argue, the president is not a helpless pawn in the hands of his bureaucratic advisers. Nixon has shown that a chief executive can in fact work his way around the ordinary executive machinery.

It should, however, be made clear that the control Nixon achieved over foreign policy has been far from total domination. The president's mastery of decision was greatest in those areas where policy least depends upon bureaucratic organizations for its execution. Summit meetings with China and the Soviet Union could be arranged through Kissinger and his National Security Council staff, and when matters of this sort were on the agenda of policy Nixon was very much in command.

Inevitably, however, a great deal of slippage occurred when Nixon and Kissinger had to rely upon the capabilities of the regular national security apparatus for the success of policy. In such situations a president's ability to achieve his goals is greatly affected by the professional skills and orientations of the bureaucrats through whom he must attempt to work his will. Allison has aptly described this kind of presidential reliance upon bureaucracy, although his analysis tends to overlook situations in which a president's policy decisions do not depend upon bureaucratic organizations for their implementation:

... existing organizational routines for employing present physical capabilities constitute the range of effective choice open to government leaders confronted with any problem. . . . The fact that fixed programs (equipment, men, and routines that exist at the particular time) exhaust the range of buttons that leaders can push is not always perceived by these leaders. But in every case it is critical for an understanding of what is actually done.[20]

There were occasions when his dependence upon bureaucratic organizations for the execution of his decisions was as frustrating for Nixon as it was for earlier presidents. In 1969 an American reconnaissance plane was shot down over North Korea, and Nixon decided to launch a retaliatory air strike against North Korean airfields. He could not do so immediately, however, since it took considerable time for the American military apparatus to deploy the forces necessary to conduct such a mission. As it turned out, Nixon changed his mind during this delay. "As the military slowly moved air and sea reinforcements toward Korea, his anger cooled and he decided against retaliatory raids."[21] In this case, the cumbersome nature of bureaucratic routines forced Nixon to reverse a major decision, perhaps in the long run to his own and the country's advantage.

The power that executive organizations command in the area of national security policy comes not only from the skills and capabilities they control but also from their ability to attract public support. This ability enables agencies to build and maintain a constituency of community groups which benefit from an agency's activities and support its efforts to maintain and expand its organizational authority. During the Nixon Administration the Department of Defense continued to exhibit the extraordinary constituency strength it has enjoyed since World War II, largely because of the economic reliance of a wide range of communities across the United States upon contracts for local defense industries or the continued presence of military facilities.

The power of the defense establishment during his administration compelled Nixon to bargain with the department to win its approval of some of his major policy initiatives. The American withdrawal from Vietnam, for example, involved Nixon in constant negotiations with the Joint Chiefs of Staff, and the pace of that withdrawal was very much affected by the advice of military officials. In order to secure Department of Defense acceptance of the disarmament agreements negotiated with the Soviet Union in 1972, the president was obliged to accede to the department's demand for the continued development of offensive capabilities. Indeed, Secretary of Defense Melvin Laird insisted in testimony before Congress that the department would oppose the arms control agreement reached in Moscow if the increased appropriations necessary to continue a weapons de-

[20] *Ibid.*, p. 79.
[21] New York *Times*, Jan. 21, 1971, p. 12.

velopment program were not forthcoming. Nixon was thus in the paradoxical position of supplementing the presentation of a disarmament treaty to Congress with a proposal for increased military appropriations.

The kind of leverage the Department of Defense exerted at the time of the SALT agreements in 1972 is a tribute not only to the political strength it draws from its own constituency but also to the prestige of the military profession in American society. This high public standing springs from the great importance Americans attach to a strong national defense, and it has survived innumerable blows that Vietnam has inflicted on the reputation of the military in recent years. Nixon was able to give short shrift to a comparatively vulnerable organization like the Department of State in his decision-making processes between 1969 and 1972, but State has always lacked a strong constituency and its diplomatic expertise is a far less impressive art in the public eye than the awesome science of war. The strength of the Pentagon's assets compelled Nixon to treat its views with respect and on occasion deference during the years of his administration and to bargain with defense officials in areas of policy generally regarded as lying within their sphere of competence.[22]

During the first Nixon Administration the bureaucracy continued to reveal its long-demonstrated capacity to defy or evade presidential control when it suited the purposes of some lower-echelon officials to do so. Perhaps the most celebrated case of this kind of bureaucratic independence involved General John D. Lavelle, the Air Force commander in Vietnam, who was retired from the armed forces in 1972 after being demoted to the rank of three-star general. Beginning late in 1971, Lavelle had sent aircraft under his control on bombing missions over North Vietnam that were in apparent violation of the rules of engagement under which the Air Force had been authorized by the president to operate in the north. These rules restricted American planes to "protective reaction" strikes upon anti-aircraft guns that had either fired at or were about to fire at them. Lavelle had initiated raids upon pre-selected targets in North Vietnam and then falsely labelled these raids "protection reaction" strikes in his official reports to his military superiors.

The Lavelle case was an unusual episode of the military seeming to take the war into its own hands.[23] But it revealed as had so many

[22] For a more complete analysis of the sources on which the Pentagon's constituency support rests, see Francis E. Rourke, *Bureaucracy and Foreign Policy* (Baltimore: The Johns Hopkins University Press, 1972), pp. 28–33.

[23] It is still not altogether clear whether the Lavelle affair was in fact a case of a bureaucrat abusing his discretion. Some observers contend that the Nixon Ad-

other earlier occurrences in Vietnam (especially the slaughter of Vietnamese civilians at Mylai) the risks that a president takes when
lower-level officials enjoy wide discretion in carrying out policies that
are general and often ambiguous in character. Very often, the outcomes that result when complex and highly specialized organizations
take over the task of executing these orders differ considerably from
the president's original intent. Military organizations are a special
problem in this regard, since they command formidable instruments
of immense and irreversible destruction. When such organizations are
set in motion in pursuit of presidential goals, it is not always certain where they and the chief executive's goals will ultimately come
to rest.

At the other extreme from the Lavelle situation, where a bureaucrat
seemed to interpret his discretionary authority very broadly, was a
case involving the Coast Guard in 1970. A Russian seaman attempted
to defect from a Soviet vessel and was returned over his own violent
objections to his ship by the Coast Guard. In this instance the bureaucrats responsible for the decision interpreted the scope of their
authority very narrowly and were reluctant to risk taking action that
might embarrass the United States by offending the Soviets. The
Nixon Administration was greatly discomfited by this episode, which
grievously offended many of its more conservative supporters.

The lesson to be drawn from both the Lavelle and Coast Guard
episodes is clear. Even a president like Nixon who is determined to
minimize the role of bureaucrats in the foreign policy process cannot
avoid leaving some discretionary authority in their hands. Inevitably,
such discretion will be used in ways that are disadvantageous to the
president. Some bureaucrats will be too aggressive, others too timid
in using the power assigned to them. A president can thus limit the
influence of bureaucrats in foreign affairs, but he can never abolish
it altogether.

The Presidential Stake in International Politics

The new approach to foreign policy which the president announced
in the early days of his administration (the so-called Nixon Doctrine) signified to many that the United States was now going to
scale down the scope of its activities abroad. Some observers even

---

ministration never did intend its guidelines to preclude the bombing of North
Vietnamese targets, when this seemed militarily advisable, and that the chief error
Lavelle made was to violate guidelines in clumsy ways that required subordinates
to falsify records—a practice which led ultimately to the disclosure of what was
going on to a Congressional committee by an Air Force sergeant.

suggested that America was about to retreat from the leading role it had assumed in international politics following World War II. During the ensuing four years the administration was often to charge its critics with being (at best) "neo-isolationists." What this charge overlooked was the extent to which the Nixon Doctrine itself supported the belief that the United States should become less involved in the international arena in the future than it had been in the past.

Discussions of the Nixon Doctrine tended to concentrate on its potential impact abroad, how it would affect our relations with our allies and those we perceived as adversaries. Generally overlooked in the discussion were the possible consequences of this doctrine for domestic politics in the United States. If these domestic implications had been fully appreciated, there would have been far less alarm over the possibility that the United States was about to retreat into an isolationist posture reminiscent of the 1930s.

The fact of the matter is that the first casualty of any large-scale retreat on the part of the United States from international politics would be the presidency itself. The dominant role presidential power has exercised in the American political arena since World War II stems in no small measure from the chief executive's position of leadership in the conduct of foreign affairs. It is this position which gives him his overpowering stature in the eyes of the public and a decisive advantage over all his political competitors. In domestic politics, by way of contrast, the president is often reduced to bargaining and haggling like any other politician, never altogether certain that his purposes and programs will prevail.

Hence it is difficult to conceive of any American president voluntarily announcing a retreat from the American posture abroad that would so clearly invite a decline in his own political authority at home. In view of the strenuous efforts Nixon has made throughout his administration to preserve and expand the scope of his power as president, it would be incredible if he intended the Nixon Doctrine to have any of the isolationist overtones commonly attributed to it. No president has seemed more jealous of the prerogatives of his office, in terms of ceremonial deference as well as substantive influence.

Perhaps as remarkable as any other aspect of the affinity of interest that has emerged in modern American politics between the presidency and an activist foreign policy is the fact that this affinity is even stronger for Republican than it is for Democratic presidents. Historically, it has been the Republicans who have been most closely linked with isolationism throughout this century. This linkage was very visible in the 1920s when Republican presidents occupied the White House. It became even more pronounced in the 1930s when isolationists mainly centered in the Republican party bitterly opposed the efforts of Franklin D. Roosevelt to align the United States with the European nations that were threatened by the rising power of Nazi Germany.

Today, however all poll data show the Republican party ranking much higher in public standing in terms of its capacity to handle foreign policy than it does in domestic affairs. This difference springs in part from the fact that the Republicans are linked with "hard times" domestically, while the Democrats are associated with American involvement in war. World War I, World War II, the Korean War, and the Vietnam conflict all began under Democratic administrations.

Coming to office in this political context, Nixon's intention from the outset was clearly that of making foreign policy the long suit of his administration. This was not entirely a matter of personal temperament, as some observers have contended. It was also a matter of solid political calculation. A Republican president is in a much stronger position in the eyes of the electorate when he is dealing with foreign policy issues than with domestic problems.

Certainly, the steps Nixon took in foreign affairs during the year preceding the 1972 election represented, whatever their eventual impact upon the position of the United States in world politics, a masterful use of presidential discretion to structure a climate of opinion favorable to his own re-election. In the past, presidents have often profited from the occurrence in election years of international crises which enhanced their political prospects. President Eisenhower, for example, is widely believed to have been helped greatly at the polls by the Suez crisis and the Russian intervention in Hungary in the month immediately preceding the presidential election of 1956.[24]

However, Nixon's success in 1972 did not reflect the emergence of crises from which he was fortunate enough to draw political profit. It was the product of events which he himself had caused to happen —the dramatic trips to Peking and Moscow followed by the negotiation of the SALT agreements with the Soviet Union enormously enhanced his public standing at a time when it could be of maximum advantage to his re-election prospects. Also helpful to Nixon's standing in the election year of 1972 were meetings with President Pompidou of France, Prime Minister Trudeau of Canada, Chancellor Brandt from West Germany, Prime Minister Heath of Great Britain, and Premier Sato from Japan.

[24] For a review of the role of foreign policy issues in recent presidential elections, see Stephen Hess, "Foreign Policy and Presidential Campaigns," *Foreign Policy* 8 (Fall, 1972), pp. 3–22.

There has long been widespread disagreement as to the precise impact of foreign policy issues on presidential elections in the United States. Many observers contend that the outcome of a presidential race turns primarily on domestic issues—such matters as the price of wheat, the level of unemployment, or the cost of groceries in the supermarket. Others argue for the salience of foreign policy in the race for the White House, and point to the election of 1952 and 1968, when the Korean and Vietnam wars seemed to exert a major influence upon voting behavior. What seems beyond dispute is the fact that the voters are very much concerned over the relative capacity of rival presidential candidates to deal effectively with foreign policy issues, even though they may have little knowledge of, or concern for, the substance of these issues. Clearly, presidential candidates themselves believe this to be the case. One of the chief ways in which presidential hopefuls demonstrate their qualifications for the high office they seek is by exhibiting knowledge and competence in matters affecting the national security of the United States. When a candidate fails to radiate a reassuring image in foreign affairs, his campaign is gravely damaged (as was the case with Barry Goldwater in 1964 and George McGovern in 1972).

Thus state governors are seldom taken seriously today as presidential candidates, largely because their executive experience does not embrace foreign affairs. U.S. Senators, on the other hand, have moved to the fore during recent years in the contest for presidential nominations, in no small measure because their role permits much greater public association with foreign policy issues. Even more advantageous in this respect is the position of the sitting vice-president, who has the opportunity to meet with foreign potentates as the official representative of the United States prior to running for the presidency. In this way he can gain a presidential stature in the eyes of the electorate that no other candidate can match.

But no one is in a position to benefit more from the voter's concern with the competence of a candidate in the area of foreign affairs than an incumbent president. He has the power to act, while his opponents can only talk, and the polls commonly show that the voters have a tendency to rally behind the president whenever he takes highly visible, dramatic steps in foreign affairs, even though the action taken may ultimately be viewed as something less than successful in its effects.[25] This rallying tendency is especially valuable in an election

[25] See John E. Mueller, "Presidential Popularity from Truman to Johnson," *American Political Science Review* 64 (March, 1970), pp. 18–34.

year, as Nixon demonstrated with the mining of North Vietnamese coastal waters and the large-scale bombing of North Vietnam in the Spring of 1972.

Even more important, however, the incumbent is at the center of national attention. His claim to have competence sufficient for the presidency has a legitimacy no challenger can match: he now holds the office and the voters perceive him as having "presidential stature" as a statesman, if only because they have seen him for nearly four years meeting with the heads of foreign states, negotiating international agreements, and otherwise exhibiting confident familiarity with the great issues of foreign affairs. The difficulties presidential aspirants face in this respect are formidable, and all other factors aside, Nixon's advantages in foreign affairs by themselves seemed sufficient to defeat George McGovern in the 1972 presidential election.

Thus, in foreign affairs the story of the Nixon years thus far is very largely a story of the president triumphant. While at the outset of the administration and as late as the invasion of Laos in 1971, it seemed that Vietnam might well be the nemesis of the American presidency, Nixon was finally able to escape a debacle in Southeast Asia with the president's power not only intact but even to some degree augmented. Once again a chief executive had proved himself invulnerable to serious challenge from Congress on major foreign policy issues and had succeeded in sustaining his authority even in the face of serious erosion of public support.

Still, even after Nixon's landslide re-election in 1972, the triumph was not without its portents of problems to come. The highly centralized White House structure for the management of foreign affairs under Kissinger may well have been a political and diplomatic asset for the conduct of well publicized "secret" negotiations designed to end the war in Vietnam. But this arrangement has not been without costs. It has led to a down-grading of a great many other executive agencies and officials involved in the framing of national security policy with inevitable damage to their morale and effectiveness. Moreover, the question of executive accountability appeared likely to come increasingly to the fore as the Vietnam war receded into the merciful past. A foreign policy controlled so completely by a small White House *apparat* seemed bound to provoke growing resistance from Congress and the public in the years ahead. In the fall of 1972, the American mood was passive and presidential power dominated the scene in foreign affairs. It was not at all certain that the inertia of 1972 would be any more permanent a feature of American politics than the activism of the late 1960s. Indeed, it was quite plausible that once Vietnam was safely behind, new challenges to presidential hegemony over foreign policy would arise, or that fear of such challenges might lead presidents to tread somewhat more cautiously in foreign affairs in the future than they had in the past.

In short, 1972 was a year in which a crisis seemed to have passed, the patient would surely recover, but the long-term impact of the illness on his constitution was far from clear. Many early predictions of the transforming effect of Vietnam upon the way in which American foreign policy is made have proven erroneous. But it still seemed quite premature to assume that the presidency had emerged altogether unscathed from the searing effects of the Vietnam experience.

It is also essential to avoid exaggerating the long-term significance of President Nixon's use of foreign policy issues to dominate the political scene in 1972. The fact of the matter is that the opportunities he seized to end the long and disheartening war in Vietnam and to make a new beginning in America's relationship with the People's Republic of China were unique opportunities afforded him by history to create foreign policy events that will not be open to future presidents. Worth remembering in this connection is Nixon's comparatively low estate in the public eye prior to his 1972 success. During all the earlier years of his administration the polls repeatedly suggested that he might well be a one-term president.

Moreover, one of the most paradoxical aspects of Nixon's performance may well lie in the fact that the way in which he and his power in foreign affairs strengthened his hand as president may ultimately make it more difficult for future presidents to make domestic political capital out of America's international involvements. Both the end of the war in Vietnam and the "normalization" of relations with the Soviet Union and the People's Republic of China suggest that foreign policy may be an area of less salient concern in the decade to come. If this is the case, presidential power in American politics will surely diminish, for as was earlier suggested the linkage between presidential ascendancy and the prominence of foreign policy issues on the political horizon is unmistakable. Thus, the prestige and power of his own office might well be the first casualty of the "full generation of peace" that Nixon repeatedly proclaimed as his major goal throughout his first term in office.

4

THE SOVIET OUTLOOK:
AMERICA, EUROPE, AND CHINA

Herbert S. Dinerstein

Since some of the major problems of Soviet foreign policy have recently been resolved, it seems possible to project the present into the future with considerable expectations of making a good guess at the direction Soviet policy will take. First, territorial and political settlements of the Central European question have been made. Although no final peace treaty has been agreed upon, the West German treaties with the Soviet Union and Poland and the negotiations underway between West and East Germany point to a reasonably permanent arrangement. Second, the Soviet Union has agreed with the United States, on a very narrow basis to be sure, to control the pace of the arms race. The two recognize each other as roughly equal in nuclear strength and accept the idea of a limit beyond which augmenting weapons systems produces no increment in security. Third, relations with China although slightly improved are still a major preoccupation for the Soviet Union as will be shortly described. Fourth, the Soviet Union, despite frequent and dramatic failures in the third world, is still convinced that it must be a power involved in the politics of the developing world. Fifth, the Soviet Union is still preoccupied with the political stability of the socialist states of Eastern Europe. The more severe problems seem to be contained at present, but the unsatisfactory economic situation, which is a major cause of the political difficulties, has not been appreciably improved.

In making the case in the following pages that we can expect, not a period of stasis, but rather a period of re-evaluation of the fundamental assumptions of Soviet policy, I shall set two defining limits on my speculations. First, the simple projection of present tendencies into the future is unsatisfactory. Such a principle of predictive analysis is always faulty in the long run.

The question is: What is the long run? By assuming that change must occur because the political actors within the Soviet Union are shifting in relative importance and making different demands upon the leadership to create a congenial international environment, while that environment itself is in flux, one can avoid the errors deriving from a static view of the world—sometimes described as always preparing for the last war or the last political crisis. But while avoiding this error, one risks another, which constitutes the second defining limit, namely overestimating the speed with which the leadership of the Soviet Union will recognize that the world has changed and how rapidly it will be able to shift course to respond to these new appreciations. The constituencies with strong interests in one or another aspect of Soviet foreign policy are numerous and powerful. Decisions in the Soviet Union, as in most countries with an elaborate political system, are reached by bargaining rather than by the solitary decision of a single person or a tiny group of advisors around a single person. The constituencies with a vested interest in the present appreciation of the central significance of nuclear weapons are well entrenched and disposed by conviction and self-interest to resist, what I shall argue is bound to happen, the relegation of nuclear weapons to second rank. In asserting that the day of the primacy of nuclear weapons is passing, I do not claim to describe the official position of a small group within or alongside the Soviet leadership nor of some Soviet leaders. I shall make the case that the balance of political forces produced by nuclear weapons in the last quarter century will be altered by non-military forces in the next quarter century.

Until now nuclear weapons have been a boon for the Soviet Union, having moved it rapidly to the rank of a superpower. Nuclear weapons seemed to proffer possible victory in war and in a later period a sure deterrent to another power's impulse to seek victory in such a war. Thus the two states differing radically in their social systems and in economic strength seemed to have become roughly equal in power and to have developed some common goals, for example, the limitation of the number of nuclear powers.

But the very acquisition of nuclear weapons by the Soviet Union and their domestication in the international system has caused the earlier criteria of great-power strength to resume something of their former significance. The international system was once regarded as a system in which war, its preparation, and its consequences occupied the central place. The relationship between the states constituting the system was constantly shifting in times of peace. A long and destructive war could lead to the disappearance of some states or their eclipse for several decades. But the system endured. Now with the existence of nuclear weapons it is difficult to imagine the international system surviving a nuclear war in which the major powers participated. The physical and political landscape would be so altered that one neither can nor wishes to guess what its features would be. Therefore as the years pass without any nuclear wars and with gradual accomodation among the major powers, the expectation is that major nuclear wars will not occur. This belief, whether it represents an accurate prediction or wishful thinking, has profoundly altered the international atmosphere. The Soviet Union has abandoned the Marxist view that wars are inevitable as long as capitalism exists; in the United States the belief is questioned that superiority in military strength, which is a function of economic and technological strength, could guarantee world order and maintain the international balance of power. The president of the United States alternates between saying that the United States needs only nuclear sufficiency and that the United States must always be militarily superior. Some still believe that changes in the balance of "assured destruction" automatically work changes in the political balance.

But this notion is antiquated or at most of only transitional importance. How otherwise can one reconcile the radical change in the weapons balance since the Cuban Missile Crisis of 1962 with the trivial changes in the political balance of power between the Soviet Union and the United States? Would the international system be very different if the United States and the Soviet Union had agreed to have no active defense systems against nuclear offensive weapons instead of only a limited number? Although powerful political groups in each of the two major nuclear countries believe that permutations in the weapons balance are critical, nuclear strength seems to be more and more a status symbol of national potency. It seems to be out of the question however, that the two superpowers would mutually agree to abandon nuclear weapons in the conviction that they mutually negate each other. Such an action would automatically make France, China, and Great Britain superior in one feature of power. For China nuclear weapons have caused an accession of power even more dramatic than that enjoyed by the Soviet Union when it acquired nuclear weapons. One cannot readily imagine inducements sufficient to make China or other states that might acquire nuclear weapons surrender their newly won advantage. Paradoxically the unprecedented destructiveness of nuclear weapons and the likelihood of their continued existence is joined with the proposition that nuclear weapons will cease to be decisive in ordering the ranking of the great powers.

A partial analogy may serve to resolve this seeming paradox. At one time railroads changed the nature of warfare, and although they continue to play a major role, they are no longer a critical measure in the ranking of power. Before World War I the capacity of rail nets to mobilize masses of men quickly and strike a knockout blow dominated the preparations for war. Thus the German, Russian, and French mobilization plans were carefully worked out on the basis of the railroad capacity, and in all the crises before World War I, the point of no return was considered to be the call for mobilization. By that time, it was believed, the die had been cast; presumably no power could mobilize and then not fight. Mobilization was considered as irrevocable then as launching a number of offensive nuclear missiles would be now. In the Franco-Prussian war the German General Staff succeeded in mobilizing a mass of men and striking a knockout blow within a few weeks, and in 1914 almost succeeded in doing so. In World War II, although railroads did not play the almost exclusive role in logistics that they had in the earlier two wars, the rapidity of the German advance in May 1940 depended on the railroad net. Thus in two wars against France, German strategy, military preparation, diplomacy, and the conduct of the war was dominated by confidence in what railroads could contribute to war. In the third German war against France, the logistic contribution of the railroads was essential yet support aircraft held the center of the strategic imagination and, in the opinion of some, together with tanks determined the outcome. If another world war is in store, nuclear weapons and their delivery vehicles will occupy center stage, but battlefield aircraft, tanks, and even railroads will still play a role.

If humanity is not disappointed in its hope that nuclear war will be successfully avoided, an unprecedented military-political phenomenon will have occurred. A new weapons system will have receded to second place in determining great-power ranking without having been employed in war, except for the anti-climax of the nuclear bombing of Japan in 1945. This comforting assumption about the future may well be incorrect. Perhaps man in his folly will continue to destroy himself and his surroundings with mounting efficiency. But this does not affect the calculations upon which the relations among great powers are now regulated, and it is with these calculations that we are concerned.

Before World War I, it was assumed that the capacity to mobilize and supply millions when joined to greatly enhanced fire power would make for an intense short war. This assumption was mistaken and World War I became the paradigm for wars of the modern period in which cost exceeds gain even for the victor. But the international system was built on that mistaken assumption, just as the international system is now being built on the assumption that nuclear war must, and therefore will be avoided. As stasis and the permanence of the military strategic relationship between the superpowers is accepted, the older criteria of economic and political strength become the touchstones of great-power ranking.

During Mr. Nixon's visit to Moscow in 1972, his foreign policy adviser, Henry Kissinger, made a comment illustrating the retirement of accepted notions about power relationships. He said that in the nuclear age a great power cannot augment an alliance system in the hope of being able to win a war, to reduce an opponent to passivity in foreign affairs, or to force concessions upon him. Although this notion has been current for about a decade, its pronouncement at a summit meeting demonstrates how far the major powers had come in their realization that alliance systems are no longer simply preparations for war but are assemblages of powers to pursue other ends.

Let us rather abruptly shift our attention to these other ends—the domestic arrangements that we are arguing no longer provide only the foundation for the edifice of power in the world but are at once the stuff of that power and its symbol. The outlook for the Soviet economy is hardly as bright as the outlook for its weaponry. The Soviet Union grows roughly at the rate of 5 percent a year, and if the military strategic sector continues to take its present proportion of the total GNP, the resources allocated to the military establishment will continue to rise in absolute terms. Unless the United States radically increases the share of its GNP allocated to arms, the Soviet Union can be reasonably confident that it will continue to enjoy—if that is the right word—nuclear parity with the United States. But the Soviet people cannot reasonably anticipate parity in living standards with West Germany, France, and Great Britain—not to speak of the United States. Although the general standard of living has risen since the Russian Revolution more than fifty years ago, especially if improved opportunities for education and improved health facilities are included, it has ceased to be a factor in popular approval of the political authority. The Soviet people, in asking what has been done for them lately, make comparisons with neighbors. In a year of poor weather conditions, such as 1972 was, the structural faults of the system obtrude; food must be imported in great quantities and food queues form in the large cities. The comparison with the United States is painful. Almost half of the Soviet population is engaged in agriculture and periodically fails to meet minimum needs. By contrast, only 6 percent of the United States population, with somewhat better soil and climactic conditions to be sure, is able to provide more food than can be consumed—and very expensive food at that. At every turn comparisons hardly flattering to the Soviet Union emerge. The large share of the American GNP devoted to services and amenities, the very high productivity and efficiency of American industry, all leave the Soviet Union far behind. That Japan, which entered the modern industrial system only a century ago, will soon leave the Soviet Union far behind is particularly galling. The Western European nations outdistance the Soviet Union by every measure of per capita performance. Perhaps even worst of all, some Eastern European countries, notably East Germany, surpass the Soviet Union. How long will storage sites full of nuclear weapons compensate for shelves empty of consumer's goods? A sally into the Soviet press at almost any time of the year demonstrates the preoccupation with poor economic performance. Exhortations abound to harvest crops before the weather changes, not to drink on the job, to work conscientiously.

Industrial inefficiency injures national self-esteem in many ways. One of the most humiliating political consequences of the poor Soviet economic performance is the prohibition on free emigration. Propably, even if the Soviet Union opened its doors, the number of people departing would not be great. The absorptive capacity of other countries is limited and the normal attachment of people to familiar surroundings tends to make them stay put. Mass emigration has most often been a consequence of severe economic deprivation, which does not exist in the Soviet Union. Large elements of the Soviet population are disgruntled but they are not desparate. Yet emigration except for special cases is proscribed in socialist countries. The Soviet leaders are afraid to discover empirically how many would leave if they could. They lack faith in the attractiveness of their own system and prefer to accept the opprobrium of being the "prison of the peoples" to risking the possibility that hordes might leave, thereby demonstrating the illegitimacy of the system. By contrast when some Western European countries were suffering a "brain drain" they never contemplated prohibiting emigration. The cure in their view would be much worse than the disease. For them restriction on the freedom of its population to come and go was incompatible with their image of a respectable state. The Soviet leaders seem to share this view because they insist that no general restrictions on emigration exist.

To inquire why the Soviet economy is so deficient would take us too far afield. Even the Soviet leadership realizes that the old arguments about the destruction of the Civil War and of World War II, while relevant for a long time, fail to explain the differences between

East and West Germany and fail to explain why Japan is gaining so rapidly on the Soviet Union. Whether a planned economy centrally managed from the top can be efficient is a theoretical question. It is a fact that planned economies in countries led by communist parties have performed badly. Professional Soviet economists are just as skillful in locating and describing the difficulties as outsiders are. They realize that without a degree of consumer sovereignty and the readiness to devolve decisions, the burden on the central planning organs, even when they are aided by computer technology, is unbearable. Perhaps professional economists in the Soviet Union are more aware of the economic costs of institutional rigidity than political leaders, but it is the latter who fear and must cope with the political consequences of the devolving economic-political authority to local non-party groups. Theoretically it could be argued that a socialist system could safely and profitably make such a dramatic shift in the locus of political power. But Soviet leaders have permitted only very limited experiments in local management, and larger scale experiments in other socialist countries have either been grudgingly accepted or repressed when they crossed over into political experimentation, as they did in Czechoslovakia in 1968.

To restore private property in agriculture is unthinkable and yet the inefficiency of agriculture drags the whole economic system down. Unless Soviet leaders are willing to assume political risks of unpredictable magnitude only minor improvements in economic performance can be expected. Some in the Soviet Union seem resigned to this state of affairs because they shrink before the risks of altering it; less sophisticated and presumably higher ranking officials refuse to believe that the structure is basically flawed.

Both groups favor the introduction into the Soviet Union of exciting Western technological innovations such as advanced computer systems. The better informed and less sanguine may have modest and realistic expectations of what these new complicated tools could perform, but they prefer them to nothing at all. The less sophisticated hope that the purchase and introduction of key elements of Western technology would make the economic system lurch forward. The psychological motivation for faith in the magic of new technology is understandable. Why face the dismal prospect that the Soviet Union will never achieve economic parity with the United States and will sink in rank relative to other powers? Why invite the host of troubles that radical internal reforms would entail? Why not just hope that the Soviet Union will become an economic great power because the superiority of socialism over capitalism is bound to produce such a result later if not sooner? Meanwhile military parity secures the great-power status of the Soviet Union. Just as the adoption of nuclear weapons catapulted the Soviet Union into the first class of military powers, so it is believed that the introduction of computer technology will close the economic gap.

A military great leap forward is more easily made than an economic leap. The military sector of the economy, large though it is, can be partitioned from the rest and accorded special treatment. Only in the military sector does consumer sovereignty prevail, for only the military consumer can reject goods that do not meet specifications. To oversimplify, in the rest of the economy the measure of performance is not meeting the demands of the market but of the plan, a very different thing. Therefore injections of capital even in the form of high performance technology does not produce the same results as in market economies. It is a case of pouring fresh water into rusty pipes. But Soviet leaders are understandably reluctant to believe that the Soviet automobile industry or the Soviet chemical industry will not benefit as much as others from the introduction of solid-state computers.

For the Soviet Union to acquire this new technology to which it attaches so much importance it is necessary for it to have relatively good relations with the most advanced industrial countries in the world. Ideological differences are no longer an impediment. Japan, West Germany, France, Great Britain, and Italy can, and want to, supply the Soviet demand for advanced technology. Consequently American businessmen now argue that it is their patriotic duty not to lose this market to countries on the other side of the balance of payments with the same intensity that they once argued that it was their patriotic (and profitable) duty to build expensive weapons systems to deter the Soviet Union. Thus the political barriers to Soviet acquisition of advanced technology are falling away.

But Soviet purchases will be limited by her reserves of foreign exchange. The Soviet system has little to sell on the world market because a country without an internal market is poorly adapted to compete on the world market. Soviet industry has no practice in satisfying the customer. Thus, for example, although Soviet aircraft are competitive in design and performance with Western aircraft, purchasers or recipients of Soviet aircraft have had discouraging experiences with spare parts, servicing, and so forth.

Soviet opportunities to earn foreign exchange are limited, and crop failures such as that of 1972 cut into these meager earnings. Thus the Soviet Union would prefer to purchase foreign technology with the returns from the sale of raw materials, particularly energy supplies, whose development costs would be covered by loans from the recipients. Capitalist countries have shown some interest in accepting such a bargain and providing capital at moderate costs because they want to husband their own energy resources, as in the case of the United States, or to assure a supplier since they have no resources of energy, as in Japan's case. But since the Soviet Union does not have a monopoly of energy supplies the price it can expect will be determined by the price of competitive sources or suppliers of energy. The gains from such trade will only purchase modest quantities of the new technology. The Soviet Union, failing a radical change in its economic (and political structure), cannot expect to solve its economic problems with the importation of the new technology that it can afford to purchase.

Yet the Soviet leaders reveal at every turn how eager they are to acquire high-performance technology. If the picture presented in the past few pages is correct, a major goal of Soviet foreign policy is to acquire foreign technology at the cost of scarce foreign exchange, but in the end the Soviet economy will be unsatisfactory. How can intelligent men be so foolish? A plausible explanation of this paradox furnishes the theme of this essay.

The Soviet leaders fear that the glory of being a great power is slipping from their grasp as the standard of greatness becomes more economic than military, and they cannot come to terms with the somber realization that their political and economic arrangements are inadequate. The choices are: to believe in the magical efficacy of the injection of some foreign technology, to face the gloomy prospect of falling behind in the contest for greatness, or to risk the hazards of revamping the system. Few national leaderships would choose the second or third alternatives without giving the first a trial. For this choice, the Soviet leadership is prepared to pay a price. No one can say flatly that in the spring of 1972, the Soviet leaders swallowed the insult of the mining of Haiphong because they did not want to jeopardize the ratification of the West German-Soviet Treaty (which seemed then to hang on a few votes) nor the visit of President Nixon to Moscow. From both events they expected improved access to advanced technology. Obviously this was not the only factor in the decision, but inability to specify just how important a factor it was should not lead to denial of its importance.

Another element in the self-image of the Soviet leadership is the political stability of the system. The defection of a group of the radical intelligentsia and the nationalities problem are particularly troublesome. Since Stalin's death small elements of the Soviet intelligentsia have manifested their dissatisfaction with the system. Some profess to want only reforms within the system; others reject the fundamental assumptions of the system. Their actions seem pathetically inadequate to their aspirations. A few demonstrations have occurred; an underground literature of protest circulates; some protesters have been tried in semi-public (but widely publicized) trials. The total hardly seems to threaten the Soviet regime, and probably does not even shake it. But memories of the past unsettle the Soviet leadership.

When one realizes that no public demonstrations have occurred for years in the Soviet Union, even a mini-demonstration in Red Square against the Soviet invasion of Czechoslovakia is a notable event and evokes memories of demonstrations like that of Bloody Sunday in 1904. The literary critiques are widely read, but only a tiny minority predict with Amalryk that the Soviet system must collapse. Solzhenitsyn is more typical in attacking the system indirectly. In his exposure of the seamy side of the Soviet system the question cries out: Can such a system be justified? In his literary works centered on the pre-Soviet period, the emphasis on traditional religious values establishes a counter-ideology to the system. Writers lose their jobs, some are jailed, some are put into insane asylums. But some now fight back as they did not while Stalin lived and continue the pre-Soviet revolutionary tradition that the revolutionary cannot offer repentance in the hope of mercy but must use the court as a platform from which to attack the system. Such tactics are not dangerous to the system, perhaps, but they are ominous and unsettling to a leadership that fears that national greatness is falling from its grasp.

The protest of the national minorities within the system also revives memories of the tsarist period. Then, as now, some national minorities combined their nationalist aspirations with claims for social justice, thus allying the national with the revolutionary movement. During the early years of the Soviet Union the national minorities fared well. The demand for educated cadres benefitted such urbanized minorities as the Jews, Armenians, and Georgians. In the backward areas of the country, heavy industry was introduced to create a reliable proletariat, but the consequence was the creation of a nationalist and newly literate intelligentsia.

But as the system settled down to slower economic growth careers were no longer as open as they once had been. The first success of the extensive Soviet program of popular education created new groups who demanded the white-collar and supervisory jobs that were the rewards of education. Now there are not enough good jobs to go around, and instead of welcoming all into the university, an unofficial *numerus clausus* has been introduced. This has been particularly threatening to the Jews, since until now their political disabilities had been balanced by their superior economic opportunities. The Jews are now the neuralgic point of the nationalities problem, and it is useful to consider their role.

At the end of World War II, the Jews of the Soviet Union were well on the way to assimilation. Secularization and the decline in religious belief and the career opportunities offered by the Soviet system made assimilation a kind of solution for Soviet Jews. Life in the Soviet Union was harsh, but they were no worse off than others. For a variety of reasons connected with the political situation in several Eastern European states and with the establishment of Israel and his conviction, largely unfounded, of the political potency of ties between the Jewish community in the Soviet Union and the Jewish community in the United States, Stalin decided that the Jewish population of the Soviet Union was politically unreliable. When this designation was followed by the execution of the intellectual leadership of the Jewish community and the harassment of large elements of the remainder, much, if not the majority, of that people began to feel that it had no future within the Soviet system. Now twenty-five years later, Stalin's fears have been made to come true. More and more Jews denied the option of assimilation have become nationalistically self-assertive and want to emigrate. The younger Jews have taken courage from the protest of the Russian and the non-Russian intelligentsia and have begun to defy the authorities in a way unprecedented for the weak and traditionally passive Jewish population of the Soviet Union. The Soviet authorities have followed an inconsistent and vacillating policy in dealing with the newly insistent and demanding Jewish population. They have permitted some of the more militant to emigrate to the state of Israel, presumably in the hope that when the most militant members of the community departed it would resume its normal behavior. Instead it only encouraged others to enter the lottery where winning meant an exit visa and losing remaining as a marked man in a group that already had second-class political rights.

A little difficulty with a scattered nationality of less than three million hardly constitutes a threat to the stability of the Soviet state, but if the weak Jews can defy the Soviet authorities, the other nationalities may also decide to do the same. If present population trends continue, the Slavs in the Soviet Union will become a minority. In the Russian and Soviet multi-national state, as in others, the dominant nationality ruled the others by dividing them. Now the non-Russians are making common cause. For the Ukrainian nationalists and the Jews to cooperate wipes out an enmity that dates back to Khelmnitsky's uprising in 1648 and 1649. Who would have expected that the communists would reconcile the non-Russian peoples of the Soviet Union at their own expense?

The developments among the intelligentsia and the non-Russian peoples in recent years evoke many memories of the last decades of the Russian Empire. It is no wonder that dissatisfaction takes traditional forms. Much of the political culture has survived. The poet is the symbol of protest; the intellectual is the surrogate victim for and the hero of the suffering masses. But these resonances of the past, heartening to some, frightening to others, can be profoundly misleading. The Russian Empire suffered defeat in war twice in a single generation before the political structure collapsed. The two situations are only superficially comparable. In the Imperial period the great mass of the population were outside the political system—the swamp is what Lenin called them. In the Soviet periods, millions of the politically inert have been activated, and derive benefits from the system. The proletariat and the better-off peasants have finally become the support of the system.

This is the cold view from the outside by a detached observer who has nothing to lose if the system founders. For the Soviet leadership, plagued by self-doubt after an all-too-brief feeling that their country had reached the first ranks, any echoes of the old revolutionary drama in a contemporary setting are unsettling.

❊   ❊   ❊

The recent visits of the American president to Peking and Moscow have been described as a complete revolution in international relations, as a retirement of the bipolar relationship in favor of a new triangular, quadrilateral, or pentagonal scheme. These rhetorical flourishes exaggerate the suddenness of the change. The novelty is not in the replacement of unmodified hostility by adversary relationships but in the formal and ceremonial recognition of what has been an evolving reality for almost a generation. The United States has recognized what the Soviet Union and China have demanded for a quarter of a century. By the SALT treaty the United States recognizes, to all intents and purposes, the Soviet Union as its military equal; the United States by giving somewhat grudging assent to West German *Ostpolitik* and to Soviet *Westpolitik* effectively acknowledged the existence of two German states and opened the path for the eventual international recognition of two German entities, thus accepting the Soviet political expansion of the immediate postwar years. These are not concessions but a belated recognition of reality. Yet this formal "acceptance of the consequences of world War II" is politically significant because it permits the beneficiaries of the status quo within both systems to press openly for its consolidation. Improved state and economic relations with the ideological opponent are no longer to be tolerated as a necessity of the balance of terror but as valuable in their own right. By recognizing the status quo, both parties realize that neither can cause dominoes to fall on the other side of the board nor need they fear their falling on their own side.

The learning process has been long. The departure, or more correctly, the ejection, of Yugoslavia from the Soviet state system in 1948 and the failure of the expected pro-Soviet forces to overthrow Tito did not cause a chain reaction in the rest of Eastern Europe. No other dominoes fell though several teetered dangerously. This feeling of vulnerability has kept alive the fear that the more politically and economically attractive West European states could upset the precariously perched regimes in Eastern Europe. But the regime in East Germany survived 1953, the regimes in Hungary and Poland survived 1956, the Czechoslovak regime survived 1968, and the Polish regime survived 1970. In none of these cases has the United States or West Germany intervened or even come close to intervening. West Germany is unable to do what the Soviet Union would like—to guarantee the internal stability of the regimes of Eastern Europe—but it is able to promise to refrain from political support of anti-communist or reformist communist movements in Eastern Europe. The journeys of Mr. Brandt and Mr. Nixon to Moscow have set an official seal on the territorial and political arrangements of Central and Eastern Europe and make it possible for the Soviet Union to regard political disturbances in the socialist countries of Europe as indigenous in origin rather than as of foreign inspiration.

Even in Southeast Asia, where the United States has conducted the war with unprecedented ferocity, it has respected the domino on the other side of the board. It has been many years since the notion of "liberating" North Vietnam was even entertained, and the United States' war aims are confined to South Vietnam. As these lines are being written the main issue between the United States and North Vietnam is the extent of the political changes, if any, to be introduced into South Vietnam. The Soviet Union for its part did not give North Vietnam large-scale military aid until the inception of the U.S. bombing campaign and the massive introduction of American ground troops in 1965 and has furthermore never provided the kinds of aircraft and missiles which would have permitted the North Vietnamese to retaliate in kind for the bombing of North Vietnam.

Since 1954, the United States has only suffered the loss of one domino, and a pretty small domino at that, namely, Cuba. The fear that the adoption of communism in Cuba would produce new Cubas was unfounded.

The agreement not to knock over dominoes on the other side of the board is a tacit agreement and each side sometimes gingerly touches or even rocks the opponent's dominoes. The degree of restraint varies with the perceived importance of the area. In Europe the United States has gone no further than making propaganda and providing some very modest trade benefits to selected countries in Eastern Europe. The Soviet Union has not eschewed propaganda to Western Europe but thus far has had very little opportunity to extent economic blandishments. For many years the Soviet Union and some Eastern European countries persisted in ascribing the most malign movites to Western Germany. But these accusations seemed to derive more from preoccupation from the threat from within than from the threat from abroad. During all the years of verbal hostilities directed against West Germany, that country's trade with East Germany has grown steadily.

In addition to the agreement on Europe, the president's visit to the Soviet Union served as the occasion for signing the SALT Agreement, analyzed elsewhere in this volume. Here it is enough to say that the SALT Agreement, like its predecessor, the Partial Test-Ban Treaty, limits only a small area, with the expectation that each side will not push very far in those areas of weapons improvement and fabrication not covered by the agreement. The agreement limits each side to a specific number of anti-ballistic missile sites and promises negotiations on limiting the development of offensive weapons. In each country, various groups, governmental and private, have argued among themselves about the national position of their country resulting from the SALT accord. Since the agreement is of such limited scope, the contest between these parties in each country can be expected to continue and its successive resolutions in each country will both reflect and cause the reciprocal developments in the other country. If political developments had permitted the conclusion of the SALT I Agreement several years earlier, mutual abstention from the development and procurement of ABM systems could have been part of the agreement. The foregoing presentation suggests that the presidential visit to Moscow has only formalized the status quo. With the increased political importance of communications, big show-biz spectaculars strengthen the domestic position of the incumbent office-holder in each country. Mr. Nixon reaps political rewards for bringing peace in the conflict between communism and the free world, a conflict whose erosion he was one of the last to recognize. Mr. Brezhnev's claims are a little more solid, since the United States has now formally recognized the political gains of the Soviet Union in Europe. But here too there is an air of trumpeting last year's victories, for the West has never acted against the Soviet Union and has long abandoned even threats. Seemingly politicians are again taking credit for events whose development they had strenuously sought to impede. The significance of the new phase of Soviet-American relations outweighs the immediate and parochial political motives of its creators. It is not the motives but the consequences that we must regard. Agreement between the two great powers has created constituencies in each society interested in widening the area of agreement. Now some elements of U.S. big business want to extract natural gas and sell computers and automobile plants to the Soviet Union. It is in their interest to discern and bring to public attention those political developments which offer promise of a peaceful Soviet Union. The emergent status quo like the old finds its defenders.

Within the Soviet Union presumably the same sort of process takes place. We know little about the political process in the Soviet Union. In the graphic description of one specialist (Professor Seweryn Bialer), the political system in the Soviet Union from the outside looks like a floor covered with a large blanket. From underneath the blanket emerge the barking and the howls of fighting dogs. We hear the noise and see the movement. What the sides are or who is winning we do not know. Our information on the Soviet political scene is only somewhat better. We know what some of the issues are and we know what causes some of the contenders espouse, but our understanding is neither precise nor detailed. Much like his predecessor Khrushchev, but more successfully thus far, Brezhnev has adjusted his political positions to reflect the balance of political forces within the Soviet political system. We know of the long drawn-out debate about developing and deploying anti-ballistic missiles. Whether to negotiate with the United States on the SALT Agreement was long argued, and the decision to seize West Germany's long-proffered invitation to settle matters was also long contended. We also know that those who favor expenditures on domestic necessities at the expense of the military budget are oriented toward detente and coexistence. Shifts in policy are incremental and therefore slow.

A new policy is not the result of a brilliant new analysis but rather the slow tipping of the political balance vote by vote. The general style is cautious and conservative, and it is looming disaster rather than glittering opportunity which impels a step as dramatic as the military investment of Czechoslovakia.

The Soviet leadership has swallowed many bitter pills to obtain agreements with the United States and West Germany. The most noteworthy were acceptance of the renewal of the bombing of North Vietnam and the mining of the harbor in Haiphong when the morale of the South Vietnamese authorities needed bolstering. In the negotiation on Germany, the Soviets had good cause to believe that a general agreement with West Germany leaving the Berlin issue aside could be reached. Only when negotiations were far along did the Soviets learn that the price of detente had gone up. They had to accept what they had refused for more than a decade—the recognition that West Berlin and West Germany were politically bound. In any matter as artificial as the status of West Berlin there is no right and wrong. What is significant is that the Soviet leadership has yielded on what it considers secondary issues for the sake of primary issues and that on the whole the primary issues can be identified with expected advantage to the power position of the Soviet Union in the non-military area. With each new increment in the ties that bind the Soviet Union to states formerly designated as enemies it takes a greater shift of power within the Soviet Union to alter these arrangements. Thus a political revolution would be required for the Soviet Union to denounce its treaties with Western Germany or to resume nuclear testing, as it has a right to do if it thinks the situation justifies the resumption. However it would take only a slight shift in the balance of forces within the Soviet Union for the negotiations between Western and Eastern Germany to stall. The same considerations apply to the United States. Once an incumbent president has garnered the political credit for putting aside the fear of nuclear war, it is difficult for him or his successors to restore the atmosphere of peril. A radical change in the external or internal environment is required. Generally, a new configuration gathers inertial force around itself. The status quo has altered: long live the status quo.

*   *   *

Although many probably agree that the presidential visit to Moscow was the culmination of a long process, the visit to Peking is often regarded as a more radical step. But the Sino-American rapprochement is also the culmination of a long process beginning with the American decision to abandon the goal of the unification of Korea.

The Chinese eagerness to make peace or, more correctly, to have the Vietnamese make peace in 1954 was an attempt to be followed by the concerted effort at Bandung the next year to achieve co-existence with its neighbors. It was all part of an effort to receive world acceptance and most importantly U.S. acceptance of the legitimacy of Chinese communist rule. The United States' willingness to respond to these overtures was somewhat slow in forming. In 1954, it was only after an internal dispute within the administration (in which Mr. Nixon lost the case for U.S. involvement in Indochina) that the United States eschewed military involvement in Indochina. But by 1958 when the Chinese started to shell the off-shore islands in the Taiwan Straits, the United States showed restraint, recognizing that the action was a limited probe. Consequently the Chinese, or at least the faction that was to emerge triumphant after the Great Cultural Revolution, learned that Chinese restraint was the key to the deterrence of the employment of U.S. military superiority. The U.S. self-limitation on use of its military power against China, a restraint exercised over many years, finally had unintended, unforeseen, and profound results. It first reduced and then eliminated Chinese dependence on the military power of the Soviet Union to ward off attack from the United States. Without this tacit American reassurance to the Chinese, the breach between the Soviet Union and China might have never taken place.

The Soviet conduct of its relations with its Chinese ally is a model of mishandling. The Soviet leaders continued to believe that the Chinese needed their protection against the United States, needed Soviet economic and political support, and that the Chinese had no alternative but to accept the alliance on Soviet terms. The Soviet conception of international relations is not too different from the style of political life within the Soviet Union. The subordinate has very little leverage in dealing with superordinate authority, and he more or less has to take what he gets. The Soviets correctly discerned the deep American resentment toward China, and calculated (correctly as it turned out for many years) that it would inhibit a reconciliation with the Chinese. But the Soviet Union failed to predict that the Chinese could learn that they had nothing to fear from the United States as long as they were moderately prudent. The Soviets reasoned that since the Chinese could not mend matters with the United States they had no place to go. They did not realize that China could simply go away and that once she had separated herself from the Soviet Union she could pursue her own interests in her relations with the United States.

Complacent in the belief that the Chinese had no course but to follow in the Soviet wake, the Soviet leaders, or perhaps more correctly, Khrushchev treated Chinese interests cavalierly. For example, the Soviet Union refused to support the Chinese in the conflict over Tibet. We now know from ex-ambassador Gailbraith's revelations that the United States was supporting the rebels in Tibet, a movement which in the Chinese view threatened the integrity of China and the legitimacy of communist rule. In 1958, the Soviet Union and China quarreled about Soviet military bases in China. The dispute is still obscure, but apparently the Chinese refused to permit Soviet submarine bases on Chinese soil without participating in the command of those ships. The Soviet Union reduced its modest economic support of China, then withdrew its technical assistance, and finally created a situation in which there was little left to take from the Chinese. The Soviets had made themselves ridiculous by their futile threats and pressures.

These familiar events are summarized here to make the point that the Soviet Union suffered a profound blow to its self-esteem. For the Chinese, who were so weak and poor, to defy the Russians undermined the reputation of the Soviet Union and the self-confidence of its leaders. It was worth a great deal to the Soviet leaders to compel compliance with their wishes.

There are other elements in the bitter Soviet enmity to the Chinese, the most striking of which is a sort of nineteenth-century racialism which owes more to Wilhelm II and Hearst's conceptions of the yellow menace than it does to Marx and Engels.

An ideological layer is imposed on top of the familiar national tension: Soviet legitimacy derives in part from the claim to be the first in a series of communist powers that will bring a more just rule to the world. This expectation of the expansion of communist rule has been modified in recent years, but the notion has not been officially retired. If the Chinese continue ostentatiously to reject the Soviet Union as an ally and to cover Soviet ideological formulations with abuse, it is clear that the vision of a band of communist brothers is invalid, at least for the present.

In addition, the Chinese possession of nuclear weapons and a delivery system has presented the Soviet Union with a serious problem. Although the rudimentary Chinese capability could not destroy the Soviet Union, it could as the theorists of the independent French nuclear capability have argued tear off a limb from the Soviet beast. For the Chinese, nuclear weapons represented an even more dramatic leap forward in power status than Soviet acquisition of nuclear weapons had.

In 1969 the Soviet press carried discussions of the possibility of destroying Chinese nuclear facilities. These scarcely veiled threats were really empty because it was unlikely that the Chinese, in contrast to the practice of all other nuclear powers, neatly piled their finished nuclear weapons against the walls of the factories that had produced them. Thus for the Soviet Union to destroy nuclear manufacturing facilities did not remove the danger that one or more Soviet cities in Eastern Siberia or Soviet Central Asia could be destroyed. It was not the first time that the Soviet Union had made empty and ultimately damaging threats to employ nuclear weapons. Although between 1958 and 1961 the Soviet Union had not specifically threatened the use of nuclear weapons if its wishes on Berlin were not met, it deliberately nourished Western fears of a nuclear confrontation. When it dropped its campaign against Berlin, its nuclear menace stood revealed as bombast. Similarly the Soviet nuclear blackmail against China diminished the authority of the blackmailer when China ignored the threats. Then the Soviet Union began to deploy troops on the Chinese border, equal if not greater in number than those on its Western frontiers. This action succeeded where bluster had failed. The Chinese consented to discuss the border issue and tension abated somewhat.

The Sino-Soviet relationship has gone from bad to worse, while the U.S.-Chinese and the U.S.-Soviet relationships have gone from bad to not bad. The worsening relations between the Soviet Union and China have strengthened the political position of those Chinese groups who argued that the main enemy was the Soviet Union and that the United States did not represent a long-term threat. It now seems clear that Mao has held this position consistently. The cult of personality around him was put to a different political use than the cult of personality around Stalin. Mao's opponents continued to deify him while ascribing to his words meanings that he was powerless to reject. On the whole Mao's opponents wanted China to modernize quickly more or less on the Soviet model. Such a decision meant the creation of an industrial and political bureaucracy to oversee that process and would have required extensive Soviet economic and technical assistance in the absence of good relations with the United States. As one would expect, this group stressed the dangers from the United States and stressed the folly of having the Soviet Union and the United States as simultaneous enemies.

Mao seems to be that rare phenomenon, a revolutionary who neither sees the necessity of a Thermidor nor seeks to create an atmosphere in which old enemies are reconciled and comfortable old habits reassumed. Mao has nourished a savage hatred for the old intellectual bureaucracy which lorded over the mass of uneducated Chinese and could not accept this elite in its new incarnation as a party bureaucracy of the Soviet type. Hence it is not surprising that Mao has insisted that China could manage without the Soviet Union, that the Soviet Union was not the model for China. Once Mao took that position, the United States had to be the lesser enemy, or in another version, the counter against the major enemy. Here Mao proved to be astute or lucky, for despite the mounting involvement of the United States in Vietnamese affairs, the United States had carefully avoided entanglement with China.

For many years in the public statements and in interviews granted to friendly Americans, Mao has indicated his interest in a rapprochement with the United States. In 1972 the United States heeded Mao's signals, largely for domestic reasons and possibly in the hope that the Chinese could force the North Vietnamese to make peace on worse terms than they thought necessary. It served Mao's purpose to make it seem as if the American president had asked to be received in order to make ceremonial obeisance to the Emperor of Heaven. In the United States, on the other hand, it served Nixon's purpose to seem to have taken the initiative to make peace with China (when there was no war).

The rapprochement between China and the United States went somewhat further than the conventional reconciliation of disputes in which the agreement essentially boils down to calling yesterday's intractable problem today's solution. Thus the Thirty Years War was settled by the Treaty of Westphalia with each side to the dispute accepting what they had earlier regarded as impossible. Similarly the intractable problem of the reunification of Germany has been settled by accepting the two Germanies as normal. In the Sino-American rapprochement, however, the United States has given way on its claim that the authorities in Taiwan represented the only legitimate government of China. Furthermore, an almost immediate consequence of the agreements between the United States and China is that the greatest power in the Western Pacific, Japan, has rapidly reversed her position on Taiwan and has gone further than the United States in meeting Chinese communist wishes on that issue. Thus from the Soviet point of view the United States has played favorites in making concessions to the Chinese while exacting them from the Soviet Union. But from the outside, as we have argued earlier, it would seem that the United States has recognized the existing state of affairs on both sides of the Eur-Asian land mass, and whether such recognition represents "defeat" or "victory" is a matter of judgment.

In the earlier discussion of the Soviet decision to come to terms with Germany, the pressures of the Chinese problem were not mentioned. Traditionally the Soviet Union has sought detente on one side of its vast borders when in difficulties on the other. Thus in 1935 when the Soviet Union appreciated the true menace of Hitler, it appeased the Japanese by selling the Japanese the Chinese Manchurian railroad at a very low price. Now in 1972, when the Chinese seem to represent an intractable problem, the value of freeing one's hands in the west seemed to be overriding.

Both the Soviet Union and the Chinese have gained from the United States' formal recognition of the extensive political gains made in the wake of World War II. They have gained this recognition at a modest price. For the Chinese to have a peace that is more than a temporary breathing spell after almost constant turmoil since 1911 is no mean accomplishment. It is also no mean accomplishment for the Soviet Union to be recognized as an equal by the United States less than two generations after the German armies destroyed a large fraction of its modest industrial establishment.

It is not suggested here that the Soviet Union and China have enjoyed unnecessary victories over the United States because the presidential incumbent threw away American advantages for narrow electoral purposes. It is no mean accomplishment to lay the ghost of devils equipped with that mysterious multiplier of power, communist ideology. A weaker communist state could over-awe or subvert a stronger capitalist state because Satan was more powerful than Gabriel. To sweep away such fears is to dispense with a major irrationality in the formulation of international policies.

The general framework of the relations of the Soviet Union with the United States and China has been described. It may now be useful to describe Soviet prospects in particular areas, starting with Western Europe. If one reads Soviet discussions of Western Europe, the divergent Soviet appreciations readily emerge. Some ascribe the present happy state of affairs in Europe largely to the strength of Soviet arms and point out that by the 1980s both sides will have new weapons systems. The implication is clear: whatever security the Soviet Union enjoys in Europe it owes to the deterrent effect of its weapons systems, and great care must be taken not to lose that advantage through unwise negotiations about mutual force reductions. The contrary view is that the favorable changes in the European political climate derive from the success of the Soviet foreign policy of co-existence and the retirement of the myth of the aggressive intentions of the Soviet Union. The implication is again clear: the main factor was the cessation of the Soviet pressure on Berlin which permitted the forces favoring detente in Western Europe to become ascendant. Thus in return for very minor concessions the Soviet Union can obtain Western advanced technology and deal with each European state individually, thus ultimately depriving the United States of its hegemonic role.

Even the advocates of this optimistic view of the future warn that one must not expect to begin the process with the end—the dissolution of the NATO alliance and the Warsaw Pact. To a certain extent this constitutes reassurance to those in the West who fear relaxation and reluctantly agree to talks in order to be able to limit their extent. But this reassurance is at least equally applicable to Eastern Europeans, who fear the political consequences to the Warsaw Pact. Agreed mutual force reductions are notoriously difficult to negotiate, entailing the equation of say a number of submarines with a number of fighter bombers, i.e. crates of oranges with gaggles of geese. Most likely both sides will agree to refrain from doing what only small constituencies on each side see advantage in doing. Even such a narrow agreement or perhaps even a statement of principles will offer political promise. Individual European states might unilaterally reduce their commitment to NATO. Ample precedent exists. One only need recall the French withdrawal or the earlier unilateral decision of Denmark and Norway not to permit nuclear weapons to be stationed on their territories. In an era of detente where the heads of states would be under pressure to claim that great progress toward peace had been made in Europe, pressures in European parliaments for further reductions in military spending would invite a Soviet response. Presumably some would argue that the time had come for reductions in Soviet military expenditures and in the numbers of the Soviet armed forces in Eastern Europe; others would contend that the new favorable balance must be maintained.

Soviet forces in Europe serve several functions. They constitute a balance to the NATO forces and are an important part of the Soviet military power which gives them parity with the United States. But they also serve the purpose of controlling whatever dissident and dangerous, from the Soviet point of view, forces might emerge in Eastern Europe. Logically these two functions can be distinguished. Supersonic planes and medium-range missiles are of little utility in riot control. Thus it is theoretically possible for the Soviet Union to entertain proposals for even radical reductions in the cost of its European theater forces without compromising their garrison function. But the proponents of large Soviet forces in Central Europe find it advantageous to collapse the distinctions between these two functions and to pretend, and perhaps believe, that any radical reductions in the cost of Soviet troops in Central Europe would threaten the political stability of that area. Since the present Brezhnev-Kosygin government derives political support from satisfying many constituencies, they risk their continued tenure in office if they follow to their logical conclusions some intellectual constructs about foreign policy. Theoretically a policy of mutual force reductions in Europe could produce great financial savings without any diminution of political control in Eastern Europe. But the open hostility of the Soviet "military-industrial complex" might well be regarded by the Brezhnev-Kosygin coalition as a political price they cannot afford to incur. Rigidities of a different kind but with the same political effect exist within the NATO forces, so that the most likely prospect is for a slow and gradual reduction in forces rather than a radical reduction based on the proposition that a balance with a much reduced price tag serves the same function as the present high-priced balance.

*   *   *

Although the rules of the road are reasonably clear in the relations between the great powers in Europe, the situation in the underdeveloped world is more ambigious. The direct security interests of the great powers have rarely been involved in the politics of the third world, Cuba being an exception. Hence more general considerations such as face, prestige, or credibility govern. These values are hard to define precisely, so that misunderstandings sometimes leading to confrontations occur.

The Soviet Union feels that it cannot and must not be indifferent to political changes anyplace in the world, since it has passed from being a continental power to becoming a world power. This new role can increase the prestige of the Soviet Union as a world power and as the leader of the communist world, simultaneously furthering the political fortunes of the faction within the CPSU that would claim credit for such an advance. The importance of being accepted as a great power has been referred to in another context. Reassurances that the shameful past of weakness is behind is sought in space exploits, in recognition of Soviet strategic strength, in insistence on receiving equal treatment on any and every international issue, and in the unremitting and almost completed effort to establish diplomatic relations with every state in the world and to be "in" on every issue of world importance. Thus the Mediterranean cannot be an American lake; the Soviet Union must have a presence in the Indian Ocean, the Caribbean, and even Anarctica.

It could be argued that having influence, clients as it turns out, in every part of the world has diminished even more in importance in the last third of the nuclear century than the incremental value of adding another second-rank country to an alliance system. It could be argued that there is no longer any gain to be garnered from ac- quiring the late twentieth-century version of a colony. At least some Englishmen profited from India, some Frenchmen grew rich in Indo- China. Some Soviet citizens see this lust for influence in far-off lands as a wasteful and pathetic effort to imitate the imperialists and fear that communism is caught in a cruel fate of its own devising—the irresistible impulse to repeat the history of capitalism, especially its failures. Communists instead of bursting forth into a new world are doomed to imitate yesterday's capitalists, while today's capitalists leave their past behind. In the Soviet Union the Gosplan bureaucrat accumulates capital at the expense of the worker rather than the Manchester mill owner; the international bourgeoisie (or perhaps even the international aristocracy) is to be replaced by the interna- tional proletariat; the party elite in Tashkent and Kaunas have given up their native language for Russian, just as the Scots and the Welsh have adopted English. The party elite in Warsaw, Prague, and Sofia are to speak Russian, as rajahs in Delhi and tribal chiefs in Lagos spoke English. The sun never set on the British Empire, no sea in the world is not to bear on its surface the proud ships of the Soviet fleet. "What a tawdry dream" say the Soviet dissident intellectuals; "Now the Soviet Union (or Russia) takes its rightful place in the world" say the portly men in the Kremlin. In the late nineteenth cen- tury, the half-starving, prematurely toothless English worker reveled in the glory of empire; today's decently fed, well-dressed English workers who holiday in Spain shed no tears for the good old days. But it will be a long time before the average Russian and his self- appointed leaders in the Kremlin cease to thrill with pride at the glory which has finally come to Russia.

The power of national pride should not be dismissed merely be- cause it has become somewhat passé in the West. The urge to erase national humiliation is persistent: speaking in 1876 five years after the unification of Germany, Bismarck contemptuously dismissed proposals for the extension of German rule to distant areas as not worth the bones of a single Pomeranian. But countless Pomeranians were to perish and Bismarck's work to be undone before his cry of "enough" was to be heeded. I am not suggesting that Soviet national history will follow the German pattern, but the analogy serves to em- phasize the power of injured pride in international relations.

I am suggesting that many of the reasons advanced for Soviet involvement in the affairs of distant and miserable peoples are partially rationalizations for the impulse to glory. The Soviet Union, we are told, wants to take over the Mediterranean and push out the United States, and a White House spokesman has said the goal of our policy is to expel the Soviet Union from Egypt. There are some sound military reasons for the Soviet presence in the Mediterranean: to counter the nuclear strategic capability of the U.S. Sixth Fleet, especially its submarine arm, but these are secondary to the simple desire to play the role the British once played there. Some Soviet leaders hope that flotillas, squadrons, gunboats, and the instruments of triumphant imperialism retain their potency in the nuclear age. The Russians, we are told, or they tell themselves, are unfolding a carefully worked-out scheme and when the Suez Canal is opened will sit astride the life-line to India. But what will it profit the Soviet Union to bear generous gifts to the ungrateful Indians?

The passion to grasp at life lines to defunct Empires cannot easily be slaked, but appetites for more prosaic things can also be discerned. The Soviet Union has greatly increased its merchant marine. Since workers' organizations in the capitalist state are more powerful than workers' organizations in the socialist state, the Soviet Union can carry cargo more cheaply than many. As we have indicated earlier, the Soviet Union earns only limited amounts of foreign exchange by the export of raw materials and cannot compete in the sale of manufactured goods. To be able to provide a service much in demand on the international market at competitive prices is a genuine contribution to the power of the Soviet state. Soviet interest in the exploitation of the resources of the ocean beds is another indication of a sensible Soviet impulse to compete with the United States in an area that brings genuine benefits to the Soviet Union rather than the empty symbols of a past age. Thus the Soviet Union, in its overseas naval policy, simultaneously pursues goals posited on contradictory principles: the source of national power and prestige is economic strength; the extension of Soviet influence is to be pursued to the furthest ends of the earth even if it entails only costs and promises but no material benefits.

In its dealings with the underdeveloped world the Soviet Union pursues another goal that has its analogue in the experience of its rivals for world power—the desire to create a more congenial, ideological environment. In this they ape the United States rather than Great Britain. A reader of literature on the Soviet Union in the last few generations could be excused for believing that the communists had invented the idea of exporting revolution, but it has a long if not always noble history. One need only recall parts of the French and American experience.

The Soviet experience with new states governed by communist parties has not been reassuring. For a while Soviet leaders could believe that the Soviet armies did not impose communism on Eastern Germany, Poland, Rumania, Bulgaria, and Hungary and that the Soviet armies had merely served as a catalyst to speed up the historical process, that the existence of the Soviet Union served as a surrogate for the existence of a large proletariat, that the order of events was only slightly changed but that the essence remained. The revolution had preceded the creation of a powerful proletariat. The proletariat to be created by industrialization would then usher in the Golden Age. But Berlin 1953, Poland and Hungary 1956, and Prague 1968, as well as the sad history of China, have revealed how hollow was the hope. But if the core of belief is hollow, the shell must be preserved. If only the shell can be preserved, perhaps belief can be reconstituted.

Active Soviet post-war involvement in the underdeveloped countries begins about 1955, and the circumstances are very similar to those in which Lenin pronounced the two-stage theory of revolution in 1920. High hopes for revolution in Poland, which would spread to Germany and end the isolation of the Soviet Union, were dashed, and Lenin hoped that the major enemies of the new state could be undermined by the loss of their colonies. The bourgeoisie of China, Turkey, and India would weaken the colonial powers by the national struggle for independence in which the fledgling communist parties of those countries would participate and grow strong enough to take power. The road to Paris was to be through Peking or Calcutta. The faith in the revolution to be in Asia was the substitute for the dying faith in the revolution in Europe.

In 1955 revolutionary possibilities in Western Europe seemed to be exhausted, and the conquests of the revolution in Eastern Europe seemed to be precarious. Perhaps this time the world of the new countries would redress the balance of the old world. No wonder the Bolshevik leaders after the unexpected assumption of communism by Castro exuberantly told the American Ambassador in Moscow that Cuba made them feel young again. But the euphoria was short lived. Communism did not spread in Latin America, then described by the chief organ of the CPSU as the most revolutionary continent in the world. The Soviet leaders would have to wait a long time, they feared, for the confirmation of their faith that communism was the hope of mankind.

They gave up their hopes only gradually. The articulators of the ideology first developed the theory that the new countries could benefit from the Soviet experience, could establish heavy industry on the Soviet model, and could thereby create a proletariat whose party would then take power protected by the growing military power of the Soviet Union. But in rapid succession Nkrumah, Ben Bella, and Sukarno disappeared. In the United States academic experts worked out theories explaining and predicting how economic growth roughly on the model of the United States would produce new democracy. Appropriately enough the sub-title of Walt W. Rostow's *The Stages of Economic Growth* was *A Non-Communist Manifesto*. The counterpart was the theory of political development whose final absurdity was the theory that the refugees caused by American bombing in South Vietnam would force the pace of urbanization and create the pre-conditions for modernization and democracy in South Vietnam. In the Soviet Union the ideologists too failed to be disheartened by the failure of the under-developed countries to develop economically according to their predictions, and promulgated a new theory on which to pin their hopes. The state bureaucratic and military strata would carry out the revolutionary duty of the proletariat and then in some unexplained way make way for the communist party.

In the Soviet Union as in the United States some persisted in their belief that somehow their society would still be the model for all mankind, but by now the Soviet attitude is essentially pre-emptive: we can't bring socialism to Egypt or Indonesia in the foreseeable future, but at least we can prevent the other ideology from getting a foothold. Indira Ghandi or Nasser are hardly socialists, but at least they call themselves socialists.

In the long run both the Americans and the Russians will realize that it is a sucker's game to collect clients, that neither communism nor democracy is exportable, that India, Egypt or Chile cannot affect the balance of power in the nuclear age. But in all probability the long run will be longer in the Soviet Union because ecumenical dreams are more necessary for faith in the political system than in the United States.

5

MILITARY ISSUES:
STRATEGIC PARITY AND ITS IMPLICATIONS

Laurence W. Martin

During the first Nixon Administration, an unusually large number of important changes took place or were more openly acknowledged in the military situation of the United States. Most pervasive in its immediate consequences was the consummation of American retreat from Vietnam under circumstances which left the ultimate verdict of political victory or defeat somewhat open but certainly could not be plausibly depicted as a success for American arms or strategy. The casualties, the expense, and the scandals, all magnified by the mass media, combined to breed a mood of profound popular distrust for military leadership and of disillusionment with the usefulness of military power as an instrument of national policy.

The other major military happening was Soviet achievement of a generally acknowledged "parity" in strategic nuclear weapons, long foreshadowed but now formally registered in the Strategic Arms Limitation Agreements of May 1972. This deal with the Soviet Union was paralleled by the Sino-American rapprochement which, though a brilliant American diplomatic coup vis-à-vis the Soviet Union, was also a recognition that the Chinese regime had successfully weathered the period of vigorous American confrontation. Combined with efforts to urge a greater degree of military burden-sharing on America's European, Japanese, and other allies, the overall effect of these events has been to dramatize the relative military decline of the United States.

A few years ago such a decline would have produced vociferous alarm. That it has not on this occasion seems to be due not only to disapproval of recent military ventures and an awareness of detente in superpower relations, but also to a more general if vague belief that the role of military power in international affairs is declining. To many it appears that the inhibiting effect of nuclear weapons has combined with revised notions of national interest to make war between states an increasingly clumsy and dangerous tool. From this

137

assumption it is easy to conclude that many of the traditional imperatives of national security can be ignored with impunity.

The Nixon Administration has certainly not subscribed to this view. On the contrary, it has repeatedly affirmed that maintenance of the military balance is a condition for the preservation of detente. On the other hand, the Nixon Doctrine does imply that American security interests have been too widely defined in the past and the military burdens of the United States needlessly multiplied as a consequence. How far the Nixon Administration believes these burdens can be lightened has been obscured by the spate of delphic doctrines with which it has deluged the public. The catchword for military policy has been "sufficiency," a word admirably calculated to suggest different things to different people. It can be used to put a brave face on retreat or to confuse the advocates of retreat while standing firm. The underlying trend, however, is one of retrenchment.

During the past twenty-five years of cold war military affairs have so dominated American diplomacy that it is hard to prevent a survey of defense policy from becoming a complete reassessment of foreign relations. Perhaps the SAL Agreements are the firmest starting point for assessing recent developments. The strategic balance has been the fulcrum of the world balance for twenty years and still constitutes the main reason for its bipolar structure. Strategic nuclear deterrence is the ultimate basis of American security, the source of the contemporary sense of stability between the two major military blocs, and the main ground for hope that force will play an increasingly remote and symbolic part in the mutual relations of the great powers.

The recent attainment of parity by the Soviet Union must be seen against the historical development of Soviet-American strategic relations. Almost ever since the Soviet Union acquired nuclear weapons in the early 1950s, all-out war between the superpowers has been regarded as unthinkable. Although supposedly unthinkable as a deliberate act of policy, nuclear war remained a possibility, as the result of escalation in crisis, and the United States retained such a degree of strategic superiority that it was able to use that possibility as a very effective way of extending its deterrent umbrella over at least its closer allies. Moreover, confidence in this extended nuclear shield, bred in the period of American monopoly and sustained into the period of mere superiority, allowed the Western alliance to forego a full matching of Soviet military power across the board at conventional level.

SALT had its origins in the Soviet erosion of American superiority and in a consequent deeper American sense that the option of strategic nuclear war had become a negative instrument, capable only of deterring nuclear aggression. Over the years, the United States had adopted a series of fall-back strategic doctrines to counter steadily rising Soviet striking power. The first, which might be called the first McNamara solution, was the concept of using American numerical and technical superiority to implement a strategy of controlled response, using 'city-sparing' counter-force strikes. Increased conventional strength for a flexible response in Europe was intended to give added depth to this range of defensive options. The continued increase in Soviet forces, however, and the emergence of hardened or submarine weapons thought to be beyond the reach of counter-force action, led to the emergence of the second McNamara solution: the acceptance of mutual vulnerability as a basis for stability. Ideally this acceptance would be reinforced by abstention from forces that could defend populations or be used in a damage-limiting, counter-force role.

The strategy of mutual assured destruction implied that no degree of superiority, falling short of a clean, disarming first strike, was worth having. In practice, however, the United States still possessed a substantial superiority in numbers and Mr. McNamara promised to maintain this. Indeed he instituted the program for multiplying the warheads on American missiles and insisted on the maintenance of the "Triad," the posture whereby each of the American forces of bombers, land-based missiles (ICBMs), and submarine-based missiles (SLBMs) could alone do an unacceptable amount of damage to the Soviet Union. Moreover, Mr. McNamara's suggestions of what would constitute an adequate level of assured deterrent destruction were set very high, being based more on a calculation of the point of declining technical efficiency of American striking forces than on any political or psychological analysis of Soviet expectations.

It was never clear whether Mr. McNamara saw real strategic advantages in numerical superiority or whether he was merely trying to defuse criticism of his underlying policy of mutual vulnerability. He took some pains to see that the numerically superior American forces were ill-suited to counter-force action and that the ballistic missile defense (BMD) system he reluctantly initiated would offer no significant protection against a Russian attack. He also seems to have assumed that the Russians were sufficiently committed to a policy of minimum deterrence—akin to his doctrines, if not his practice—to be resigned permanently to a numerical inferiority. In a notoriously incautious comment in 1965, Mr. McNamara declared that "the Soviets have decided that they have lost the quantitative race, and they are not seeking to engage us in that contest. . . . There is no indication that the Soviets are seeking to develop a strategic force as large as ours."[1]

This, as we now know, was a gross miscalculation, and the idea of a more or less self-sustaining balance of mutual vulnerability based on a plateau of strategic technology succumbed to the twin influences of a determined Soviet increase in strategic forces and a new round of technological ingenuity, resulting in higher accuracies, multiplication of re-entry vehicles, and much improved prospects for the performance of strategic defensive systems. None of this meant the inevitable erosion of mutual vulnerability; it did mean that this vulnerability might only be attainable at the price of continued and rising investment in strategic systems. Soviet determination also suggested that no plausible level of expenditure could perpetuate the kind of superiority the United States had hitherto been able to enjoy. For the time being, however, the installation of multiple warheads on American missiles and insistence on more subtle ways of calculating the balance enabled an appearance of American advantage to be maintained. This was only the latest in a series of typical American efforts to use faith in technical sophistication to offset a deterioration in the strategic position when measured by the cruder but, one suspects, often more politically effective indices of power.

This was very roughly the strategic situation at the beginning of the Nixon Administration. Strategic analysts were laboriously absorbing the significance of the new technologies and the vigor of the Soviet strategic build-up. At the same time, uneasiness was being expressed in several quarters about the deeper implications of a posture of strategic vulnerability—an uneasiness which provided much of the support in both superpowers for programs of missile defense. The basic Nixon doctrine for defense policy was the typically delphic concept of sufficiency. When applied to defense policy in general, the term either indicates a willingness to cut margins unusually close to the bone or is simply platitudinous: "there is an absolute point below which our security forces must never be allowed to go. That is the level of sufficiency. Above or at that level, our defense forces protect national security adequately. Below that level is one vast undifferentiated area of no security at all."[2]

[1] U.S. News and World Report, reprinted in Congressional Record, April 7, 1965, S-7271.

[2] Richard M. Nixon, U.S. Foreign Policy for the 1970s: Building for Peace, February 25, 1971, p. 167.

For strategic forces the phrase has a useful ambiguity: it seems to reassure those who believe the former insistence on numerical superiority was excessive and those who fear that primacy is being too readily conceded to the Russians. Other statements suggest, however, that the Nixon Administration has been very much alive to the disadvantages of depending solely on the deterrent effect of a last-resort capacity for destroying Russian cities. Defining the purpose of American nuclear strategy as "the maintenance of forces adequate to prevent us and our allies from being coerced," President Nixon continued: "I must not be—and my successors must not be—limited to the indiscriminate mass destruction of enemy civilians as the sole response to challenges."[3] This remark presumably meant in particular that the United States needed some option other than a suicidal strike against the Russian population in the event of a limited counter-force first strike by the Soviet Union, however unlikely, and some capacity to initiate a limited strategic nuclear action, however incredible, in response to nuclear or large-scale conventional attacks on American allies. In the first of his annual foreign policy statements, the president claimed to have identified "four specific criteria for strategic sufficiency."[4] These criteria, though not immediately spelled out, were thought to be: an adequate second strike capability to deter surprise attack; a posture giving no incentive for the Soviet Union to strike first in a crisis; the ability to prevent the Soviet Union being able to inflict more damage on the United States than the United States could effect in return; and a capacity to protect the United States from suffering substantial damage from small nuclear attacks or accidental missile launches.

SALT offered the possibility of putting the strategic balance on a satisfactory basis by agreement rather than by free competition. American motives in seeking a SAL Agreement were mixed. Among them were: a political desire to placate the arms control lobby and be seen to respond to the obligations imposed on the nuclear powers by the Non-Proliferation Treaty; hope of restraining the Soviet strategic build-up and, if possible, freezing the position of superiority enjoyed by the United States at the outset of negotiations; and the belief that such a freeze would relax international tension, reduce the chance of war arising from an unstable balance, and save a great deal of money.

The belief that any initial SAL Agreement would reinforce peace was largely a matter of rhetoric, for there was little reason to believe

[3] *Ibid.*, p. 170.
[4] *United States Foreign Policy: A New Strategy for Peace*, February 18, 1970, p. 93.

that either power was about to let itself slip into a situation in which war would seem a remotely attractive option to the other. The argument from economy was, however, real enough, not merely because of popular pressures for greater spending on domestic welfare, but also because sharply rising military costs meant that without a politically unattainable increase in the military budget, greater investment in strategic systems would come at the expense of severe cuts in general purpose forces. There was also the specific embarrassment that the very costly Safeguard BMD system was highly unpopular and was unlikely to be successfully financed to completion. A limit on BMD could turn this system into a bargaining counter and permit the abandonment of the program without loss of face.

Soviet motives in SALT can only be surmised, and any evaluation of the agreements must be correspondingly tempered with the cautious reflection that we do not know what the Soviet leaders believe they have achieved. The Soviet Union certainly seems to have come to accept that the nuclear superpowers share a common interest in avoiding nuclear war. Perhaps the most striking token of this was the security-conscious Soviet Union's formal acceptance of the principle of "verification by national means" in the ultimate agreements. Despite their success in closing the strategic gap between themselves and the United States, Soviet leaders must retain a healthy respect for American military potential. The American multiple warhead program, the Safeguard system, and the American escape from the burdens of Vietnam must have made the moment seem ripe for freezing the strategic balance at its now favorable level. As it was, by energetically continuing its build-up during negotiations, the Soviet Union succeeded in striking a far better bargain then seemed likely at the outset. Even so, the decision to reach an agreement was apparently highly controversial in Russian ruling circles and the build-up of the Soviet strategic stockpile to its present high level may well have been the condition for the acquiescence of the Soviet hawks.

The agreements that emerged from these negotiations upon the president's visit to Moscow are complicated and open to contrary interpretations. The treaty on BMD essentially cuts off the further deployment of BMD altogether. Thus, unless the treaty is abrogated, the policy of mutual assured destruction is enshrined for all time. Rather illogically the treaty permits two BMD areas in each country, one around an ICBM field, the other around the national capital. This anomaly is presumably due to the investments already made on each side and perhaps to a residual Russian attachment to the notion of defending the center of national power, which in their case also embraces a force of ICBMs. By complex regulations as to size and position of BMD systems and particularly the associated radars, the parties guarantee that they will not provide a defense for their national territory nor a base for such a defense in future. Special efforts are made in the treaty and the accompanying interpretive statements to preclude the upgrading of anti-aircraft missiles, for which the extensive Russian SAM system would offer promising opportunities against older American re-entry vehicles. Not only present methods of BMD, but also any future devices, such as lasers, are renounced. On the other hand, and again rather paradoxically, the development of better and new systems is specifically provided for. Presumably the justification for this provision lies in the difficulty of verifying compliance with restrictions on research and development. The provision may also reflect an underlying reluctance to abandon forever all hope of providing an effective national defense. Thus, a loophole remains for taking advantage of a technological breakthrough or for reacting to the rise of other nuclear powers.

Accompanying the BMD Treaty are the Interim Agreement and the Protocol restraining the further deployment of launchers for offensive ICBMs and of ballistic missiles on submarines. The agreement freezes deployment at the level of July 1, 1972. No numbers are specified for ICBMs, but the United States has declared that the relative ceilings are 1054 for the United States and 1618 for the Soviet Union. Modern "heavy" ICBMs are subject to a special freeze at the July 1 level. No definition of "heavy" is agreed but the term means the Russian SS-9 and perhaps a few somewhat larger launchers constructed for a follow-on type. Again no numbers are specified but informed American sources cite a total of 313. The number of permitted submarine-launched ballistic missiles is spelled out in the protocol. The United States had 41 boats with 656 missiles operational on July 1, 1972; the Soviet Union is credited with 740 missiles on submarines operational or under construction. Additional SLBMs may be deployed up to ceilings of 710 on 44 submarines for the United States and 950 on 62 submarines for the Soviet Union, provided such additions are replacements for ballistic missiles on older submarines or for ICBMs of types deployed before 1964. The Russians are believed to have some 90 eligible missiles on older diesel submarines besides a considerable number of older ICBMs; the possible small American increment represents solely the 54 *Titan II* missiles.

The agreement does not restrict qualitative improvement, including the multiplication of re-entry vehicles. Bombers and cruise-missiles are similarly unrestricted. The Soviet Union refused to include a ban on mobile, land-based missiles. A unilateral American declaration asserts that deployment of such weapons would be incompatible with the agreements, but the Soviet Union has not responded. Many of the ingredients of the strategic balance, including such crucial elements as accuracy and yield, are thus left unrestricted as avenues for future technical ingenuity.

Nevertheless the SAL Agreements are major landmarks by any standards. The mere achievement of agreement on such critical and complicated issues goes far beyond what many observers believed possible between major adversaries. It remains to be seen, however, whether further progress will be made and what the effect of the existing agreements will be on the strategic balance and the future of international politics. For the obstacles envisaged by many skeptics have been surmounted only at the cost of considerable ambiguity.

In crude numbers of the items regulated, the United States has concluded a far worse bargain than might have been expected. Two arguments justifying the bargain are difficult to refute because they are highly speculative. The first is that the political benefits of the agreements will more than compensate for the technical concessions made; in extreme form, this argument suggests that in the atmosphere of improved detente the precise details of the military balance are of declining interest. The second argument is that the initial SAL Agreements are only a preliminary to a further pact on offensive weapons that will rectify the shortcomings of the first. Indeed the American delegation to SALT, perhaps uneasy at some features of their handiwork, explicitly declared that failure to reach a more comprehensive agreement on offensive weapons would constitute the kind of "extraordinary event" permitting withdrawal from the BMD treaty. The same consideration dictated the five-year limit on the interim agreement.

There are certainly features of the agreements that seem somewhat out of line with the original American approach to the negotiations. The overall numbers favor the Soviet Union and in some respects, such as the estimate of existing SLBMs, indicate a generous interpretation of the meaning of "under construction." The BMD agreement would seem to negate the previously alleged purposes of the American BMD program. Defense against China may perhaps be dismissed as technologically impractical in the long run and out of keeping with the assumption of Chinese rationality implied by the Sino-American rapprochement. Dealing with accidental launches may be regarded as relatively unimportant and as partly provided for by the September 1971 Soviet-American agreement for co-operation to reduce the chance of mishap. Nevertheless both purposes were still cited in the president's February 1972 foreign policy statement.

More important, perhaps, was the declared main purpose of the *Safeguard* system, to protect the *Minuteman* sites against counter-force attack, which was otherwise thought to offer the growing Soviet SS-9 force a high possibility of success. This danger was a prime reason for American insistence earlier in the negotiations that limits on BMDs should be closely linked to curbs on offensive missiles. While a curb has been imposed, it is of a less binding nature, is at a high level, and does nothing to restrict the technological developments needed to perfect the SS-9 as a counter-force weapon.

There are a number of possible answers to these misgivings, in addition to the more general rebuttals already described. For those who believe a second-strike capability for assured destruction is all that matters, regardless of the enemy's force levels, the present and prospective performance of the American Triad is ample. Not even the most alarmist critic can envisage the American deterrent being eroded within the next few years to the point at which a Soviet first strike could be launched with impunity. To those who believe in the importance of relative strength above the level of assured destruction, it can be pointed out that the United States enjoys a superiority in several weapons systems not restricted by the interim agreement— notably intercontinental bombers and forward-based tactical aircraft capable of reaching the other superpower from land bases or aircraft carriers. The Russian advantage in SLBMs might also be regarded as offset by the Soviet Union's greater problems with regard to basing and deployment and by the superior characteristics of existing and currently projected American missile firing nuclear submarines (SSBNs). Above all, the United States has an apparently substantial lead in the development and deployment of multiple re-entry vehicles, especially those of the advanced, independently targetable variety (MIRV). Consequently, despite the Russian advantage in gross numbers of missiles, the "force-loading" balance greatly favors the United States, especially when account is taken of weapons on bombers.

This American lead is likely to increase over the next few years, as *Poseidon* and *Minuteman III* enter the force. Nothing in the SAL Agreements prevents this, while the Russian program of installing added missiles is now cut off. Thus it has been claimed that the agreements favor the United States by forbidding the continuation of the kind of force multiplication hitherto pursued by the Russians, and permitting that preferred by the United States. In the longer term, however, the present agreements might favor the Soviet Union much more decisively. For while the United States has already exploited much of its total missile payload with re-entry technology, the Soviet Union has only to match present American technological achievements to attain truly immense force-loadings on its large and numerous ICBMs. A follow-on missile within the weight limits permitted for SS-9 replacement, for example, might carry up to twenty 500 KT warheads. Indeed, in his annual report for FY 1972, the Secretary of Defense specifically declared that "future significant development in Soviet forces for intercontinental attack will probably lie in qualitative improvements in their ballistic missile forces."[5] This might suggest that the Soviet Union was thought likely to switch from multiplication of missiles to the refinement of re-entry vehicle technology even in the absence of a SAL Agreement.

It is patently difficult to determine the net effect of the SAL Agreements on the strategic balance. This difficulty is not merely the result of the degree of secrecy and technical complexity surrounding the components of the balance. It is also due to the fact that what constitutes a deterrent, what conditions might tempt a nuclear power to strike first in a crisis, and what kind of forces it would be desirable to have should strategic nuclear war turn out to begin in a controlled rather than all-out fashion, are still calculated chiefly on the basis of arbitrary and highly debatable assumptions.

The ultimate verdict as to whether the first SAL Agreement is an aberration or heralds a new dawn for arms control and reason will be much affected by what happens to the strategic balance during the next five years and what further agreements, if any, are concluded. Both parties have made it clear that they intend to exploit the residual permitted forms of armament vigorously. All past experience suggests that Soviet programs will be energetic. The Russians will presumably push forward with their new 3000-mile-range SLBM, their heavier ICBM, and their swing-wing bomber, *Backfire*. They will also pursue improved warhead technology. The United States, while continuing to deploy *Poseidon* and *Minuteman III*, has laid new stress on the B-1 bomber and the *Trident* submarine, which will become available about 1980. Airborne ballistic missiles and cruise missiles offer avenues to explore if, as one may expect, the effect of SAL is to divert technology from forbidden into unrestricted areas. Of particular significance in view of President Nixon's plea for options for controlled response are the projects for improved airborne National Military Command Centers and for development work on new and

---

[5] Melvin Laird, *Annual Defense Department Report*, February 22, 1972, p. 41.

more powerful warheads capable of counter-force strikes against Soviet military targets.[6]

Programs of this kind are calculated not merely to strengthen
American forces but also to create a strong bargaining position for
the coming rounds of SALT. The dissatisfaction expressed with the
existing agreements by Senator Henry Jackson and his Congressional
allies, and their demand that no future agreement be concluded on
offensive missiles that does not secure numerical parity, will also have
some effect on the bargaining. More important, however, will be
whether sustained support for the "safeguarding" programs is forthcoming. The initial response of the Congress was favorable but the
pressure, not merely of domestic calls on the budget, but also of
other military requirements, may well prove formidable. So long as
SALT negotiations continue, however, administrations will be able to
argue their need for a good bargaining position. Indeed a cynic
might suggest that so far the SALT exercise has done more to ac-
celerate than to restrain strategic arms procurement on both sides.
Financial savings from the first round are likely to be very modest
and may well disappear altogether if the new weapon projects reach
the stage of production.

In the light of all these considerations, it seems wisest to reserve
judgment as to whether the SAL Agreements have reinforced the
security of the United States and the peace of the world. Any immediate misgivings about the details of the agreements are, of course,
very much muted by the general belief that the atmosphere of dé-
tente, of which the agreements are at once a source and a product,
makes any prospect of nuclear war appear remote. Quite apart from
all the details, however, there remains a more fundamental reason for
doubting the long-term stability of the present arrangements. This
doubt lies in the permanent acceptance of strategic vulnerability entailed in the ban on all forms of ballistic missile defense. It may well
be that this unprecedented abandonment of any attempt at defending the American people is the appropriate and inevitable response
to the nuclear weapon. It is, however, difficult to suppress the feeling
that the search for security through defense—the only recourse
against accident or irrationality—will prove politically and psychologically irresistible in the long run and that the dialectic of offensive
and defensive technology will offer recurrent encouragement to that
search.

Perhaps only rapid and impressive progress toward much more
drastic restrictions on offensive systems can ensure the continued ob-

[6] See New York *Times*, August 5, 1972.

servance of the BMD Treaty. Further SAL Agreements are, however, likely to be increasingly difficult to devise. Any more rigorous restrictions on numbers of missiles and a start on an actual reduction may require agreement on controlling qualitative characteristics that may be hard to verify. The suggestion of curbs on anti-submarine warfare, perhaps by means of sanctuary areas for SSBNs, raises the problem that ASW is a dual purpose activity related to conventional as well as nuclear war. It is also an activity indulged in by nations other than the superpowers. The same difficulty will arise in much more acute form when attention turns to the NATO forward-based tactical systems (FBS) which so concern the Russians, and to the Soviet MRBMs, which threaten Western Europe. Hitherto the SALT negotiations have been bilateral. The next stages will have to be multilateral, for the FBS, many of which are dual purpose, form part of the local military balance in Europe. Indeed the Soviet attempt to link the French and British SSBN forces to the allowable total of the United States has already multilateralized the strategic problem. Possibilities for disruptive effects within the Western alliance are obvious. The administration credits itself with having successfully avoided sowing suspicion among its NATO allies during SALT, so far, by adequate consultation. While there is much truth in this claim, it would be foolish not to realize that the Europeans have held their peace largely for fear of irritating the Americans on issues that they could not hope to influence. This does not mean that the Europeans cannot tell the difference between being consulted and being informed. As the issues come nearer to their own interests and to questions on which they have effective influence, a more genuine multilateralism will probably assert itself.

Strategic nuclear weapons are, of course, not merely instruments which the nuclear powers might use to destroy each other. They are also symbols of prestige and umbrellas under which the rest of their possessor's foreign and military policy operates. This being so, fundamental transformations in nuclear relationships are likely to have far-reaching repercussions.

In many respects the exact nuclear balance as measured by esoteric expert analysis may be less important than the general impression in the world at large. Over the past few years this impression has been one of relative Soviet advance. The world in the early 1970s is perhaps best characterized, if not as one of American nuclear inferiority, then at least as one in which the United States has ceased to be clearly superior. Because the Soviet Union has been accustomed to operate from inferiority and the United States has enjoyed superiority, it must be supposed that, if adjustments to the new balance are necessary, they will be more painful for the latter. How far such adjustments are in fact necessary will depend on whether margins of nuclear strength can be translated into advantage at lower levels of political or military conflict. Only experience can answer this question conclusively. The American administration has argued that nuclear superiority is not a useful instrument for trying to assuage alarm about rising Soviet strength. It has, however, talked differently on occasions, most notably perhaps in the president's expressed anxiety about being deprived of options and his requirement that the American capacity to deal out destruction should not fall below the Russian. The Chairman of the Joint Chiefs of Staff categorically stated the dangers of inferiority when he declared that "we will pay a very high price in the effectiveness of our diplomacy if we permit the Soviet Union to achieve a clearly evident overall strategic superiority, even were that superiority to have no practical effect on the outcome of an all-out nuclear exchange."[7] Whatever the technical merits of this assertion, it is a fair assumption that others will give some credit to such a view when it is expressed by the senior American military officer.

Most expert observers of the Soviet Union seem to agree that the Russians themselves derive great satisfaction from their newly won strength. Their strategic parity and their ever widening naval deployment, when coupled to their long-established conventional superiority in Europe, justify considerable self-confidence. This is supported by a military budget that, when adjusted for prices and particularly for the cost of manpower, now equals or perhaps exceeds that of the United States. While economic pressures undoubtedly bear on Soviet as on Western defense expenditures, there is little evidence to suggest that such considerations are allowed to constrain seriously desired Soviet military enterprizes. The Sino-Soviet dispute, though a potential problem, has so far been mastered by the Soviets without their having to reduce active military strength elsewhere. Pointing from strategic parity to Vietnam, the Middle East, and their extended naval presence, Soviet leaders may well conclude that their military outlays have brought them handsome political dividends. This contrasts sharply with the chastened and suspicious American approach to military questions.

But even if the American military position has deteriorated in relation to that of the Soviet Union, the notion that military power is of less value in the world today can always be adduced to argue that

---

[7] Admiral T. H. Moorer, *U.S. Military Posture for FY 1972*, March 1971, p. 14.

no unpleasant consequences need follow. With anything approaching a credible retaliatory force, the United States should be safe from direct attack. It follows from this that the significance of the military balance elsewhere, and of which nations dominate what potential military resources, has radically altered from the pre-nuclear age.

When the United States made its first decisive commitment to NATO, Europe was seen as the base from which an attack on the American homeland could be launched and as a vital economic contribution to the military potential to do so. The extended American perimeter was thus being manned in defense of the United States itself. Now, however, even the most important areas overseas have to be valued for their contribution only to more subtle and indirect conceptions of American welfare: for such purposes as commercial access and the sense of living in a congenial and relatively amicable world. Threats to overseas friends and allies are thus no longer considered direct threats to American security.

The belief that overseas interests are less essential to the core of American security can be coupled to the theory that, in any case, military power is less necessary than it once was for the protection of such interests. After more than a quarter century in which nuclear weapons have not been used, the great powers have not fought each other, and the only prolonged conventional war was that in Korea, the belief that war is ceasing to be a usable instrument of inter-state conflict has a certain plausibility. Other forms of struggle are coming to the fore, notably economic influence, subversion, and manipulation of the mass media. The professed aims of national policy are increasingly oriented toward the cultivation of material prosperity, and commerce and investment rather than conquest are seen as the ways to pursue such ends. Fears of being cut off from access to materials and markets have dwindled at a time when the advanced industrial countries are progressively less dependent on the rest of the world and when sheer self-interest is confidently expected to curb any tendencies to prolonged commercial discrimination against the major industrial nations. Moreover, constant frustration in efforts to maintain influence over the third world has converted many Western analysts to the view that any effort by the communist states to bring that world within a closed system will be similarly defeated by the spontaneous force of national determination and pluralism.[8]

[8] For a thorough examination of the diminished role of military power, see Klaus Knorr, *On the Uses of Military Power in the Nuclear Age* (Princeton: Princeton University Press, 1966). For a narrower discussion of American interests in these terms, see Robert W. Tucker, *A New Isolationism: Threat or Promise* (New York: Universe Books and Potomac Associates, 1972).

There undoubtedly are trends working to modify the role of armed force in international politics. Force is increasingly used in carefully modulated ways and all of the great powers have frequently shown a marked reluctance to become formally involved in hostilities. Military assistance, subversion, and covert intervention have become the typical forms of military struggle between the great powers. These forms, however, have become increasingly common, and as armed struggle has come to be regarded as dangerous and reprehensible in its more overt forms, it has also become almost continuous in its lower-level manifestations. Moreover, although there may be deep sociological trends inhibiting the resort to force, it must never be forgotten that the relative restraint of recent years has been experienced in a world based on a highly structured bipolar balance of power. This balance was also one in which the predominantly *status quo* protagonist was dominant in both strategic nuclear power and world-wide mobility. It would be foolhardy and premature to take it for granted that stability would persist if one party to the balance precipitately ceased to exercise its role. Nor should anyone doubting this judgment fail to discount the inevitable temptation for a war-weary nation to be uncritically receptive to theories suggesting that the burdens of world power could be laid down with impunity.

A special form of this wistfulness may partly inspire the suggestion, sometimes espoused by the administration, that the strategic world is shifting from its long bipolarity into a pentagonal form in which China, Japan, and the European Community can share the balance with the Soviet Union and United States. China has always been regarded as a potential superpower and her split with the Soviet Union compels treating her as an independent factor. Her present strength is, however, very limited. Europe and Japan have certainly reached a high degree of economic power and now assert themselves with vigor in that respect. The two are, however, closely nestled under the military wing of the United States, and insofar as they show any signs of groping toward military independence, it is almost entirely the result of American urging. Their spontaneous leaning in that direction is small. If their foreign policies enjoy a certain new latitude it is from within the framework of the bipolar balance.

Nor is it at all certain that the United States would really welcome a truly pentagonal world. The logic of such a configuration is full nuclear self-reliance by the component powers. Japan's inhibitions in this respect are well known and Europe is far from the necessary degree of political unity. It is very possible that American proponents of non-proliferation exaggerate the difficulties of establishing a minimally effective deterrent, and the ultimate logic of emerging global trends probably is toward a multiplicity of nuclear powers. For the moment, however, this seems more likely to be a goal than a reality, and while the Nixon Administration, particularly in private, speaks more sympathetically of such a prospect than its predecessors did, it is far from easy to imagine this sympathy translated into a policy of active encouragement and assistance. The force of immediate arguments for non-proliferation, the known prejudices of the Congress, and the newly acquired problem of not appearing to undermine the spirit of SALT, are likely to override any more grandiose speculations about multiple patterns of world power. Nor do the European and Japanese allies of the United States show any very vigorous enthusiasm to exchange the theoretically more rewarding privileges of independence for the reassuring and familiar security of American hegemony.

Consequently the United States is, and for several years is likely to remain, the only military power capable of offsetting what would otherwise be the overwhelming predominance of the Soviet Union. Moreover the Soviet Union itself clearly prefers a bipolar framework. This preference underlies the Soviet Union's approach to SALT and its pained reaction to the Sino-American rapprochement. There is nothing surprising about the fact that around this dominant bipolar military balance, an increasing multipolarity characterizes other aspects of world politics. On the contrary it has been quite common in the past for lesser powers to enjoy a considerable latitude deriving from the mutual stalemate or the indifference of the leading states. This phenomenon may be reinforced in the present world by the increasing importance of non-military forms of power. Nonetheless the bipolar nuclear balance, if essentially negative in its mutually inhibiting effect, is not rendered negligible thereby. On the contrary, it is the necessary condition for the resulting multipolarity.

Although the United States has the potential to sustain this role, it is always possible that, in its present disillusioned mood, the United States might fail to do so. On balance there are, however, good reasons to suspect that it will not. Among these reasons are: the range of formal commitments and habitual concerns which the United States has acquired during decades of behaving as a great power; American aversion to the idea of a world increasingly dominated by hostile states and a consequent solicitude for the survival of kindred nations, a disposition especially marked with regard to Western Europe and Israel; the belief that even today American economic well-being could be harmed by loss of access to freely trading overseas

areas either by the installation of hostile regimes or by denial of
the use of the seas, a belief reinforced by the energy crisis and a
possible future need for foreign oil; the fear that, even if some of the
accepted reasons for American foreign involvement and military efforts are outmoded, too precipitate an abandonment of established
American policies would produce dangerous instability. President
Nixon laid particular stress on the last principle when he asserted
that "others judge us—and set their own course—by the steadiness of
our performance as well as the merit of our ideas. Abrupt shifts in
our policies—no matter how sound in concept—are unsettling. . . .
If we acquired a reputation for unsteadiness, we would isolate ourselves."[9]

Thus the Nixon Administration has promised consistency and continuity of policy and has announced its loyalty to the multitude of
American defense treaties. On the other hand, it has issued a re-
minder that its observance of those commitments will be guided by
American interests; the Nixon Doctrine itself, with its emphasis on
curtailed military involvement and increased burden sharing by allies, is recessive in spirit. Leaving strategic nuclear policy on one
side, therefore, the prospect for American military policy might be
described as less of the same.

The need for the American military role in the world to be somewhat less ambitious is dictated not merely by a suspicion that the
previous scale of support and intervention has been excessive and is
now less necessary, but also by the severe physical constraints under
which the armed forces of the United States will have to operate
over the next few years. Although the military budget has apparently
remained surprisingly steady during the run-down in Vietnam, in
1973 dollars the total obligational authority has fallen from $99.7 bil-
lion in 1969 to $82 billion in 1972. A substantial amount of real
resources has been transferred to domestic programs and the military
share of GNP has fallen from about 9 percent to 7 percent. Within
limits, budgetary restriction on defense policy is a voluntary choice
for such a rich nation as the United States, but in the absence of
some dramatic rise in international tensions it is unlikely that the
share of GNP allocated to defense will increase, given the heavy demands of domestic federal programs, the saliency of military spending in the readily "disposable" part of the budget, and the rather
high propensity of the United States, by modern world standards,

[9] Nixon, *U.S. Foreign Policy for the 1970s: Building for Peace*, p. 15.

for private consumption. Indeed the principle of "Net Assessment," introduced by the Nixon Administration, whereby defense programs are supposed to be weighed against alternative domestic proposals, is an explicit injunction to regard defense as less than an absolute priority.

As we have seen, SALT cannot be relied upon to curb the rising trend in expenditure on strategic nuclear weapons. In particular, the uncertainties inherent in an imperfectly policed system of mutual restraints create a strong case for a sustained program of research and development. Budgetary pressure will consequently bear heavily on general purpose forces, which already account for some two-thirds of defense expenditure. Much of this expense is attributable to manpower, which in turn reflects the fact that the problems of the armed services have sociological as well as economic roots. On the one hand, the price of labor in the United States is extremely high; on the other, military life appeals to only a limited number of young Americans, and this number has been at least temporarily reduced by the bloodshed and appearance of incompetence that characterized Vietnam. The unpopularity of the draft and the military inefficiency that the training and short-term service of conscripts entail have produced the decision to have an all-volunteer force. This means a drastic fall in numbers; the armed services will have declined from some 4,250,000 to less than two-and-a-half million between 1970 and 1973; forces overseas have declined from over 1 million to less than 500,-000. Even so the voluntary recruitment at the remaining level of manpower will be very expensive. The draft has been a concealed tax for the benefit of the military that now must be carried openly on the budget. Pay and emoluments at the new, higher levels now make up well over half of the defense budget, but it is as yet far from certain that even the reduced force levels can be sustained.

Obviously the new scarcity of manpower will impose hard choices. If the costs of military equipment continue to rise more rapidly than the general price level and if military manpower must be paid at premium rates, a military establishment confined to a fixed proportion of the GNP must either contract or be less well equipped. A completely fresh look will have to be taken at the trade-offs between man- and machine-intensive strategies, and ingenuity must be applied to devising new career patterns for the military. As some compensation, all-volunteer forces ought to reach much higher levels of efficiency if they can be recruited without too much reduction in human standards. This has been the British experience. All-volunteer forces may also be usable without some of the political and emotional constraints suffered by drafted forces. Above a certain level of operations, however, this advantage may be offset by the increased reliance on reserves proposed as a supplement to depleted regular units.

Having considered the new constraints on the armed services, the Nixon Administration has announced that the McNamara aim of preparing for "2½ wars"—that is, preparing to fight a major war simultaneously in Europe and Asia, plus a little one somewhere else—is replaced by planning for 1½ wars. Because adequate forces for 2½ wars were never constructed, this announcement in itself does nothing to facilitate a reduction in forces. In practice, however, the kind of force maintained for use in the intense European battlefield is very different in character from the force suited to Asian operations. Both the rhetoric of the Nixon Doctrine and the evidence of force reorganization carried out during the early years of withdrawal make it clear that in practice the 1½-war principle means reduced preparations for land war in Asia. Garrisons in Korea, Japan, Taiwan, Okinawa, and, of course, Vietnam, have been sharply cut and it may not be long before no American forces designed for ground operations are to be found in Asia at all.

Despite this priority for the European theater so far as ground forces are concerned, the Nixon Administration has professed determination to honor American commitments in Asia as elsewhere. But the administration has adopted a line of reasoning similar to that with which the British covered their own retreat from Asia: to reaffirm commitments in principle, but to claim discretion as to how they shall be discharged. Henceforth the main form of American military intervention in Asia is supposed to be by equipping and training local forces. American forces will not normally be committed to counter-insurgency, and direct American military action will therefore come only at the stage of overt conventional aggression. Over the whole edifice, however, hangs a promise of protection against nuclear threats or attacks.

Insofar as this policy is more than a cover for retreat, it rests on a set of optimistic assumptions drawn from various recent experiences. The relative success of Vietnamization encourages faith in local forces. China's preoccupation with her Soviet border, her interest in American diplomatic support, and a generally revised estimate of Chinese aggressiveness raises hopes that she can be deterred from launching "theater war." The happy accident of a new and more amiable regime in Indonesia removes another potential source of large-scale aggression. Emergence of embryonic regional alignments such as ASEAN affords some hope of a local security system rather like those the British have tried to leave in their wake in Malaysia and the Persian Gulf.

Nevertheless a policy of reliance on local forces and on an offshore maritime presence involves some substantial risks. The difficulty of drawing the line between insurgency and aggression has been at the heart of American troubles in Asia, and the present formula offers no clear guidance for specific situations. Providing limited assistance by way of supply and the performance of sophisticated military functions, such as air support, may be a way of retaining limited liability, but as Vietnam itself demonstrated, it may also offer opportunities for progressive involvement. Yet such a policy may be less effective as a deterrent than a more formal, standing presence. There is a clear conflict between the requirements of deterrence and the principles of flexibility and limited liability.

In the aftermath of Vietnam, however, the Nixon Doctrine is intended to set a high threshold for the re-introduction of American ground forces to Asia, even at some considerable risk to the Asian balance of power. This risk is partly discounted by the belief that, on the one hand, the United States has less at stake in Asia than was once thought, and on the other hand, that the self-equilibrating forces likely to frustrate any would-be military aggressor are stronger than was previously credited.

Insofar as the United States continues to take its military obligations in Asia seriously, it is likely to put a heavy emphasis on maritime forces. Maritime forces, organized around aircraft carriers, offer an obvious device for maintaining a capability for strike and intervention without the rigidities of a land-base structure. Their flexibility provides a solution to the problem of preparing a limited force to meet a wide range of unpredictable contingencies. It is not surprising, therefore, that the enunciation of the Nixon Doctrine has been accompanied by a rise in naval expenditure. Leaving on one side the apparently secure place of seaborne strategic systems in the defense budget, spending on general purpose naval forces has risen quite sharply to over $16 billion. Expenditure on procurement of ships has reached twice the annual rate of the late 1960s.

The case for naval expenditure has been advanced not only by the prospective shift to an offshore role in Asia but also by the conspicuous development of the Soviet navy as an arm of Soviet policy. Whatever the arguments for believing that the spontaneous forces of multipolarity and economic logic will keep the trade routes open, even isolationists in their approach to foreign intervention become uneasy at the prospect of leaving the protection of sea lanes to the self-restraint of the Soviet navy.[10] This concession is more far-reaching than it at first appears, for technology has not yet rendered sea-power entirely independent of a network of footholds on the land. Open attacks on American or indeed other Western shipping except in all-out war are, however, improbable. For those who still attribute importance to the competition for spheres of influence between the superpowers, the greater significance of the Soviet navy lies in its contribution to extending Soviet political interests. In this respect the Soviet fleet has both a positive and a negative function. Negatively, its presence may inhibit the employment of Western naval forces to influence local situations; positively, naval forces are used to show the flag or even, as in the Mediterranean and West Africa, to intervene actively, if so far non-belligerently, in local conflicts.

It is not easy to establish a proper level of response to this Soviet naval activism. Contrary to common belief, the Soviet navy, except in its SSBN force, has not grown much in recent years. It has certainly been modernized but the Western rate of building has been considerably higher. Moreover the United States Navy possesses in its carriers a costly and valuable asset which the Soviet Union could not hope to match for many years to come. Looked at in strictly naval terms, the Soviet navy is a force designed to deny the seas to a more powerful force. For this reason it is not technically an ideal force to undertake interventions. But the political effect of navies is not determined by expert naval analysts, and it is the increasingly ubiquitous presence of the Soviet navy that has earned it attention.

So long as the Russians, who were previously parochial in their naval practice, choose to spend their time and money on a widely deployed pattern of maritime operations, there is little that can be done to prevent a rise in their prominence relative to the older established naval powers. Nor should it be forgotten that the Soviet naval presence is only part of a much more diversified policy of penetration, orchestrating naval power with military aid, training missions, and commercial enterprise. It would not be sensible, therefore, to regard Soviet naval activity as simply calling for equivalent adjustments in the Western naval order of battle. On the other hand,

---

[10] Thus my colleague Robert W. Tucker writes that "the withdrawal from commitments on land in no way reduces the need to retain sufficient naval power to move unhindered at sea. However improbable the contingency of denial of free movement of U.S. ships at sea, that contingency must be guarded against." *A New Isolationism*, p. 88.

the rising Soviet naval presence has undoubtedly contributed to the general impression that the Soviet Union is in the strategic ascendant.

Exactly what inhibiting effect the Soviet presence has on American policy is hard to determine. It is commonly said that another Lebanon expedition on the model of 1958 could not be mounted for fear of collision with the Russian fleet. Yet in 1970 the Sixth Fleet was used to deter Soviet-supported Syrian intervention in Jordan under circumstances that the president later declared to have entailed a real danger of war.[11] The lesson presumably is that, under deterrence, determined naval operations can still be executed, but the decision to initiate them must be considerably more difficult to take when the possibility of direct conflict between the superpowers exists. Yet by its wide naval deployments, the Soviet Union is acquiring its own capability to intervene and, although cautious, has shown in the Middle East that it will commit forces to combat overseas. To reduce American naval deployments would therefore be to confer to the Soviet Union precisely the freedom of action enjoyed by the United States during its years of naval monopoly.

While the Nixon Doctrine frankly envisages a less intimate American involvement in the military affairs of Asia, it proposes a virtually unchanged involvement in Europe, provided certain conditions are met. Although, as we noted earlier, Europe has lost much of its earlier significance as the first line of defense for the security of the United States itself, it still retains a prime position in the balance of political, economic, and military world power. Europe has also played such a pre-eminent part in the Soviet-American competition that its passage from the American to the Soviet sphere of interest would be the single most decisive symbol of American decline imaginable.

That Europe was no longer an essential component of American physical security has been obvious for a decade or more. Recent events, however, have illuminated this hitherto unduly neglected change more vividly. The registration of American strategic vulnerability in SALT, the Soviet-American rapprochement, and the Congressional pressure for a reduction in American forces in Europe have reminded observant Europeans that their importance to the United States, though still great, is conditional. Talk of a pentagonal world also suggests a diminished European role, for it would mark a decline

[11] He called it "the greatest threat to world peace since this Administration came into office." U.S. Foreign Policy for the 1970s: Building for Peace, p. 127.

from being the prime American partner to one among several pieces
to be moved around the board of American diplomacy. Fortunately
for the Europeans, the pentagonal notion has its limitations and,
from time to time at least, the American administration still speaks
in terms of a special relationship with Europe. The generation of in-
stinctive Atlanticists who once shaped American policy has gone, but
looking to European unity, President Nixon still declares in words
reminiscent of the Kennedy era that: "Two strong powers in the
West would add flexibility to Western diplomacy. Two strong powers could increasingly share the responsibilities of decision."[12] In specifically military policy, Europe is also favored. For where Asia is
handed over to an offshore presence and military assistance, Europe
is promised the undiminished contribution of American ground
forces. Indeed the lower American profile in Asia relieves the Europeans of a long-standing fear that the United States might allow its
Asian entanglements to distract it from Europe or to drag it and its
European allies into an unnecessary war.

It is also very clear that the Soviet Union puts a special value on
Europe. Viewed from Moscow, Europe is a peninsula of the Asian
heartland which the Soviet Union ought to dominate. The American
presence violates the Russian preference for small neighbors, just as
the rise of China violates it in the East. For the moment Soviet military policy dictates domination over Eastern Europe as a defensive
glacis and as room for the deployment of Soviet troops which would
attempt to overrun Europe in the event of war. Though anxious to
avoid a military conflict with the United States, the Soviet Union
would welcome the ultimate withdrawal of American troops. Unless
Europe had developed its own deterrent military strength in the
meantime, the result would be the so-called Finlandization of Western Europe. This would probably take the form, not of military conquest, but of a steady increase in Western European deference to
Soviet preferences in both foreign and domestic policy. Moreover,
while deliberate aggression is highly unlikely so long as a semblance
of balance remains in Europe and would probably be unnecessary if
it did not, there are several areas of potential political instability in
Europe that may produce spontaneous outbreaks of violence.
Among these are Spain, Italy, Yugoslavia, and even, perhaps, France.
The Irish situation has demonstrated how even the most traditionally
stable of states may suffer from the modern phenomenon of civil
strife. While dealing with such problems is best left to national pol-

---

[12] U.S. *Foreign Policy for the 1970s: Building for Peace*, p. 30.

icy, the European countries' capacity to do so would be severely hindered if the framework of international security were also suspect.

A military balance is therefore essential for the political health and independence of Europe. Measured by the simple indices of wealth and population the Europeans, as Senators have been eager to suggest, ought to be able to balance the Soviet Union by themselves. It is generally acknowledged, however, that Europe lacks and cannot quickly muster the will to mobilize the necessary resources and the unity to employ them effectively. For this deficiency the United States is partly responsible, for its protective presence, while perhaps preserving Europe from Soviet domination, has warded off the pressures that might have compelled the Europeans to bestir themselves.

The American contribution to European defense contains two elements: a nuclear guarantee and a contribution to an initial level of resistance—the so-called flexible response—intended to make the guarantee credible to both friend and enemy. The initial conventional response is commonly supposed to work by making the risk of escalation obvious to the enemy. It is less commonly recognized but probably more important that the semblance of a conventional defense blurs the stark risk of the nuclear guarantee to American eyes. It is thus of profound importance that recent events are eroding both aspects of the American posture. Nuclear parity and the registration of mutual vulnerability in the SAL Agreements take the incredibility of an all-out American nuclear strike on behalf of Europe a significant stage further. To some eyes the SAL framework constitutes an implied doctrine of no-first-use. Yet the pressure on general purpose forces raises a question about the continued viability of the conventional phases of flexible response.

Innumerable attempts to calculate the military balance in Europe fail to obscure the overall inferiority of NATO. Whatever the superficial figures of peace-time strength in Europe, Soviet superiority in tanks, tactical aircraft, and, above all, in capacity for reinforcement leave no doubt as to the true balance under most imaginable circumstances. Moreover, NATO strength should probably be discounted for the lack of "agility" entailed in being a coalition with mixed equipment and somewhat irrational deployment. An additional handicap is imposed by the need to affect a strategy of forward defense to console the exposed West Germans.

Most experts agree with the judgment of recent British and German White Papers on Defense that the present level of NATO forces is just sufficient to make the strategy of mounting an initial conventional resistance to aggression plausible. Any reduction in allied strength would thus pose the double danger of undermining the flexible response and thereby exposing the American guarantee as a stark policy of massive retaliation that might well prove politically insupportable. The Nixon Administration has pursued several lines of approach in search of a solution to this dilemma.

The first and most obvious is the demand for increased burden-sharing. If the Europeans would do more in their own defense, it would on the one hand afford an answer to Congressional objections to an inequitable burden, and on the other hand make it possible for even much-reduced American forces to be incorporated into a workable strategy for postponing the moment of nuclear decision. How few American troops would serve to make American commitment fully credible is an open question, but many Europeans believe that the number could fall as low as 100,000 without losing all practical and symbolic value.

American contributions to European defense do indeed impose a considerable burden on the United States. Estimates vary but perhaps a third to a half of American general-purpose forces are primarily maintained for use in Europe, at a cost of from $14 to $20 billion. Not all of these forces would be eliminated if the European commitment were abandoned, and those that are stationed in Europe are probably less expensive than if they were in the United States. Overseas stationing does, however, pose balance of payments problems, and even if these are not inherently serious when studied from the viewpoint of economic theory, in the imperfect world we actually inhabit they create serious difficulties for fiscal management. By one device or another West Germany offsets some 80 percent of American foreign exchange costs, but the expedients, including the purchase of arms and bonds, involve various fictions and constitute a permanent source of mutual irritation.[13]

Efforts to get the Europeans to do more have borne some fruit. The European Defence Improvements Program of December 1970, and its successor the following year, involving a total of some $2 billion in extra defense expenditure over five years, while partly a disguised response to inflation, were at least steps in the right direction. If the Europeans have not energetically increased their efforts, they have resisted a rapid decline. Domestic pressures on defense budgets are, of course, strong in Europe, and a United States whose own defense programs are constrained by domestic factors cannot

[13] The best single discussion of these issues is John Newhouse, ed., *U.S. Troops In Europe: Issues, Costs, and Choices* (Washington, D.C.: The Brookings Institution, 1971).

realistically expect European behavior to be dictated purely by strategic theory. It must also be remembered that, while the average percentage of GNP spent by Europeans on defense is low, that of the larger countries is around 5 percent, so that general exhortations have quite different implications for particular nations. Nor are the Europeans free of the sociological pressures on military manning, and a trend to voluntary service is pushing up manpower costs in Europe as in the United States. Thus, for a variety of reasons, the trend in European force levels is likely to be downward. The trend has, however, been much slower than might have been expected a few years ago, and the old European belief that greater efforts might counter-productively encourage the United States to do less has been finally scotched.

A long-established variant of the effort to get the Europeans to do more involves encouraging them to co-operate for greater efficiency. The extreme form of such co-operation would be the creation of a European strategic nuclear force capable of taking over the task of deterring Soviet attack or blackmail. Numerous familiar difficulties beset this project. The SAL Agreements may have somewhat reduced the technical difficulties by removing the prospect of a thick Soviet BMD program but the pace of technological innovation surrounding the whole SAL enterprise has served to emphasize the costs of nuclear forces designed for the big league. Europe's lack of political unity makes it unlikely that the Europeans can soon muster the energy to pursue the development of a nuclear force or the cohesion to wield it credibly. On the other hand, national nuclear forces do exist in France and Britain, and there is little prospect of their being readily abandoned.

Which direction the further development of those forces will take could be much affected by American policy. Spokesmen for the Nixon Administration, at least in private, take a more generous line toward the possibility of American assistance than those for previous administrations. But Congressional attitudes remain suspicious, and the general arguments for non-proliferation may now have been reinforced by a sense that assistance to other nuclear powers would run contrary to SALT. The logic of multipolarity, of a lower American profile, and of technological and political possibilities all point toward an ultimately nuclear Europe, but its emergence will not be in time to solve the immediate strategic problems of the alliance.

In the meantime the move toward European unity in defense is likely to take the form of modest and *ad hoc* improvements in the coherence of strategic doctrine and continued joint projects of mili-

tary procurement. The enthusiasm of some European leaders to follow up the enlargement of the community by steps toward greater
political coherence is stronger than some skeptics believe, and one of
the sources of this enthusiasm is the desire for a weightier voice in
world affairs. As we have already seen very vividly in the area of
monetary policy, a concerted European policy is not always to American liking. In defense, however, the European sense of deference
to American predominance is likely to last as long as the United
States chooses to exercise leadership. For several years an independent, united European defense policy will probably remain the goal
inspiring pragmatic forms of co-ordination rather than an institutional
reality.

Another possible source of relief from American military problems
in Europe is seen by some in the complex project for Mutual Balanced Force Reductions (MBFR). Now that it has been taken up by
the Russians, this idea, which was once a NATO defense against
Soviet proposals for a European Security Conference ignoring all the
real security questions, must be taken seriously. American motives
have been ambiguous. In one dimension the possibility of negotiating
a reduction in Soviet forces has held out a tempting formula for reducing American forces in Europe without worsening the military
balance and even, on a wildly optimistic view, while improving it.
From another perspective the prospect of negotiations and the need
for a good bargaining position have been cited to still domestic critics of high American force levels in Europe and to urge sustained
military efforts on the Europeans. The latter tactic has been reinforced by European fears that if they do not keep up their contributions, the United States might strike a bilateral bargain with the
Soviet Union.

On strictly strategic principles, the chances of negotiating a better
military balance with the Russians appear negligible, although there
may be some hope of minimizing the bad effects of unilateral Western force reductions impelled by domestic motives. This is chiefly
because the Soviet margin of superiority is such that even equal percentage cuts in forces on each side would bring about a deterioration
in the Western position. Not only do percentage reductions tend to
inconvenience a smaller force more than a large one, but also Western forces are now very close to the minimum level necessary to man
the required frontages, almost regardless of the strength of the opposition. On the central front, divisional sectors cover about twenty
miles, which most soldiers would regard as an absolute maximum for

mounting a conventional defense. Even proportionately larger reductions in Soviet forces, which are not likely to be negotiable, would not eliminate this problem. Moreover at all levels of reduction, a great difference between American and Soviet proximity to the central front enhances Soviet superiority in reinforcement capability. This consideration must be related to the fact that only if withdrawn American units were disbanded would the United States enjoy a real economic benefit from force reductions. Some Soviet units might be demobilized—a difficult matter to verify—but more would probably become a central reserve which, given Soviet internal lines of communication and lift capability, would considerably increase the Soviet Union's flexibility in dealing with its eastern and western fronts. Moreover, as there is no likelihood that Soviet territory would be included in the zone of restricted force levels, much of the deployment required for an attack could be carried out without technically violating an MBFR agreement. Unilateral intelligence might reveal what was happening, but there remains the problem, which bears on the whole of MBFR, of how readily NATO would respond to the breach of an agreement once concluded. The influences dragging Western troop levels down and the problems of consensus in a coalition would very probably make for sluggish and perhaps divisive reactions.

Fundamental difficulties of this kind overshadow the great technical complexity of designing a formula for equitable force reduction. The problem is much more complicated than that encountered in SALT, and it must be addressed in a multilateral forum. Very possibly only a crude formula, such as gross number of men to be withdrawn, could be agreed upon, leaving it to each side to translate that into practice. But the process of negotiation could offer the Soviet Union ample opportunity to exploit divisions within NATO. There is an obvious source of dispute between the Americans and the Europeans as to whether reductions should be in indigenous or stationed forces. Perhaps the most dangerous issue of all, however, concerns the forward-based nuclear systems. Whether the FBS are dealt with in the framework of SALT or of MBFR, the Europeans will suspect that any American concessions to the Soviet Union are founded on a bilateral deal. On this, as on many other arms control issues, suspicion is reinforced by European dependence on American sources for much intelligence information about Soviet forces.

For Europe, perhaps the most beneficial result that could emerge from MBFR would be for the United States to regard an agreement as constituting a positive commitment to maintain the residual level of forces as a minimum. To secure this, the Europeans might be well advised to permit all the reductions to be made in stationed forces, for many believe that uncertainty about American intentions has done more damage than moderate actual withdrawals would do. In practice no agreement could effectively bind an administration intent on further reductions. An MBFR agreement would, however, strengthen an administration that wished to maintain force levels in its dealings with domestic critics.

Perhaps the most dangerous aspect of MBFR and the parallel European Security Conference is that, by becoming institutionalized East-West consultative mechanisms or by virtue of explicit agreements, they might give the Soviet Union a legal pretext for intervention in Western strategic debates, which are notoriously difficult enough as it is. Given the fact that any force reductions would require painful readjustments on the Western side and that the next few years are critical for the political and military integration of Europe, such intervention would come at a particularly awkward moment. Existing German tenderness about *Ostpolitik,* American concern for the bilateral SALT relationship, and French absence from the NATO framework would all increase Russian leverage. Such an intrusion, coming at a time of partial American withdrawal, would have the appearance and perhaps the reality of a start on "Finlandization." No such opportunities are likely to exist in reverse.

Given the declared policies of the Nixon Administration, no precipitate large reduction in American force levels seems likely over the next three or four years, barring some dramatic outcome to MBFR. The general trend for both American and West European forces will, however, almost certainly be downward and this raises a real question about the future of the present strategy of flexible response. Leaving the tactical nuclear component aside for the moment, the flexible response means fighting a conventional war for as long as possible. Great and unresolved confusion surrounds the supposed duration of such a conventional resistance, and while such spokesmen as the former British Minister of Defence, Denis Healey, talk of five to ten days, NATO naval forces still reflect the expectation of a prolonged battle to keep the Atlantic line of communication open. A more fundamental question, however, is whether the whole idea of manning a conventional front will have to be abandoned if Western forces decline any further.

All Western armed forces are under financial pressure from the combined influences of rising costs of weapons, declining enthusiasm for military service, and consequently soaring rates of military pay.

The crucial case here is West Germany, which supplies the greatest single contingent of manpower on the central front. Efforts to eliminate politically insupportable inequities in the draft have compelled the Bundeswehr to the drastic expedient of cutting the period of service to fifteen months, with all the attendant losses in efficiency and burdens of training. A longer-range proposal, however, envisages a two-tier structure in which the core of the Bundeswehr would be professional, supplemented by a militia on Swiss lines. A move of this kind has much to recommend it, but it would certainly dictate a different kind of strategy.

Some students of NATO strategy draw encouragement from a supposed shift in the technology of conventional warfare to favor the defense. Light anti-aircraft and anti-tank missiles, greatly improved delivery accuracies for conventional warheads, and new kinds of area interdiction weapons such as minelets and cluster-bombs are seen as an answer to the rapid armored advances envisaged by Soviet strategy. But while there is some truth in this, the theory is disturbingly reminiscent of all the other transient technological promises with which the West has assured itself that security can be had at low levels of effort. In particular, we have yet to see what countervailing technological ingenuity can do for the offensive.

The need to find a strategy compatible with the imperatives of national manpower policies in the West has therefore lent increasing interest to a new strategic concept whereby militia units of the kind envisaged by Germany, joined perhaps in the interests of deterrent solidarity by allied special forces and armed with some of the new light anti-aircraft and anti-armor weapons, are relied upon to provide a barrier defense behind and through which the professional armored and air cavalry forces, including Americans, would mount a mobile defense or counter-attack. The military effectiveness of such a strategy is a matter of debate but considerable professional opinion is ready to give it a serious hearing.[14] Politically the strategy has the merit of providing the necessary appearance of a forward defense without binding the main force into an untenable posture. Whether such a strategy will survive the prolonged analysis of the military experts remains to be seen. In any case it is rather unlikely that any such radically new strategic concept will be adopted formally and at one stroke, given the cumbersome processes of NATO and the many national views to be accommodated. It is possible, however,

[14] See *inter alia*, D. M. Pontifex and E. A. Burgess, *British Army Review*, August 1970.

that the alliance will arrive at such a situation piecemeal, as national policies remold the forces at NATO's disposal.

It remains to turn briefly to an old and familiar aspect of the search for technological solutions, that of tactical nuclear weapons. This issue unfortunately exposes a divergence of American and European interests. Both sides of the alliance concur in giving tactical nuclear weapons a crucial part in the mechanism of deterrence by flexible response. The two sides arrive at this agreement, however, from somewhat different perspectives. For the United States, tactical nuclear weapons are a device to implement a nuclear guarantee while postponing the decision for strategic nuclear war. This prompts a search for ways to employ tactical weapons without crossing the strategic threshold. Conversely, the Europeans, for whom any substantial tactical nuclear engagement would be a disaster, prefer to regard tactical nuclear weapons as a fairly delicate trigger on the strategic forces. It is not, of course, that the Europeans would welcome a strategic nuclear war. It is simply that any large-scale war in Europe, conventional or nuclear, would be a catastrophe for the Europeans. They therefore favor a rather incredible strategy of forward defense, to save them from becoming a battlefield, and a policy of nuclear deterrence to prevent the strategy from being tested.

In his first foreign policy statement, President Nixon noted that the deterioration in the strategic balance required a reassessment of the role of tactical nuclear weapons.[15] Clearly, the more incredible American initiation of strategic war becomes, the less convincing it is to regard the use of tactical nuclear weapons as a brief stage on the ladder of escalation. Discussions initiated by the Europeans in the Nuclear Planning Group (NPG) have produced agreement on initial uses of tactical nuclear weapons in ways intended to be useful as tactical blows and warning demonstrations. But even the briefest discussion with the authorities involved reveals that the processes for executing the initial uses are unwieldy and fraught with impracticalities. At the same time, a complete lack of agreement exists on the question of follow-on use. This question involves deciding whether to escalate by turning to strategic weapons or by intensifying the use of tactical weapons, and thus strikes directly at the divergence of European and American interests.

Many NATO spokesmen assert that uncertainty itself acts as a deterrent. This has some validity, but there is a difference between uncertainty in the mind of the enemy and muddle in one's own think-

15 *United States Foreign Policy: A New Strategy for Peace*, pp. 21–22.

ing. In his 1972 foreign policy statement, President Nixon returned to the tactical nuclear issue to make precisely this point: "Doctrines cannot be improvised in times of crisis and left to chance." At the same time he reiterated his warning that parity had changed the basis of European security: "In an era of strategic balance between the U.S. and U.S.S.R., the more plausible threats were those below the threshold of strategic nuclear war."[16] Thus the pressure of parity on the logic of an American nuclear guarantee to Europe is opening up the question of tactical nuclear doctrine, however much those who know the present illogicalities and future disruptive potential of NATO policy would prefer to leave it closed. Moreover the place of the FBS in SALT and MBFR will force the question open in a forum where NATO would be unwise to explore its own internal differences.

Part of the problem is that there is some logic in the Soviet Union's effort to treat the FBS as strategic systems, because they can hit Russian territory, and in regarding the MRBMs as not strategic, because they cannot hit the United States. This view is not equitable as between the two alliances, but it does reflect the situation when regarded only from the narrow self interest of the superpowers. The FBS with deep interdiction capability merge the NATO tactical response imperceptibly into the American strategic strike. This gives them precisely the deterrent effect the Europeans want, but equally endangers the American search for a tactical option that will not bring on strategic nuclear war. The Russians would obviously like to get rid of the FBS and thus decouple the American strategic deterrent from Europe.

When considering the ultimate security of the United States, American strategists also want decoupling; but, when trying to deter an attack on Europe which Western forces are not ready to meet in conventional terms, the FBS serve to suggest that once at war the United States might drift into a response which cold analysis of American interests would condemn.

One escape from this dilemma, a full scale NATO conventional defense, has never proved attainable even when, in the early 1950s and again exactly a decade later, the United States tried to construct one. In theory there is one other escape, now being earnestly advocated by its proponents. This is the application of small, short-range nuclear weapons to compensate for deficiencies in conventional forces and make the prospect of an effective defense rather than re-

[16] U.S. *Foreign Policy for the 1970s: The Emerging Structure of Peace*, February 9, 1972, pp. 44 and 43.

taliation the deterrent to aggression. The short-range weapons could not threaten Soviet territory and would therefore not provoke an attack on the United States. Being nuclear, they would presumably retain some of the deterrent aura of a class of weapon not used since 1945. But their prime role would be to make defense credible.

There are many objections to this strategy, and they have so far proved sufficient to raise overwhelming opposition. For Europeans such a development would seem to destroy almost the last semblance of protection by American strategic forces and raise the specter of a prolonged and destructive nuclear campaign in Europe. To assuage such anxieties it would be necessary to convince the critics, first, that the new small nuclear weapons now available could be used without severe collateral damage and, second, that they would in fact contribute to a winning defensive strategy. A difficulty here is presented by the Soviet tactical nuclear arsenal and tactical doctrine which supposedly calls for the large-scale use of high-yield weapons and confidently asserts that such an approach will favor the offensive. One expedient for deterring the Soviet Union from escalating a constrained Western use of nuclear weapons might lie in the European national strategic forces, for the use of these forces might be credible at the point when high yield Russian tactical and theater weapons were in use. In this conception American strategic forces would deter a Soviet strike at the United States, European national forces would deter the MBRMs and set limits to other theater weapons, while small, unmistakably tactical, battlefield nuclear weapons would stiffen the conventional defense.

The Western allies have long skirted the issue of tactical nuclear weapons because of the illogicalities and mutual differences a thorough-going examination might expose. Some progress has been made in the NPG in recent years, but the fundamental dilemmas remain unsolved. Now it is possible that SALT and MBFR will drag the problem into a dangerous East-West forum before NATO has reached a clear consensus of its own. In view of all the difficulties and the widespread conviction that obscurity has its own deterrent effect, it is unlikely that any radical new doctrine will be formally adopted in the next year or two. The United States may very well adjust its tactical arsenal so that decoupling could be attempted if deterrence fails, but it is far from easy to see how complete reassurance of this could be conveyed to the Russians so long as dual-capable aircraft remained part of the American force in Europe.

If the United States moves in this direction, it seems probable that the Europeans will see a reinforced need to preserve their national nuclear forces to influence the rules of tactical engagement. The United States might view the European forces with some misgiving in this respect, for fear that they might re-establish the linkage from local response to global nuclear war that the readjustment of American strategy was intended to break. Short of a total withdrawal of the American commitment to Europe, however, and an abrogation of Article V of the North Atlantic Treaty, some linkage is inevitable, and if President Nixon, in his four criteria for sufficiency, can envisage a limited strategic exchange between the United States and the Soviet Union, moderated by fear of a full-scale response, it does not seem far-fetched to believe that the Russians would recoil from retaliating upon the United States for a European escalation of the theater war.

There is an air of unreality about all discussions of strategies for the last resort. In the present atmosphere of detente this air is pervasive. Although the logic of underlying strategic reality may drift in the direction just indicated, the declared policy of NATO and the United States will probably change little and the resulting fuzziness will serve as an effective deterrent. It would only be if new and unexpected tensions developed in Europe or the Middle East that the leaky joints in Western nuclear doctrine would begin to cause concern beyond the narrow circle of professional strategists.

One is led to the overall conclusion that the early 1970s are a period when fundamental changes in the global military balance are in gestation but not yet ready to emerge. Their emergence may be all the slower because the United States and its allies have many incentives to postpone painful adjustments to new realities. The two dominant influences on the American strategic position, the loss of nuclear supremacy and the urge to shed commitments after the debacle in Vietnam, will inevitably alter the United States' relations with all its allies in the medium term, but President Nixon is certainly correct when he warns that doing anything precipitously would be disturbing and unsettling for the central balance of power on which the whole present sense of stability rests. If the range of American military commitments and interventions with which the United States has burdened itself since 1947 has been excessive, it would not be fanciful to blame it on an exaggerated indoctrination with the "lesson of Munich." The belief that failure to take a strong stand early enough leads inexorably to disaster has inspired American policy since the beginnings of containment. If this was an uncritical application of a sound lesson, however, it would be no less dangerous to make too much of the lessons of Vietnam and allow one failure to condemn a quarter century of diplomacy. The error, if error it was, has not been the decision to play an active role in the world balance but to exaggerate the importance of the third world and to overestimate the possibility of organizing it on old-world lines.

The more significant parts of American efforts to develop a structure of collective self-defense have been thoroughly vindicated. In this respect the Nixon Doctrine's discrimination between Europe and Asia accords with the best strategic principle of cutting losses and reinforcing success. The path to self reliance for Japan, as well as Western Europe, is now open if not short. If the United States does not allow its strategic ties with those outposts to break prematurely, a lower military profile elsewhere is unlikely to bring disaster.

6

THE DIPLOMACY OF ALLIED RELATIONS:
EUROPE AND JAPAN

Robert E. Osgood

Detente and the Structure of Power in U.S. Alliances

Next to the transformation of America's relations with the Soviet Union and the People's Republic of China, no peaceful international development would affect American foreign policy more than a change in the basic configuration of power and interests (the "structure of relationships," as the Nixon Administration would call it) between the United States and its major allies: the chief NATO countries and Japan. The greatest change in this relationship that one can reasonably anticipate would be a shift from the military dependence of these allies upon the United States to substantial military autonomy. Even if such a development continues to seem unlikely, the United States will be faced with a new phase of adjustment in relations with its allies. For the relationship between the United States and its allies that served American interests in the era of confrontation is not likely to serve them so well in an era of negotiation.

In the last quarter century the most important structural characteristic of international politics that has shaped American foreign policy has been the configuration of power and interests among the five principal centers of actual and potential power in the world: the United States, the Soviet Union, Western Europe (chiefly, the United Kingdom, France, the Federal Republic of Germany, and Italy), Japan, and China.[1] Six major developments have shaped this configuration: (1) the polarization of international power and conflict between the United States and the Soviet Union, accompanied by the organization of the principal second-rank states as their allies; (2) the economic resurgence of Western Europe and Japan; (3) the extension of America's Europe-centered animosity and competition with the Soviet Union to communist China in Asia; (4) the transformation of

---

[1] China's ranking among the five is based more on the size of its population and on its geographical position than on its industrial or even its military capability. Its role as a major actor on the international stage, however, is based not only on material factors but equally on ideological zeal and political determination and on its critical position in the configuration of interests between the superpowers.

Sino-Soviet relations from those of nominal partners to real adversaries; (5) the movement of U.S. relations with the Soviet Union from confrontation toward detente; (6) the movement of U.S. relations with the People's Republic of China toward rapprochement.

A major change in one set of relationships among these five centers of world power affects the other relationships. Thus the Sino-Soviet split has affected U.S. relations with both countries, and U.S. relations with each has affected their relations with each other. So far, however, the basic relationship of power and interests between the United States and its major allies has remained remarkably stable despite momentous changes in the other relationships and despite the resurgence of the economic power and self-assertiveness of these allies.

Recent developments, however, raise questions about the perpetuation of this relationship: How will the consolidation of detente with the Soviet Union and the pursuit of rapprochement with China affect U.S.-European and U.S.-Japanese relations? Should the American government seek to alter the basic structure of power and responsibility between the United States and its allies, or should it concentrate upon adjusting the modalities of this relationship to changing conditions in order to preserve the existing structure? How far can the United States retrench militarily without undermining this basic structure?

Clearly, the Nixon Administration has sought to preserve the basic structure of power and responsibility within the two major U.S. alliances as the basis for elaborating a more comprehensive *modus vivendi* with adversaries. True, it has applauded the tendency of its allies to become more self-reliant and has even urged them to free themselves from American tutelage on the grounds that only more independent allies will feel a stake in becoming more effective and responsible participants in the less polarized international order that is emerging. On the other hand, in this stage of detente the administration would regard any movement of its allies toward full-scale military self-reliance as upsetting to the diplomatic equilibrium. In the name of creating an invigorated partnership with its allies, it indirectly discourages complete self-reliance by combining concessions to allied independence with new bonds of consultation. At the same time, however, it asks them for increased burden-sharing and it pressures them to adjust their trade and monetary policies to American interests.

American military retrenchment, like the division of military responsibility in the alliances, is integrally related to detente. The success of detente will permit the United States to preserve its global interests at a lower level of effort and involvement, but retrenchment is clearly subordinate to detente. Unilateral retrenchment is regarded as the consequence, not the instrument, of a successful era of negotiation. If retrenchment should go too far too soon, it would undermine the stable structure of relationships underlying detente. Not the least reason for this danger, in President Nixon's view, is that such retrenchment would undermine the confidence of America's allies in American leadership and lead them toward military separatism or demilitarized neutralism.

Thus the Nixon Administration's answers to the questions posed above are reasonably clear and consistent. They reflect an overall strategy of American leadership in a more moderate and pluralistic diplomatic environment in which the principal objective is to orchestrate a comprehensive *modus vivendi* with the Soviet Union. But the long-run success of this strategy depends on unforeseen developments as well as on calculated intentions. A process of diplomatic accommodation, rapprochement, and retrenchment, once started, may lead in directions not anticipated. In the very success of the Nixon-Kissinger design, there may be the seeds of its undoing. If only for this reason, it is not too soon to examine the pros and cons of the only real alternative to the present structure of relationships: the orderly devolution of power and responsibility from the United States to its major European allies and Japan.[2]

The Nixon Strategy in Europe

In no other respect has the Nixon Administration more clearly subordinated retrenchment to both diplomatic accommodation and alliance cohesion than in its European policies. In doing so, it has felt compelled to bolster the existing structure of power between the United States and its allies, even while applauding their increased self-reliance. While advocating a redistribution of burdens and responsibilities from the United States to its NATO allies, in practice it expects this redistribution to take place within the existing organization of military power, in which the United States retains the preponderant voice.

The logic of this position is clear: the first priority is detente. But a European detente, if it is to be more than atmospheric, depends on preserving the military balance that has made detente possible.

[2] Unilateral withdrawal and disengagement is also, theoretically, an alternative, but it is not one that any president will explicitly and consciously adopt. On the other hand, it may well come about by default or through a piecemeal process of attrition. This prospect and its consequences are assessed, along with the alternative of devolution, in the analysis that follows.

This military balance, in turn, depends on preserving the organization of military power that established it.[3] The cohesion of NATO under American leadership is considered essential to this organization.

The administration views with favor Western Europe's move toward greater cohesion and independence in the economic and political realms, even to the extent of looking forward to the formation of a European defense community eventually.[4] In the practical future, however, it sees a compelling need to stabilize America's dominant security role in Europe. To this end conflicting economic interests must be accommodated (without jeopardizing U.S. trade and monetary interests), American troops in Europe must remain at about the same level (pending East-West agreement on balanced force reductions), and the allies must assume a sufficiently larger share of the burden of collective defense to make the maintenance of America's role acceptable to the American Congress.

Of course, the Nixon Administration did not invent detente, but the consolidation and elaboration of detente in terms of the accommodation of concrete interests has turned out to be the primary thrust of its European policy. The active pursuit of accommodations in Europe began in bilateral trade and diplomatic relations (most importantly, between the FRG and Eastern European countries) and in U.S.-Soviet preparations for Strategic Arms Limitation Talks (SALT) several years before the Nixon Administration came into office, only to be almost frozen by Russia's intervention in Czechoslovakia in the summer of 1968. In pursuit of a global *modus vivendi* with the Soviet Union, the Nixon Administration cautiously restudied the bases for a strategic arms agreement and finally, in November 1969, began the series of bilateral negotiations that culminated in the "interim" arms limitation treaty signed at the Moscow "summit" in June 1972.

[3] "Western collective defense in Europe has deterred war for more than two decades and provided the essential condition of security in which free European institutions could revive and flourish. Today, the military balance underpins the overall stability on the Continent which makes detente feasible in the 1970's. East-West diplomacy in Europe is more active today than at any time since the Second World War; new hopes and new complexities are emerging. This is hardly the time for the West to abandon the very cohesion and stability that have brought these new opportunities about." Richard M. Nixon, *U.S. Foreign Policy for the 1970's,* February 9, 1972, p. 42.

[4] "We continue to feel that political and defense cooperation within Europe will be the fulfillment of European unity. European and American interests in defense and East-West diplomacy are fundamentally parallel and give sufficient incentive for coordinating independent policies. Two strong powers in the West would add flexibility to Western diplomacy, and could increasingly share the responsibilities of decision." *Ibid.,* p. 40.

At the same time, West Germany resumed its *Ostpolitik*, begun some eight years earlier; and Chancellor Willy Brandt, elevating *Ostpolitik* to a major national program, took energetic efforts to normalize relations with the Soviet Union, Eastern Europe, and eventually East Germany on the basis of formal recognition of the status quo. These efforts resulted in Bonn's Eastern treaties with Moscow and Warsaw, which essentially recognized the territorial political status quo. Bonn's coalition government, partly in deference to its right wing, then made Germany's ratification of these treaties contingent on the Soviet Union's agreement to a satisfactory four-power treaty on Berlin (to be elaborated by agreements between the two Germanies and between the GDR and the Berlin Senate) in order to affirm and improve rights of Western access and communication. The four powers reached such an agreement in November, 1972; and shortly afterward the Federal Republic of Germany and the German Democratic Republic agreed to establish normal relations.

In the United States, as in West Germany, completion of the Berlin treaties, depriving Russia of a primary lever against the status quo, became the test of the further development of *Ostpolitik* generally, including America's willingness to participate in a conference on European security and pursue negotiations at the summit in Moscow. The Soviet Union, in turn, made its willingness to sign the final protocol of the Berlin agreements contingent on the West German parliament's ratification of the treaties with the Soviet Union and Poland.[5] The eventual acceptance by all parties of these linkages and counter-linkages cleared the way for completion of the Berlin agreements through negotiations between the two Germanies. It also cleared the way for a conference on european security, which the American government now calls a conference on security and cooperation in Europe (CSCE). Poland and other East European countries have enthusiastically promoted CSCE, the Soviet Union has endorsed it (initially, without American participation), and the United States has skeptically agreed to go along with it, contingent first upon the Berlin accord coming into effect and, then, upon agreement to parallel discussions of an agreement on mutual balanced force reductions (MBFR).

At the same time, President Nixon did not neglect America's own *Ostpolitik*, which had proceeded under the banner of "peaceful en-

---

[5] For a concise analysis of the politics of these linkages and counter-linkages and their relationship to Brandt's *Ostpolitik*, see Kenneth A. Myers, "Ostpolitik and American Security Interests in Europe," The Center for Strategic and International Studies, Georgetown University, 1972.

gagement" in the previous administration. Seeking new levers of constraint against the Soviet Union as a proximate goal and, as an ultimate goal, the evolution of an all-European "system of security" resting on the "normalization" of Soviet relations with East European countries as well as the "reconciliation" of Eastern and Western Europe (including the two Germanies), he became the first president to visit Romania and Yugoslavia; and he received their heads of state in Washington in return.

More substantial in its ostensible objective than any of these moves toward European detente is the project of negotiating MBFR. But in MBFR the objective of achieving the counterpart of a SALT agreement in European conventional and tactical nuclear arms merges uneasily with the more immediate domestic political objective of preventing the premature unilateral reduction of American troops. First proposed by the North Atlantic Council in June 1968, MBFR was initially embraced by the Nixon Administration as a counter to the Soviet Union's disturbingly vague proposal for a European security conference and to Senator Mansfield's pressure for the unilateral substantial reduction of U.S. troops in Europe. But then, to the administration's surprise, Brezhnev announced, in Tbilisi in May 1971, that the Soviet Union was ready to discuss MBFR. This announcement gave credence to the administration's argument against the unilateral withdrawal of American troops, but it also compelled the American government to approach the technical and political complexities of this subject with the intention of preparing a serious negotiating position—a task that almost all the experts viewed with profound skepticism.[6]

The U.S.-Soviet agreements at the Moscow summit in June 1972 gave a new momentum to CSCE and MBFR. Therefore, in the summer of 1972 it seemed that a broad range of European issues might be on the agenda of East-West conferences, ministerial meetings, international standing committees, and similar forums for years to come. If there is a common international aim underlying this process

[6] The technical/political problem of negotiating MBFR arises principally from the asymmetrical functions and capabilities of Eastern and Western forces, particularly because of Russia's proximity to Central Europe and its larger more rapidly mobilizable reserves. But some kinds of arms control provisions, like those that might regulate the reintroduction and reinforcement of forces, would pose more political than technical obstacles to agreement, and not only from the Soviet Union's standpoint. The implications of MBFR for intra-allied relations, particularly with respect to West Germany's position, would constitute another realm of political difficulties. The best treatment of this subject is Christoph Bertram, *Mutual Force Reductions in Europe: The Political Aspects*, Adelphi Papers No. 84, (London: International Institute for Strategic Studies, January, 1972).

of accommodation and normalization, it is not to produce a grand settlement formally ending the division of Europe into opposing blocs. It is, first, to ratify the territorial/political status quo and remove it from international contention and manipulation and, second, to mitigate the tensions and rigidities of international relations across East-West boundaries so that the military concerns that led to the formation of opposing blocs will no longer be a major factor in European international relations.

If the expanding network of negotiations and agreements on East-West issues should succeed in this objective, it would seem to vindicate the strategy of containment and the whole structure of military power underlying it, although in a way that was scarcely foreseen at the outset of the cold war. Consequently, President Nixon, like the allied leaders, was inclined to keep the familiar military structure—American troops and all—intact at least until the process of accommodation is further advanced. Accordingly, for the sake of European security and the cohesion of NATO he pledged to maintain and improve American forces in Europe and promised not to reduce them except through reciprocal reductions negotiated with the Warsaw Pact by the United States and its allies.

Primarily to counter domestic pressure for retrenchment, the Nixon Administration made the fulfillment of this pledge contingent upon an "improvement" in forces. In December 1970, the European allies agreed to add $1 billion to their collective annual defense contributions for the next five years. In December 1971, they decided to add another $1 billion for the fiscal year. In addition, the FRG agreed to pay $2 billion in 1972-73 for the maintenance of American forces in order to help offset U.S. balance of payments deficits. This payment fell short of the American objective of maintaining its forces in Europe "with balance of payments consequences no different from those of maintaining the same forces in the United States."[7] But the increased allied contributions to collective defense, combined with the prospect of negotiations on MBFR, did succeed for the time being in fending off Senatorial pressure for substantial unilateral reductions.

[7] Nixon, *U.S. Foreign Policy for the 1970's*, p. 45. This objective is a response to the view that, although America's European defense burden in budgetary terms is neither onerous nor disproportionate to America's relative wealth or security benefits, the maintenance of American forces in Europe does impose an economically and politically significant balance of payments cost (accounting for about one-half of America's net liquidity deficit). On the balance of payments problem and burden-sharing and how to deal with them, see Timothy W. Stanley's testimony of October 27, 1971, in U.S. House of Representatives, 92d Congress, 1st sess., *Hearings*, Special Subcommittee on North Atlantic Treaty Organization Commitments, House Committee on Armed Services, pp. 12842-72.

Theoretically, an alternative to maintaining the existing structure of military power in NATO as the basis for European security and detente was to create a European defense community within the alliance that could substantially relieve the burden of American troops and even on American military leadership in Europe. Maximizing European self-reliance in securing Western Europe had been the basis of Congressional support for European unity at the outset of the cold war. The Nixon Administration was more receptive to the concept of a united Western Europe with full self-reliance (as opposed to various formulas of European federation or confederation within an Atlantic partnership dominated militarily by the United States) than previous administrations. Declaring not only the "end of American tutelage" but also the "end of the era of automatic unity" in relations with the European allies, the president reaffirmed America's support for the growth of European unity, even at the possible price of increased economic competition; and he did so for larger geopolitical reasons, not merely to reduce America's economic and political burden.[8]

[8] The administration's basic rationale for European unity was the promotion of Europe's vitality, independence, and responsibility, on the supposition that a truly self-reliant Western Europe would act more effectively in its own behalf and add flexibility to Western diplomacy. It recognized that such a united Europe might also more effectively pursue policies unfavorable to some American interests but held that the overall benefit would be worth the cost. Thus in the president's first report he said, "We consider that the possible economic price of a truly unified Europe is outweighed by the gain in the political vitality of the West as a whole." (Nixon, *U.S. Foreign Policy for the 1970's*, p. 32.) In muted form the administration's advocacy of European unity reflected the view that Henry Kissinger had written shortly before coming into office in the Brookings Institution's study, *Agenda for the Nation*, although his view stressed the limits of American power more than the president's: "It is not 'natural,'" he wrote, "that the major decisions about the defense of an area so potentially powerful as Western Europe should be made three thousand miles away. It is not 'normal' that Atlantic policies should be geared to American conceptions." (p. 597) "Such a relationship is not healthy in the long run. Even with the best will, the present structure encourages American unilateralism and European irresponsibility. This is a serious problem for the United States. If the United States remains the trustee of every non-communist area, it will exhaust its psychological resources. No country can act wisely simultaneously in every part of the globe at every moment of time. A more pluralistic world—especially in relationships with friends—is profoundly in our long-term interest. Political multipolarity, while difficult to get used to, is the precondition for a new period of creativity. Painful as it may be to admit, we could benefit from a counterweight that would discipline our occasional impetuosity and by supplying a historical perspective, modify our penchant for abstract and 'final' solutions." (p. 599) "Central Issues of American Foreign Policy," in Kermit Gordon, ed., *Agenda for the Nation* (Washington, D.C.: The Brookings Institution, 1968).

In practice, however, President Nixon made the first priority of European policy the development of detente. This priority determined that a movement toward West European military coalescence would be an objective distinctly subordinate to maintaining the existing military structure in Europe and attaining force reductions by East-West agreement. It meant that no West European defense coordination would disturb the existing structure of military responsibilities in NATO. If the process of intra-European coordination should eventually lead to an integrated European defense force and even an Anglo-French nuclear force in the service of the European allies, the United States would not be displeased. Indeed, it might even cooperate. But the process would have to spring from the Europeans' own efforts, not from an American grand design or from American initiatives and pressures. European military autonomy, if it were feasible at all, would probably be the final stage of a process of economic and diplomatic coalescence that still had a long, hard way to go.

The Strength of Existing American Relationships with Europe

At this time the NATO allies clearly regard the continuation of American preponderance in the management of Western Europe's military security as the most satisfactory relationship for the indefinite future. Differences of military strategy and defense policies no longer trouble this relationship, partly because a rough consensus has been achieved over the years, but largely because military security is no longer an immediate or lively concern. Differences on trade and monetary policies have largely replaced military issues as a source of tension between the United States and its European allies, but so far these differences do not seem to jeopardize the structure of military responsibilities. Similarly, substantive and procedural diplomatic issues between the United States and its allies loom larger than before, but they do not provoke movement toward European military independence. The European allies remain sensitive to any indication that the United States might be entering into understandings and agreements with the Soviet Union that affect their interests without informing or consulting them; but the United States has been sufficiently attentive to these sensitivities to preserve allied defense cooperation. Allied fears of U.S.-Soviet "collusion" have been mitigated, if not dispelled, by intra-alliance consultations on bilateral negotiations, such as America's extensive briefings to allies on SALT. The winding down of America's involvement in Vietnam and America's military retrenchment in Asia have overcome European concerns that Asian entanglements will distract the United States from attention to Europe. By ceasing to importune the allies with grand designs and self-righteous advice, the Nixon Administration has removed an irritating feature of American preponderance, especially in its relations with France.

Indeed, the European allies are not only satisfied with the structure of military relationships in NATO, they are quite explicitly anxious to keep as strong as possible what they regard as the key to this structure—the American military presence. As one would expect, the West German government has declared that American troops are essential to European security and the success of *Ostpolitik*. More noteworthy is France's position. Whereas General De Gaulle had complained about American hegemony in Europe's defense, formally severed France's relations with the military organization of the alliance, and declared France's nuclear force the only reliable guarantor of French security, now French leaders (carrying out a shift of policy that began before De Gaulle left office) are in the forefront of those calling for the maintenance of the existing level of American troops in Europe, ostensibly on the same strategic grounds that Secretary of Defense McNamara used to propound. The French military in many ways has quietly coordinated its plans and exercises with NATO's. France's nuclear force has ceased to be a point of political leverage or contention. The United States government has permitted the French to acquire some of the militarily sensitive information and equipment that it used to withhold.

The dominant role of the superpowers in European diplomacy indicates that military preponderance still translates into political influence, but the allies apparently accept the disparity of power between them and the superpowers as an unavoidable fact of international life. Besides, their military dependence does not prevent them from playing roles on the diplomatic stage that are consonant with the scope of their interests and ambitions. America's initiatives in detente have opened the way for America's allies to pursue their own *Ostpolitik*. America's rapprochement with China has encouraged the allies to explore communication with the PRC, as China openly supports the strengthening of the Common Market and opposes East-West accommodations that might relieve Soviet armed forces for service in the East. Much to Soviet concern, West German visits to Peking have raised the possibility of Bonn using rapprochement with Peking (including the prospect of diplomatic recognition) as leverage against the Soviets in *Ostpolitik*—for example, to induce them to put pressure on the East Germans in the Berlin negotiations.[9]

As American "hegemony" seems to be no hindrance to allied diplomatic maneuvers, neither is it regarded as an obstacle to West European aspirations to unity. Within the existing structure of power there has been enough progress toward West European coalescence in the economic and political fields to provide a sense of movement toward European unity and to sustain a feeling of collective identity separate from the United States. Britain's entry into the Common Market has raised more tangible hopes of European unity than were ever afforded by the theory that political spillover from economic integration would produce a European federation. The success of the relatively unheralded "Davignon processes" of exchanges of information and regular consultations among foreign ministers shows that interstate policy coordination on the model of the old Fouchet Plan is a more fruitful path toward European unity than the functionalists or federationists envisioned.[10]

But this process of economic and political coalescence shows few signs of extending to commensurate military integration. The problems of non-military coalescence, such as those attending the effort to form a European monetary union, seem challenging enough without being complicated by the problems of fully integrating defense establishments. To be sure, there have been increasing bilateral and multilateral consultations on military questions among the major allies (for example, in the Eurogroup, a committee composed of the Defense Ministers of ten European allies minus France), but these measures of intra-European military coordination are quite secondary to the coordination that takes place under American guidance in NATO. Efforts toward joint arms production and procurement, once viewed by champions of European unity as the most promising way to begin military integration, have proved to be very difficult politically and rather unrewarding economically. As for the more ambitious project of forming an Anglo-French nucleus of a European nuclear force, despite Prime Minister Heath's endorsement of the idea before he assumed office and indications that President Pompidou is at least not opposed to the idea in principle, the British and French

[9] On these developments, see the interesting columns of Victor Zorza; for example, those in the *Washington Post* on August 5 and 8, 1972.

[10] A good account of the dominance and adequacy of intergovernmental cooperation and coordination of national policies in Western Europe is Theodore Geiger, *Transatlantic Relations in the Prospect of an Enlarged European Community* (London: British-North American Committee, 1970).

governments have evidently concluded, after intermittent and unsatisfactory discussions of the matter, that any effort to negotiate such a project would be premature. Their caution is in line with the prevailing assumption in Europe and the United States that, although an integrated European military force might naturally follow the establishment of a European concert or confederation, to try to achieve the former before the latter would probably doom both to failure.

Thus, although the present process of non-military coalescence may prepare the foundation for the eventual military coalescence and independence of Western Europe, this eventuality is evidently not going to materialize simply as the natural outgrowth of economic and diplomatic cooperation. Rather, it will depend on the organized political will of the major West European governments deliberately concerting their military resources and policies in order to acquire collectively the full attributes of a new center of power in the world. At this point in the era of negotiation the driving motives for European unity seem too limited, cautious, and pragmatic to inspire such creative energy. External relations are preoccupied with economic objectives and East-West diplomacy. Domestic economic and environmental concerns absorb any surplus energy that might be applied to the construction of a European superpower.

Thus there are many signs of satisfaction with, or at least complacent acquiescence to, the familiar structure of power and responsibility in NATO and no signs of an alternative emerging. On the other hand, the general satisfaction of the United States and its allies with the familiar structure is no assurance that it will endure. It might erode from its very success.

The Weakness of Existing American
Relationships with Europe

Let us suppose that the military balance comes to seem so stable that the conditions for maintaining it cease to concern Western governments. That is close to the present situation. Under this condition the FRG, despite its genuine professions of prior attachment to the West, will feel free to devote its total energy to the alluring objective of reconciliation with the GDR. Alternatively, West Germany's *loss* of confidence in American and allied protection might compel its leaders to seek security almost totally through *Ostpolitik*, but present trends indicate a growing not declining German self-confidence.

The Soviet Union, by making its sanction of German reconciliation conditional upon West Germany's cooperation with Soviet conceptions of European security, will be in a position to discourage further FRG integration into a more self-reliant West European bloc and even to loosen the FRG's Western ties. But with the Federal Republic's security ties to the West no longer providing much of an incentive for diplomatic cooperation between Germany and its allies, and with the GDR matching the FRG's pace of rapprochement as it seeks to establish its status as one of the world's major powers, the Soviets need hardly be concerned about West Germany's ties to the West. They may even begin to regard these ties as a useful constraint. In any case, the British and French are likely to find the pace of intra-German rapprochement disconcerting, with the result that they may in effect isolate the FRG diplomatically and leave the United States as the only Western tie and constraint upon West Germany.

Maintaining an American presence in Europe for the major purpose of restraining Germany, however, would not be likely to recommend itself to the American government for long under these conditions. Nor would it be a role calculated to promote constructive relations with either Germany or France and Britain. Thus many who would regard reconciliation of the two Germanies as a desirable goal in itself might regard it as a threat to the European equilibrium if it were pursued at the expense of Germany's attachment to its Western allies.

It is impossible to predict in detail but not hard to foresee in general how, by some such route, the present period of diplomatic maneuver could erode the structure of relationships that made it possible. If the crux of erosion were Germany's detachment from the West without some compensating reduction of power in the East or increase of power in the West, the prospect of stabilizing a revised structure of relationships in Europe would be dim.

One need not carry the scenario to this length to see how the success of the present structure may carry the seeds of its own decay. Suppose, for example, that MBFR proves to be as difficult to negotiate as the experts now believe. How long will it be before the European allies come to place so little value upon maintaining a military force of anything like present dimensions that they are unwilling to pay the price in support costs, defense contributions, and accommodation of American economic interests that is needed to keep the Americans from unilaterally withdrawing most or all of its forces in Europe? Might not the Russians facilitate this outcome if they offered unilateral withdrawals from Eastern Europe as a *quid pro quo* or, more likely, if they simply withdrew their forces and demanded reciprocity?[11]

In any event, the standard arguments for maintaining troops in Europe are likely to become less and less convincing with the passing of time. In protracted detente the argument that one should not remove the military condition that made detente possible will tend to become too abstract to counter the argument that detente makes that condition obsolete. The argument that American troops must not be reduced unilaterally pending the achievement of internationally agreed reductions would become threadbare if the problems of achieving reductions that are genuinely "balanced" to the satisfaction of both sides and America's allies seem insurmountable.

But let us assume that all but symbolic numbers of American troops are unilaterally withdrawn under these circumstances. The prevailing assumption now in all the NATO countries is that the substantial unilateral withdrawal of American troops from Europe, whatever the effect on European security and diplomacy might be, would certainly not move the European allies to compensate materially for this withdrawal or to assume the primary responsibility for their own defense. It would merely convince them that the communist military threat to Europe no longer requires sustaining more than token conventional forces. Then they would find themselves rushing to Moscow for security, perhaps in pursuit of beguiling but fruitless schemes for "neutralizing" Central Europe. And they would grow increasingly divided over the military and political balance among themselves.

Of course, this kind of scenario may be quite fanciful, and there is a distinct tactical motive in the assurance with which it is predicted by anxious proponents of the status quo. Nonetheless, it is no less plausible than the supposition that unilateral American withdrawals would shock the allies into coalescence when the incentives for coalescence are otherwise so weak. The very fact that over the years everyone has attributed so much political weight to the presence of American troops in Europe makes it all the more likely that the unilateral and uncoordinated withdrawal of these troops would fulfill the dire prophecies.

This is not to say that even the total withdrawal of American forces would cause some political or military disaster. That, too, is

[11] Quite apart from possible political dividends, the Soviets might find such withdrawals worth taking in order to concentrate military resources on the China front if they believed that the various East-West agreements and negotiations assured the passivity of their Western front.

quite unpredictable. Nevertheless, one can understand why responsible policy makers dare not operate on the optimistic assumption that the resulting imbalance of military power would have no adverse effects. Rather, prudence impels them to assume that Europe's self-confidence, its sense of security, its harmony, and even its progress toward economic and political coalescence would be jeopardized in ways that are no less likely because they cannot be precisely known. And yet, although it is widely believed that American troops *will* be unilaterally withdrawn before long, no one prepares to adjust Europe's own defense efforts to that contingency, partly because the allies suspect that the greater their efforts to organize a separate defense community, the more inclined Americans will be to withdraw.

The Alternative of Devolution

Those who worry about the long-run instability of the present structure of relationships in NATO and who are also anxious to preserve a convincing equilibrium of power in such a critical and historically troublesome area as Europe must either look toward ways of strengthening the existing structure or toward ways of creating a new structure consistent with such an equilibrium, recognizing that in either case a stable structure of relationships in Europe will depend as much on harmonious economic and diplomatic relations among the Western allies and upon East-West accommodations as upon an adequate military balance. Today the conventional prescriptions for revitalizing the alliance are almost entirely in the first category: strengthening the existing structure.[12] But they have little or nothing to say about the organization of military power.

Closer to revision but also much less specific in content is the proposal to create a kind of trilateral economic and political condominimum among the United States, the Common Market core, and Japan.[13] But this proposal, too, in addition to its vagueness and dubi-

[12] They include the Europeanization of burden sharing, the coordination of Western *Ostpolitik*, the institutionalization of regular Atlantic summit meetings, the formalization of the Eurogroup as a European defense caucus within NATO, and various proposals for revising Atlantic trade and monetary relations. See, for example, Curt Gasteyger, "Europe and America at the Crossroads," Atlantic Papers 4, The Atlantic Institute, March, 1972, and U.S. House of Representatives, 92d Congress, 1st sess., *Hearings*, Special Subcommittee on North Atlantic Treaty Organization Commitments, House Committee on Armed Services, October 1971 to March 1972.

[13] Former Under Secretary of State George W. Ball advocates, as he has for a number of years, "building a coalition of major non-Communist industrialized nations by first turning the United States-Japanese Mutual Security Treaty into a

ous feasibility, fails to address the issues of the military balance and the division of labor in maintaining it, except to urge the maintenance of American forces in Europe. It is, in fact, based on opposition to greater West European or Japanese military independence, which it identifies with a Gaullist nuclear posture.

If we look for plausible revisionist conceptions that pertain directly to the structure of military power in the world, there is really only one: the orderly devolution of power and responsibilities from the United States to a West European defense community. Scarcely anyone has proposed putting this conception into operation immediately;[14] but it is worth considering, if only because examining it illuminates the conditions underlying the present state of affairs and points to an idea whose time may come, even if it comes too late.

The case for devolution, on grounds of immediate American interest, is simply that it would enable the United States to maintain its essential security interest in Europe under a reduced military, economic, and political burden. This point is commonly accompanied by an argument of equity which objects to the "anomaly" of the United States maintaining its dominant military role and presence in Europe this long after World War II when its European allies, hav-

mature coalition, then progressively integrating that relationship into an expanded Atlantic partnership that would include in its purview the Far East as well as the West." "We Are Playing a Dangerous Game with Japan," *New York Times Magazine*, June 25, 1972, p. 38. Zbigniew Brzezinski advocates a trilateral "community of developed nations" with a "Council for Global Cooperation" on the model of a higher-level OECD, which might be expanded to include other developed nations, and finally, even communist countries. But this community would be organized to cope with technical, economic, and environmental cooperation rather than to coordinate military-political policies: *Between Two Ages: America's Role in the Technetronic Age* (New York: Viking Press, 1970), pp. 293ff.

[14] The most persuasive exception is David Calleo in *The Atlantic Fantasy: the U.S., NATO, and Europe* (Baltimore: The Johns Hopkins University Press, 1970) and his testimony on October 27, 1971, in *Hearings*, Special Subcommittee on North Atlantic Treaty Organization Commitments, pp. 12873–12903. In *The Discipline of Power* (Boston: Little, Brown & Co., 1968), George Ball advocated that Western Europe become a "second Western area power capable of sharing with the United States the burdens and decisions of the West in a way the individual European nations can never do." (p. 347). But until Western Europe were united, he strongly opposed even the existing British and French nuclear forces as dangerous, divisive, and ineffective and proposed absorbing them into a seabased multi-lateral force in which the United States would have exclusive control over the decision to use nuclear weapons. Ball was typical of the most ardent advocates of a more equal partnership with Western Europe in that he was also most vigorously opposed to President de Gaulle's assertion of French and "European" independence.

ing more than recovered from the war, are materially capable of taking care of their own security. But the case for devolution can be put on broader grounds of mutual self-interest as well:

1. Without devolution the strength and cohesion of the present structure of power and responsibility will erode, leaving Europe weak and divided and the United States isolated.

2. Through devolution Western Europe could attain a level of power and responsibility commensurate with its capabilities, and the United States could maintain its commitment to Europe at a level of effort more compatible with America's revised conception of its world role, thereby stabilizing the division of labor between the United States and its allies for the long run.

3. Devolution would release the latent energy of Western Europe for the responsible pursuit of collective external interests and would give the constructive task of coalescence new stimulus, whereas the perpetuation of European dependence on the United States in a protracted period of detente will lead to growing apathy, irresponsibility, and parochialism in Western Europe (much of it transferred to resentment and suspicion of the United States) and will obstruct the momentum of coalescence with growing intra-European divisions.

4. West German integration into a strong, cohesive, and self-reliant West European political and defense community would eliminate the potentially divisive conflict between *Ostpolitik* and *Westpolitik* in the FRG and deprive the Russians of a lever for isolating West Germany from its European allies.

5. It would also relieve the United States of the political burden of being the exclusive protector and container of Germany in a period in which German diplomacy will be the potentially disturbing focal point of East-West politics in Europe.

6. The creation of a West European political and military entity that could act as a new pole of power would further constrain Soviet behavior, enhance the independence of Eastern Europe, and create new diplomatic opportunities to construct a network of agreements and understandings embracing all five major centers of power in the world.

7. Underlying all these points is the assumption that the principal interests of the West European allies and the United States are sufficiently convergent so that the allies' increased freedom of action would not disadvantage the United States but would revitalize the alliance.

These reasons for devolution, like most basic considerations in the political world, depend heavily on intangible values and on intuition,

scarcely susceptible to proof or disproof. It is not surprising, therefore, that the arguments against devolution generally concentrate on
allegations of practical infeasibility. But the feasibility of devolution,
of course, depends on what devolution is.

It is not easy to say exactly what would constitute devolution. Making a West European collectivity primarily responsible for its own
security is ultimately a matter of creating a new center of military
and diplomatic self-confidence, initiative, and influence—a center that
would view its military and foreign policies less in terms of eliciting
American support than in terms of pursuing its own interests. But
this is an intangible political objective that cannot be measured in
relative numbers of troops or the distribution of military commands.
Moreover, even the most cohesive, decisive, and autonomous European structure, to be successful, would still have to depend to an
important extent on America's nuclear guarantee and on harmonizing
its political and military policies with the United States. Despite the
difficulty of defining precisely the conditions of independent power
and influence, however, one would readily recognize the multiple internal and external signs of their existence if the hypothetical European structure were to emerge. One would recognize the emergence
of a cohesive new center of power and decision just as one recognizes that the West European allies are now a fragmented military
and (to an important extent) diplomatic dependent of the United
States.

Would devolution necessarily require a unified European military
force? Perhaps not if West European military security could be taken
for granted and if military power ceased to be relevant to the central
issues of international politics. But unless East-West relations should
become as harmonious as intra-Western relations, military security
will continue to be at least a latent concern in Western Europe.
Therefore, the extent of the allies' dependence on American military
protection seems bound to affect their freedom of action. Since the
central issues of international politics in Europe include the distribution of military power in the present context of multilateral arms
control negotiations as much as in the previous context of military
deterrence and confrontation, one cannot assume that traditionally
the principal instrument of national sovereignty in external relations
has become obsolete.

The kind of military force—its size, composition, structure, and organization—that would be needed to implement devolution is too
large a question to deal with here. But undoubtedly the European
allies collectively have the economic, technological, and human re-

sources to create an adequate armed force if they want to. Would this force have to include a centrally controlled or coordinated nuclear force? Perhaps the argument that nuclear independence is essential to political independence is less compelling with respect to a European grouping than when General De Gaulle made it in behalf of France. But it is still hard to imagine a center of power claiming anything like equality with or independence from the United States without the capacity to compel the Soviet Union to regard it seriously as an independent source of a possible nuclear decision.[15]

The pragmatic argument against devolution is simply that it would be imprudent to upset the existing structure of allied relationships, which has worked so well, when the feasibility of substantially transferring power and responsibility from the United States to a new West European political and military entity is so doubtful and the advantages of such a transfer are so hypothetical. In this view the historic political obstacles against states of roughly equal power concerting their military forces in peacetime are compounded by the atmosphere of detente and the concomitant domestic opposition to new defense projects (particularly if they would raise defense budgets). The obstacles to nuclear coalescence seem particularly formidable, not only because of the problem of joint British and French control but also because of the problem of giving Germany associate membership without a share of the decision to use nuclear weapons.[16]

Many Americans who openly support the goal of European unity, a more nearly equal trans-Atlantic partnership, and the like are profoundly—and perhaps too smugly—skeptical of the capacity and will of the West European states to assume and discharge such a formidable responsibility. But they also regard devolution as undesirable even if it were feasible. Not only do they fear that an independent

[15] This leaves open the question of how large a nuclear force would be needed to convince the Soviet Union that a West European coalition were more than merely symbolic or an adjunct of America's nuclear force. Without going into the technical, strategic, and political intricacies of this question, it can be said that what would be needed is not a force that could supplant the U.S. nuclear force but only one that could credibly inflict a sufficient cost upon Soviet military operations and civilian values to add a decisive inhibition to hostile Soviet actions. There is no technical or economic reason why the European allies could not, in a few years, and even without American material assistance, build such a force around nuclear submarines and tactical nuclear weapons.

[16] A closely-reasoned and detailed analysis of the technical, legal, and political problems—with the emphasis on the political problems—of creating an Anglo-French nuclear force is Ian Smart, *Future Conditional: The Prospect for Anglo-French Nuclear Co-operation*, Adelphi Papers 78 (London: The Institute for Strategic Studies, August, 1971).

and united Europe would clash with American economic interests and complicate American diplomacy in an area that is as important to us as Alaska. They also fear that a European nuclear force sufficiently strong to be used independently would dangerously complicate the bilateral strategic balance and jeopardize all the bilateral technical and procedural checks against accidental, unauthorized, hair-trigger, spasmodic, and unlimited employment of nuclear weapons.

To these arguments against devolution another one has been added in this period of intensified diplomatic accommodation and maneuver: the effort to create a new center of military power in which the FRG were an integral member would intensify the Soviet Union's consistent animus toward European unity and therefore threaten to upset detente. To this prospect the obvious retort is: So what? Moscow might make threatening noises, but would Soviet opposition to a European defense community really take precedence over its interest in freezing the European territorial and political status quo? Might not the Soviets actually become more obliging when faced with the prospect of serious West European coalescence? In any event, what could the Soviet Union do in East-West relations to damage vital West European interests?

This defiant reasoning raises a valid point, but it is not one that is likely to appeal to European governments—or, for that matter, to an American president—who have invested so much political capital in detente. Moreover, in some respects the effort to seek security through East-West accommodation and the effort to seek security through intra-Western devolution are contradictory—in political reality, if not in logic. To try to undertake devolution within the context of MBFR, for example, could complicate an already extremely difficult problem of formulating a genuinely negotiable allied position on force reductions.[17] If an MBFR agreement were achieved, the Soviet Union might construe it as a right to intervene continually in NATO decisions and policies designed to strengthen and adjust the West European defense posture on the ground that such measures would

[17] It can be argued that the necessity of formulating allied force reductions for MBFR could serve as a stimulus to plans for devolution, but in political reality it would be extremely difficult to combine the process of international with the process of intra-alliance negotiation. In practice, either one or the other would have to take precedence in determining Western positions on such questions as whether to apply cuts and limitations to foreign-stationed or to indigenous forces or both, whether to apply arms reductions to the two Germanies or to a larger geographical area, how to deal with tactical nuclear weapons and "forward based [air] systems," and how to control the reintroduction of forces.

alter the balance. Correspondingly, any project to create a European nuclear force, particularly with American material assistance, would run afoul of Soviet objections that the conditions of its adherence to the bilateral strategic arms agreement were being violated.

For these reasons those who are concerned about preserving the strength and cohesion of the North Atlantic alliance may understandably choose to shore up the existing structure and avoid the risk that futile efforts to transfer power and responsibilities would only precipitate America's withdrawal without creating any European substitute. Even those who look forward to devolution in the long run may conclude that the priority of East-West accommodations and the rudimentary stage of West European coalescence render premature any move in that direction now.

Yet waiting for the ideal time for devolution may only lead to missed opportunities. For all we know, 1973 through 1977 may be the optimum time to start the process. At the head of the United Kingdom and France are statesmen who might take the crucial initiatives that are needed to give devolution a proper start. American troops have not yet been unilaterally withdrawn. The European allies are still confident of American protection but have resigned themselves to eventual troop withdrawals. East-West tensions are low, and the Soviets are still constrained by their eagerness to complete the settlement of the territorial/political status quo. At the same time, the process of East-West accommodation has gone far enough, with enough success, to enable the Western states to turn to the problems of intra-Western reconstruction as a harmonious concomitant rather than an obstacle to detente. But be that as it may, can governments be expected to abandon familiar working relationships with known problems in order to embrace bold new designs with unknown problems? Their general reluctance to do so may reflect as much prudence as inertia.

The Nixon Strategy in East Asia

President Nixon's foreign policy has reaffirmed the primacy of Western Europe in America's international scale of priorities. In doing so, it has in effect lowered the relative value of the Far East with the exception of Japan. It is no accident, therefore, that first and foremost, the Nixon Doctrine has been applied to East Asia since the president first enunciated it at his Guam press conference in July 1969. The reason is clear. Because of the disparity between the magnitude of America's involvement and interest, East Asia became the area of America's most controversial containment efforts, including two large and unpopular local wars. It is the area in which the United States most distinctly overreached itself in exclusively assuming the burdens of protecting the "Free World" from communist incursions. It is the area in which the United States became massively entangled in a miserable war that threatened to undermine the internal and external underpinnings of its dominant global position.

In East Asia, unlike Western Europe, the Nixon Administration has undertaken a substantial military retrenchment. In more farreaching terms it has coupled retrenchment with an announced policy of transferring America's security responsibilities to the countries in the area. But it has also refrained from transferring regional security responsibilities to Japan, the one center of allied power that could discharge such responsibilities. As in Europe, it has refrained not only because the ally is opposed to devolution but also because it does not wish retrenchment to take place at the expense of a diplomatic equilibrium that facilitates a global *modus vivendi* with the Soviet Union. So in East Asia, too, the continuation of America's preponderant role in managing the security of its major ally is, in effect, the condition for maintaining a stable structure of international relationships in a period of diplomatic accommodation and maneuver.

In applying the Nixon Doctrine to East Asia the emphasis lay, at first, on American military retrenchment and a redistribution of security burdens from the United States to its allies and other friendly countries. The nature and scope of retrenchment soon became clear —so clear, in fact, as to call into question America's commitments to its allies and require their reaffirmation—but the nature and scope of the redistribution of burdens was somewhat ambiguous. On the one hand, the rationale for redistribution could be taken to justify a full-scale devolution of security responsibility. In this case, Japan would have to take on most of America's burden. On the other hand, the administration refrained from pushing the logic of devolution beyond Japan's undertaking a larger share of the close-in defense of the home islands, saying that the precise relationship among Japan and the other three major powers involved in East Asia would remain inchoate pending further policy developments.

In a massive withdrawal of troops from Vietnam, President Nixon reduced American forces from over 500,000 to less than 3,000 in his first term and eliminated America's ground combat role. He also withdrew about 20,000 of the 60,000 U.S. military personnel in South Korea; 12,000 from Japan and 5,000 from Okinawa (leaving about 27,000 and 43,000 respectively); 16,000 from Thailand (where, however, some forces were restored in 1972 as they were withdrawn from Vietnam), and smaller numbers from the Philippines and Taiwan. The deactivation of two divisions returning from Vietnam and one returning from Korea left only about four divisions available for Asian contingencies. Secretary of Defense Laird announced in the annual Defense Report for 1971: "With regard to U.S. force capabilities in Asia, we do not plan for the long term to maintain separate large U.S. ground combat forces specifically oriented just to this theater, but we do intend to maintain strong air, naval, and support capabilities. . . . In the future, we expect the emphasis in Asia more and more to be placed on U.S. support to our allies who themselves provide the required manpower."[18]

In some respects, this retrenchment spoke for itself, but its place in the larger context of foreign policy needed explanation. President Nixon and his Assistant for National Security Affairs, Henry Kissinger, explained that military retrenchment is the obverse of an overdue political and psychological retrenchment. But retrenchment, they held, is not an end in itself. It is the prelude to the reconstruction of a new international order in East Asia within which the United States can safely transfer much of its overinflated security burden to the indigenous countries. The purpose of retrenchment, the president's report said, is not so much to reduce America's physical burden as to relieve Americans of the political and psychological strain of formulating the plans and programs and making the decisions for others who ought to be taking responsibility for their own security and sharing the task of building a structure of peace, in which they all have an equal stake.[19] To this end the president pledged military and economic assistance to Asian allies and friends, pointing to the example of the U.S. agreement to help modernize South Korean armed forces as part of the decision to reduce the American presence by 20,000.

Full revelation of the nature of the new structure of peace within which the United States hopes to transfer its responsibilities, the administration advised, must await decisions not yet made by the major countries involved. But the structure, it held, must rest on two pillars: regional groupings of the small states (which were touted by the president's annual reports with an optimism that was unique in his government); and the policies of the four large states with major

[18] *Defense Report on President Nixon's Strategy for Peace*, Statement of Secretary of Defense Melvin R. Laird before the U.S. House of Representatives, 92d Congress, 1st sess., House Committee on Armed Services, March 9, 1971, p. 77.
[19] Richard M. Nixon, U.S. *Foreign Policy for the 1970's*, February 25, 1971, pp. 11–12.

Asian interests and power, none of which would have a dominant influence.[20] Looking beyond the Nixon Doctrine, the president anticipated that the restructuring of America's posture would lead to the "readjustment of the whole international order in the Pacific region," based on a new equilibrium reflecting the renewed vigor of the smaller states acting in regional groupings, the expanding role of Japan, and the changing relationships between the Soviet Union, the PRC, Japan, and the United States.[21]

In the construction of this new international order, the administration assigned a key role to the emergence of communist China from its diplomatic isolation. President Nixon made this point in his first report and two years later noted that he had foreshadowed it in his article in the October 1967 issue of *Foreign Affairs*. He implemented this diplomatic innovation through two years of small conciliatory steps and other signals, which culminated in Kissinger's visit to Peking in July 1971 and his own visit in February 1972. The administration has not yet publicly defined the role it expects Peking to play, beyond looking toward China's participation in the more evenly balanced quadrilateral diplomatic equilibrium emerging in East Asia and taking pains to deny that the policy of "opening a dialogue" with China is aimed at exploiting Sino-Soviet tensions or that it need disrupt U.S.-Soviet detente. But since the convergent interests of China and the United States in constraining Russia are at the root of the Sino-American rapprochement, it is reasonable to suppose that in American eyes China's principal role lies in supporting the overriding objective of inducing the Russians to cooperate in the consolidation of a global *modus vivendi*.

This whole far-reaching rationale for lowering America's posture in East Asia might well be taken as a case for the full-scale devolution of America's regional security role to Japan. Indeed, this is just what anxious Asian friends and foes alike initially suspected. The administration's conceptual framework seemed to anticipate Japan's becoming a pole of power with the normal functions of state sovereignty possessed by the three other major participants in the multipolar Asian balance of power, instead of remaining a military dependent, constitutionally forbidden to take care of its own regional security. Official words and actions specifically pertaining to Japan gave credence to this interpretation.

The Nixon Administration said much about the necessity of Japan, which had become the world's third greatest industrial power, shed-

[20] *Ibid.*, p. 92.
[21] *Ibid.*, p. 98.

ding the outworn habits of subservience acquired under American tutelage and assuming an autonomous role in the construction of a new international order in East Asia. It presented America's treaty with Japan for the reversion of Okinawa to Japanese administration (but permitting the United States to use Okinawan bases on the same terms of advance consultation as the remaining bases in Japan), which was signed in 1971 and put into effect in 1972, as a necessary adjustment to Japan's growing strength and pride. Partly to facilitate the ratification of the treaty by the Senate, President Nixon got Prime Minister Sato to join him in a communique (in November 1969) that further supported the logic of devolution by stating that the security of South Korea is "essential" to Japan's security and that Taiwan is "a most important factor for the security of Japan."

As special evidence of Japan's outward-looking role in shaping the East Asian international environment, the administration hailed Japan's increasing contribution to economic development in Asia, marked by its prominent role in the Asian Development Bank and by the pledge of one percent of its GNP (gross national product) to assisting less developed countries.

In July and August of 1971, the American government inflicted what the Japanese called twin "shocks" when it announced the visits to Peking without giving Tokyo advance notice and imposed a temporary 10 percent surcharge on dutiable imports. The president's 1972 report acknowledged that these actions were shocks, called them regrettably unavoidable, but declared that they "only accelerated an evolution in U.S.-Japanese relations that was in any event overdue, unavoidable, and in the long run, desirable" because the trend toward more autonomous policies is "a necessary step in the transformation of our relationship to the more mature and reciprocal partnership required in the 1970's."[22]

Even more directly affirming the logic of devolution, the Nixon Administration, like its predecessors, urged the Japanese to strengthen their conventional defense forces as a concomitant of the consolidation of American bases and the reduction of American forces in the home islands and Okinawa. Secretary of Defense Laird's advocacy of increased Japanese defense budgets, in particular, gave credence to the supposition that the United States might be turning over regional security responsibilities to Japan, since he and other members of the Department of Defense failed to make precisely clear the limits to the military role they were urging Japan to support more vigorously. The fact that Laird's position coincided with an internal debate in

[22] Nixon, *U.S. Foreign Policy for the 1970's*, February 9, 1972, pp. 52 and 58.

Japan over the magnitude of Japan's Self-Defense Force (SDF) accentuated the suspicion of those opposing increases in the SDF that the United States was trying to push Japan into a larger military role.

In spite of all these indications of an American policy of devolution, however, in reality the U.S. government stopped far short of adopting the full logic of its rationale. Although it did not unmistakably affirm the limits upon Japan's military role until the twin "shocks" and the controversy in Japan over the five-year defense budget made disavowal of any larger objective imperative, the White House had always viewed the enlargement of Japan's regional role in economic, not military, terms. The only transfer of America's military security functions that it envisioned was to regional groupings of the smaller Asian states. The transfer to Japan, as to the European allies, was to be confined to a redistribution of the allied defense burden under continuing American regional preponderance. In East Asia, moreover, the United States reaffirmed its exclusive responsibility for nuclear protection of the area and explicitly opposed the acquisition of nuclear weapons by its ally.[23] As in Western Europe, there were some compelling reasons for this reaffirmation of the status quo.

Japan's Inhibited Military Role

In East Asia, as in Western Europe, the fear of American withdrawal had the immediate effect of reinforcing the desire of America's allies to keep the United States engaged. But whereas the concomitant prospect of devolution in Europe was widely regarded as theoretically desirable, although in fact improbable, the prospect of transferring regional security functions to Japan, although quite hypothetical, alarmed the Japanese and other nations, since it evoked painful and frightening memories of Japan's prewar adventures. Consequently, the immediate effect of the emergence of this prospect in the wake of the Nixon Doctrine was to reinforce the pressures to preserve America's preponderant security role in East Asia.

The Nixon Doctrine, coming after two decades of intense American involvement in Asia and after twenty-five years of unquestioned American tutelage over Japan—and coming also in the context of Vietnam-induced retrenchment—inevitably raised expectations of a

---

[23] In a press conference in Tokyo on June 12, 1972, during a three-day visit, Henry Kissinger said, "It is not the policy of the U.S. that Japan should go nuclear," and he avowed that the Nixon administration, while expecting Japan to play a wider role in defense of the home islands, does not envisage a Japanese military presence elsewhere. It would be incorrect to infer from Japan's world economic power, he was reported to have said, that Japan is or should be a world military power. *Washington Post*, June 13, 1972, p. A18.

radical change in America's whole position in East Asia. Congressional and public sentiment for retrenchment, as well as official policies, raised doubts in Japan about America's will to uphold its security obligations in South Korea and elsewhere. There doubts were reinforced by the knowledge that President Nixon had staunchly pledged to keep American troops in Europe indefinitely while proudly undertaking military retrenchment in Asia. In this context of doubt, President Nixon's journey to China raised persistent suspicions that Washington and Peking might make some deal against Japan's interests. All the talk about a multipolar balance of power might mean that the American government regarded its commitments to Japan as subordinate to its global interest in devising a rapprochement with China. The balance that required bolstering Japan at one time might require bolstering Japan's competitor at another.

In conjunction with these doubts and suspicions the recent consciousness in Japan and the world at large of Japan's immense GNP and its exploding world trade and investments, accompanied by the doubling of its projected fourth five-year defense budget for 1972-76, raised the prospect of Japan becoming a full-scale superpower.

Although Japan's defense budgets have been less than 10 percent and a declining proportion of the total government budget since 1960, and have been only 1 percent or less of the GNP, this proportion was enough to increase the controversial budget proposed for fiscal year 1972–73 by 19.7 percent. It was enough to create a sizable modern force, including jet fighters with a range greater than the B-24 bombers of World War II and a capacity to carry nuclear bombs. Moreover, there could be no doubt that by the end of the 1970s Japan could readily produce a more-than-token nuclear force with a long-range missile delivery system within two or three years of a decision to do so.

Japan's emergence as a full-scale superpower gained further credence because of the general supposition that military power eventually follows the expansion of economic interests and because Japan's rapid creation of economic dependencies in East Asia evoked memories of the Greater East-Asian Co-Prosperity Sphere.[24]

[24] Presumably, the expansion of Japan's trade and investments in East Asia gives it an interest in protecting trading areas from internal and external disruption. But it should be noted that Japan is much less dependent on its Asian trading partners than they are dependent on it. For example, Japan conducts over 6 percent of its trade with South Korea and Taiwan, but they trade from 40 to 45 percent of their combined exports and imports with Japan. This pattern of dependency characterizes Japan's pre-eminent and pervasive economic presence throughout East Asia. See, for example, the report on this phenomenon in the New York *Times*, August 28, 1972, pp. 1ff.

The combination of American retrenchment and Japanese resurgence raised the specter of devolution. To the Japanese, as to others, America's regional military preponderance had provided the indispensable assurance that Japan's military role would remain restricted. Confidence in America's nuclear umbrella and conventional shield had enabled the Japanese to avoid the internally divisive and externally provocative issue of supplanting America's military protection with its own armed forces. Consequently, the announcement and implementation of the Nixon Doctrine not only shook Japan's confidence in American protection, it also threatened to raise an issue about Japan's role that most Japanese did not want to face. Thus, the very plausibility of devolution led Japanese leaders to reaffirm the nation's renunciation of a larger military role more vigorously, lest fears of Japan's military resurgence upset the domestic and foreign political conditions of Japan's non-military ascendance.

Japan's renunciation of the status of superpower is codified in Article IX of its postwar Constitution. Reflecting the trauma of defeat and nuclear destruction in World War II, this article is interpreted to restrict Japan's military objectives to "self-defense" and to prohibit "offensive" weapons.[25] It gains political force from the massive domestic consensus against stretching or amending the Constitution to permit a larger role than insular defense. The consensus springs partly from opposition to the resurgence of "militarism" and partly from perception of the practical advantages of keeping defense budgets (and, equally important, manpower levels) low but, more fundamentally, from the desire to avoid provoking and frightening other nations with whom Japan is eager to enjoy favorable economic and diplomatic relations.

[25] Article IX provides that "the Japanese people forever renounce war as a sovereign right of the nation and the threat or use of force as a means of settling international disputes. In order to accomplish the aim of the preceding paragraph, land, sea, and air forces, as well as other war potential, will never be maintained. . . ." The Japanese Supreme Court has upheld the prevailing view that this article does not deny the inherent right of self-defense and preparation for self-defense against armed attack. But it is also generally interpreted to prohibit overseas dispatch of forces and the possession of weapons that might take offensive action against other states, such as long-range missiles. Nuclear weapons are also considered to be prohibited, but officially the legal obstacle to nuclear weapons production lies in Article II of Japan's Atomic Energy Act and in the government's adoption of the three nonnuclear principles of not manufacturing, possessing, or importing nuclear weapons. The government has said that "small" or "tactical" nuclear weapons designed for self-defense only would not violate the Constitution, but it has renounced acquisition of such weapons as a matter of policy. See the so-called Defense White Paper, *Japan's Defense*, issued by the Japanese Defense Agency in October, 1970.

While reaffirming these constraints upon its military role the Japanese government also anxiously sought reaffirmation of the primary international condition that makes the constraints viable: American responsibility for Japan's regional security. It sought to keep the United States engaged but on terms appropriate to the abandonment of tutelage: Japanese military and administrative autonomy in the home islands and Okinawa and closer consultation with the United States.

Only a much more serious loss of confidence in American protection, coupled with a greatly intensified fear of a Chinese or Soviet threat to Japan's regional security, might lead Japan to reconsider its military dependency on the United States; and even then Japan might not choose the option of projecting its military power overseas. In reality, however, the Japanese see no serious military threats to their security and find it hard to imagine them arising in the future. As inhabitants of an insular nation that has never been invaded, they are not disposed to worry about foreign attacks. Understandably, they find it hard to imagine China or Russia attacking Japan. For geopolitical and historical reasons many Japanese would regard the PRC's recovery of Taiwan as a threat, but the chance of this occurring by armed force seems too remote to be of practical concern. Perhaps the withdrawal of American troops from South Korea without a reliable all-Korean settlement would raise the specter of China or Russia filling in the vacuum and shock the Japanese into reappraising their military role; but for reappraisal to lead to devolution one would have to posit other unlikely conditions, such as a South Korean invitation to Japan for assistance.

Underlying this assessment of Japan's inhibited military role, however, there is the implicit premise that only a tangible and compelling security motive could induce Japan to take on the full military attributes of a superpower. This premise does not take account of the larger motives of status and pride and influence that usually mingle with considerations of security in the higher counsels of powerful nations. With the passage of time Japan's war-born inhibitions against full-scale military autonomy may fade. With the experience of acting on the central stage of world politics Japan seems bound to acquire more of the psychology of a great power as opposed to the psychology of a defeated dependent. Already the Japanese have largely overcome their "nuclear allergy," in that they approach the issue of nuclear abstention or armament as a practical political, economic, and strategic choice rather than as an emotion-laden taboo. Prime Minister Tanaka's trip to Peking in the fall of 1972 to apologize for Japan's past transgressions and establish diplomatic relations, and

Moscow's not unrelated moves to improve relations with Tokyo (possibly on the basis of returning the war-occupied islands north of Japan in exchange for Japanese economic assistance in Siberia), portend an active independent diplomatic role, which is more likely than Japan's enlarged economic role to lead to an expanded military role. So the view that in strictly pragmatic terms there seems to be no compelling reason for Japan to abandon its military inhibitions begs the question of whether, in addition to their pragmatism, the Japanese may develop an irresistible taste for independent power and influence that can only be satisfied by military self-reliance.

This question cannot be answered merely in terms of traditional historical generalities about *Realpolitik* or in terms of psycho-political theories about Japanese behavior. Nor can one assume that new modes of international politics are developing in which military power will be irrelevant to foreign policy or that Japan's undeveloped military potential can indefinitely supplant forces in being as an instrument of policy or status. As profound as these considerations may be, Japan's military role is likely to depend very much on the specific pattern of conflict, competition, and alignment that develops among the five major centers of power in the world and upon the relations of the United States and Japan within this pattern. At this time, however, the configurations of international politics are still so rudimentary and tentative and the possibilities are so broad in range that one can only elaborate conjectures.[26]

Partnership or Devolution

The one thing that is fairly clear about the developing pattern of international politics in East Asia is that the break-up of the cold war pattern of confrontation, coupled with the explosion of Japan's economic strength and influence, will draw Japan into a more active diplomatic role. The immediate effect of this new activism, however, is evidently not to lead Japan and the United States deliberately to loosen the bonds of alliance but rather to prompt their governments to seek ways of strengthening these bonds. For loosening them would accentuate fears of Japanese "militarism" or at least "Gaullism" and thereby threaten to supplant one era of confrontation with another.

The fear of an expanded Japanese military role, whether justified or not, would be acute if the United States were to withdraw its

[26] The author briefly undertakes this exercise in conjecture in *The Weary and The Wary: U.S. and Japanese Security Policies in Transition* (Baltimore, 1972: Johns Hopkins University Press), chapters 10–13.

troops from South Korea before a reliable *modus vivendi* between the two Koreas were achieved. Indeed, American withdrawal might create a situation in which the Japanese as well as the Russians and the Chinese would each fear that one or the other would try to fill the vacuum, and their fears could upset the diplomatic equilibrium. On the other hand, for the United States to remain credibly engaged in South Korea's behalf presupposes not only the maintenance of an American trip-wire but, more important in the long run, a high degree of coordination of military policies between the United States and Japan, if only because without such coordination the United States cannot count on reliable access to Japanese bases which are essential to provide air support for Korea but which the Japanese now control.

Therefore, the American and Japanese governments are likely to formulate the policy question that faces them in terms of how to strengthen the bonds of alliance on the basis of the existing distribution of military responsibility while Japan pursues an increasingly independent, differentiated, and influential set of foreign and economic policies. The official answer of both governments to this question will almost surely be a combination of trying to improve consultation on a wide range of economic, political, and military issues— that is, the standard prescription of a closer partnership—while bargaining more vigorously with each other with respect to increasingly differentiated, though not necessarily incompatible, policies. Accentuation of the second course, however, will tend to limit the efficacy of the first. So the question underlying the prescription of partnership is whether the interests and policies of these two countries—and, more fundamentally, their political cultures and modes of communication— are sufficiently convergent to sustain the kind of close working relationship that has existed between the United States and its major European allies in NATO.

Between these two nations there are neither the institutionalized forms of collaboration nor the underlying political, cultural, and personal affinities that have made highly-developed forms of cooperation possible in NATO. It is too early to gauge the magnitude of the political burden and strain on the Americans or the Japanese that the forthcoming era of diplomatic maneuver and economic politics will impose. But it would not be surprising if the political and psychological burden of trying to maintain an international environment congenial to mutual interests in a period of Japanese economic ascendance and diplomatic resurgence should lead both nations to seek a looser alignment instead of a closer partnership. If neither the magnitude of American interests nor their convergence with Japan's interests is sufficient to sustain the NATO path of collaboration, the vitality of the alliance may come to depend on a much larger measure of Japanese self-reliance and American detachment than the rhetoric of partnership presumes. In any event, if there is a reasonable case for an orderly devolution of regional security responsibility to Japan, it must rest on this kind of political consideration. For unlike the situation in Western Europe, Congressional pressures do not threaten to compel the unilateral withdrawal of American forces from Northeast Asia, and substantial withdrawals have already been made.

The case for devolution, beyond the generalized argument for loosening the formal bonds of the alliance in order to preserve its essential cohesion, must rest on the assumption that America's vital interests in East Asia—primarily, the security of a peaceful and democratic Japan—will be protected best in the long run by Japan itself; and that these interests will be protected by Japan operating in a more structured multipolar diplomatic equilibrium in which the United States could substantially relinquish its military concerns within the defensive perimeter defined before the Korean War. This assumption depends on an orderly devolution, as opposed to devolution by shock or erosion. Orderly devolution would have to eschew a sudden and total transfer of security responsibilities or the unilateral abandonment of American military obligations. It would begin with political agreements and understandings between Japan and non-communist East Asian states, supplementing economic ties that are already well advanced. Japan might then undertake to protect sealanes far from Japanese shores. Military and technical assistance agreements might follow. But only in the final stage of devolution would Japan enter into formal military commitments to supplement or supplant American commitments, and even then the stationing of Japanese armed forces overseas would almost certainly be excluded.

Japan's gradual assumption of an overseas military role would make more likely its decision to produce nuclear weapons, particularly if China had deployed an impressive nuclear force as a constraint upon Japan as well as the Soviet Union. But since there are quite special inhibitions against a Japanese nuclear force, and since Japan's conspicuous nuclear potential serves most of the political purposes of an actual force while avoiding the political liabilities, it is not a foregone conclusion that devolution would entail nuclear proliferation.[27]

[27] It is another question whether the opposition inside and outside Japan to Japan's acquisition of nuclear weapons is justified on grounds of the generalized fears that are commonly expressed. The proponents of these fears offer no reasons

Unlike the prospect of devolution to America's European allies there can be no doubt about the political as well as the material capacity of Japan to take on the burdens of military self-reliance. But the internal and external political constraints against Japan doing so are much greater than in Europe. Under present conditions any explicit move toward devolution or even any suspicion of it would be profoundly divisive in Japanese political life. Therefore, it is hard to foresee any Japanese government either openly or covertly moving toward devolution unless there were some striking increase in the perceived danger to Japanese security or a radical change in Japan's heretofore stable consensus politics.

One would also have to posit a radical change in the attitude of other states to imagine their requesting a Japanese military commitment, let alone a Japanese nuclear force. Under present conditions the prospect of Japan's extending its military role would surely create a foreign reaction that would set back the government's whole postwar effort to advance its wealth, influence, and status in an atmosphere of international acceptance. This being the case, the United States will certainly not want to bear the onus of encouraging devolution.

If planned devolution, therefore, is even less likely than the formation of an intimate U.S.-Japanese partnership, the outstanding feature of U.S.-Japanese relations in the next decade, as in the case of U.S.-West European relations, is likely to be a succession of improvised efforts to adjust an increasing number of policy differences while both parties try to maintain the present structure of power and responsibility between them amid the strains of an era of detente and diplomatic maneuver. If this structure should basically change, it will be in spite of the plans of governments, not because of them.

---

to think that Japan's possession of nuclear weapons would make it more expansionist or adventurous than the present five nuclear powers, and they take no account of the technological and political developments that have radically changed the internal and external environment of Japan's foreign policy since the Second World War. The opposition to a Japanese nuclear force on the general grounds of preventing the spread of nuclear weapons to other states is more plausible, but here too the unconvincing and unexamined assertions that are usually made in favor of non-proliferation (particularly, the quantitative projection of nuclear dangers in proportion to the number of nuclear states) seem so abstract and oversimplified as to suggest that the real bases of opposition lie in national antipathies, the desire of the nuclear haves to exclude the have-nots, and other non-rational motives.

7

THE POLITICAL ECONOMY OF ALLIED RELATIONS:
THE LIMITS OF INTERDEPENDENCE

David P. Calleo

1

For the past few years, it has been fashionable to see a growing pluralism in the world's political system, to note that the superpowers are increasingly restricted, that the age of "bipolar" duopoly is giving way to a world of five great powers, or threatens to disintegrate into an unstructured world of nationalist individuality. Those who share this view tend to see the principal task of American foreign policy as a substantial and orderly devolution, to be accomplished in such a fashion that the world-wide "structure of peace" developed in the bipolar era can be transformed before it collapses. As World War II's destruction and demoralization brought an overwhelming pre-eminence and responsibility to the United States, so, it is argued, the end of the post-war era of reconstruction should return an appropriate share of the burdens of world order and development to others. The United States should henceforth devote a greater measure of attention to its own domestic problems. Otherwise, the growing anomaly between America's swollen responsibilities to the international system, and the growing power of others within that system, will make world order increasingly precarious.

In its foreign policy pronouncements, the Nixon Administration generally appears to honor this view. The annual presidential foreign policy reports to the Congress repeatedly have organized themselves around the need for new policies and institutions to effect an orderly transition from balanced duopoly to balanced pluralism.[1] Nixon's efforts to cultivate good relations with Paris, and now Peking, might seem to suggest recognition of emerging pluralism. The Nixon Doctrine suggests an important shift of responsibility for defense.

[1] See President Nixon's recent foreign policy reports to the Congress, *United States Foreign Policy for the 1970's: A New Strategy for Peace*, February 18, 1970, and *United States Foreign Policy for the 1970's: The Emerging Structure of Peace*, February 9, 1972.

But while the Nixon Administration has clearly articulated the need for a change, and has been at pains to show the innovative character of its policies, the same bipolar conceptions of American interest that dominated the previous twenty years have, in fact, dominated American foreign policy in the early 1970s. A Republican administration has continued the old Democratic policies, but tried to reduce the costs. Innovation has been restricted to means and seldom ventured to a fundamental reconsideration of ends. Indeed, Nixon's foreign policy calls to mind the old "more bang for the buck" principle of Eisenhower's day.

Nixon's policy toward Vietnam is, of course, the most obvious evidence for this view. Under Nixon, the troops have left but the war has continued. Whatever may have happened finally, the Nixon Administration can hardly be said to have moved with alacrity toward ending a commitment long considered unworthy and unnecessary. Instead, in four years, nearly all the old alternatives were tried at least once more.

Vietnam is undoubtedly special. It can always be argued that the American disengagement from the universal confrontation of the old bipolar system cannot be so precipitate that we seem unable to protect our interests anywhere. Such an abrupt American abdication from old commitments, it can be said, is likely to result not so much in a plural world system, as in a revival of Russian imperialism. The creative side of the Nixon Administration's policy inevitably lies elsewhere than in Vietnam. But even the administration's greatest initiative in the Far East, the spectacular visit to Peking, does not so far confute those who see the administration as concerned primarily with the appearance of change and not with fundamental alterations in America's world role. American moves toward a genuine accommodation of long-standing differences with China, or toward encouraging a new role for Japan, are, at the moment, hard to detect. Instead, our new relations with China seem more a move in the old bipolar contest with Russia than the beginning of a new multipolar game.

The other grand Nixon initiatives—the mutual arms limitation agreements and presidential summit meetings with the Soviets—hardly represent a departure from the bipolar foreign policy of the Kennedy, Johnson, or indeed Eisenhower Administrations. On the contrary, the pursuit of detente and bilateral agreement with the Soviets has long been the cornerstone of the old policy of duopoly.

But what would constitute a policy that genuinely accepted pluralism and sought a corresponding reduction in America's commitments? Devolution of an exaggerated world role would mean, above all, establishing new relations not with our old adversary the Soviet Union, but with our old allies, in short with Japan and above all Western Europe. The nations of Western Europe are as domestically stable as any in the world, blooming with prosperity and united in a rather effective regional organization. If there is any place in the world ripe for a devolution of American responsibilities, it is presumably there.

Nowhere, however, has the conservative continuity of America's foreign policies under Nixon been more apparent than in Europe. The United States has stoutly resisted any changes in our European military protectorate, assumed during the most anxious days of the cold war. Like its predecessors, the Nixon Administration has discouraged initiatives to build a separate European nuclear force around British and French components, or even any European military coalition separate from the hegemonic arrangements of NATO. And while, with our own predilection for bilateral negotiations with the Soviets, we could hardly oppose European initiatives to settle the unresolved political questions which still keep the continent's peace uneasy, the French and German initiatives toward the East have had only our tepid and nervous acquiescence. In brief, we have worked steadily to delay serious general negotiations on European security questions. Even our assent to the Berlin agreements, which did little but consolidate the status quo, required considerable pressure from both Bonn and Paris. Meanwhile, on the economic front, America's hostility to Europe's economic bloc and our spoiler's role in preventing its consolidation has become increasingly unrestrained.

In short, whatever movement has occurred toward a more self-sufficient and unified Western Europe, or toward a settlement to end Europe's cold-war divisions and blocs, has not been at our initiative, and has had, at best, only our grudging support. On the contrary, we have sought to conserve our own "Atlantic" bloc, and with it the predominating role and responsibility which we have assumed in European affairs since the founding of NATO. Thus aside from the president's professed admiration for de Gaulle—an admiration which, thanks to Malraux, need not be extended to de Gaulle's policies as carried on by his successor—the Nixon Administration's European policy is remarkably similar to that of the Johnson Administration in its later years.[2] Both policies have been tenacious and sluggish. Both have sought to preserve and consolidate the postwar Atlantic system,

[2] For Andre Malraux's denigration of Pompidou and his policies, see *Felled Oaks* (New York: Holt, Rinehart and Winston, 1972).

and along with it, the hegemonic role assumed by the U.S. in European affairs since the war's end.

To say that our European policy has remained the same in its essentials is not, of course, to condemn that policy, nor to deny that Nixon's Administration may pursue it effectively. Any assessment of Nixon's European policy must consider not only the goals being sought, and their prospects for success, but also the likely alternatives.

In its fundamentals, America's European policy is neither haphazard, nor unself-conscious. On the contrary, it reflects the design for an Atlantic system which has been maturing in the American political imagination over several generations. Since World War II, we have been in a strong position to shape events to fit our ideals.

The outlines of America's Atlantic ideal are familiar enough, although the grandeur of the whole conception is frequently missed or distorted by the tendency to consider the political, economic, and military dimensions in isolation. But an understanding of the whole requires not only considering the parts together, but understanding the various stages in the evolution and implementation of the over-all post-war design.

America's post-war plans for reconstructing the world's political-economic system strongly reflected the persistence of the general Wilsonian vision in the American political imagination, and particularly, the influence of those ideals promoted so assiduously since the 1930s by Roosevelt's Secretary of State, Cordell Hull. In Hull's old-fashioned liberal vision, economic relations were all-important for peace. In particular, all restrictions on the free flow of goods and money were anathema. It had become an article of faith that economic blocs inevitably lead to political rivalry, militarism, and war. Hence, in Hull's ideal world, free trade was to be accompanied by free convertibility of money and freedom for investments and capital movements.

Hull's ideal economic system, of course, called for a parallel political and security system. International economic institutions and international political institutions were mutually dependent elements in the over-all international order. Thus, along with the IMF to manage the world's money, and the ITO (transformed into the GATT) to guide the world's trade, there came the U.N. Security Council to guard collective security. America, in short, would use its moment of historical dominance to build a liberal world order—open economically and politically—and organized through permanent international institutions.

Of course, America's Wilsonian ideal soon foundered on the rock of Stalinist intransigence. The Russians were hostile to all capitalist "penetration" and were determined to consolidate their brutal sway over Eastern Europe. Moreover, the "loss" of China removed another huge part of the world from what was to have been a universal liberal system. Soon decolonization, neutralism, and economic underdevelopment separated much of the third world. In effect, by the late 1940s, the Wilsonian-Hullian system was effectively applicable only to the developed capitalist countries. The Wilsonian world system had been transformed into the Atlantic community.

Not only had the Hullian system shrunk, but the cold war greatly altered its character. For, in its formative postwar years, the Atlantic community became primarily preoccupied not with transatlantic economic integration, but with European military security.

After the Russians promoted the communist coup in Czechoslovakia in 1948 and acquired nuclear weapons in 1949, the United States and its European clients turned to building a mutual security system. An American guarantee for Europe's defense was to discourage Russian pressure and calm Europe's domestic turbulence. With the outbreak of the Korean War, the United States established a virtual protectorate over Western Europe. General Eisenhower was sent to build an inter-allied staff of wartime proportions; European national armies were to be integrated under the elaborate military and political apparatus of NATO, a system which institutionalized American military hegemony. A re-armed United States covered Europe with air bases, sent an army to defend Germany, and placed a large fleet in the Mediterranean.

At the same time, the self-evident failure of Hullian liberal policies to promote rapid economic recovery in 1946–47, plus the dangers of communist subversion in a starving Europe, all prompted American compromise with Europe on economic matters.[3] Thus, our early attempt to promote Europe's reconstruction through "liberal" policies of free trade and convertibility, a policy both unpopular and unsuccessful, gave way to a policy combining American aid with European protectionism. To rebuild their industries and markets, while establishing the stable welfare economies which their people de-

[3] For a discussion of America's immediate postwar European economic policies, in particular the Anglo-American Financial Agreement and its transition, see Richard N. Gardner *Sterling-Dollar Diplomacy* (Oxford: Oxford University Press, 1956), pp. 210–23; also David P. Calleo and Benjamin M. Rowland, *America and the World Political Economy* (Bloomington, Indiana: Indiana University Press, 1973), particularly chapters two and five.

manded, European governments needed not only massive inflows of American aid but restrictive measures on trade and money. Hence the Marshall Plan and the birth of America's Europeanist policy. Whereas Hull had opposed all protectionist "blocs," by the late 1940s and throughout the 1950s, the United States, opposing Britain, was strongly encouraging European economic integration, even if it discriminated against American trade. A European political-economic bloc became America's goal rather than her nightmare. In the revised American vision, Europe's economic integration became the prelude to its federal political integration. As a united Europe emerged, the United States would have a worthy partner in world order and Soviet communism would be decisively defeated.

Nevertheless, the old ideal of a single Atlantic economic system persisted throughout this Europeanist phase of American policy, especially in the State Department's economic bureau. Europe's customs union was to be only a phase in the evolution toward Atlantic economic integration. Similarly, Europe's political integration was to result, not in a Europe separating from American hegemony after a period of convalescence, but a Europe which was America's partner in upholding the world's new "system of peace."[4]

American policy toward Japan went through a rather similar evolution.[5] After an early period when American policy combined retribution with doctrinaire economic liberalism, the cold war plus the urgent demands of Japanese recovery led not only to a formal American military protectorate, but also to economic concessions permitting Japan to control her own foreign trade and domestic investment. At the same time, the United States opened its own markets to Japanese goods and tried, without much success, to persuade Europeans to do likewise. As we saw it, pan-Atlantic world partnership was to encompass not only Western Europe, but also Japan, and we began a long campaign to get her into the GATT.

By the late 1950s, with the Soviet menace at least contained and both Europe and Japan well on the way to recovery, American policy began to return to its earlier goal of a liberal world economic community. The prospects seemed promising. By the late 1950s, the European states had returned to convertibility; Japan rather unwill-

[4] For a discussion of conflicting American aims, see Harold van Buren Cleveland, *The Atlantic Idea and Its European Rivals* (New York: McGraw-Hill, 1966).

[5] See Jerome B. Cohen *Japan's Economy in War and Reconstruction* (Minneapolis: University of Minnesota Press, 1949) and also his *Japan's Postwar Economy* (Bloomington, Indiana: Indiana University Press, 1958).

ingly followed in 1960. Within the GATT, a series of trade negotiations, beginning with the Dillon Round in 1960, gradually reduced American and European tariffs to the lowest rates since before World War I. Trade among the developed capitalist countries grew to record levels. A great boom in international investments, in particular the spread of American corporations to Europe, began to point to an entirely new degree of economic, and ultimately political, integration among the Atlantic powers.

With the return of the Democrats in 1960, the reviving Hullian spirit in American policy became increasingly articulate. Kennedy's "Grand Design," with its "Declaration of Interdependence," was meant to inaugurate the new era of transatlantic political and economic integration.[6] Britain was to join the Common Market, thus diluting France's "inward-looking" predilections, and a new round of tariff cuts, the Kennedy Round, was to eliminate virtually all tariffs among the Atlantic nations. At the same time, as the United States and Russia entered a new period of confrontation over Berlin and Cuba, American policy sought to revitalize the military alliance. A major program of rearmament, including a major increase in American forces in Germany, accompanied a new series of doctrines emphasizing the importance of Atlantic military integration and centralized control. At the same time, the United States remained firmly opposed to independent European nuclear deterrents.

In short, the Grand Design not only presupposed the indefinite continuation of an anti-communist Western political bloc, over which the United States would sustain its hegemonic protectorate, but pressed forward with the old plans for transatlantic economic integration. The period of Europe's consolidation into the Common Market was ready, we argued, to evolve into the consolidation of the Atlantic community, an economic system that was to stretch to Japan. Kennedy's Administration also saw a revival of American economic interest in the third world. As Europe and Japan had been nursed to liberalism, so the countries of the third world—after a long period of development to capitalist modernity—would ultimately join the grand Wilsonian construction.[7]

Kennedy's vast scheme for pan-Atlantic economic, military, and political interdependence presupposed a relationship far more imperial, at least in its economic aspects, than when both Europe and Japan

[6] For a fuller discussion and numerous citations, see Calleo and Rowland, *America and the World Political Economy*, chapter 4.

[7] See W. W. Rostow, ed., *The Economics of Take-Off into Self-Sustained Growth* (New York: St. Martin's Press, 1965).

were completely dependent on the United States. Ironically, Kennedy's revival of Wilsonian liberalism came at the very moment when Europe was growing both more restive at American political and military tutelage, and more capable of resisting it. Thus, as it happened, the age of Kennedy in America coincided with the age of de Gaulle in Europe.

America's failure to impose the Grand Design was not surprising. Whatever the chances for an Atlantic system when the United States was militarily, politically, and economically dominant over a prostrate and terrified Europe, the Atlantic ideal was unlikely to prevail after the economic and political revival of Europe, particularly in an era of detente. But if France was strong enough in the 1960s to ruin the Grand Design, she has not been strong enough to galvanize Europe into an independent coalition. Thus the past few years have been a period of increasing mutual frustration. We have been strong enough to discourage European constructions but too weak to revitalize our own Atlantic alternatives. A European military coalition is stillborn—the United States is discouraging Britain's nuclear sharing; but NATO remains in "disarray"—Western Europe's major military power still refuses to participate. Even if Western Europe has not built an effective structure to coordinate national policies, the Atlantic alliance's pretentions to collective "detente management" have grown more and more self-evidently unreal.

The same analysis hold for economic institutions. If the Common Market's unity is increasingly shaken by America's trade policies, and if the European Monetary Union remains a most precarious construction in the face of American pressures, the old Atlantic institutions—the GATT and the IMF—are also gradually breaking down. Protectionism spreads and monetary convertibility becomes more and more uncertain.

How long will this period of mutual frustration last? Will it end in decisive victory for either the Atlantic or the European ideal, or will the frustrated ideals eventually reach a mutually tolerable and stable accommodation?

The question suggests three logical alternatives. One is an Atlantic Europe, in which some version of the Grand Design would ultimately prevail.[8] In this alternative, the transatlantic economic integration paced by big business continues inexorably; the dollar standard is finally accepted; the logic of the single nuclear deterrent continues

[8] For perhaps the best discussion of the Atlanticist ideal, see Eugene V. Rostow, *Law, Power and the Pursuit of Peace* (Lincoln, Nebraska: University of Nebraska Press, 1968).

to prevail; the European nation states increasingly lose their functions and authority, but remain incapable of a union strong enough to end American predominance. Even if, along with continuing American hegemony in the West, the Soviet Union continues to hold symmetrical sway over its bloc in the East, the climate produced by the tacit truce of the superpowers allows relations between Europe's two halves sufficiently tolerable to avoid serious conflict.

The second alternative sees a Europeanist solution.[9] Western Europe develops into a bloc sufficiently solid to resist domination by either superpower. This European bloc, increasingly integrated into a sort of confederal economy, reasserts control over its economic environment and expels or controls disturbing alien elements, like footloose American corporations or dollars. Hence, both Europe and America tend to become more self-contained and inclined to protectionism, although the tendency may be kept in hand if transatlantic trade and monetary problems can be brought back to equilibrium. In any event, a European Monetary Union puts an end to the dollar's hegemony. Politically, such a Europe remains on friendly terms with the United States, but takes an increasingly independent and cooperative line toward the East, and works toward some version of a Europe from the Atlantic to the Urals. Militarily, such a Europe remains allied with the United States in a looser Atlantic alliance, but builds a military coalition of its own, armed with some kind of collective nuclear force to replace the American hegemony of NATO. Such a Europe probably would become an increasingly powerful economic and political force in the world at large, and might gradually reassert its old influence in the Middle East, Africa, and even in the Far East and Latin America.

The third alternative is the untidy residue if neither the Atlantic or European alternatives prevails. It sees essentially a perpetuation of the status quo: "nobody's Europe." The Brussels institutions continue to coordinate intra-European economic affairs and to handle trade negotiations with the world outside. But even if coordination extends to a monetary union, divisions among the Europeans inhibit their forcing any fundamental changes in the international monetary system. The dollar continues its shaky hegemony and the Europeans continue to resist but not to overcome. Periodic currency crises run their course and provisional arrangements continually patch up the system. Militarily, Europe continues to rely on NATO, even if the organization

---

[9] For a powerful version of the Europeanist idea, see Franz-Josef Strauss, *Challenge and Response* (London: Weidenfeld and Nicolson, 1968).

becomes more and more a shell, and even if the French, and perhaps the British, continue to build a separate nuclear deterrent. Active, uncoordinated Western initiatives continue toward the East, all helping to improve the atmosphere, but all limited by Russia's unwillingness to countenance any serious threat to her close hegemony.

In this third view, Western Europe, or rather Pan-Atlantica, becomes a kind of latter-day Holy Roman Empire, with America in the Hapsburg role. Hegemony is loose and limited and prevails only with considerable difficulty. All the old historical elements remain active, even if new forces occasionally appear. In the end, the general framework proves capable of defeating any initiative for serious change. Such a world might be called "plural," but it is not a pluralism of equal and independent states in a common system. Rather it is the kind of hegemonic pluralism which Metternich sustained so well until, of course, the whole system blew up in domestic revolution.

American foreign policy toward Europe since the collapse of the Grand Design finds its most convincing rationale not as a pursuit of the first, Atlanticist, alternative, but as an anticipation of the third, Hapsburgian, Europe. While American policy-makers might prefer a more integrated Atlantic construction, Europeanist resistance remains too great, at least for the present. But by frustrating the Europeanists in turn, the United States can retain sufficient influence in European affairs to prevent initiatives which might threaten America's economic well-being or disturb the truce between the superpowers. If we occasionally feel guilty at a spoiler's role, we can always argue, not unreasonably, that we cannot ourselves forge for the Europeans those collective institutions needed to replace America's military or monetary hegemony. Even if such European constructions may come in due course, the United States should not meanwhile withdraw its comforting presence and risk a disintegrating panic among the Western states, which might well make them an easy prey for Russian penetration. Our European interests are too great. With the political instability on the other side of the Iron Curtain, the risk that some sudden deterioration might suck the United States into an escalating military confrontation is still considerable. Therefore, the need for the United States to control the local military in Europe remains. In the face of such vital political and military interests, the United States cannot afford to let short-term economic considerations dictate overall policy. Specifically, it is up to the protected Europeans to make those adjustments needed to put the American balance-of-payments in equilibrium and to permit the dollar to return to convertibility.

Such arguments make a prudent and powerful case and easily find wide acceptance. They reconcile a conservative perpetuation of the status quo with the recognition, in principle, of an eventual need for disengagement—while nevertheless guarding the possibility of an Atlantic Grand Design in the end. What, if anything, is at fault with such a policy?

The most serious criticism argues that postponing and resisting American disengagement from remaining European hegemony greatly increases the dangers of a general collapse in transatlantic economic, military, and political relationships, and indeed threatens European unity itself. In the end, according to this view, the present American policy will endanger basic transatlantic ties far more than a purposeful and resolute American withdrawal from hegemony. Indeed, a pruning of untenable American commitments and privileges would renew and revitalize America's European role. Thus, American policy should deliberately seek to recast Atlantic relations into a new, non-hegemonic mold, appropriate for a revived Europe in a plural world.

The validity of such a critique depends upon two assumptions. First, that the revisionist forces are such that the present quasi-hegemonic system will continue to deteriorate and, second, that acceptable alternative arrangements are feasible, should we withdraw in part. The first assumption is easier to deal with than the second. What are the forces which have been eroding the status quo or which endanger it in the forseeable future?

Aside from the domestic unrest which occasionally bedevils all advanced industrial societies, three major revisionist trends present themselves. First, the diplomatic restiveness of the major continental states—initially France and now Germany. Second, American "neo-isolationism." Finally, the steady deterioration of America's international economic position. The three trends are, of course, related, even if too often studied in isolation.

With Europe split between the superpowers and Germany divided down the middle, the restiveness of the major continental powers is hardly surprising. As the European states have recovered their domestic prosperity and morale, evolved stable national political systems, and linked them in various intra-European organizations, their impulse to escape from external tutelage is natural—however skillful, benevolent, and gentle that hegemony may be. As the threat of Russian invasion and subversion has appeared to recede, close incorporation into an American-dominated Atlantic community has had less and less to offer. Even the British, long addicted to Atlanticism, have grown weary of playing junior partner.

France, never flattered by a special relationship, has been the most articulate of Europe's revisionists.[10] After acquiring a strong and determined government, the French moved vigorously to re-establish direct and increasingly cordial relations with Russia and Eastern Europe, while withdrawing selectively from the institutions of Atlantic hegemony, NATO in particular. At the same time, France has sought to build intra-European institutions into effective coalitions both to resist American economic and political hegemony and to prevent any grand settlement of Europe's affairs between the superpowers over the heads of the Europeans themselves.

French revisionism has drawn strength from its claim to speak with a European as well as a national voice. The claim, given some substance by France's general pre-eminence within the European Communities and her special relationship with the Federal Republic of Germany, derives its moral force from de Gaulle's own Grand Design for Europe, a vision which challenges the American counterpart in nearly all its essential elements. In de Gaulle's view, Europe's nations could never reach any satisfactory accommodation so long as the United States and Russia confronted each other across the middle of Germany. Detente organized essentially between the superpowers would merely stabilize the rival blocs and hence consolidate Europe's division and subordination.

To escape, the Europeans should disengage from the superpower confrontation and move toward a system of their own—a "Europe from the Atlantic to the Urals." A Western European bloc, loosely allied with the United States, would coax the Russians toward a pan-European system. While de Gaulle expected Russian hegemony to persist in Eastern Europe, time, he hoped, would relax and humanize the Soviet grip, both at home and abroad. Meanwhile, the natural advantages of intercourse with a friendly, but strong and independent Western Europe, would slowly draw Russia into normal and relaxed relations within a pan-European system. Detente would be succeeded by entente and finally by cooperation.

Gaullist diplomacy focused not only upon the Soviets, but especially upon the Germans. A resolution for the German question was an essential element in de Gaulle's ultimate pan-European system. West Germany, he believed, would never stay firmly bound within any Western European bloc, pan-European system, or continuing Atlantic alliance which by its very nature precluded Germany's national reunification. The pull of nationalism was too powerful to be resisted

[10] For an authoritative version of France's foreign policy in de Gaulle's regime, see Maurice Couve de Murville, *Une Politique Étrangère, 1958–1969* (Paris: Plon, 1971).

indefinitely. If everyone knew reunification would take a long time, still, no friend of Germany's should push her to renounce her own national integrity or seek to design a European future which left the German nation forever separated. Instead, de Gaulle hoped to use Germany's desire for reunification as the lever France needed to pry her neighbor loose from American hegemony. As long as West Germany remained merely a forward outpost of American military power, with no active diplomacy of her own, de Gaulle argued, no satisfactory solution to the German problem was possible. Detente organized by the superpowers would only consolidate Germany's division. Thus Germany's salvation lay not in perpetuating the cold war Atlantic bloc, and the Soviet-American confrontation across Europe, but in building a pan-European system in which a Western European bloc maintained close but independent relations with both superpowers. Only within such an environment would the Russians gradually relax their grip on the East. But without a close Franco-German accord, no solid Western European bloc could exist to counter-balance the Russians within the pan-European system, or counter-balance the United States within the capitalist world.

In de Gaulle's time and since, the French have pressed their design upon both the Russians and the Germans, with what long-range consequences only time can tell. In recent years, French policy has scored notable success in the economic sphere, through the Common Market. Gradually, a gathering European economic bloc has used its power to assert European interests to counter American designs. Spurred on by the French, Europe has challenged, if not ended, the hegemony of the dollar.

While French revisionism has become increasingly preoccupied with economic affairs within the Atlantic world, German diplomacy has launched a major campaign to promote not only detente, but also the beginning of a European diplomatic settlement. The West German strategy is both complex and obvious. By renouncing claims on the Sudetenland and the territories east of the Oder-Neisse Line, and by signing non-agression pacts and offering economic blandishments, the West Germans have sought to cultivate normal relations and expanding influence among their eastern non-German neighbors. At the same time, especially since the Russian intervention in Czechoslovakia, the West Germans have been careful to defer to Moscow's Eastern hegemony and hence not to appear more ardent in their relations with the lesser Eastern states than with the Russians themselves. Finally, and perhaps of greatest significance, the Federal Republic has moved to recognize the East German state and establish intimate all-German relations.

It is difficult to know where such policies, once begun, may finally lead. If the West Germans have formally accepted the status quo, they have also tenaciously insisted on their right to peaceful reunification. Thus, while the Russians doubtless see Germany's recognition of the status quo as an end in itself, some West Germans see it as the first step toward change. The attractive power of the Federal Republic's economy and culture will, it is hoped, loosen the constraints that prevent easy intercourse and perpetuate the rigid divisions of the cold war.

But to come back to our original question: Do the revisionist policies of France and Germany seriously threaten America's hegemony in Western Europe? According to one view which is now widespread, they do not. If it is true that both France and Germany have now become revisionist powers, it is also true that their policies toward the United States still contradict rather than complement each other. France's European formula calls for a cohesive Western Europe, allied with the United States, but disengaged from its military control. Germany's Eastern campaign bases itself upon a continuing American nuclear and military protectorate. The French formula suggests a Western European military coalition and the end of NATO in its present form. Consequently, the Brandt coalition has resolutely resisted the French program.

Brandt's reasons are not difficult to understand. Quite apart from its inherent difficulties, a more self-sufficient European military bloc might well involve not only a certain expansion in Germany's military capacities, but also open the Pandora's Box of Germany's nuclear status—all of which would disturb domestic opinion in Germany, provoke unease in the United States and Western Europe, and cause great alarm in Eastern Europe. Hence the Brandt-Scheel government's unswerving loyalty to NATO. In effect, Germany's revisionism in the East leans upon her conservatism in the West. So far, in an era of superpower detente, Germany's conservative Atlanticism has not been difficult to reconcile with her adventurous *Ostpolitik*—indeed it has been its military foundation.[11]

Of course, as Germany pursues more intimate relations with the East and seeks, in effect, to move from a detente based on recognition of the status quo to a fundamental recasting of European relations within a new cooperative system, the tensions will rise. For unlike Germany, the United States has no great interest in dismantling the postwar European settlement. And certainly, whatever the long-

[11] See Willy Brandt, *A Peace Policy for Europe* (New York: Holt, Rinehart and Winston, 1969) and especially pp. 75–93.

range tension between Atlanticism and *Ostpolitik*, Germany's heavy reliance on the United States grows more and more incompatible with her close participation within a Western European economic and political bloc with France.

Sparked by France, the Common Market has clashed increasingly with the United States, above all over the special role of the dollar. A European monetary union now is widely seen as the next major step toward European integration. Germany is caught in the middle. Basing *Ostpolitik* on Atlanticism gives the United States powerful leverage on German policy. Germany finds it difficult to join with France in effective action to dethrone the dollar, especially as American troops abroad are in themselves a principal cause for the United States' basic balance-of-payments deficit.[12] While successive German governments have been unable or unwilling to contribute enough directly to end the American military deficit, they nevertheless have always been willing, in the end, either to accept surplus dollars or to revalue the Deutschemark—both actions increasingly incompatible with any European monetary union which includes France.[13] In short, Germany's Atlanticist *Ostpolitik* clashes directly with further progress toward Western European integration.

But while these tensions between European goals and American military hegemony are logically obvious, many people find it difficult to see them ever upsetting the status quo. To begin with, many believe that all grand designs, French or German, for reconciling Europe from the Atlantic to the Urals will be blocked by Russia's iron determination to maintain tight control over the East. Should a more intimate association with the West inspire revisionism in some East European regimes, those regimes will be crushed like Dubček's government in Prague. In a nuclear world, no one in Europe, Germany included, will risk a war to change this harsh reality. In the end, no

[12] In 1970, for example, the United States was running a basic balance-of-payments deficit of $3.38 billion. That same year foreign exchange expenditures of the United States for military purposes were $4.8 billion. After military sales were deducted, they were $3.37 billion. In Europe, foreign-exchange expenditures after transactions in military equipment, were $1.28 billion, of which $700 million was spent in Germany alone. See John Newhouse, ed., *U.S. Troops in Europe*, (Washington: Brookings Institution 1971). See also Secretary of the Treasury John Connally's analysis in his speech to the Finance Ministers of the Group of Ten in London on September 15, 1971.

[13] In 1961 the Federal Republic of Germany revalued its currency by 5 percent. Throughout the rest of the 1960s, the Germans had tried to control the monetary effects of their constant surplus, but in October 1969 heavy selling of dollars and francs for marks forced the Bundesbank to revalue the mark by 8.5 percent. By the time of the Smithsonian agreements, the mark had revalued by 13.6 percent against the dollar.

Western European government, France included, will give up its comfortable American protectorate for the sake of chimerical hopes for a new pan-European system. The French play with these ideas only because geography allows them to take the Atlantic protectorate for granted. Should the Americans ever withdraw, leaving France yoked to Germany to face Russia, no one would be more disconcerted at their success than the French themselves. In this view, France's Eastern policy, like Germany's, bases itself upon America's continuing its European protectorate. France's measured disengagement in no way threatens the continuation of that protectorate; it merely gives France the best of both worlds.

Hence, according to this view, Brandt's Atlanticist *Ostpolitik* only follows the path blazed by de Gaulle a few years before. No European government seriously wants to change the present Atlantic bipolar system, but wants only to exploit the possibilities for maneuver within it. In a nuclear world, no one will risk real change, or renounce a comfortable status quo. Furthermore in this post-Gaullist era, it is said, no European government has the political will or authority to embark upon such an adventurous course. If anything, the major European states appear headed for a time of domestic economic, social, and political instability. Moreover, Britain's joining the European Communities may well dilute France's ability to mobilize Europe against American policy. In any event, the inevitable disruption of the communities from enlargement will greatly enfeeble Europe's capacity for a concerted external policy. Enlargement will also increase America's ability to interfere and inhibit unfavorable policies, as de Gaulle predicted long ago. In short, the revisionism of the European powers will continue to be what it has been—a minuet, in which all the shifting partners return, at the end, to where they were in the beginning. Thus, it is easy enough to argue that the revisionist diplomacy of the European powers, far from uniting them against the Atlantic protectorate, only increases their differences with each other and, hence, their dependence upon the United States.

No one can easily assess the relative weight of these various complex arguments and considerations. Still, the complacent view that discounts the significance of tensions between European goals and Atlantic hegemony bases itself upon a number of arguable assumptions. It presumes that neither the Gaullist nor the German revisionists are seriously discontented with things as they are. It takes for granted that the Russians are uninterested in any real accommodation with the Western Europeans, that Czechoslovakia is and will remain the definitive Soviet response to Eastern European revisionism, that Western Europeans will continue to feel both threatened and helpless militarily. In addition, the complacent view tends to assess European revisionist attitudes in isolation from the other two major dynamic elements in the over-all situation: the internal pressures which may encourage the American government itself to contemplate a military withdrawal from Europe, and, closely related, America's growing economic weakness and the consequent threat to Europe's domestic economies. Neither of these considerations can properly be ignored, as they may well be crucial for the future.

In recent years, signs that the United States itself might be tiring of the protector's role have brought a new and dynamic element to European calculations. How seriously should these signs be taken? Do they really threaten the status quo?

Were these signs limited to general public opinion, it would be easier to discount them as transitory "neo-isolationism"—part of the reaction aroused by the Vietnam war and unlikely to persist beyond it. Both the Nixon and Johnson Administrations have been able to defeat Senator Mansfield's various resolutions and amendments calling for a substantial reduction of our European garrison.[14] Even if Mansfield's proposals should pass the Senate in some form, a determined administration might expect to thwart Congressional pressure until it recedes. Yet the pressures for reduction are not only political, but military and financial.

The next few years are likely to see a radical reorganization of America's military forces and budget. In the face of public resistance to the draft and increasing disciplinary problems within the military, the Nixon Administration early committed itself to an all-volunteer army.[15] Conventional forces, of the type used lavishly in NATO garrisons, are already extremely expensive and will become more so with a professional army. With the national budget in huge deficit, the apparent progress of Soviet-American detente and the urgent pressure of domestic needs, a significant jump in the military budget seems improbable. Military resources, including manpower, will grow increasingly straitened. The military is committed to developing vari-

[14] Senator Mansfield first introduced his resolution on August 31, 1966, in which he spelled out the basic arguments for European troop reductions: recovery of Western Europe, unequal military commitment by different members of NATO, fiscal and monetary problems of the United States, changes and improvements in techniques of modern warfare, new potential for quick transportation of troops. Senator Mansfield's subsequent resolutions on January 19, 1967, December 1, 1969, and January 24, 1970, reiterate these arguments in the light of new developments.

[15] See Schultz, Fried, Rivlin, and Teeters, *Setting National Priorities: the 1973 Budget.* (Washington: Brookings Institution 1972), p. 61. The study estimates changing to an all-volunteer army will demand an increase of $4.5 billion in annual expenditure.

ous expensive new weapons systems, which have powerful support among industrial interests. How much longer, therefore, can military planners see the NATO garrison as a justifiable use of 300,000 scarce and expensive troops? The poor morale and training of these forces, particularly of the 200,000 man garrison in West Germany, is not likely to commend itself to military planners.[16]

The balance-of-payments cost of the European garrison presents yet another reason for reducing it. The dollar outflow for military forces abroad has always been a major factor in the United States' basic balance-of-payments deficit. In 1970, for example, official figures assign military forces stationed abroad some $4.5 billion in outflow—a sum half again larger than the entire basic deficit for that year.[17] Both the Johnson and Nixon Administrations have pressured European and Japanese allies to buy American arms to offset the military balance-of-payments losses. But even deducting all U.S. military sales abroad from the exchange costs of forces abroad, a highly questionable form of accounting in any case, these arms purchases have never succeeded in meeting more than a third of the annual military losses. Thus, in 1970, net military outflow still constituted an exchange loss of over $3 billion. Moreover, even in recent years, forces stationed in the NATO region have been responsible for from a third to a half of this military exchange outflow.

The significance of this fact, of course, depends on the importance assigned to America's continuing inability to reach a balance-of-payments equilibrium—a large subject to be addressed in a moment. It is worth noting, however, that the inability to bring our balance-of-payments deficit under control has already led to restrictions upon American investments abroad and, more generally, may come to threaten the whole position of America's vast overseas corporate operations.[18] At the very least, if the exchange costs of NATO forces

[16] See Haynes Johnson and George Wilson, U.S. *Army in Anguish*: three separate articles in the *Washington Post*, September 12, 1971, "U.S. Army: A Battle for Survival"; September 13, 1971, "G.I. Crime, Violence Crime Overseas"; and September 14, 1971.

[17] See E. R. Fried, "The Financial Cost of Alliance," in Newhouse, *Troops in Europe.*

[18] Restraint of private capital outflows began in 1963 with the Interest Equalization Tax on United States resident income from foreign securities; in 1965 "voluntary" restraints sought to discourage foreign lending by United States banks and direct foreign investments by United States businessmen, and in January 1968 direct investment restraints became mandatory. See United States Department of the Treasury, *Maintaining the Strength of the U.S. Dollar in a Strong World Economy* (Washington, 1968), pp. xii–xiii.

affront an increasing number of other American interests, domestic forces pressing for substantial reductions are likely to grow. In short, when these military and balance-of-payments factors are considered, national policies, our own included, which presuppose an indefinite continuation of the present NATO garrison, perhaps rest on a shaky foundation.

Even if the American forces in Europe are cut, however, it need not mean the end of America's hegemonic military role. A substantial reduction of American forces would not, in itself, necessarily force a reorganization of the alliance involving a major devolution to Europe of the responsibility for its own defense. No one seriously expects the Russians to invade Western Europe. Presumably, even if our garrison were substantially reduced, we would not disavow our NATO pledge to Europe's defense and the American nuclear guarantee would not altogether lose its credibility.[19] If the Europeans could not have American troops, they might be glad to have at least an American commander. The Nixon Administration, of course, has invested so much of its prestige and general credibility in maintaining the American NATO forces at their present level that it will be awkward to de-emphasize the significance of some future reduction. The administration has been painting itself into a corner.

Many observers believe Nixon counts on negotiations with the Russians for "Mutual and Balanced Force Reductions" to cloak substantial American withdrawals. If these have been the administration's expectations, they do not seem well-founded. In view of the considerable size of Western European forces, and the instability of the Eastern European regimes, the Russians are unlikely to regard their own forces in Eastern Europe as excessive.[20] Nor are they likely to

[19] Senator George McGovern in "A new Internationalism," an October 5, 1972, address before the City Club of Cleveland, describes this relationship as follows: "We no longer need to maintain 319,000 American troops in Europe to deter aggression. If we make some force reductions there is nothing the Soviet Union can do to weaken us or our Allies or to reduce our security."

[20] Western European armed forces in 1972 totalled 2,703,500, broken down as follows: Belgium, 96,500; Britain, 364,600; Denmark, 40,500; France, 501,000; Greece, 159,000; Italy, 414,000; Netherlands, 116,500; Norway, 35,900; Turkey, 508,500; West Germany, 467,000.

Eastern European armed forces, without the Soviet Union, totalled 987,000, broken down as follows: Bulgaria, 148,000; Czechoslavakia, 185,000; East Germany (GDR), 126,000; Hungary, 103,000; Poland, 265,000; Rumania, 160,000. The Soviet Union has total armed forces of 3,375,000. Estimates for army forces place 310,000 Russian troops in other Eastern European countries, and 600,000 to 900,000 in European Russia. (*The Military Balance: 1971–72*, IISS, London; for Russian estimates and their problems, see Calleo, *The Atlantic Fantasy*, pp. 146–48.)

reduce them sufficiently enough to cover a major American withdrawal. In any event, geography being what it is, the need to counter-balance Russian conventional forces will remain even if the great bulk of Soviet troops withdraws to Russia. In short, a credible Western European defense against the Soviet Union will need either an American protectorate or some form of military coalition among the Europeans themselves. If the United States sought, through troop withdrawals, to transform the protectorate into a more traditional alliance, what would be the European reaction? Would there be a compensating European defense coalition?

The European reaction would probably depend primarily on the general state of relations among the West European states themselves. A common view anticipates widespread panic culminating in disarmament and neutralism—the "Finlandization" of Europe. But nothing in the objective military situation seems to demand an outcome so obviously contrary to the national interests of the Europeans themselves. The major states have large conventional forces in being; Britain and France have at least the makings of a serious nuclear deterrent. There is no inherent reason either for panic or recrimination. In view of the obvious common interest in mutual defense, and the long experience of intimate inter-governmental cooperation within the Common Market, Europe might be expected to rise to the occasion.[21]

On the other hand, the present American policy of perpetuating hegemony by fostering divisions among the Europeans might seem calculated to make our ultimate devolution as traumatic and dangerous as possible. Why then do we not seize the opportunity for an orderly devolution from a transatlantic protectorate to a transatlantic alliance?

Such a question, of course, merely restates the fundamental issue which bedevils transatlantic relations. The United States is reluctant to give up its military hegemony over Western Europe. The ideal of a closely integrated economic and political pan-Atlantic community dies hard in the American imagination. To give up NATO, that part of the Atlantic community already in place, would seem retrograde and foolish, a burst of irresponsibility jettisoning the major accomplishment of a great generation of American world leadership. Fear of nuclear proliferation, moreover, can always be invoked to support these Atlanticist arguments. Ironically, it can always be added that there has still been no European settlement, that the United States

---

[21] For further views on the possibilities of European integration, see the author's *Atlantic Fantasy* (Baltimore: The Johns Hopkins University Press, 1970), chapter 8, pp. 123ff.

cannot withdraw leaving Russia on the field. Finally, vigorous opposition to withdrawing the American forces can always be counted on from among the European governments themselves. Even the French, while refusing to return to NATO, and calling periodically for Europe to organize a defense coalition, are clearly in no hurry to precipitate developments. In fact, France formally opposes American troop withdrawals.

None of this should be surprising. Europeans would understandably prefer to avoid the thorny issues which a European defense coalition would raise, for as long as the American protectorate seems credible and its economic and diplomatic costs to Europe are not too high. For France, as for Britain, the price seems minimal. Regardless of their feelings toward NATO, neither has felt inadequately protected, nor severely constrained in diplomatic or economic policy. Both, of course, have turned a deaf ear to American pleas for balance-of-payments' support for the troops, while nevertheless demanding, with increasing force, that the United States end its payments deficits.

No doubt the French see this contradiction clearly enough and ultimately expect the Americans to leave. Meanwhile, France builds up her own nuclear forces, carries on desultory talks with Britain about nuclear cooperation, and with Germany about a strategy for tactical nuclear weapons. But with France's own nuclear arms gradually developing, the longer Europe's coalition waits, the better France's relative position among her neighbors. Meanwhile, the American deterrent remains more than adequate against a threat which, for the moment at least, no one takes seriously.

British policy seems similarly ambivalent and leisurely. Prime Minister Heath came to power after several years of urging a joint Anglo-French nuclear force.[22] Talks have been held, but the British apparently still insist that the resulting forces be placed under NATO control. When the Nassau agreements are reviewed in 1973, perhaps the British will be more receptive.

Whereas the Pompidou and Heath Governments, refusing to pay any political or economic price for the American protectorate, have at least contemplated the possibility of an American withdrawal, and made some steps to prepare for it, the Brandt Government, apparently basing its *Ostpolitik* upon the assumption that U.S. forces would remain in Europe indefinitely, has made itself more vulnerable than ever to American pressure over economic and monetary issues.

[22] See Prime Minister Edward Heath's article, "Realism in British Foreign Policy," *Foreign Affairs*, October, 1969, pp. 46–47, as well as his recent book, *Old World, New Horizons* (London: Oxford University Press, 1970).

Germany's regular acquiescence before American demands is probably the principal obstacle to a concerted European policy toward the dollar. The tension has been mounting for the past several years. Thus, the policy which any German government would probably prefer—to be increasingly European in economic and monetary affairs, but remain resolutely Atlantic in military affairs—becomes less and less viable. The steady deterioration of America's international economic position, and the increasing strain which it puts on transatlantic relations, makes it increasingly difficult to separate the military and the economic spheres. The logic of military and economic inter-dependence presses Europeans to choose a parallel orientation for both.

Deteriorating economic relationships are probably the most significant of the forces undermining America's European position. Unlike diplomatic or military revisionism, which often appeals only to limited elites, the causes working for economic revisionism engage a wide range of domestic interest groups, affect the general standard of living, and bear significantly on the ability of national governments to control the economic environment for social purposes. However limited its initial concerns, economic revisionism is bound to have a powerful influence on political and military relationships.

In many respects, the problem troubling economic relations across the Atlantic is similar to the problem troubling political relations: the United States has been seeking to sustain, indeed increase, the degree of inter-dependence and control at the very time when Europe's resurgence, and America's relative decline, demand greater mutual autonomy.

It is also worth noting the similarity between America's economic tensions with Europe and those which disturb our relations with Japan.[23] Indeed, American economic difficulties with Japan form a somewhat sharpened parallel to our European problems. At the war's end, Japan became an American military protectorate. As the cold war developed, our fear of Japanese domestic dissaffection quickly brought an end to our insistence upon free-trade and often punitive economic policies. For several years, the Japanese, like the Europeans, were encouraged to foster their recovery through protection and were given easy access to the American domestic market. Japan

[23] For a general study of Japanese-American postwar relations, see Jerome B. Cohen's *Japan's Postwar Economy* (Bloomington, Indiana: University of Indiana Press, 1958), and Martin E. Weinstein's *Japan's Postwar Defense Policy, 1947–68* (New York: Columbia University Press, 1971).

was to be part of the pan-Atlantic Grand Design. Otherwise, we feared economic necessities might draw Japan into the Chinese and Soviet spheres, or revive that Japanese regional imperialism which had brought us into conflict in World War II. But not until the late 1950s, after European currencies had returned to convertibility, did we begin to pressure the Japanese seriously to enter into the liberal world system we had hoped to build all along. Since the 1960s, Japan has been pushed strongly to open her domestic markets to foreign goods and especially to foreign investment. Europeans, meanwhile, have been pressed to open their markets and share with us the burden of competing with Japan.

So far at least, the pan-Atlantic policy has failed on all counts. It is not acceptable to Japan, which does not want foreign investors undermining the extraordinarily complex corporatist system by which her industry and society are controlled; nor is it acceptable to Europe, which has no desire to compete in its home market with Japanese goods; nor finally to the United States, which can no longer afford to absorb the swelling product of the Japanese export industry.[24]

Japan's military dependence has, of course, given us extraordinary leverage in Japanese policy. As a result, most of Japan's monetary reserves are in depreciating and inconvertible dollars. At the same time, the outflow of dollars for Japanese defense makes our return to equilibrium all the more difficult.[25] We have sought relief from our spiralling trade deficit with Japan by pressing for an appreciation of the yen, while we ourselves depreciate the dollar. But despite a dollar depreciation of nearly 17 percent against the yen, the American trade deficit with Japan in 1972 appears to be greater than before. Meanwhile, a series of acrimonious negotiations among the Japanese, ourselves, and the Europeans have spawned a proliferation of "volun-

[24] America's merchandise trade deficit with Japan has steadily increased since 1965. Recent figures (in millions of dollars) are:

1967	1968	1969	1970	1971
−304	−1100	−1398	−1223	−3206

Negative sign indicates U.S. deficit

Source: U.S. Bureau of the Census, *Highlights of the U.S. Export and Import Trade*, Report FT 990, December, 1971 (released January, 1972), pp. 44–46, 86–88; U.S. Bureau of the Census, *Statistical Abstract of the United States 1971* (Washington, D.C., 1971), pp. 768–71; and *Statistical Abstract of the United States 1969* (Washington, D.C., 1969), pp. 808–11.

[25] United States Defense Expenditures for goods and services in Japan in millions of dollars:

		Jan.–June		
1965	1966	1967	1968	1969
346	484	538	581	320

Source: U.S. Department of Commerce, *Survey of Current Business* 49, no. 12, p. 44.

tary quotas" for Japanese exports to the United States.[26] Thus, economic elements reinforce a reviving Japan's impulse to resume diplomatic independence. At the same time, the cooperative economic patterns built since the war are beginning to unravel. The military hegemony to which we cling appears to have lost its economic base.

Our economic relations with Western Europe, and the Common Market in particular, have shown similar deterioration throughout the 1960s. While we have continued to enjoy a trade surplus with the Communities, our overall balance-of-payments deficit has made the Europeans our principal creditors. Thus, America's pretention to a continued economic and military hegemony, pressed in the Grand Design, has grown more and more anomalous with the dollar's weakness. The system's fundamental disequilibrium, reflected in a precarious dollar, has increasingly strained the institutions of both transatlantic and intra-European cooperation. Throughout the period, the United States has proved unable either to adjust to the relative decline in its financial position, or to reverse it.

The history of the postwar monetary system shows the degree of hegemonic integration which the United States has exercized over Europe and also explains the current malaise. The monetary system built around the IMF was an integral part of the post-war American world design. While the Bretton Woods Conference formally embraced multilateralism, the system that actually developed was hegemonic. Since the early 1950s, the United States has run a balance-of-payments deficit almost every year. Through 1970, we have had a trade surplus, as well as a large repatriated net income from foreign investments. But troop costs and new industrial investments have consistently gone beyond that surplus. By 1971, the trade surplus itself had disappeared. All this time, the constraints presumed to bring a deficit country back to equilibrium simply did not apply to the United States. Even after American monetary reserves were far from adequate to cover the huge and mounting pile of American short-term external obligations, the dollar remained universally acceptable. The European nations and Japan simply added more dollars to their reserves. The system that had developed was, in fact, a dollar standard. The United States was, in effect, acting as the world's central bank, determining the international money supply by its balance-of-payments deficits.

As long as the dollar was freely acceptable, the system constituted

[26] For an enumeration of earlier American-imposed trade restrictions, as well as a short history of US-Japanese trade relations, see Williams Commission, *Report*, Papers II (Washington, D.C., 1971), pp. 186–88.

liberalism without tears. As the international money supply has been constantly increasing, most states have had ample reserves and thus have been able to maintain convertibility without heavy deflationary constraint on domestic employment and growth. Indeed, the system has if anything encouraged inflation. In short, unlike the interwar period, national growth and international trade have gone forward hand in hand. Moreover, the system has been a particularly favorable environment for the spread of international corporate investment, American corporate investment in particular. Unhampered, at least until the later 1960s, by serious currency restrictions, most large American corporations have made substantial direct investments abroad. Many now draw an important share of their annual net profits from these investments. This corporate migration has, of course, helped push Europe's rapid economic growth, spread American technology and management, and further "integrated" the Atlantic economy.

Not only has the monetary system had popular general economic effects, but it has been a vital mechanism for the over-all transatlantic military and political relationship. American monetary hegemony has provided the means for financing American overseas military commitments. Every year, the foreign exchange costs for America's overseas forces have generally equalled or surpassed our basic payments deficit.[27] Not unreasonably, those who have received the protection have been expected to accept the surplus dollars. Military hegemony and monetary hegemony have gone together.

While the post-war monetary system had numerous advantages for everyone, it suffered from an obvious fundamental flaw. As the overall system required a continuing American deficit, our monetary reserves predictably grew smaller in relation to our short-term external obligations. Hence the dollar's convertibility has appeared increasingly uncertain and the system has grown increasingly precarious.

Much of our diplomatic policy in the 1960s and 1970s has consisted of ingenious attempts to persuade foreigners to go on accepting dollars, despite our continuing deficits and shrinking reserves.

At the same time, a more daring official policy has worked persistently to demonetize gold. Arguing that, if the American deficit were ended, some new form of regularly increasing international li-

---

[27] A comparison of the statistics for U.S. basic balance-of-payments and outflow for net military transactions from 1965–1970 proves the point:

	1965	1966	1967	1968	1969	1970
U.S. Basic Balance	−1814	−1614	−3196	−1349	−2879	−3038
U.S. Net Military Outflow	−2122	−2935	−3138	−3140	−3341	−3371

Source: U.S. Department of Commerce, *Survey of Current Business* (June, 1971), table 1.

quidity was essential, the United States has demanded a new form of international money issued and distributed annually by the IMF, the Special Drawing Right. Although the SDR scheme was duly installed, two developments frustrated the American expectation of enough new money to cover our debt. The French, using their Common Market position to gain leverage, successfully insisted that the United States and Britain not be allowed to use their majority control in the IMF automatically to determine the amount of SDR created.[28] More significantly, by 1967, the American balance-of-payments deficit began to grow to astronomical proportions. After 1970, the spiralling deficit reflected not only the growing nervousness of dollar holders, but a marked deterioration in the American balance of trade.

American strategy shifted to demands that the burden of adjustment should fall upon "surplus" countries, in other words that Europeans and Japanese should revalue their currencies so that American goods and investments would be more competitively priced. American pressure plus waves of speculation, has, in fact, forced our German protectorate into significant revaluations. Nevertheless, speculation against the dollar quickly resumed. Finally, in August of 1971, the dollar was forced to float and later to devalue formally.

The dollar's crisis in 1971 provided a virtuoso display of American monetary improvisation. The American government was widely expected to find a dollar devaluation intolerably damaging to its prestige. Instead, Secretary of the Treasury John Connally, forced to suspend convertibility, demanded a massive dollar depreciation, and imposed an import surcharge to reinforce his demands. Connally called for a depreciation calculated to bring a $13 billion turnaround in American trade—big enough not only to redress our trade deficit, but also to cover all our outflow for military and investment purposes.[29] In effect, Connally's policy offered the Europeans and Japanese the alternative either of accepting the dollar at its old parity— even if it remained inconvertible—or else allowing the dollar to depreciate on a free market until an American trade surplus covered

[28] The original IMF quota and voting arrangements of 1945 gave the U.S. and Britain combined a near majority and the original EEC countries a relatively small role, doubtless a reflection of the time's political and economic realities. In the machinery for creating Special Drawing Rights, the Six, as the world's major creditors, are given a collective veto. New SDR creation requires 85 percent of the total votes and the Six presently have 16.9 percent.

[29] See Secretary Connally's statement to the Finance Ministers of the Group of Ten in London, September 15, 1971.

the cost of all American outflows. The first course meant acknowledging frankly America's unique exemption from any restraint on external spending. The second course, permitting a dollar depreciation adequate to end the deficit, promised serious damage to European trade.

For the Europeans to escape the dilemma Connally set for them, they would logically have to follow one, or perhaps a combination, of two difficult alternatives. They could impose restrictions, either to stop the rush of inconvertible dollars or to discourage the sale of American goods cheapened by drastic devaluation. Or Europeans could help end the American deficit by taking direct action to compensate for, or supplant those non-commercial American outflows, especially military, which made the American deficit inevitable.

At first glance, controls seemed the easiest course. But apart from the practical difficulties, those European countries with liberal traditions and important extra-community trade, like Germany, understandably opposed restrictions which would have invited retaliation.

Although the Europeans could not agree on controls, neither has any agreement seemed in sight for any adequate direct subsidy to cover the exchange costs of overseas American military commitments. But America's overseas military commitments doubtless weighed in the crisis. For it was our two military protectorates, Germany and Japan, who revalued in 1971. And fears that a tough European monetary policy toward the dollar would force or induce the Americans to withdraw troops was very likely a major consideration in the Brandt Government's decision to revalue unilaterally.

With such conflicting interests at work among them, Europeans in 1971 were once again unable to agree on any collective position toward American demands. Each went its separate way. The Germans floated and revalued and the French imposed controls. A few months later, the Smithsonian agreements ratified a series of currency changes involving a substantial devaluation of the dollar and a substantial revaluation of the yen and the Deutschemark. Supposedly, time was gained both for a fundamental reform of the world monetary system and for a firm monetary union among Europeans.

Despite a good deal of brave talk, neither world reform nor European union as yet shows much progress. To be sure, experts have broadly agreed about the outlines of a new world monetary system. Many see the need for a European monetary bloc—to maintain firm rates among its closely interdependent members and a common stance toward the dollar. Many propose that the huge pool of dollars now held by foreign central banks should somehow be funded, so as no longer to menace the American balance-of-payments, and thus safely permit the dollar's convertibility to be restored. Nearly all can agree that in the future, the United States, as well as any other member of the system, should be expected to keep payments in broad balance. Many also believe a regular creation of SDR should be used to provide adequate liquidity to finance short-term deficits. Wider bands and more frequent parity changes are now popular means to facilitate the rapid adjustment of persistent deficits or surpluses.

Rather perversely, however, all these plausible schemes ignore the main problem in the monetary system. Any system which presupposes American equilibrium is likely to work only if the United States, in fact, keeps its official outflows at a level which can be matched by a current account surplus acceptable to her trading partners. At the moment, that condition would appear to mean either a much heavier subsidy to the United States for its troops, or a substantial diminution of America's military role in Europe and Japan. While this vital matter is unresolved, world monetary reform seems likely to remain only an aspiration and European monetary union only a fair-weather construction.

For many observers, any firm resolution of the military issue seems so improbable that they cannot therefore take seriously the prospect either of a durable European monetary union or of any profound change in the world's monetary system. In particular, many believe Germany will continue to accept surplus American dollars, or to revalue the mark periodically, rather than risk the withdrawal of American military forces. In this view, the economic costs of the monetary system are not great enough to override the military and political interests that sustain Germany's ultimate allegiance to the status quo—in other words, to America's tenacious if shaky hegemony in Europe.

Moreover, despite a continuing basic deficit, the short-term market prospects for the dollar may very well improve. Europe's current rapid inflation suggests that, in the immediate future, world markets may judge the dollar more stable than continental currencies. Even if continuing official expenditures preclude redressing the basic deficit in the American balance-of-payments, short-term capital movements, or the flow of investment funds, may cover more fundamental disequilibria. In other words, in the monetary sphere—as in the diplomatic and military—expectations of a continuing status quo are neither improbable nor unattractive.

Nevertheless, a number of powerful considerations press the European states toward close monetary cooperation to revise the present system, in particular the special position of the dollar. To begin with, the costs of monetary disunity for Europe grow heavier. Continual failure to concert policy in monetary crises is beginning to threaten the morale and credibility of the European Communities. It is difficult for intimate trading partners, whose economies are closely tied together, to function indefinitely with constantly changing parities among themselves. Their Common Agricultural Policy becomes more and more complex to manage. Floating upward while partners remain relatively stationary considerably magnifies the costs of revaluation. For this reason, German resistance to further unilateral revaluation is likely to stiffen. Probably most important of all, many Europeans believe the present monetary situation endangers the internal economic balance of European states, and makes their domestic economies increasingly unmanageable. Why?

The United States is accused, by the French in particular, of "exporting inflation." By this, the French mean not that the domestic American rate of inflation is higher, but that the United States, by exporting surplus dollars, has been causing inflation in other countries—particularly those which have received such lavish American investment in the past two decades. Reinforcement for the French argument has come from the fantastic growth of the Eurodollar Market, that great, volatile pool of credit which has frequently frustrated European governments attempting to regulate domestic money supplies. Thus governments have felt handicapped in their efforts to stifle inflation or in general to exert effective control over domestic economic environments.

European reactions, of course, have been ambivalent in this respect as in others. Many interests use, and profit from, the Eurodollar Market, and many defend it. In Europe, as in the United States, a powerful business ideology defends the present monetary system. The Eurodollar Market, it is said, exists not so much because of America's excess, but because of Europe's need. Big business has long gone beyond the nation state and demands a pan-Atlantic capital market. Traditional states must or ought to give way before the internationalization of business corporations. Behind these arguments lies the familiar case for laissez-faire: scarce resources should go as the market dictates; economic allocations can achieve maximum efficiency only when not "distorted" by political interference.

Such arguments, of course, make it easier for Americans to ignore the forces gathering against the monetary status quo. Nevertheless, the view appears to overlook the general tendency of post-war history. While no one can sensibly overlook the increasing role of international corporations, these corporations are unlikely either to doom the nation state or to liberate economics from politics. The great accomplishment of the post-war era, after all, has been the taming of economics by politics. In all advanced capitalist countries, and certainly in most of Europe, government is expected to take the commanding role in the economy in order to provide security both for the individual and for business. Economic growth has to be planned, stimulated, regulated, and shared according to political forces and ideas which permeate the political-economic system. The social conflict which now begins to perturb all Western societies probably means increasing political intervention. Above all, the need to protect and shape the physical environment in Europe's crowded countries will demand more and more conscious political direction.

The present monetary system, with its continual disruption of European domestic economies, and the capacity of their governments to direct them, therefore runs counter to what would seem to be the fundamental evolution of modern political economy. Any national political economy constitutes a delicate and often precarious working balance of domestic political-economic forces. Unpredictable and uncontrollable external forces which seriously disturb that equilibrium are likely to be rejected. Under the circumstances, the more relevant question is not whether the internationalization of business will sweep away the nation state, but whether the domestic needs of all advanced societies will force them to abandon a liberal world economy—that world economic system, symbolized in the GATT and the IMF which is the creation of these years of American hegemony. At the present time, such dissociation seems the general drift of events. The same impulse seems at work in American policy, for example, which has pushed the European Communities toward a separate monetary and trading bloc. As our hegemony fades and American basic payments deficits continue and foreign resistance to the dollar standard becomes effective, the United States may well be driven to recurring dollar depreciation and import restrictions. Of course, in theory, the United States could impose a rigorous deflationary policy on itself at home and thus hope to generate a sufficient trade surplus. Quite apart from foreign reaction, such a course is politically most unlikely. For the United States, the whole foreign sector is not important enough to call the tune for the domestic economy. Short of war or dictatorship, no political economy, particularly one so self-sufficient as our own, will easily tolerate severe external interference with its own domestic goals and balances. In short, when the dollar is under pressure, the United States will float or devalue. Faced with such policies, an increasingly self-sufficient European bloc, to prevent its own domestic disruption, will very likely impose serious controls over foreign trade and capital movements. If the Europeans cannot manage to do this collectively, then their own economic union will break up and they will return to the more primitive form of nationalist protectionism typical of the inter-war years.

None of these extremities would, of course, be necessary if the United States could bring its payments into balance without demanding so enormous a trade surplus from its Atlantic partners. With the American economy inflating no faster than the European, even a floating dollar presumably need not depreciate if the system were first cleansed of destabilizing non-commercial factors such as the foreign exchange costs of military commitments. Today, troops seem to be playing the same role in deranging the market's adjustment mechanism as war debts and reparations in the 1920s. But as then, a liberal international system among independent states is unlikely to work if it must carry such heavy political burdens.

Such an analysis strongly suggests that the present economic, and ultimately the military, status quo is unlikely to persist. An American administration enlightened by such a view would presumably press rather more for devolution and rather less for the preservation than either the Johnson or first Nixon Administrations. It has never been difficult, of course, to construct a convincing rationale for America's long-range interest in a European economic, political, and even military bloc. A European bloc seems an almost essential element in any world system that is not only plural, but stable and peaceful. Once disengaged from too close economic integration with the United States, European governments ought to be able to get their national domestic economies in order and adjust mutual relations well enough to preserve the obvious advantages of the Common Market. A European military and political coalition, allied loosely to the United States, but not its creature, ought to dispose sufficient weight to live amicably but securely next to the Russians. While the unsettled state of Eastern Europe makes the future uncertain, an independent Western Europe is hardly any more likely than the United States to unleash a nuclear war to "liberate" the East from the Soviets. If it is possible to take a more hopeful view of the evolution of Eastern Europe, then an independent Western Europe bloc, no longer a forward outpost of American military power, may well be the arrangement most likely to coax the Russians into a more creative approach to their own problems of devolution.

But a policy of devolution obviously carries risks. Official imaginations dwell on the dangers of "Finlandization," if the American he-

gemony recedes. Western European powers are feared to be so dis-
united that the Russians can dominate by playing one off against
another. The danger might be real enough if the whole movement
toward Western European cohesion disintegrated at the same time
as America's European role diminished drastically. But that may well
happen anyway if the present mutual frustration of Atlantic and
European policies continues. Eventually, transatlantic institutions are
likely to break if American-European tensions remain unresolved;
meanwhile the struggle will divide and embitter the Europeans seriously enough to poison cooperation among them. Moreover, as some
suspect of Brandt's *Ostpolitik*, Atlanticism can provide the cover for
nationalist and anti-European policies among the Europeans themselves.

According to many observers, of course, Europe is already hope-
lessly divided. The great post-war crusade for union has deteriorated
into a sort of league for commercial collusion. Surely the details of
military and diplomatic affairs present no clear picture of durable
and comprehensive unity among the European powers. France and
Germany have made perhaps the most serious efforts to concert their
policies. Yet among the European states, they have most often been
the principal exponents of conflicting views. Moreover, the economic
and social troubles of Britain and Italy may seriously compromise
efforts to sustain even Europe's present economic integration.

But Europe's disunity can easily be exaggerated. Many of the serious intra-European divisions of recent years have arisen over relations with the U.S.—in particular the future of NATO and the dollar.
If America were to step back from military and monetary hegemony,
at least one major cause, or at least pretext, of disunity would greatly
diminish.

In general, American observers have been too quick to equate European unity with progress toward achieving the particular organizational formulas so popular in the heyday of Monnet and Hallstein.
Their preoccupation with supra-national forms leads many American
observers to underestimate the extent and significance of Europe's
actual integration. Any European bloc will be a coalition of sovereign
states. They are unlikely to abandon or attempt to devolve their political legitimacy to some supra-national political construction. But if
national states have not disappeared, they have nevertheless created
a remarkable series of institutions which force them to consider and
resolve together an increasing range of vital national decisions. The
result is an extraordinary political system, whose real significance
has not been enough appreciated. At the very least, the shortcomings

of our own experiment with a relatively centralized "federal" government over a continental state should make students more open-minded toward Europe's attempts at a looser "confederal" arrangement. In any event, it can hardly be argued that the Europeans have shown no talent for agreement, or that the whole experiment of the Common Market prefigures the demise of European union. Quite the contrary.

To return to an earlier point: if devolution which anticipates a European bloc carries risks for American interests, so indeed does a policy aimed at maintaining the status quo. While the present quasi-hegemony may seem to many a situation that serves American interests well, no one should overlook the danger of a general breakdown, particularly if economic relations continue to deteriorate. Numerous uncomfortable parallels link the current state of international economic disorder, particularly in the monetary field, with the deterioration of the late 1920s. An Olympian perspective, of course, might see a crash in transatlantic affairs as the necessary prelude to the formation of a genuine European bloc and a sensible readjustment of transatlantic relationships. The risk is high that such a breakdown would lead, as in the inter-war period, to incalculable domestic political disruptions, and that European economic unity might itself be an early casualty.

It is this larger historical parallel which lifts America's European relations beyond the familiar range of cold war issues. For in our future relations with Europe much more will be decided than whether the United States can gracefully divest itself of its now unnaturally swollen defense burdens. It will also be decided whether, out of the post-war episode of our hegemony, there can emerge a lasting system of organized international cooperation among the developed capitalist countries—a system which can survive our hegemony's inevitable decline. The issue goes back to all those questions of the inter-war years, questions for which the 1930s failed so disastrously to find an answer. Can a liberal international system be combined with orderly, contented domestic societies? How can international liberalism and the mercantilist welfare state come to terms with each other? One thing seems certain. The solutions will be found, if they are to be found, in the future pattern of relations between the United States and Europe.

8

ECONOMIC POLICY AND DEVELOPMENT:
THE CASE OF LATIN AMERICA

Benjamin M. Rowland

Introduction

Nineteen seventy-one was the "year of crisis" for our foreign aid policy, and President Nixon, in time-honored political fashion, was laboring to apportion the blame. The dollar crisis, he noted in his annual foreign policy message, had obliged him to make a 10 percent reduction in aid expenditures. This was not meant as a signal of lessening U.S. commitment. Above all:

It did not justify the action taken by the Senate in November which almost abolished our entire aid program. This action, subsequent Congressional treatment of the aid program, and the large cuts in the aid levels I requested are of serious concern to those of us who realize the importance of this program, and to friendly nations who look to us for assistance.[1]

Who was to blame? Accusing Congress for the collapse of foreign aid was not without foundation. Aid was unique among the instruments of our foreign policy. It required Congressional approval. The disenchantment with aid, like a fever chart, reflected the growing frustrations of a Congress unable to impose its will on the administration. A vote against aid translated easily into a vote of protest against the conduct of our foreign policy in general.

For some Congressional critics the protest ran deeper. Aid was more than the administration's vulnerable foreign policy flank; it was a carrier of the same disease infecting our foreign policy in its entirety. The policy responsible for Vietnam and the policy which promoted foreign aid were cast from the same cold war mold. Our aid policy, projecting American interests and American power into every corner of the third world, contained the seeds of many Vietnams. It supported corrupt, elitist regimes and committed us to their

---

[1] Richard M. Nixon, U.S. *Foreign Policy for the 1970's: The Emerging Structure of Peace*, February 9, 1972, p. 77.

241

survival.[2] Simple withdrawal from Vietnam would not rescue our aid program from its critics. There must be no more Vietnams—no more engagements in regions of peripheral importance where passions might erupt and interests entangle.

While the Congressional attack on aid clearly exceeded the wishes of the administration, in a broader sense Congress was merely extending to an economic plane what had, in fact, already occurred on a politico-strategic level. However steadfastly we were holding our ground in other quarters of the world, we were indeed withdrawing from the third world. Certainly, in a strategic sense, our participation in the third world was well below the massive involvement which characterized United States policy in the early 1960s. Opportunities to become involved were not wanting—in Nigeria, India, Chile, the Middle East. In each of these areas, it seemed, we were showing an uncommon degree of forbearance. Like the Johnson Administration before it, though to a lesser extent, the Nixon Administration seemed determined to change the foci of superpower rivalries away from the peripheries of the third world, where the imponderables were many, to the more highly developed and hence presumably more rational main arenas of world power. In this respect, Congress, even as it exceeded the intentions of the administration, was faithfully reflecting the broad strategic shifts in American foreign policy.

For Congress, however, the attack on foreign aid seemed to be revealing a disenchantment not only with the excesses of the past but with the pretensions of the future, with the broad outlines of the Nixon Doctrine itself. Explaining that policy, the president said: "I have repeatedly emphasized that the Nixon Doctrine is a philosophy of invigorated partnership, not a synonym for American withdrawal."[3]

But was there a basis for an invigorated partnership with the third world? Whatever the prospects for that strategy in the world at large, for our third world policy the line between orderly devolution of responsibility implied in the notion of partnership, and outright withdrawal, seemed perilously thin. What was there to retain our commitments and keep us from "neo-isolationism?" The exuberantly critical mood of Congress in 1971, it must be said, left little room for maneuver.

The United States was not the only party engaged in a reappraisal. If for the United States the collapse of economic assistance and other concessionary economic policies reflected the waning importance of

[2] See, for example, Sen. Frank Church, "Farewell to Foreign Aid: A Liberal Takes his Leave," *Washington Post*, November 7, 1971.

[3] *U.S. Foreign Policy for the 1970's: Building for Peace*, February 25, 1971, p. 258.

the third world in our overall strategy, rising economic nationalism in the third world reflected not only the decline in the volume of our economic blandishments, but a growing tendency by third world countries to assert their national political integrity through economic means. Hence the double dilemma of the Nixon Doctrine: Could we, with less to offer, hope to contain the third world's apparent growing restiveness?

Focusing on our relations with Latin America, this essay will attempt to assess the future course and impact of our economic policies toward the third world. Latin America emerges as the proper object of such a study for a variety of reasons.

First, there seems a greater likelihood of sustained U.S. interests in Latin America than elsewhere in the third world. When the Asian adventures which have enmeshed succeeding postwar administrations are no more than a dim, bitter memory, Latin America, if only from proximity, will continue to command substantial American attention. Geopolitical reasoning dies hard, even as the motives which have sustained it in the past fade away. Whatever the difficulty in demonstrating the precise nature of the threat to our security posed by erring Latin American republics, American policy will predictably maintain a vigorous interest in being surrounded by a group of amiable client-states.

Second, and of growing importance, Latin America represents the biggest American economic stake in the third world. Latin America has always been a major trading partner. Until less than twenty years ago, it was the principal site for United States foreign investment. It provides strategic raw materials for the U.S. economy and is, in turn, a key consumer of American output, capital, and expertise.

Third, Latin America emerges as a proper object for study because, of all regions of the third world, it has passed most unambiguously beyond the realm of the cold war. The only power which might be more embarrassed than the United States by the emergence of another Cuba, it is sometimes said, would be Russia herself. Hence, in removing the aura of superpower conflict from Latin America, it seems plausible to argue that "normal" American interests and concerns will stand a greater chance of gaining the ascendency.

Finally, Latin America is both important and representative for the simple reason that we choose to make it so. To cite President Nixon: "If we cannot build partnerships in the relationships with developing countries in this hemisphere, then this task will indeed be formidable elsewhere in the world."[4]

4 *Ibid.*, p. 359.

The prospects for a successful "partnership," or, indeed, for a civilized relationship of any sort, will increasingly turn on the nature of our economic policies. Economics, it is often noted, is the basic stuff of peace-time diplomacy. Economic issues deemed secondary in a time of protracted conflict acquire new importance in a time of peace. For the third world, President Nixon has noted: "The predominant issues in their relations with us are the style and content of our economic relations."[5] He might have applied the same broad logic to the United States. In Latin America during the heyday of the Alliance for Progress, as in Europe under the Marshall Plan, it was our policy to purchase allies with economic concessions. We would appease our clients economically, demanding only political loyalty in return. But by the later 1960s, the various economic blandishments designed to command third world allegiance seemed superfluous. In the cold war aftermath, we betrayed a growing eagerness to return to economic "normalcy." America under the Nixon Doctrine yearned for business as usual.

Given its present disarray, what is to be the likely future course of our economic policy toward Latin America? Will it be concessionary or punitive? Will it revert to the old "liberal ideal" of economic openness which has played so important a role in ordering American perspectives on international economic relations, or will it adjust to Latin America's evident economic revisionism?

The study which follows weighs the prospects for sustained cooperation between the United States and Latin America in the light of the past and apparent future course of our economic policies.

United States–Latin American Policy in Perspective

Our Latin American policy during the 1960s—based on the Alliance for Progress, with its emphasis on economic development, political reform, and social engineering—represents a significant departure from a policy which, in general, has always been a minimalist one. Over the 150 years since America's unilateral declaration of the Monroe Doctrine, we have rarely exercised ourselves seriously on Latin America's behalf. From the vantage point of history, the Alliance for Progress is the clear exception for which the "low-profile" policy announced by President Nixon upon coming to office forms the general rule. In essence, the Monroe Doctrine expressed our intention to exclude from the hemisphere serious rivals for the atten-

[5] *Ibid.*

tions and loyalties of the Latin American republics. Twice during the twentieth century, rivals appeared to challenge our hegemony in the hemisphere—Germany in the late 1930s and Russia in the late 1950s. Both occasions inspired concessionary economic policies to strengthen wavering loyalties and bring erring states back in line. As the challenges were removed, our interests and initiatives have tended to decline accordingly.

During these periods of hemispheric siege, in effect if not in intent, the United States relaxed the customary strictness of its economic policies. Many Latin American nations were not slow to capitalize on our temporary weakness. In the late 1930s, Mexico and even Bolivia took advantage of the heightened political atmosphere to nationalize the foreign oil holdings within their countries, confident, ultimately, of the moderate American response which followed.[6] Similarly in 1960, after a long battle, Mexico nationalized several American-owned utility companies, again confident that America's pre-eminent concern with Castro and desire for hemispheric solidarity would allay punitive reprisals.[7]

The policy of economic appeasement in exchange for political solidarity was not limited to the Western Hemisphere alone. Indeed, it emerges as a dominant theme in America's postwar economic diplomacy, of which the Latin American case is only the most recent example. As in Latin America, moreover, it was a policy we adopted only in circumstances of extraordinary urgency, and, as in Latin America, it was a policy we abandoned as soon as circumstances permitted.

If economic appeasement was the exception to our favored economic policy, what was the ideal from which it deviated? The notion of an "ideal type" presents a number of obvious intellectual problems. Nonetheless, in economics, perhaps more so than any other aspect of our policy, the American ideal was clear. The American economic ideal embraced openness. Like an uncertain ingenue, it feared and grew uneasy in front of closed, exclusive groups. Our fear of closed blocs, we argued, grew out of our interpretation of the inter-war experience. Economic blocs grew into political blocs. Political blocs enhanced the likelihood of war. The necessary complement to the "open" political system of the United Nations was the open economic system sanctioned in the Bretton Woods Agreements.

Whether our advocacy of that policy stemmed from a peculiarly

---

[6] See Bryce Wood, *The Making of the Good Neighbor Policy* (New York: Columbia University Press, 1964), pp. 168–282.

[7] See Raymond R. Vernon, *Public Policy and Private Enterprise in Mexico* (Cambridge: Harvard University Press, 1964).

virulent strain of American naiveté or from cold-blooded calculations of national self-interest remains a central point of contention among interpreters of post-war American foreign policy. Neither view is particularly flattering. In any event, few outside the United States shared our open internationalist vision.[8] Russia, although a signatory at Bretton Woods, had no intention of tying her economic fate to the West. Britain, no doubt more sympathetic to the general principles of Bretton Woods than Russia, nonetheless made clear her preference for a protected regional arrangement in which she could recover from the war without being overwhelmed by America's economic power. Although Russia removed herself from the system, American power was sufficient to batter Britain into acquiescence. For a loan of three and three-quarters billion dollars, Britain agreed to allow her currency to become convertible by the summer of 1947. A major run on sterling in July and August 1947 led to inconvertibility—a condition from which Britain emerged only in 1958.

Reassessment of the war's disruption and the growing menace of Russia led America to abandon her ideal policy. Only a major infusion of capital would save Europe from chaos and communism. Only a Europe united politically and economically would feel strong enough to face the U.S. openly once recovery had been achieved. Hence the new American policy encouraged Europe to form an economic group and openly discriminate against the dollar. The OEEC, formed to dispose of Marshall Plan aid while forcing the Europeans into close consultation, was followed by the European Payments Union, a clearing mechanism to aid Europeans in marshalling their scarce dollar reserves.

In only slightly altered form, the same general shift occurred in American policy toward Japan. Until late 1947, America adopted a policy of lofty vindictiveness toward Japan. Again, the threat of communism combined with profound economic dislocations led to a shift mirroring the change in our policy in Europe.

During this period, to be sure, the rhetoric of America's open "liberal" system was never entirely obscured. There was no reassessment of our economic ideals, only the belief that they had been prema-

[8] For radical scholars of American foreign policy, our quest for an open economic world is taken as evidence that America conforms to the Leninist scheme of an advanced capitalist society—a country driven to mortal economic combat abroad to protect the structure of society and distribution of wealth at home. For a discussion with particular reference to Latin America see Robert W. Tucker, *The Radical Left and American Foreign Policy* (Baltimore: The Johns Hopkins University Press, 1971).

turely applied.[9] Nearly all concurred that the essential liberal principles should be honored, even in their breaching. The price of our aid was political loyalty. Full recovery, we hoped, would usher in an age when the wisdom of an open liberal system would be clear. In the meantime, our economic diplomacy would insure that when the time was ripe, that liberal solution would still be a possibility.

Nineteen fifty-eight marked the beginning of the end of our economic appeasement of Europe. By late 1958, the principal European currencies had left the shelter of the European Payments Union and resumed convertibility. Japan followed suit two years later, albeit reluctantly and with many qualifications. European integration, still with America's blessing, continued to press forward, although now, as before, America did not hesitate to insist that the European movement be "outward-looking."

More interesting for the purposes of this essay, the cycle of American policy now appeared ready to repeat itself in the third world. From the end of the war until about 1958, American policy toward the third world bore a general correspondance to her European policy from 1945 to 1947. We would sanction no special deals nor create special institutions for the economic problems of the third world. To be sure, general conditions at the outset seemed to justify such an approach. America's resources were not inexhaustible. Europe lay in ruins; the third world did not. In Latin America, for example, the war was a positive stimulus to most domestic economies. War-time scarcity and the disruption of shipping forced the development of native industries where few had existed before. Heavy war-time demand for Latin America's raw materials swelled gold and foreign currency reserves. Having little to buy with their foreign exchange, many Latin American nations emerged from the war with the strongest reserve positions they had ever enjoyed. High commodity prices, continuing buoyant through the Korean War, added to the general optimism and made the curtailing of war-time economic co-operation seem less painful. By around 1954, however, the value of the leading commodities plummeted. With their reserves sorely depleted, poverty unrelieved by the prospect of rapid growth became the ruling condition.

The rising incidence of revolutionary activity in Latin America reinforced the Marshall Plan thesis that communism fed on poverty and that massive infusions of capital could effect the proper cure.

[9] For a supporting view, see William Y. Elliott *et al.*, *The Political Economy of American Foreign Policy* (New York: Holt, Rinehart and Winston, 1955).

Thus, by 1958, our policies toward the third world began to show striking similarities to our earlier policy toward Europe. And, as our apprehensions grew, our economic policies toward the third world began to acquire some of the same "flexibility" which they had shown in the earlier European recovery period. In 1959, we endorsed a regional development bank for Latin America, a concept pressed energetically by many Latin Americans since the beginning of World War II but until then resisted with equal force by the United States. A new receptiveness to the idea of commodity agreements formed another major departure from traditional American policy. To cap it all, we officially sanctioned third world economic regionalism, reversing a barely disguised earlier hostility to the notion.

Not surprisingly, the new currents showed themselves in the international organizations as well. In 1958, Gottfried Haberler led a team of prominent economists to the conclusion that third world development demanded a radical revision of the rules and practices governing international trade.[10]

By late 1960, the ground had been laid for the most massive change of all—the Alliance for Progress—a kind of "moral Marshall Plan," as one of its principal architects, Adolf Berle, described it.[11] At the heart of the Alliance was the assurance of the new president to commit no less than $1 billion annually for a period of ten years to the South American continent.[12] As he announced to a group of Latin American diplomats gathered in the White House:

I have called on all the people of the Hemisphere to join me in a new Alliance for Progress—*Alianza para Progreso*—a vast co-operative effort, unparalleled in magnitude and nobility of purpose, to satisfy the basic needs of the American people for homes, work and land, health and schools— *techo, trabajo y tierra, salud y escuela.*[13]

It is perhaps too easy to be cynical about the motives behind the Alliance, as, indeed, many Latin Americans were at the time. Genuine idealism, no doubt, underlay much of the new president's poli-

[10] Gottfried Haberler *et al., Trends in International Trade* (Geneva: GATT, 1958).

[11] Arthur M. Schlesinger, Jr., *A Thousand Days* (Boston: Houghton Mifflin, 1965), p. 182.

[12] The assurance was actually given by Treasury Secretary Douglas Dillon at the Punta del Este Conference in August, 1961. Later in the same conference, Dillon stated that Latin America might expect to receive $20 billion in external, although not necessarily American, assistance over the coming decade.

[13] Quoted in Schlesinger, *A Thousand Days*, pp. 204–05.

cies. Kennedy's adviser, Arthur Schlesinger, Jr., in all likelihood reflected the general mood: "To a surprising extent," he said, "the slate has been wiped clean. . . . The atmosphere is set for miracles."[14]

Of all the motives which fed the initiation of the Alliance, it is hardly controversial that anti-communism was the strongest. The famous Nixon "good-will" visit to Latin America in 1958, culminating in an assault by a murderous crowd in Caracas, brought home the perilousness of America's position with dramatic urgency. Cuba confirmed our worst fears. If the germ of an Alliance for Progress existed before Castro's turn to the left, as Milton Eisenhower,[15] among others, steadfastly maintained, no action of consequence was taken until after Castro's appearance. The chronology of events amply demonstrates the correspondence: *January 1959*—Castro assumes power; *April 1959*—at a meeting of the "Committee of Twenty-One," the U.S. offers support for a Latin American Common Market, offers to discuss commodity agreements, and agrees to the idea of an Inter-American Development Bank; *February 1960*—World Bank's "Soft Loan" window opens; *March 1960*—Eisenhower adopts contingency plan to overthrow Castro; *July 1960*—Eisenhower announces U.S. support for Latin American social reform; and *September 1960*—in the Act of Bogota, the U.S. commits $500 million for Latin American social reform.

Contradictions in the Alliance

Although it took Gaullism, a superpower detente, and finally an American financial crisis to expose the contradictions of the policy which began with the Marshall Plan, the weaknesses of the Alliance for Progress surfaced quite rapidly. The Latin American campaign— even before it started—suffered three deficiencies which were not present in the Marshall Plan. It was more ambitious, more amorphous, and enjoyed less public and governmental support.

Whereas the Marshall Plan had merely attempted to restore a wartorn society to a former level of achievement, the Alliance was charged to construct, from hitherto rigid, unyielding materials, a totally new order. It was to do so, moreover, without abruptly unseating the old. Even more remarkable, in retrospect, than our formula for a "non-violent revolution from above" was the limited nature of the investment we believed necessary to accomplish our goals. How-

[14] *Ibid.*, p. 170.
[15] Milton Eisenhower, *The Wine is Bitter* (Garden City, N.Y.: Doubleday, 1963).

ever vast the undertaking, however unparalleled in pretension, the architects of the Alliance nonetheless sold it as a project finite in time and financial commitment—a venture from which the United States could extricate itself without jeopardizing its ultimate success.

That we were able to think in such terms at all is attributable to nothing so much as the remarkable school of economic-development theory which flourished around Walt Rostow and his "Charles River Group" in Cambridge, Massachusetts.

At the height of the cold war, in 1952, the Center for International Studies at the Massachusetts Institute of Technology launched a major research program into the prospects for promoting non-revolutionary economic growth in the third world. The costs of such a program, Rostow and his colleagues reckoned, would be "somewhat larger than current spending for economic aid," but "insignificant compared with the costs of waging limited war."[16] The United States was at a crossroads, confronted with revisionist countries eager for growth, susceptible to the lures of communism, and in imminent danger of concluding "that their new aspirations can be realized only through violent change and the renunciation of democratic institutions."[17]

In fact, the authors asserted, America had much to offer to countries in the process of development, for had we not "developed more successfully than any other nation the social, political, and economic techniques for realizing widespread popular desires for change without either compulsion or social disorganization[?]"

A vast program of "world development," led by the United States, would not only save America abroad, but would be our moral redemption at home, saving us from the "stagnation of smug prosperity." Such a program would "give fresh meaning and vitality to the historic American sense of mission—a mission to see the principles of national independence and human liberty extended on the world scene."[18]

Every vast bureaucratic undertaking needs a simplifying thesis—a buffer between its practitioners and squirming reality—and this Rostow supplied with admirable success. In essence, he argued, a relatively small amount of seed capital, adroitly placed and carefully monitored, could create a self-sustaining process of growth. It was no longer necessary to be paralyzed to inaction by the great gap in per-capita incomes which separated the rich from the poor. To close

[16] Max F. Millikan and Walt W. Rostow, *A Proposal: Key to an Effective Foreign Policy* (New York: Harper & Row, 1957), p. 2.

[17] *Ibid.*, p. 5.

[18] *Ibid.*, p. 8.

the gap, we would not have to supply the difference—only that relatively small amount needed to bring aggregate savings up to a level of around 10 percent. From there, the inexorable dynamics of an economy in "self-sustaining growth" would take over the task.

There were, to be sure, two main versions of the Rostow thesis, one for scholarly and one for popular consumption. The first, "The Take-off into Self-sustained Growth," appeared as a learned article in the *Economic Journal* and inspired no small amount of informed controversy.[19] The second, which went through an extraordinary seven printings between 1960 and 1962, was a distillation of the scholarly piece, lacking the nuances and the carefully-worded qualifications of the original. In the transformation, the title changed as well to *The Stages of Economic Growth: a Non-Communist Manifesto.*

Anyone might be allowed to indulge in a little hyperbole. Indeed, exaggeration may well play an indispensable role in mobilizing the inchoate forces which make up a government. Rostow, however, was not only a leading publicist but a high priest of the administration—a role which his critics may have found less easy to forgive.

The Alliance sought to be both a social revolution and a vehicle for rapid economic growth. While debatable whether the Alliance would have succeeded limiting itself to the far less exacting task of promoting economic growth alone, as a vehicle for social reform, it has almost universally been judged a failure. The five social targets enumerated by Kennedy—land, jobs, housing, health, and education—were to give the program its popular orientation. Somewhere, rather early on, the revolution lost its way.[20] For if the goals of the Alliance were revolutionary, the means were not. There was an inevitable tension between Kennedy's revolutionary Alliance rhetoric and the implications of Rostow's economic prescriptions. One or the other had to give way. It is fair to say the problem did not go unnoticed. Lincoln Gordon, an economist and our Ambassador to Brazil during the early 1960s, advanced the argument that the two sides of the Alliance were mutually reinforcing:

Social investments, properly conceived, are complementary to economic investments and are major elements in an effective development program. In addition, both social investments and structural reforms are essential to the

[19] See, for example, Berthold Hoselitz, "Non-Economic Factors in Economic Development," *American Economic Review, Papers and Proceedings,* May 1957, p. 28.

[20] For an excellent treatment of this theme by a former AID official and a journalist, see Jerome Levinson and Juan de Onis, *The Alliance that Lost its Way* (Chicago: Quadrangle, 1970).

national cohesion and sense of popular identification which the success of the Alliance for Progress requires.

But the essence of his argument was that welfare would take second place to growth:

Where average standards (of living) are low, mere distributive measures add no significant real income to the masses. They add only the psychic income of seeing the once mighty laid low.[21]

Gordon, in short, did not speak to the immediate dilemma of choosing between growth and popular welfare. If poverty bred communism, then massive public welfare spending of the sort envisaged by Kennedy seemed the appropriate cure. But a "self-sustaining" growth system—one which could combat communism without permanent outside support—required massive investments, not spending on welfare. The political conditions likely to inspire such investments—conditions which would coax locally-owned capital out of its strong-boxes in Switzerland and the United States, or inspire foreign investors looking for a likely site to place their surplus capital—were not those called for in Kennedy's program of sweeping social reforms. In fact, they seemed quite the opposite. Faced with a choice between stability and social reform, the Alliance quite simply took the former path. Where countries seemed set on pursuing social reform measures at the expense of stability—political or economic—institutions like the IMF were on hand to lead erring members back to the paths of orthodoxy.[22] While our social rhetoric angered the conservatives, the absence of substantial accomplishments inflamed the revisionists. Friends were few.

The Fruit of Contradiction

The initial contradictions of the Alliance spawned two reactions. One argued that if there was to be social reform, and if orthodox economic policy impeded its realization, then those economic policies were expendable; the other held, in effect, that if social goals conflicted with growth, the realization of those goals could be deferred. One of the early manifestations of the problem was the scholarly

[21] Lincoln Gordon, A New Deal for Latin America (Cambridge: Harvard University Press, 1963).

[22] For a description of IMF requirements for "stand-by loans" see Joseph Gold, "Aspects of the Relations of the IMF with its Developing Members," Columbia Journal of International Law, Fall, 1971, pp. 267–302.

debate which came to be known as the "monetarist-structuralist con-toversy." Intricate in detail, in its essential technical parts it was an argument over the virtues of inflation as opposed to stability as a stimulus for growth.[23] For the monetarists, who were amply repre-sented by the technicians of the IMF, only the serene climate created by a "stable" monetary policy could inspire the savings necessary to achieve "take-off."

Spiralling inflation, which in some Latin American countries was 100 percent and more a year, clearly discouraged investment. No lo-cal capital markets could develop. Those with money would place it in inflation-proof investments such as land and real estate—invest-ments which contributed little to productivity. Or they would simply send it abroad.

The structuralists, who counted among their number many of the so-called "radical" Latin American economists, such as Osvaldo Sun-kel and Aníbel Pinto, while decrying the runaway inflation experi-enced in Brazil and Chile in the late 1950s and early 1960s, nonethe-less claimed that "moderate" inflation was necessary to energize the dormant quarters of the economy.[24] It was, as some were frank to call it, a "leap of faith" strategy. It provoked demand before there was an assured supply to meet that demand. It was a strategy of some risk, which, even if it succeeded, would cause some amount of excess-demand inflation, with abundant money bidding up the price of scarce or non-existent goods. Moreover, by aggravating the de-mand for imports, it risked "external disequilibrium," as the price disparity between what could be purchased at home and abroad grew more pronounced.

The structuralists did not have a satisfactory answer for each of the monetarist complaints. On the other hand, they were arguing from a different frame of reference and hence attached different weights to the monetarist criticisms. Better to have excess demand, they argued,

[23] For a discussion of the major issues involved, see Roberto Campos, "Two Views of Inflation in Latin America," David Felix, "An Alternative View of the 'Monetarist'–'Structuralist' Controversy"; and, especially, Joseph Grunwald, "The Structuralist School on Price Stability and Development: The Chilean Case," in Albert O. Hirschman, ed., *Latin American Issues* (New York: Twentieth Century Fund, 1961).

[24] In Grunwald's words: "The essence of the 'structuralist' argument is that price stability can be attained only through economic growth. The basic forces of infla-tion are structural in nature. Financial factors may be important, but only as forces propagating inflation and not originating it. It is admitted that monetary policy can be easily managed and has relatively quick effects, but it attacks only symptoms and therefore cannot cure." *Ibid.*, p. 96.

than allow the economy to produce below its potential. And if the structuralist program caused balance-of-payments problems, these might be controlled by a variety of manipulations at the border—by quotas and tariffs, multiple exchange rates, or outright devaluation. Thus insulated from external competition, the inflated prices of domestic goods should not unduly hamper growth and development. In fact, they would stimulate the domestic market, whereas stability would only invite stagnation.

Whatever the merit of the respective arguments, the monetarist-structuralist dispute was at heart a political one. Beneath the technical drapery there lay significantly different visions not only of what was possible domestically but of what constituted a proper world order and the role of the third world within it.

A strategy of inflation at home played a key political role. Indeed, it reflected and hence implicitly recognized the struggle for modernization and social reform taking place in the developing countries. Inflation, as Latin American scholars have noted, has its roots in political instability.[25] Whatever its immediate economic causes, it is an accurate mirror of the rising demands of new interest groups for a greater share of the national wealth and the intransigence of the vested interests in refusing to give it to them. Structuralism might thus be considered a reflection of governmental weakness—a policy for governments too feeble to eliminate the social conflicts within their domains by more direct means. Alternatively, it could be considered a policy of moderation. By this latter view, it was not surprising that inflation should accompany reform, especially moderate reform, which ruled out the economic annihilation of entire interest groups or their challengers. Hence, on the domestic level, structuralism recognized the essential vulnerability of governments attempting to transform the balance of their societies, whereas monetarism called for a degree of discipline which few could countenance.

On the international level as well, the two doctrines implied equally great differences. The monetarist school, in essence, provided a framework for development compatible with the master plan of the Bretton Woods system. By that system, if only national governments would agree to maintain domestic monetary policies consistent with a reasonable balance in their external accounts, the world might once

[25] See, for example, Celso Furtado, *The Economic Growth of Brazil*, de Aguiar and Drysdale, trans. (Berkeley: University of California, 1963); and Furtado, *Diagnosis of the Brazilian Crisis*, S. Macedo, trans. (Berkeley: University of California Press, 1965).

again come to enjoy an integrated, self-adjusting international economy. Behind such a view, of course, lay a number of critical assumptions. Foremost was the belief in the virtues of international liberalism—that ideal American policy noted earlier—that an international economy, freed of most government controls, would be the most efficient from a cosmopolitan perspective. That system, presumably, could also be adopted by each national government, whatever its stage of development, as best serving its own national interest. Thus, the monetarist prescriptions were based on the premise that all countries could participate in the liberal system on an equal footing, enjoying equal rights and incurring equal obligations, despite gross differences in economic health, cultural background, and degrees of political and economic effectiveness. The rise of structuralism suggested that many third world countries were now beginning to challenge these premises.

As the monetarist position reinforced the cosmopolitan economic viewpoints of Bretton Woods, so the structuralist school supported the growing movement in the third world toward economic nationalism. In the tradition of Henry Carey and Friedrich List, structuralism gave strength to the notion that states in the process of development must either receive privileges and exemptions from the rest of the world, or be allowed to pursue their policies from within a closed environment. The liberal Bretton Woods system did, in fact, grant a number of exemptions to the third world, which came increasingly to regard them as partial or insufficient. Orthodox economics had, for example, long recognized the so-called "infant-industry thesis." It was legitimate to protect high-cost industries at the outset if they showed a reasonable chance in the long run of becoming efficient producers. The development of infant industries, on the other hand, if pursued on any scale at all, was almost necessarily going to be inflationary (a substitution of high-cost for low-cost production) and destabilizing to the balance of payments (through a shift of investment away from the traditional exporting sectors and an increase in capital imports).

Structuralism, most of its supporters argued, was a transitional strategy. In time, perhaps, these states could join a liberal world. But one had to be national before becoming liberal. Structuralism, with its permissive attitude toward inflation, allowed a greater role for government intervention in the affairs of the country, and hence contributed to the national integration deemed of primary importance by third world statesmen. If deficit spending by the government led to inflation, it was also the easiest, if not the only, way to tax and redistribute the national wealth. Structuralism was thus, for all its technical flaws, a serious attempt to provide an economic framework compatible with the social goals of the Alliance.

The Political Dimension of the Alliance: The "Democratic Left" and Its Decline

For the group of liberals surrounding Kennedy, the principal executors of the Alliance were to be the "Democratic Left," a collection of Latin American politicians including Alberto Lleras Camargo of Colombia, "Pépe" Figueres of Costa Rica, Eduardo Frei of Chile, Rōmulo Betancourt of Venezuela, Victor Raúl Haya de la Torre of Peru, and others. Our own view of the Latin American political scene at the onset of the Alliance distinguished between a right wing, which was traditional, overbearing, and contemptuous of popular rights and aspirations, and a left wing, eager to lead the Latin American republics into communism. Neither group suited us. The right blocked reasonable reform and opened the door to radicalism. Castro gave us a vivid example of what we could expect on the left. Between the two we hoped to interpose progressive, reforming leftist democrats, moderate at home, liberal and cosmopolitan abroad.

The background of the leftist democrats was diverse. Some, like Lleras Camargo, came from ancient, wealthy families with long histories of national prominence. Others, like Haya de la Torre or Rōmulo Betancourt, were mellowed radicals from an earlier era. Betancourt, once a member of the communist party of Costa Rica (from which he was expelled for being too independent), had long been an opponent of military dictatorships. Haya de la Torre, a former outspoken critic of American "imperialism" in the hemisphere, had enjoyed a large following in Peru for many decades as leader of the APRA party, but never held office. He was the author of *Aprismo, Marxism and Historical Time-Space,* a metaphysical work which asserted Latin America's uniqueness in the face of the United States, Europe, and Russia. Haya, like Betancourt, had migrated perceptibly to the right over the years, losing some of his support along the way, but enjoying the increasing favor of the United States.

Few questioned the Alliance's determination to combat communism. Hence, it was in providing an alternative to traditional militarism that the Alliance and its leftist democratic strategy was to be judged. Kennedy, indeed, invited the judgment: "[S]even years ago," he pronounced in 1961, "there were fifteen strongmen in Latin America dominating the lives of their countries. Today there are only five. Three years from now there won't be any."[26]

Kennedy's distaste for militarism in Latin America was very nearly as strong as his dislike of communism. Militarism was the right-wing aberration for which the Alliance was to provide a meaningful alternative. In the event, Kennedy's boast of 1961 proved premature, for by 1962, the trend in Latin American politics was turning unmistakably toward militarism. In Peru, in June 1962, Haya de la Torre, the hemisphere's original left democrat, was prevented from taking office by a military coup. In 1963, military coups in Guatemala, Ecuador, the Dominican Republic, Honduras, and Argentina followed one another in swift succession. The United States, to be sure, tried to discourage the trend. In the wake of the coups in the Dominican Republic and Honduras, Secretary of State Dean Rusk announced that the United States viewed the recent military takeovers "with the utmost gravity."[27] In the interests of leftist democracy, we suspended both economic and military assistance to the offending regimes, while Senator Wayne Morse, reflecting the views of a large number in Congress, nearly succeeded in passing a bill which would have curtailed military aid to Latin America altogether.

By 1964, the key year in Kennedy's prediction, the United States faced a challenge to its Alliance philosophy from which it never truly recovered. In April 1964, Brazil, the largest and, to American policy-makers, most important of the Latin American countries, followed the pattern set by its smaller neighbors and installed a military regime.

Just how we imagined our military assistance fitting in with the rest of the Alliance is worth a brief digression. To begin with, Kennedy's distaste for Latin American militarism was not shared by everyone in his administration. Men like Adolf Berle could not contain their suspicion of the Kennedy school's social engineering, and certainly did not trust it as the sole American input into the Alliance. Berle, schooled in the New Deal and tempered in the cold war, argued that where communism was an active adversary, one could not "merely remove the conditions of poverty and unrest" and expect countries to evolve along the course we desired. In the Alliance for Progress, as in the Marshall Plan, "the companion problems of construction and

---

[26] Quoted in Simon G. Hanson, *Dollar Diplomacy Modern Style: Chapters in the Failure of the Alliance for Progress* (Washington, D.C.: Inter-American Press, 1970), p. 3.

[27] Quoted in William D. Rogers, *The Twilight Struggle,* (New York: Random House, 1967), p. 128.

defense must be simultaneously solved." The Kennedy liberals, he implied, had taken a "sound idea" to the point of "escapism." "Preparations for a major offensive in Latin America," Berle solemnly intoned, were "if anything more complete in 1962 than were Soviet preparations for the capture of Europe in 1947."[28]

Berle justified his paramount concern for Latin American security as a key element in America's grand design. There remained the immediate goals—to stave off communism, to protect American trade and investment—but Latin America's place in global strategy was far greater. Latin America was to have been an integral part of America's great vision for the free world—the Atlantic community. A Latin America solidly linked to the U.S., and through the U.S. to Europe and Japan, would swing the balance of population and land mass to the side of the West. Latin America provided "the key to whether the 21st century will be the Asian or the Western century."[29]

But if militarism was a declared enemy of the Alliance, how could we integrate our ongoing concern for security with the Alliance's ostensible main goals of growth and social reform? Our desire to blend security with social reform led to a number of novel programs. One was the plan for "civic action." We would contribute to the upkeep of Latin America's military forces. These forces would turn their men and equipment to the tasks of economic and social development. By 1963, Defense Secretary McNamara was pleased to announce that of the $50 million in military aid going to Latin America for 1963, fifteen percent was going to support civic action programs.[30] A similar sleight-of-hand justified our founding of the Inter-American Defense College in 1963. Confronted with the project, the Mexican Ambassador to the United States reacted with amused incredulity: "Give me the names of those first 60 students, and I'll pick your presidents in Latin America for the next 10 years." Delesseps Morrison, our ambassador to the Organization of American States and a promoter of the college, responded that the curriculum of the institution was "progressive" and included courses on democratic theory. Given such good men with such good training, he continued, Latin America should count itself fortunate if they *did* become the future leaders of the continent![31]

[28] Adolf Berle, *Latin America, Diplomacy and Reality* (New York: Harper & Row, 1962), pp. 113–14.

[29] *Ibid.*, p. 5.

[30] Rogers, *The Twilight Struggle*, p. 126.

[31] Delesseps S. Morrison, *Latin American Mission* (New York: Simon and Schuster, 1965), p. 228.

With the Brazilian episode, the era of blissful inconsistency among the various strands of Alliance policy seemed rapidly drawing to a close. Brazil, to be sure, raised problems which might have vexed the most open-minded of American administrations. In 1962, after enraging the right wing in Brazil by his public praise for Castro, Jánio Quadros resigned and was replaced by his vice president, João Goulart. The United States viewed Goulart's leftist sympathies with alarm, and Goulart's highly publicized journeys to Cuba and China (Goulart, in fact, was in Peking when Quadros announced his resignation) fed America's misgivings about Brazil's loyalty to the "hemisphere idea." In April 1964, the armed forces turned Goulart out of office and installed their own candidate, General Castillo Branco. The United States moved quickly and within 48 hours extended official recognition to the new militarist regime.[32]

By what standards should the U.S. move be judged? Goulart had certainly been less than prudent. The Brazilian economy, weakened by an orgy of public spending in the late 1950s, was a shambles, with all the classic symptoms of raging inflation and mounting overseas indebtedness. Financial prudence seemed to call for a period of domestic austerity, but in the Brazil of the early 1960s, no leading public figure had the will or the authority to institute such a program. The military government had both and enjoyed strong American support as well. From 1960 to 1964, AID funding to Brazil had been $178.6 million. For 1965 to 1971, the figure was $1.1 billion. Senator Frank Church has estimated that overall United States aid to Brazil —including Food for Peace, Export-Import Bank loans, etc.—since 1964 has been around $2 billion.[33] Brazil, meanwhile, embraced the stringent economic policies insisted upon by the IMF as a precondition to obtaining "stand-by" loans in support of her balance of payments.[34] On the political front, the Brazilian government dispensed

[32] For the alleged U.S. role in the coup, see Thomas E. Skidmore, *Politics in Brazil, 1930–1964* (New York: Oxford University Press, 1967), pp. 322–30. Meanwhile, Brazilians, justly famous for their political humor, were reportedly saying: "Elect Lincoln Gordon and eliminate the middle man." Quoted in Hanson, *Dollar Diplomacy Modern Style*, p. 22.

[33] *U.S. Policies and Programs in Brazil.* Hearings before the Subcommittee on Western Hemisphere Affairs, Committee on Foreign Relations, U.S. Senate, May 4–5, Dec. 11, 1971, p. 145.

[34] On Brazil's early reluctance to use IMF stand-by facilities, see Skidmore, *Politics in Brazil,* pp. 176–82, 270–72. By March, 1965, Brazil was second only to India among the non-industrialized countries in its use of the stand-by arrangements. See *Fund and Bank Review: Finance and Development* 2, no. 2 (June, 1965), p. 126.

with the faint-hearted measures of its predecessors, suppressing the "excess demands" which had been burdening the Brazilian political economy over the past several years. Political expression was contained in two official parties. Dissent was rewarded with prison or exile.[35]

The results were electric. Investor confidence was restored and foreign capital flowed into Brazil in unprecedented volume. By 1968, Brazil was riding a boom. From 1968 to 1972, Brazil's economy grew in real terms at the rate of 8 to 9 percent per year. Inflation sank to the historically moderate level of around 20 percent. In her international economic policy, Brazil seemed to be falling in step with the general Western prescriptions. There was a major tariff reform which won general approval.[36] But for all her stunning economic successes, few in the U.S. were willing to cite Brazil as an example of successful Alliance policy. The taint of political repression was too strong. Some, indeed, were inclined to argue that Brazil proved the Alliance's moral bankruptcy.

It is not the argument here that there is a necessary relationship between the economic and political policies of the Brazilian regime, although it would equally be a mistake to dismiss any relationship as coincidence. At a minimum, the case of Brazil illustrates that the necessary relationship between political and economic policies as predicted in the early days of the Alliance had clearly failed to materialize. Robert Alexander, a Latin Americanist from Rutgers University and a member of Kennedy's Latin American Task Force in 1960, had been a key figure in shaping U.S. expectations for the leftist democratic strategy. His *Prophets of the Revolution,* written in 1962, concluded with the observation that

if these countries can rapidly develop their economies and pass on to their citizens the benefits of this economic growth in the form of higher levels of living, then there will be little chance that the peoples of Latin America will decide that it is necessary to sacrifice the democracy which only a few of them have ever enjoyed in order to obtain social justice and material prosperity.[37]

[35] For a chilling account of political repression in Brazil, see Amnesty International, *Report on Allegations of Torture in Brazil* (London, 1972, mimeo). The report contains over a thousand documented cases of political torture since the onset of the military regimes in 1964.

[36] Richard N. Cooper, "Third World Tariff Tangle," *Foreign Policy,* Fall, 1971, p. 46.

[37] Robert Alexander, *Prophets of the Revolution* (New York: Macmillan, 1967), p. 304.

Within only a few short years, our earlier ebullience was gone, and Alliance rhetoric took on a new and more guarded form. AID Director David Bell, testifying before Congress in 1963, noted, for example, that while economic progress could not guarantee democracy, "it seems clear that without economic progress the chances for strengthening democratic processes in the less developed countries would be greatly diminished."[38] The change was subtle but far-reaching. We could not, in fact, have any confidence in what we were getting for our money; but without our money we would get nothing.

The notion that economic improvements would not necessarily lead to the installation of democratic regimes, or even friendly regimes, was a rude shock to the social engineers in Washington. Indeed, every combination and permutation of possible relationships between economic growth and the style of politics seemed to blossom forth in Latin America with a splendid disregard for theory. In Venezuela economic growth did, indeed, seem to coincide with the gradual democratization of the political system. And, in a country like Paraguay, stagnation seemed the fruit of the repressive military dictatorship of General Stroessner, or in Haiti, of the voodoo-ridden demagoguery of "Papa Doc" Duvalier. But there was also the case of Uruguay which, with Costa Rica, had long been considered a model of Latin American democracy, yet was the only Latin American country to experience a sustained negative growth rate throughout the 1960s. Finally, there was Brazil, combining economic triumph with political repression.

Judging from the lavishness of our official aid, we did not take long adjusting to the political changes in Brazil. But Brazil was not the only country to abandon the leftist-democratic ideal. In 1968, the Peruvian armed forces removed President Belaunde from office and replaced him with a military junta led by General Velasco Alvereda. In 1969, the Bolivian army deposed acting President Luis Adolfo Siles Salinas and installed General Alfredo Ovando Candia in his place. The new regimes shared many common tendencies with Brazil. They were run by military men. They showed a similar impatience with parties and parliaments. Each promoted a corporatist style of politics. From American perspectives, however, there was a critical difference. The new regimes were not only anti-democratic but seemingly anti-liberal as well. Among its first official acts, the Velasco regime in Peru nationalized the International Petroleum Co. Later it seized lands belonging to the W. R. Grace and the Cerro de Pasco

---

[38] As quoted in Schlesinger, *A Thousand Days*, p. 523.

Mining companies, and then took over the Lima telephone system (although, in the latter case, paying compensation to its owners, ITT). In a like fashion, General Ovando's first official act was the nationalization of the Gulf Oil interests in Bolivia. With the emergence of the new regimes, American policy in Latin America had arrived at a new crossroads. Now, it seemed, our paramount concern in the hemisphere was no longer communism, but economic nationalism.

The gradual changes in Alliance strategy which were unfolding in the middle 1960s stemmed not only from the course of events in Latin America but also from shifting perspectives within the United States. Kennedy's death in November 1963 provided the occasion for both a reappraisal of Alliance philosophy and a general purging of Kennedy men in the Alliance hierarchy. The new trends in the Alliance came together in the person of Thomas Mann. Under President Johnson, a long-time friend, Mann assumed the old roles of former Assistant Secretary of State for Inter-American Affairs, Edwin Martin, and former Alliance Director, Teodoro Moscoso.

Mann's tenure produced two significant changes in the course of the Alliance. First, it signalled an end to our discomfiture over the proliferation of military regimes. While reserving the right to take strong action against communism, Mann stated:

We cannot put ourselves in a doctrinaire straight-jacket of automatic application of sanctions to every unconstitutional regime in the hemisphere with the obvious intention of dictating internal political developments in other countries.[39]

Mann's second major change was to make the Alliance a more congenial place for private enterprise. "How many times," he asked in a speech in May 1964, "have we seen governments, in order to gain an imaginary short-term political advantage, destroy the confidence that the legitimate rights of their own private capital, and even the government's contracts, will be respected?"[40]

As a major concession to Latin American sensibilities, early Alliance rhetoric had treated the subject of private enterprise with extreme diffidence. Mann's rescue operation earned him the applause of the business community. As one businessman observed, "not until Tom Mann came back in 1964 did the business community feel it was 'in' again with the U.S. government."[41]

[39] *Department of State Bulletin* 50, 1964, p. 999.
[40] *Ibid.*, p. 862.
[41] Levinson and Onis, *The Alliance That Lost its Way*, p. 72.

Big business did not bear exclusive responsibility for our growing concern over economic nationalism. But its concern merged easily with, and hence reinforced, the traditional American concern with preserving an international liberal economic order. What were the connecting threads between America's liberal economic policy and our policy for the Alliance? Simply stated, we professed to believe that whether a country could or could not be moderate at home depended in large measure on whether it was liberal abroad.

Liberal economic theory told us quite clearly that a nation sealed off from the world could not prosper. Markets could not develop to their fullest potentialities. Without competition from abroad, countries would allocate their resources poorly, with large profits for a few and high prices for all. Most important, without the economic growth which international liberalism was best suited to provide, political gradualism could not work. With growth, violent social revolution might yet be avoided. Growth, by permitting the old elites to be replaced gently, gradually, and without abrupt extinction, could make political revolution obsolete and avoid the excesses of violent upheaval. Mollified by a growth which distributed new wealth without confiscating the old, the existing power structure could absorb new interests and peacefully transform itself. The political system would acquire from its new elements greater efficiency as well as stability. Thus, in our view, an outward-looking economic policy was the key to the moderate internal reform we hoped to promote.

Rendering a judgment on so broad a vision is perilous in the extreme. To dismiss it as a mere façade for powerful private interests, or as a vehicle for American "imperialism," risks overlooking a certain nobility of purpose which also informed our third world policy. Perhaps, as with the nineteenth-century doctrine of Cobdenism which our arguments so closely resembled, it was less our intentions than our vision itself which was flawed. There were two major flaws. First, our belief in the general virtues of business internationalism led us to overestimate the price Latin Americans would be willing to pay to join our liberal world. Second, our belief in the fundamental soundness of trade expansion led us to overestimate the price we ourselves would be willing to pay to let them achieve it.

The Alliance and External Economic Policy

In its economic dimensions, the record of the Alliance was no better than mixed. With the world as a whole as the frame of reference, Latin America fell behind in many key sectors, especially in the rate of growth of her foreign trade. In 1950, Latin America's share of world trade had been 11.1 percent. By 1968, it had fallen to 5.1 percent. On the other hand, comparing Latin America's economic performance in the 1950s and her record in the 1960s, Latin America under the Alliance made many substantial advances. According to OECD figures, Latin America's overall annual growth rate from 1960 to 1970 was 5.5 percent. Because of phenomenal increases in population, the per-capita growth rate figure was considerably lower, only 2.4 percent, but even this lower figure compares favorably with the annual average per-capita growth rate for the period 1950 to 1961, which was only 1.6 percent (Table 1).

The onset of the Alliance coincided with a particularly trying time for the Latin American economies. From 1958 to 1962, Latin America ran a cumulative balance-of-payments deficit of $2.8 billion, not large in comparison to the massive American deficits of recent years, but substantial for a group of countries which were not only poor, but would have to pay out real reserve assets to cover their excesses. By contrast, for the years from 1963 to 1970, Latin America was in surplus by $3.6 billion: for 1970 alone, the surplus was $1.14 billion. Some countries fared better than others. For the period from 1963 to

Table 1

Income and Rates of Growth in Latin America

| | | Growth rates, 1960–69 | |
	GNP per cap 1969	*Population %*	*GNP per cap %*
Mexico	580	3.5	3.4
Guatemala	350	3.1	1.9
Haiti	....	2.0	−1.0
Dom. Rep.	280	3.0	0.4
El Salvador	290	3.7	1.9
Honduras	260	3.4	1.1
Nicaragua	380	3.5	2.8
Costa Rica	510	3.3	2.9
Brazil	270	3.2	1.4
Argentina	1060	1.6	2.6
Colombia	290	3.2	1.5
Peru	330	3.1	1.4
Venezuela	1000	3.5	2.5
Chile	510	2.5	1.7
Ecuador	240	3.4	1.2
Bolivia	160	2.6	2.4
Uruguay	560	1.3	−0.8
Paraguay	240	3.1	1.0
Panama	660	3.3	4.8

Source: World Bank *Atlas*, Washington, D.C., 1971. World Bank figures are generally somewhat lower than the OECD's, the source for the aggregate figures in the text.

1970, six countries, led by Brazil, accounted for 96 percent of the surplus.[42]

Balance-of-payments figures alone do not, of course, tell how well a country or a region lives. Strictly speaking, they do not even show if it is living within its means. In fact, the Latin American surplus, even during the relatively prosperous 1960s, was of a very precarious kind, sustained largely by overseas borrowing. Of all the countries with a surplus in their balance of payments, only two, Argentina and Venezuela, had a surplus on current account. All of the others increased their reserves by increasing net foreign indebtedness, and thereby increasing their future obligations to repay. From the mid-1950s to 1970, new publicly guaranteed foreign lending to Latin America increased at 11 percent a year—a modest rate compared to other areas of the third world, but one which contributed substantially to the already large debt inherited from previous periods. For the single year of 1970, however, debt service payments due were 17 percent of the public debt outstanding at the beginning of the year.[43]

In other words, the inflow of new lending was no longer adequate to cover even repayments on past lending. By other measures as well, debt servicing cut deeply into Latin American resources.

Table 2

Adjusted 1–15 Year Average Debt Service as a Percent of

	Exports *1967–69 av.*	*Gross nat'l savings* *1967–69 av.*	*Current gov't revenue* *1967–69 av.*
Brazil	10.7	7.1	4.8
Chile	15.5	25.9	12.5
Colombia	13.6	11.4	13.9
Dom. Rep.	8.4	20.3	11.2
Mexico	11.8	7.0	17.7
Peru	11.3	17.5	16.2

Source: OECD, *Development Assistance, 1971 Review* (Paris): OECD, 1971, pp. 156–157.

If foreign borrowing postponed an immediate crisis for Latin America, it nonetheless called attention to a problem shared by nearly all developing countries—the shortage of foreign exchange and the in-

[42] Brazil 39 percent, Argentina 20 percent, Venezuela 16 percent, Chile 10 percent, Colombia 3.6 percent. See ECLA, *Economic Survey of Latin America*, Pt. 1, The Latin American Economy in 1970. (ELCA. 12/868; New York: United Nations).

[43] OECD, *Development Assistance, 1971 Review*, Paris 1971, p. 98. The high debt service ratio reflected Latin America's heavy reliance on high-cost private financing—about 50 percent of the total.

ability to earn more of it. How to increase Latin America's foreign exchange earnings thus became the core problem of the Alliance's foreign economic policy. In theory, any, or a combination, of three broad measures might have sufficed—increasing aid (or improving its terms), increasing the flow of foreign private resources, or expanding the scope for Latin American trade.

Aid and foreign investment could make an important contribution to growth and development, but there were associated problems. Each, to a degree, compromised local control over development, and neither promised, except in the short run and at a potentially great future cost, to make a contribution to the foreign exchange problem. Indeed, the opposite was likely to occur. Even when granted on "concessionary" terms, aid still required repayment. If new aid remained high, or if old payments could be rescheduled, Latin America might continue to postpone a final reckoning. In fact, by 1970, as the previous section has demonstrated, aid was no longer large enough to cover the foreign exchange costs of servicing the external debt which already existed.[44]

Direct investments also brought an inflow of foreign capital, but the annual outflow for royalties and repatriation of profits exceeded that inflow by a wide margin. For the period 1960 to 1967, for example, new U.S. funds invested in Latin America totaled $985 million, as against $6.7 billion in dividends sent abroad.[45] The two figures, to be sure, were not strictly comparable. The new investments covered a limited time period, while the returns were based on the sum of all previous investments. Moreover, foreign investments, especially in the extractive industries, were large foreign exchange earners in their own right, while manufacturing industries saved foreign exchange by expanding the scope of domestic production. Nonetheless, the dividend and royalty outflows represented the

[44] Such a calculation, of course, assumes that the Latin Americans would have been free to apply their aid receipts to servicing old debts. As a general rule, they were not. Instead, seeking maximum leverage from our limited funds, we frequently tied our money to specific projects rather than general balance-of-payments support. On the other hand, when we did allow our aid to be applied to broader balance-of-payments purposes, we frequently attached so many conditions as to render the whole exercise politically difficult in the extreme. For a discussion of the relative merits of "project" versus "programs" lending, see Angus Maddison, *Economic Progress and Policy in Developing Countries* (London: Allen & Unwin, 1970), pp. 239–52.

[45] Arturo O'Connell, *The EEC and Latin America*, A discussion paper for the Royal Institute of International Affairs (Summer, 1972, Mimeo), p. 7.

"cost" of having major sectors of the Latin American economy in foreign hands—a cost which, obviously, would not occur if the companies were owned domestically.

In any event, the case against the corporations scarcely rested on the economic issues alone. Latin American history is filled with examples of the expropriation of foreign-owned companies, and it is a reasonable assumption that the officials responsible deliberated long and hard before being moved to such an extreme position. Following the war, when Argentina was flush with foreign exchange, Peron used a large portion of his country's reserves to purchase the assets of several of the most conspicuous foreign-owned corporations. American analysts in particular have never ceased to point out his error. Had he invested the money wisely in new ventures rather than buying out the foreign owners, they say, Argentina would have emerged well ahead of the game. Instead, the money created no new productive resources. There was merely a transfer payment.[46] Others less purposefully obtuse had pointed out that there may well be a gain involved. Economists like Harry G. Johnson use the phrase "psychic income" to describe the gains of such a transaction.[47] Still others argue that growth means little unless it is matched by autonomy. The former Chilean ambassador to the U.S., Domingo Santa Maria, develops this idea with eloquence and passion:

I do not believe that economic development is the distinct characteristic of this world, but precisely the will for independence that has a higher spiritual and political essence. . . . This aspiration and will for independence, by the fact that they are consubstantial to life itself, are morally latent in all the nations of the world. . . .

A second element of the national will for independence is the notion and the search for its own identity. This supposes a degree of self-awareness as a nation. . . .

A third element is the determination to control economic resources that make possible the organic development of these units: nations and States. To aspire to this control, to search for this control, to be capable of this control, characterized these nations that intend to have, or have . . . a minimum or maximum of self-respect which constitutes prestige. Not only do they have the awareness of themselves and of their possibilities, that is national identity, however primitive and still without substance, but beyond

[46] See, for example, William Withers, *The Economic Crisis in Latin America* (New York: Free Press of Glencoe, 1964), pp. 172–77; and Robert J. Alexander, *The Peron Era* (New York: Columbia University Press, 1951), pp. 154–69.

[47] Harry G. Johnson, *Economic Nationalism in Old and New States* (Chicago: University of Chicago Press, 1967).

that, the faculty of progressively transforming pretensions and intensions [sic] into actions, precise, defined, planned actions.[48]

The American reaction to such statements typically falls somewhere between condescension and scorn. This is a serious mistake for those who would understand the bases of Latin American discontent. Statements such as the one by Santa Maria reflect with great accuracy a predominant Latin American state of mind. The Latin Americans have a grievance which we are ill-advised to ignore. Moreover, the case for national control was often more than philosophical, for it was not difficult to tie foreign control of particularly sensitive industries to serious domestic economic and political problems. Foreign ownership of utilities, for example, not only irritated the millions of Latin Americans who paid monthly bills to a company with a foreign name, but frequently interfered with national development strategies of the host governments. Governments often favored inexpensive electric power to encourage industrialization or as a part of social welfare programs, raising a clear conflict of interests with the profit-maximizing foreign companies. Companies could either attempt to defy the government's policy or, faced with declining or negative profits, allow their plant and equipment to fall into disrepair. The latter, in fact, was precisely what happened before the Mexican government nationalized the holdings of the American Light and Power Co. in 1960.[49]

Nor was it entirely far-fetched that companies might offer a more direct threat to national institutions, as the ITT incident in Chile dramatically demonstrated.[50] The foreign corporations disposed of huge resources which often exceeded the national budgets and occasionally the gross national products of their host Latin American countries. So large a body of capital could rarely afford to be neutral, especially if it believed its own interests threatened by a radical government. It was not entirely unreasonable, therefore, that

[48] His Excellency, Domingo Santa Maria, "Legal Issues Raised by Recent Property Takings in Latin America," Speech, University of Virginia, March 13, 1970, as quoted in Colin I. Bradford, Jr., *Forces for Change in Latin America: U.S. Policy Implications* (Washington: Overseas Development Council, 1971), p. 10.

[49] Raymond R. Vernon, ed., *Public Policy and Private Enterprise in Mexico* (Cambridge: Harvard University Press, 1964).

[50] In the wake of the ITT-Republican Party scandal, Washington columnist Jack Anderson revealed that ITT in Chile had attempted to enlist the aid of the CIA and State Department to prevent the Allende government from coming to power. The documents, whose authenticity has not been challenged, are reprinted in *Subversion in Chile: A Case Study in U.S. Corporate Intrigue in the Third World: ITT-CIA* (Nottingham, England, 1972).

Latin American governments viewed them with trepidation. At a minimum, borrowing the prudent axiom of military planners, it was essential to weigh the adversary's capabilities as well as his intentions.

The case against aid and investment made the case in favor of trade expansion all the more compelling. Trade expansion, moreover, offered the supreme advantage of assuring access to foreign exchange with a minimum of outside control. But how could Latin America, with her stagnating primary economies and over-priced industries, compete favorably in the world at large? The solution, demanded by Latin Americans with a growing vehemence, was for nothing less than a fundamental revision of the rules governing international trade. Liberal trade, they argued, might work among equals, but it left unequals forever the hewers of wood and drawers of water. If the rich nations truly had the interests of the developing world in mind, they would concur not only in the principle of trade expansion, but alter existing trading frameworks so that trade expansion could take place.

Trade expansion meant not only altering the rules but the composition of trade. There was little future in the bulk of third world exports. As Raúl Prebisch had been arguing for nearly two decades, not only were their growth prospects less promising than industrial goods, but the countries which concentrated their exports in primary commodities faced declining "terms of trade," obliging them to export more primary goods to obtain a constant quantity of imported finished goods.[51] In order to increase exports and hence foreign re-

---

[51] Many reputable economists treated Prebisch's doctrines with scorn. For Gottfried Haberler, Prebisch's "attempted explanation of the alleged facts is fallacious, and there is no presumption at all that the alleged unfavorable tendency of the terms of trade will continue in the future." See Werner Baer, "The Economics of Prebisch and the ECLA," *Economic Development and Cultural Change*, January, 1962, pp. 169–82. For Jacob Viner, any deterioration in the terms of trade for the third world would merely reflect differing rates of product improvement. Thus, whereas tractors, tires and automobiles had grown "incomparably superior in quality," primary commodities remained the same. Jacob Viner, *International Trade and Economic Development* (Glencoe, Ill.: The Free Press, 1952), p. 143. Others explained Prebisch's data, insofar as they did not reject it as grossly insufficient, by pointing to the different methods of customs valuations or the declining costs of ocean transport. Paul T. Ellsworth, "The Terms of Trade between Primary-Producing and Industrial Countries," *Inter-American Economic Affairs*, Summer, 1956, pp. 47–65.

Nevertheless, the Prebisch thesis struck a responsive chord among politicians and publicists in the third world and it thus grew steadily more popular. The explanation Prebisch offered for their economic stagnation was plausible, even if controversial. Moreover, blaming the rich countries at the industrial center was good politics.

serves, the third world would have to gain a greater share of the
more rapidly growing trade in industrialized goods.

Table 3

Commodity Structure of Exports 1955, 1960, 1965, 1968
(in percent of total exports)

	Primary Goods				Manufactured Goods			
	1955	1960	1965	1968	1955	1960	1965	1968
Developing Market	87.1	85.7	82.4	78.0	12.9	14.3	17.6	22.0
Economies (fuels)	(25.2)	(28.0)	(31.2)	(33.7)				
Developed Market	35.5	31.4	28.4	24.7	64.5	68.6	71.6	75.3
Economies (fuels)	(5.5)	(4.0)	(3.4)	(3.3)				
Centrally Planned	49.9	43.1	37.8	36.3	50.1	56.9	62.2	63.7
Economies (fuels)	(12.0)	(10.9)	(10.7)	(10.2)				

Source: UNCTAD, *Supplement 1970, Handbook of International Trade and Development
Statistics*, (New York: United Nations, 1970), p. 26, table 4.1.

Thus was born the plan for generalized preferences. Poor countries,
so that they could compete, would gain preferential access to the
markets of the rich, but make no concessions in return. At the first
UNCTAD conference in May 1964, Prebisch made his case for generalized preferences with disarming simplicity: developed countries
should not find such a preferential system alarming, he argued:

It is not a matter of controversy among economists that national protection
of infant industries is justifiable whenever such industries might have a long-
term prospect of reaching a high level of efficiency. ... The case is thus a
logical extension of the infant-industry argument.[52]

But the response of the developed nations was less than enthusias-
tic. France joined Belgium in trying to redirect the assault to the safer
field of complementary economic arrangements.[53] Britain alone saw
merit in the proposal, presumably because it might allow her to
dilute the burden of Commonwealth preferences.

The evolution of the U.S. position on generalized preferences illustrates not only the heavy influence of liberal-internationalist perspectives on our thinking, but how, in pursuing them, we failed to con-
sult the essential domestic base without whose support such a
policy would not be possible.

[52] Rául Prebisch, "Towards a New Trade Policy for Development," *Proceedings
of the United Nations Conference on Trade and Development* (New York: United
Nations, 1964), vol. II, p. 35.

[53] This was the so-called "Brasseur Plan." See Statement by H. E. Mr. Maurice
Brasseur, *Proceedings of the United Nations Conference on Trade And Development* (New York: United Nations, 1964), vol. II, p. 110.

In its initial stages, our stand on generalized preferences seemed keyed more closely to our European than to our third world preoccupations. The Europeans, busily building a preferential trading system with their former African colonies, were in our eyes playing light with the very mainstay of America's postwar foreign policy—the notion of an open economic Atlantic community. If we remained steadfast in our support of most-favored-nation trade, we stood to lose our leverage over Europe. Unless we could offer a system of "generalized preferences," to counter Europe's selective preferences, Europe would consolidate her bloc and turn inward. Others, we feared, would follow, and soon we would face that hostile world of economic blocs which had been the constant preoccupation of American statesmen from Cordell Hull to George Ball. It was not until 1969, and then only with the greatest reluctance, that we gave our endorsement to generalized preferences. Even then, we made a heroic effort to minimize its effects. Preferences would be only temporary, lasting no more than ten years. In no way were they meant to be a sign that we had abandoned our ultimate liberal goals. Meanwhile, American officials would refer to the new scheme as the "two-tiered most-favored-nation system."[54]

Even as we backed generalized preferences, circumstances were eroding our third world economic policy at its very foundations. The shifting focus of American diplomacy away from the third world and toward the principal centers of international power accelerated during the Nixon Administration, and our interests in placating the third world economically declined accordingly. As grand strategy made the logic of such a policy less compelling, new problems on the domestic front made the apparent costs loom larger. The inflation which seized the U.S. economy with the escalation of the Vietnam war showed no signs of abating. Inflation was also under-cutting the competitiveness of our own exports. The hemorrhage of dollars pouring into the world's financial markets left our balance of payments precarious in the extreme. The effect of these changes on our own endorsement of improving the trading prospects of the third world, highly qualified to begin with, was overwhelming. Indeed, the changes called into question not only our commitment to generalized preferences, but our commitment to economic liberalism itself.

In Washington, dedicated liberals tried to reconcile the major difficulties in the trade expansion theory. The United States, it was said, was on its way to becoming a "mature creditor economy," and hence

[54] Jerome Fried, "How Trade Can Aid," *Foreign Policy*, Fall, 1971, p. 52.

should no longer be concerned with maintaining a favorable balance of trade. In our new incarnation we could fertilize the world with our capital and technology. Labor-intensive or technologically mature industries could migrate to the low-cost peripheries of the third world, as indeed they had already begun to do in large numbers. The money we lost on our trade account we would regain on our capital account as earnings from our overseas operations.[55]

World economic efficiency no doubt would be served if these industries could dismantle their operations in the United States, move to low cost areas and export their product to the developed countries. But such a strategy confronted two major problems. The third world, happy to gain the industries, was increasingly loath to accept the foreign control which went with them. On the domestic side, such corporate migrations threatened to leave a residue of labor not easily absorbed into other sectors of the economy.

Under more promising domestic conditions, expanding trade in general, and third world exports in particular, might have enjoyed a broader basis of support. If the domestic economy had been more buoyant, the "Adjustment Assistance" strategy favored by many in the administration might have sufficed to check domestic opposition. Adjustment Assistance would provide funds for companies and workers who were injured by foreign competition, giving them time to rationalize or shift to more promising sectors of the economy. But in the general recession which haunted the Nixon Administration, few sectors seemed promising enough to absorb a new influx of the unemployed. Thus the confluence of domestic and international developments—recession at home and detente abroad—militated strongly against pursuing the course on which we had set out in a more promising age.

The one constant theme emerging from the general wreckage of our third world economic policy was continued and indeed growing support for our foreign business interests. It was almost as though the Nixon Administration was driven to reconfirm the historic affinity between the Republicans and big business. Of the new third world economic policies announced by President Nixon, nearly all contained a special fillip for American private enterprise. Business was treated to a greatly expanded investment guarantee program—the Overseas

[55] For a projection of the United States balance-of-payments for 1975, which reflects these assumptions, see Hendrik S. Houthhakker, "The United States Balance of Payments—A Look Ahead," in Commission on International Trade and Investment Policy, *United States International Economic Policy in an Interdependent World* (Washington, D.C., 1971), Papers, vol. 1, pp. 31–50.

Private Investment Corporation. Increased supplier credits from the Export-Import Bank encouraged U.S. export expansion (although with little regard to how the third world would pay). Our advocacy of third world regional movements was coupled with our entreaties that American corporations not be denied equal access to the larger markets regionalism would create. Even the one ostensibly major change of the Nixon Administration—our agreement to abandon "additionality" and permit hemispheric purchases with our aid money—seemed to reflect nothing so much as the growing presence of U.S. corporations within the Latin American region.

The strategy we were adopting appeared to tie our interest in gaining a favorable climate for overseas corporations to the growing Latin American interest in trade expansion. But there was little evidence of success. In May 1969, the Special Latin American Coordinating Committee (CECLA), a group formed in 1963 to promote the common interests of Latin America at UNCTAD, announced its famous Consensus of Viña del Mar. The document, presented to President Nixon with a covering letter from the Chilean Foreign Minister, was an unusually candid expression of Latin America's general discontent with the economic status quo.

Economic nationalism was also spreading to the Latin American regional movements. In its "decision 24," the Andean bloc announced a regional investment code which placed foreign investments at a distinct disadvantage to domestic capital. In sensitive areas such as banking, mining, and retailing, the Andean group announced that new foreign investment would be prohibited altogether. In all other areas, foreign investors would be limited to minority participation in local enterprises. If he failed to comply beyond a set date—which varied from one country to the next—the foreign investor would not enjoy the benefits of tariff reductions within the Andean region.[56] Although the new investment code abounded with loopholes, and the allegiance of some of the Andean bloc countries to its more contentious provisions remained in question (in the spring of 1972, for example, the Colombian legislature was still bitterly debating the "constitutionality" of a discriminatory investment code), the new Latin American posture did not go unnoticed in the United States.

More disturbing was the wave of expropriations of key American corporations which swept Latin America in the late 1960s, accompanied by little indication, in most cases, that the Latin Americans

[56] For details, see ECLA, *Economic Survey of Latin America, 1970* (New York: United Nations, 1971), pp. 50–54.

were inclined to pay the "prompt and just" compensation called for by the United States. According to one estimate, from 1968 to the beginning of 1971, some $2 billion in American property was expropriated by Latin Americans, a sum exceeding all the expropriations in the hemisphere, including Cuba, for the preceding decade.[57]

Nixon reacted strongly. In early 1972, he announced the "presumption" that the U.S. would deny bilateral and overrule multilateral assistance to the offending parties.[58] Others in the administration were even more emphatic. Speaking personally, Treasury Secretary John Connally wished that when American companies were faced with expropriation, the U.S. Government would say: "You don't negotiate just with U.S. business enterprise. You negotiate with the United States Government."[59]

By March 1972, less than one month before UNCTAD III was to convene in Santiago, the U.S. announced that, regretfully, it would for the time being withdraw its earlier support of generalized preferences. In case Latin Americans failed to see the connection, Under Secretary of State John Irwin removed the remaining ambiguities. The administration would suspend its commitment to generalized preferences, he announced to an audience of Latin Americans, until the domestic American climate changed enough to give the measure "a real chance of passage without crippling amendments." Irwin then lashed out at the expropriations of American companies. If U.S. aid were to continue, other nations would have to preserve "an investment climate in which investors . . . can count on investment protection and fulfillment of contractual obligation. . . . I cannot overemphasize how important it is for all of us who are interested in the common development goals of the hemisphere to come to an understanding on this issue."[60]

Against Latin America's growing determination to restrict our overseas economic interests, we weighed our own determination to impose sanctions in trade and aid until they ceased doing so. In this manner, by the spring of 1972, we approached the nadir of our relations with Latin America.

[57] Peter Schleisser, "Restrictions on Foreign Investments in the Andean Common Market," *The International Lawyer*, July, 1971, pp. 586–98; and Schleisser, "Recent Developments in Latin American Foreign Investment Laws," *International Lawyer*, January, 1972, pp. 64–87.

[58] Extending our "get-tough" policy to the World Bank and other international institutions tended to make a sham of our professed desire to multilateralize our aid program. Rather, as many have noted, it seemed we were trying to nationalize the multilateral agencies.

[59] New York *Times*, April 19, 1972.

[60] *Journal of Commerce*, March 20, 1972.

Summary and Conclusions

As our preferred formula for Latin American politics overestimated the usefulness of democracy in development, so our preferred economic policy did not fully consider the constraints which were operating not only in Latin America but in our own country as well. Our leftist democratic strategy failed to grasp that democracy was a luxury which poor countries striving for rapid development could ill afford. Even our "fall-back" position for the Alliance which emerged in the mid-1960s—a policy of endorsing strong governments as long as they were anti-communist and economically liberal—did not appreciate that the mainstay of national strength might well be economic nationalism itself. But perhaps our main failure lay in not consulting what we ourselves were capable of doing. Our loud allegiance to international liberalism misled the Latin Americans even as it misled ourselves. A program of trade expansion might well have appeased the forces of nationalism in Latin America, but our interest in a liberal Latin America was not worth the domestic cost. The whole episode seemed a classic example of our ideas rendering us blind to our interests.

Without trying to affix blame, the two sides of the problem were clearly related. Faced with massive seizures of our overseas property, the Nixon Administration, keen to the pressures of the business community, did not react unreasonably. The same might be said for Latin America. For more than a dozen years, the international community had affirmed the legitimacy of trade expansion for the third world as the most promising means for solving its foreign-exchange problems. Encountering a glacier-like pace of reform from all the developed world, and from nowhere so much as the United States,[61] Latin America might well be forgiven the brashness of her actions. There had been no shortage of warnings. As early as 1954 and several times thereafter, Raúl Prebisch had warned that indifference from the developed world might drive the third world to extremism. The warning had not been an idle one.

In the general sizing up of positions in U.S.-Latin American relations, we remain the stronger party by a great margin. We have the power, perhaps, to make them bow to our demands or, perhaps, if they resist, to drive them to new and more desperate alternatives. Are we wise in exercising that power?

---

[61] The United States is the largest, but also the most slowly growing, export market for Latin America. From 1960 to 1969, the share of Latin American exports to the U.S. as a percentage of total exports declined from 42 percent to 30 percent. O'Connell, *The EEC and Latin America*, p. 2.

Chile's experience since Allende has come to power suggests, among other things, the extreme vulnerability of a country which pursues radical domestic social and economic reform. Two years of attempting to redistribute wealth and increase domestic demand have left Chile with a raging inflation, a substantial balance-of-payments deficit, and a precariously weak internal political position. If Allende were to reassert economic stability and satisfy his foreign creditors, he would almost certainly lose the loyalty of those groups which brought him to power. Many groups on the left as well as the right await Allende's demise. Perhaps they would be unable to seize power, but we should hardly applaud the violence likely to accompany the struggle.

By the conventional wisdom, Chile erred in her economic extremism. Now she must pay for her folly.[62] Chile may have exceeded the bounds of prudence, although no doubt there were compelling political reasons for her doing so. How is the United States to react?

Nothing, of course, obliges us to follow a policy of restraint. But, it might be argued, it is precisely at this point that the need for U.S. understanding and restraint is greatest. In all likelihood, restraint would be a thankless task. The sheer weight of the United States in hemisphere affairs makes us a target for Latin American recriminations, whatever our policies. But if respect for social change and national self-assertion—for that pluralism so highly advertised in the Nixon Administration and so necessary if we are to play a less domineering role in the affairs of the world—means anything, this would be a most opportune time for it to show itself. Above all, sincere respect for political pluralism requires, especially in the third world, a greatly expanded tolerance for what might be called "economic pluralism." Otherwise, the former will lead a considerably straitened existence. We might, indeed, also reach the same conclusion by purely "rational" calculations of self-interest, for is it not a fundamental lesson of our postwar experience that only nations reasonably at peace with themselves at home and certain of their place abroad can afford to participate in our ideal interdependent economic world?

Unfortunately, a highly misleading theory still governs the thinking of many American officials on this subject. It derives from the British economic liberal experience. At the heart of that doctrine was the

[62] On Chilean reactions to U.S. pressures following the expropriating of American copper companies, see "Statement by the Hon. Alfonso Inostrosa, at the Joint Annual Discussion of the International Monetary Fund and World Bank," (press release no. 64.), Sept. 28, 1972.

notion that political differences need not interfere with economic intercourse among nations. That idea was a powerful one and helped bring down Britain's mercantile empire. But how apt is the analogy to today's "plural world?" It is certainly repeated often enough. As one prominent international theorist recently asserted, the idea of a world community may be utopian on the "diplomatic chessboard," but it is essential on the economic.[63] But many in the third world are not only politically but economically revisionist. In fact, economic nationalism has, in many instances, become the prime instrument for asserting political independence. The assertion of economic nationalism in the third world is bound to conflict with 'our notion of self-interest. But how seriously? After the blows have been struck, trade will go on. No doubt there will be room for investment as well, if along somewhat altered lines. When countries come of age, it should not be surprising that they seek to expel their former overlords and assert sovereignty over their own domains. Generosity in these trying times may raise myriad short-run problems. Annoying as they may be, it will be well to remember that for us they are marginal problems, even as they are matters of urgent political and economic necessity for the third world. In such circumstances generosity could prove the greater wisdom.

[63] Stanley Hoffmann, "Weighing the Balance of Power," *Foreign Affairs*, July, 1972, especially pp. 631–36.

9

THE THIRD WORLD:
REGIONAL SYSTEMS AND GLOBAL ORDER

George Liska

Introduction: A Doctrine for Two Seasons

The third world, even more than Europe, is the key trial ground for the political strategies intimated in the Nixon Doctrine. In the absence of major inner-generated events in the third world, the picture it presented to the United States during the past four years returned rather faithfully the doctrine's own *clair-obscur* bias. The doctrine retained, from its enunciation at Guam through the first three presidential reports to Congress and the nation, a steadiness of formulation which, in matters political, can result only from the absence of testing and twisting crises. A Republican president made the not atypical pledge of greater efficacy, and he neatly balanced the pledged reduction of U.S. involvement with a summons to greater self-reliance of politically, if not economically, independent small states of the third world, while giving a perhaps deceptively green light for political initiatives by economically competitive industrial allies. The complementary setting of a prospective "structure of peace" accommodated, finally, nuclear (and naval?) parity for the Soviet Union with diplomatic promotion of the People's Republic of China. "Negotiation" to this end replaced "confrontation" with a Eur-Asian communist monolith, incompatible with the now governmentally certified emergence of global multipolarity.

In all administration pronouncements, lesser-state self-help and American self-effacement are expected to meet in the substitution of economic and military aid for physical U.S. intervention in other than nuclear contingencies and, perhaps, direct transfrontier assaults by greater on weaker, but sturdy, powers. At the same time, benevolent references to the major communist powers are offset by reservations about the actions of the Soviet Union in the third world. If the *dosage* has all the marks of deliberation, the same cannot be affirmed for the varying emphases on third-world regionalism, especially of the economic kind. Still, regionalism is the only tentatively approved *ism* (next to idealism for the weak and the young) replacing moribund ideology; yet another is the administration's own restrained realism, contrasted favorably with likewise discredited past utopias. Finally, in what may be meaningful or only accidental, references to the goal of a "structure of peace," to be painstakingly evolved from a gradual liquidation of the Vietnam conflict, are numerically overshadowed in the third and latest presidential report by references to an "international system" to be sustained by, and itself sustain, a commitment of the lesser and less-developed states as well as the greater ones in the forthcoming "generation of peace."

Both restatements and changes in nuance have been reflected in the reduction of U.S. military capability for intervention while screening the limited range of actual reductions of American presence. Reductions have been few relative to the possible implications of the doctrine and to the administration's symbolic initiatives aimed at redirecting relations with the communist great powers. In the process, U.S. acceptance of a relatively worsening American position in the naval balance with the Soviet Union has affected third-world conditions more directly than the controversially modified nuclear-strategic balance. Among the actual manifestations of retrenchment and devolution of responsibility was to be counted the reduction of U.S. troops stationed in Korea, the suspension of naval patrols in the Taiwan Straits, and the nominal reversion of Okinawa to Japan. A new American restraint in the third world has been evidenced by forbearance with at least one more, Pueblo-like provocation by North Korea; it showed more significantly in American reluctance to propose economic-development panaceas for an increasingly nationalist Latin America in the wake of the near-defunct Alliance for Progress, and for the scattered members of the once-united Afro-Asia in the aftermath of progressive neutralism. In addition, the administration claimed to have reduced efforts to mold the conditions of political processes in independent third-world countries and to manipulate the actual components of such a process even in so dependent a country as South Vietnam. And finally, the administration took pride in avoiding interference in awkward politico-military confrontations with conflicting racial and strategic overtones in Southern Africa. On the side of actual interventions, restraint took the shape of mere naval demonstrations in the Jordanian-Syrian and the Indo-Pakistani conflicts, underlined as to efficacy in the first case and discreetly understressed in the second. The blockading naval deployments, reinforcing massive air action aimed at North Vietnam, could finally be regarded as restrained, in the context of the stepped-up conventional warfare in 1972, when measured against the scenario of an actual U.S. landing implementing an enclave strategy in the north.

More detrimental to an assessment of the practical bearing of the Nixon Doctrine than the limited scope of actual and asserted retrenchment and restraint, however, was the absence of a new crisis situation in the third-world tailored to test the doctrine's internal means-ends economy. Neither success nor failure of Vietnamization, the most dramatic instance of devolution of responsibility for security, could serve as a reliable test case prior to the termination of overt hostilities. Apart from the many peculiarities of that insurgency-cum-invasion phenomenon, the antecedence of a massive U.S. involvement to the doctrine's enunciation entailed both liabilities and possibilities of action that would be absent from any broadly comparable future case. In the actual course of events, massive conventional operations by North Vietnamese regulars beyond the demilitarized zone in 1972, both elicited and facilitated by prior Vietnamization, created a warrant for the revival of direct U.S. counteraction under the doctrine; but to give the doctrine such drastic application would militate against its underlying suggestion that a Nixon Administration directly succeeding Eisenhower's would not have incurred the Vietnam experience—had it only been in possession of lessons generated by the intervening Democratic administrations.

The paradoxes of the Vietnam war- and peace-making have not elucidated the bearing and likely prospects of the Nixon Doctrine in the third world. Neither could this be done conclusively by an abstract analysis testing the doctrine's internal equilibrium in terms of (its supposed assumptions concerning) new mixes of surviving or adjusted U.S. interests, commitments, and capabilities, relative to the capabilities and self-restraint of the Soviets and to the less-developed countries' capacities for self-reliance. Only a series of consistent U.S. actions, reflecting an actually implemented role, could validate or invalidate the posited basic trends, confirm or disconfirm the neatly counterpoised assumptions held to underlie the doctrine, and strengthen or weaken its plausibility as a practicable strategy.

At the close of the first Nixon Administration, the doctrine represented an intellectual and diplomatic effort to overcome the pretended two main, and largely interrelated, pitfalls of past U.S. foreign policy: activism and pragmatism, presumably inclining past policymakers to do too much while (or, more properly, because) reacting too often. The doctrine's long-range promise has rested on the ability of policy-makers to coordinate future U.S. foreign policy on three levels: one, of major programs, such as the recasting and implementing of key economic- and military-assistance policies to individual, selected third-world countries; two, of critical problems, such as the resolution of conflicts in the Middle East and South and Southeast

Asia; and three, of comprehensive process, including the formation of both individual third-world states and regional systems in the several segments of the third world as a whole.

To this end the U.S. approach to programs and problems will have to encompass efficaciously three pairs of processes. One pair encompasses devolution of responsibility for order and security from the U.S. to lesser powers and organisms in the third world, and politico-economic development of key third-world countries; each of these requires deliberate rational effort. The second intrinsically contrary pair of processes comprises politico-economic stagnation and overall retrogression of third-world countries in both internal and external action, as spontaneous reversions to pre-colonial patterns of collective existence. The third pair of processes, finally, which complements the first while setting limits to the internationally tolerable scope of the second, consists of the formation or evolution of regional balance-of-power systems on the one hand and, on the other, of post-postcolonial reapportionment of third-world countries in spheres of influence or even control by the great powers. Systemic evolution would consummate the decolonization of henceforth more than nominally independent actors in the pluralistic politics of multi-tier balances of power involving small, middle, and great powers; while reapportionment, related to the diplomatic equilibrium and consequent pressures toward co-responsibility for order of the great powers themselves, confirms decolonization as being a multi-phase process in which self-assertion alternates with more or less benign forms of reversion to dependent or client status. A critical test for the doctrine is to come to terms in actual strategies with the partially, but by no means wholly or lastingly, conflicting implications of regional system formation and the reformation of spheres of influence for the small and great powers alike.

Hardly reducible to dichotomies à la negotiation versus confrontation and development versus security, the practical equations have only begun to take shape at the end of the first Nixon Administration, while their "solution" has clearly been deferred to the second term in a carefully laid-out design of historic greatness to emerge from successful implementation of a doctrine of realistic modesty.[1]

---

[1] The following discussion of conflict in the third world is indebted to many monographic sources and, in particular, to essays in S. Spiegel and K. N. Waltz, eds., *Conflict in World Politics* (Cambridge, Mass.: Winthrop, 1971) and to articles by Pierre Hassner and Samuel P. Huntington in *Civil Violence and the International System* (Part II), Adelphi Papers Number Eighty-Three (London: The International Institute for Strategic Studies, 1971).

The Lesser and Less-Developed Powers:
Conflict and Regional Systems

If regional system formation and the concertation of responsibilities among balanced world powers are the logically discrete but practically complementary implications of the Nixon Doctrine, the question which of the two strands to stress more, in what sequence, or in what tactically contrived interrelations is not one that permits a ready answer. As a matter of fact, until crises have compelled a creative manipulation of the two strands, the most useful preliminary task is to identify the diverse constraints which will predictably condition the application of the Nixon Doctrine in the only analytically separable realms of the lesser- and the major-power relations. One such "constraint" consists in the historically validated patterns and requisites of evolving state systems, to be discussed now in relation to the lesser states in the third world; another, to be taken up subsequently, bears on the interplay between greater and lesser powers as a problem for order-maintenance or "managed" evolution. The most that can be attempted, within the short post-colonial perspective, is to try to see whether the record of third-world countries can be discussed at all meaningfully in terms of general ideas concerning system evolution; and, if so, whether the most fragile positive elements are sufficient to warrant a great-power policy incorporating their promotion into an overall strategy. While the following discussion is but tentative, it does support a qualifiedly positive answer to both queries. Moreover, the reservations expressed will have to do as much with the great-power responses to trends in the third world as with the innate potential for evolution along traditional lines of the third-world countries themselves.

The Structures of Regional Systems. The basic structures of third-world regions and subregions are still ill-defined as to membership and boundaries, and are only tentatively interrelated for the most part. This matches the still incomplete, but on balance growing, basic homogeneity of representative third-world actors (territorial states or those unambiguously acting in their behalf) and the similarly evolving specificity of controlling contacts and conflicts among them. Disparities in "power," so far mainly expressed in economic potential and growth, are on the increase between the actually "developing" and the "poorest" LDCs. But radical or root heterogeneity has declined along with "transnational" prophets and goals; the consequence has been the unquestioned confinement to the territorial-state framework of continuing polarity between governments oriented toward stability and revolutionary forces in and out of power. As a result, in part, of a trend toward relatively disciplined means-ends calculus in second-generation conflicts revolving around post-post-colonial economic and political survival or aggrandizement of both regimes and states, there has been some differentiation of roles. At least potentially strong indigenous states have tended to replace acutely ambitious pre-eminent leaders as credible aspirants to leadership positions in the several regions; relatively weaker, marginally situated, or internally heterogeneous states (such as, say, the Sudan or Uganda in Africa or Malaysia in Asia) gravitated toward an intermediary position between geographically or racially defined areas, not least as a means to secure extra-regional leverages against an unfavorable congealment of a regional "empire"; and the relatively weakest or most unstable countries were consigned to buffer roles, implemented through the extremes of integral passivity or feverish activism in all promising directions at once or alternately.

Such trends were manifest in both Africa and Asia, as they had been at an earlier stage in Latin America. They took the form of an incipient crystallization, and fluctuating interconnections, of West, North, and East African "sub-systems" interacting less with one another than with the Middle East (including the Red Sea and Persian Gulf areas) and Southern Africa as areas of relatively more intense conflicts and more important stakes. Similarly, the South Asian, Southeast Asian, and Northeast Asian areas were at once relatively autonomous and, depending on course and outcomes of local conflicts, potentially interacting with one another or (especially the South Asian one) with the Middle Eastern conflict area. It is useful to segregate provisionally such lesser-state conflicts and relationships, however inchoate or dormant, from great-power contentions and impingements, because the latter are no longer the sole integrators of the several regions into a global system. By themselves alone, the inter-regional tremors and consequent linkages of internal needs and external conduct have brought into near-alliance and roughly parallel enactment of conflict such locally major states as Israel and Ethiopia, both alien and acquisitive in regional terms, in opposition to counter-expansionist or revisionist, but conventionally weaker, Egypt and Somalia, respectively. A related two- or multi-party interplay involved such proximate lesser states as Iraq and South Yemen as well as such a remoter bigger state as Iran, constituting moreover a possible link eastward toward the South Asian area and its Indo-Pakistani conflict series. So far at least, the African conflict-alliance axis and inter-regional network has not effectively extended all the way down to

Southern Africa despite such potential mediator countries as Tanzania and such meddlesome activities as Israel's in Black Africa and Egypt's in Moslem Africa. Instead, South Africa has displayed, to a larger extent than the more pluralistic subregions, the either anachronistic or else futuristic features of a relatively isolated subsystem revolving around a single "middle power" in principle only capable of eventually being linked with comparable core-powers elsewhere in a transregional balance-of-power network.

Unlike the relatively well-defined identity of key actors, the indeterminate status of individual regions or subregions and their interlinkages has reflected the fluid status of conflicts. Only a few conflicts, such as the Arab-Israeli and Indo-Pakistani conflict and the conflicts centered on South Africa and Indochina, have been regionally dominant in the sense that a conclusive outcome would define the structure and politics of the relevant region for the following phase. Their unfolding, consequently, weighed on the definition and enactment of other, relatively subsidiary conflicts of either intra- or inter-state character even where these latter were more immediately influential in determining specific short-term policies. Insofar as uncertainties continued to surround the identities of policy-determinant and, to a lesser extent, regionally dominant, conflicts, the formation of regional systems and, incidentally, viable actors was inhibited. But, as a compensation, the conflicting attributes and manifestations of individual stakes of conflict, such as communal or tribal as against "national," domestic as against interstate, and "ideological" as against pragmatic, also inhibited the derailment of conflicts into unproductive dead-ends of pure tribalism, integral parochialism, or inflexible dogmatism. By and large, the gradual if uneven crystallization of the different regions and areas in the third world has displayed some promising traits and trends, notably in the Middle East–Persian Gulf–East Africa area and in South and Southeast Asia, increasingly structured internally and even inter-regionally by particular conflicts and corresponding alignments involving both intra- and inter-state issues.

Regional *systems* were emerging to the extent that such structures entail essentially predictable, because externally constrained, conduct in relation to concrete and intrinsically manageable, because finite, objectives. Conditioning the *evolution* of such systems is a spectrum ranging from initial readiness for conflict rooted in the resource base to terminal resolution of conflict typically marked by the reallocation of resources; and it passes through the actual generation and enactment of conflict. They all are crucial in linking pre-existing with prospective structures; and they are the dramatic occasions for, and evidence of, either abortive or successful adaptation to the impingements of both ideal and material changes and challenges.

Readiness for Conflict. Readiness for conflict evolves in terms of both material capacity and psycho-political disposition to engage in conflict. If the first is related, in modern terms, more to economic development, the latter bears principally on political development. As states and state systems evolve, the overall trend is toward more deliberate creation, coordination, and projection of material resources as compared with intangible and as it were accidental assets such as the longevity, legitimacy, or charisma of a leader. In the third world the tendency has been inhibited, but not yet either blocked or made irrelevant, by several factors. Among them have been the low or unstable level of its commodity prices, of locally available or externally supplied capital, as well as initial precipitation into industrial development and subsequent reversion to slower-moving manufacture- and agriculture-based strategies for development. These adverse factors affected least the third-world countries which disposed of foreign-exchange producing mineral resources (e.g., Algeria), had foreign-aid generating strategic importance (Iran and Turkey), were involved in a military conflict of interest to a great power (Taiwan and South Korea), and, finally, had a middle-power potential (Mexico and Brazil) on the basis of exceptionally favorable resource-base or management.

More complex than material capacity is disposition to conflict. It is related to an ongoing interplay between key surpluses and deficiencies of a state on the levels of both elites and mass, politics and economics. The surplus of unemployable semi-educated personnel in the third world has been a growing, and possibly principal, problem for governments; it has increased proneness to more or less violent, domestic and external, revolutionary and conventional conflict. The generalized impact of job-deficiency, replacing food-deficiency as the crucial third-world economic problem, was nakedly manifest when a government (Egypt's after the war of 1967) was politically unable to discharge unemployable urban conscripts.

If surplus has been mainly in human raw-material, deficiencies concerned chiefly material resources and the but slowly evolving (and in places retrogressing) governmental capacity effectively to attend to domestic tasks as the historically principal means for reducing pressures for compensatory activities abroad. So far at least, any shortage of exploitable or revenue-producing land per se in a pre-industrial, agricultural, or pastoral, context, played a smaller role in predisposing third-world countries to conflict than has deficiency in territorially located assets important for modern industrial economic development. As indicators of waxing and waning disposition to engage in conflict, contests over territories harboring marketable mineral resources, such as oil, natural gas, and phosphates in North Africa, were more than matched by those over maritime access and exit ports and routes on the West African coast and in both the Red Sea and Persian Gulf narrows and the Strait of Malacca in Southeast Asia.

By and large, the growing trend in the third world to treat material and tangible resources as the primary assets, stakes, and stimuli of conflict was matched by an evolution toward more secular and inward-turned leadership elites, with long-range consequences for disposition to conflict. In the process, one-man political messiahs and one-party machines tended to be replaced by civilian and military administrators as the key reconcentrators of power dissolved in post-independence delirium. The unifying trait remained authoritarianism, tempered by incompetence and corruption. The relatively unequal alliance between the military and the bourgeois-bureaucrats took the place of repressive charismatics in some countries (Ghana) or coexisted in time as a practical alternative to more free-wheeling party politics in other countries (e.g., Kenya and Israel and India) with different, moderating or stimulative, effects on conflict readiness. Even where political frameworks remained in force (Kenya and Tanzania), the political formations underwent considerable bureaucratization while the civilian regime tried to integrate the military into the political structure (Tanzania) or keep it neutral (Chile under Allende) rather than drive it into revolt by futile attempts to neutralize it by countervailing paramilitary formations (e.g., Ghana and Mali, on the Peronist pattern of Argentina). Bureaucratic management of resources and policy should militate against disposition to adventurous expansionism, while engendering the resources which can sustain conflicts resulting from internal group upheavals attendant on economic development or inspired by the growth or survival needs of the state itself. Especially in relatively strong LDCs (such as Brazil) military-bureaucratic complexes, while apt to be at first only internally expansive in the sense of extending themselves into ever-widening circles of modernizing activities both urban and rural, metropolitan and regional, are potentially expansionist at a later stage when they have met, or discovered they could not peacefully meet, what they themselves defined as the requisites of the ultimately coveted greater-power status.

The net effect of the second-generation leadership on the formation of regional systems by way of evolving readiness for conflict will also depend on its turnover and changing social makeup. An unavoidable passing of first-generation elites has tended to promote individuals deriving from ever lower social or more provincial backgrounds; this has patent consequences for outlooks and priorities. Excessive provincialism in leaders ascending to the national level is apt to produce a dangerous withdrawal from readiness to face interstate conflict into a temporarily restful isolation—until such time as dormancy yields to an explosively particularistic or overcompensating nationalistic bias, depending on the scope of available material capacities. Post-Nehru India may be within this spectrum. Furthermore, it is important whether circulation of elites will be attended by an acceleration or deceleration of the presently quite frequent turnover in personnel on the commanding heights. The rate of turnover is more important than its mechanism, whether turnover occurs by more or less simulated elections, efficacious coups, or authentic revolutions. A slow-down would seem to be required to permit the takeoff of foreign-policy formulation and execution into some continuity even if not yet stability. Such continuity is in large part dependent on a few initially serviceable, simplified traditional axioms emerging from protracted (if not necessarily always belligerently enacted) conflicts and consequent alignments with particular states. Such tradition-formation may be underway in relatively regime-stable and manageably embattled countries as Ethiopia and Malaysia. In a highly fluid environment, protraction of conflicts will more than usually depend on regime stability; by the same token, regime instability is apt either to foster disposition to prematurely terminate immediately unprofitable conflicts, or else give rise to a temptation to project internal divisions onto foreign states as the immediately opportune enemies (thus Uganda's President Obote accused a previously friendly Israel, as many another upset leader accused Western imperialism, of responsibility in a successful military coup which overthrew him).

The Generation of Conflicts. The issue overlapping with conflict readiness is the actual generation of conflicts in the third world. It has tended to fortify the impression of some evolutionary advance derived from basic, material and dispositional, readiness for conflict. The key distinction with respect to generation of conflict is between concept and contact. "Contact" entails friction—whether from a territorial frontier issue or ethnic or other fragmentation (and mobilization); "concept" encompasses a variable measure of fantasy and frustration, associated with materially ill-founded aspiration to hegemonial sway.

Early post-colonial concepts instrumental in generating conflicts evolved along a line leading from regional imperialism for nation-building by way of nativist varieties of pseudo-socialism (or, in Castro's case, communism) to a species of racialism. The latter was as intent to present itself in the guise of counter-racialism as native imperialism and socialism were to assume the clothing of anti-imperialism. All were comparably thwarted in effective expression by more potent particularisms and resulting antagonisms. Pseudo-hegemonial doctrines were simultaneously doing duty for genuine drives while aiming at such conglomerates as Greater Indonesia or Egypt or Ghana under the disguise of Pan-Malay, Pan-Arab, or Pan-African linguistic or cultural community. The resulting policies implemented the personalist phase of interstate evolution as the precursor to geopolitical and institutional or bureaucratic governing principles of action. Regional empire-building, as well as more localized efforts by less ambitious LDC regimes, was impelled by the desire to quickly erect "political kingdoms" as the near-automatic begetters of nationhood within and material sustenance from without. They were the largely symbolic acts of self-assertion by leaders and regimes in need of periodic renewal of fading legitimacy if not youth. And they resulted in doctrinal schisms and grand-stand confrontations rather than in efficaciously enacted specific conflicts between states.

The conflicts generated by concepts faded in part because they had failed to relieve post-independence frustrations. Along with them receded the vocally ineffectual, highly personal indigenous imperialism with anti-colonial overtones and social-revolutionary trappings as the leading formula for nation-building. But it did so only after exhausting its real if limited potential to provide an initial galvanizing framework for the interaction of new "states," lacking any sense of geopolitical orientation, either political or economic cohesion, or even discernible structure. Moreover, it expired only after it had replaced the myths of pre-colonial grandeur with the merely half-legendary residues of abortive but, because indigenous, legitimate imperial exemplars. These can be more systematically re-enacted and resisted in a later phase of authentic hegemonial conflicts, should the third world ever reach one. An early inkling of such conflicts may be discerned in the neo-Ghandiite drive for a greater Indian regional sphere, contrasting both with Nehru's futile exercises in the leadership of Afro-Asianism and with Sukarno's pathetic confrontationism.

The founding fathers' gropings set the stage for the second generation of salient conflicts, rooted in different forms of actual contact and resulting frictions. Differentiable from conflicts originating in essentially political concepts even when they partially overlap with them in time, these conflicts between and within states have been largely conditioned by economic factors. If they derive from this fact their specificity, their concreteness flows from the substitution of re-emergent group conflicts and divisions for grand-stand ideological confrontations. The further fact that intergroup conflicts occur within the however nominal framework of the *nation*-state tends at once to exasperate the contentions over the materially tinged issue of political predominance between groups and to provide a possible framework for their eventual resolution.

Whereas the "communalism" or "nativism" of inter-group conflicts in the third world sets it back to the pre-colonial era, the retrogression is qualified by the conflicts' potential for promoting evolution. It resides in the frictions within or across frontiers being henceforth consciously related to the territorial state in a frame of mind and action either impersonal or at least multi-personal. The transition is symbolized in the difference between Nasserite Pan-Arabism and Palestinian statism, as the *idées-force* of the Arab side of the Middle Eastern conflict, and in the chasm between Nkrumah's Pan Africanism and the Congo's and Nigeria's tension between tribalism and centralism, as the determining factors of African international relations. This is progress of sorts, in the perspective of state system formation, complementing the even more authentic geopolitical impetus behind conflicts involving such third-world middle powers as Israel, post-Nehru India, and South Africa. At the same time, however, the provisional "territorialization" of conflict-generating concepts remained vulnerable to "re-ideologization" of notably intra-state conflicts engendered by contacts, as the growing differentiation of the global ideological setting presented an increasingly wide spectrum of choice for the concurrently growing ideological opportunism.

In principle at least, inter-group conflicts can promote the political development of states or nations, and thus advance systems evolution, when victors succeed in combining hegemony with appeasement and the defeated parties at last abandon all thought of secession as a live option, while internal turmoil is siphoned off into intensified or more effectively managed conflict or competition with other states. The key advantage of internal hegemonial conflicts over the first-generation contests for dominance is their very confinement within a smaller arena that is manageable in terms of both material and immaterial resources derived from within or infused from the outside. In the longer run, however, the future of the third world depends largely on what key factor will sustain the third generation of conflicts. Such might be, along European lines, territorially based nationalisms, if and when they emerge from the void between the trans- and the sub-national levels, as the viable middle term. Such reorientation may be at once post-catastrophic if it were preceded by civil war (as in the U.S.A. itself), and pre-conditional to an effective generation of interstate conflict which, paradoxically in concept but not in practice, is at once necessary to consummate nationhood and is impeded from taking effective shape in its absence. As ethnically or socio-economically fragmented societies move toward that phase, they will gravitate from isolationism to expansionism and back again to an intermediate posture, in function of their growth and the evolving setting. Visible prospects are the war-forged united Vietnam (Indochina) or Nigeria on one side of the spectrum; on the other, a Brazil emerging into consolidated nationhood from a foreign-policy fantasy of a Quadros, or Indonesia from Sukarno's and India from Nehru's, all followed by internal turmoils and foreign-policy reactions. Such relatively powerful nation-states should in due course be ready for "hegemonial conflicts" with regional peers and extra-regional great powers, while thus transmitting system-formative impulse also to less well endowed or developed smaller states related to them by inescapable contact rather than by prematurely formulated concepts.

The Enactment of Conflicts. The capacity and disposition of third-world countries to engage in conflict and the factors generating such conflicts are basic to the political and economic development of third-world countries and the systemic evolution of regions. On the other hand, the enactment and resolution of conflicts are more immediately conspicuous and as such are relevant to the policy formulation of the great powers, notoriously poorly equipped for concerning themselves, preventively or otherwise, with the deeper-seated determinants of diplomatically at all manageable surface events. Consequently, from the viewpoint of the Nixon Administration's doctrine (and more or less closely related first-term policy), the posture chosen and applied to the enactment of third-world conflicts, and their resolution, is crucial for the doctrine's internal coherence and the policy's long-term prospects, insofar as they reflect any thought-out relationship to system-evolution in the third world and *its* prospects.

The enactment of conflicts typically revolves around, and in part also evolves between, two analytically opposite types of conflict: cathartic and catalytic, as regards their political function, and, as regards actual military operations, symbolic and catastrophic, oriented respectively toward more or less decorous stalemate or decisive subduing of the weaker party. A cathartic conflict is distinguished by the initiating party's more or less controlled release of tensions as the primary purpose while the party initiating a catalytic conflict aims more self-consciously at clarifying or restructuring an existing balance of forces.

In the relatively recent past, cathartic conflicts between third-world countries have comprised the Morocco-Algerian war, the first Indo-Pakistani war in 1965, Somalia's conflict with Ethiopia (and Kenya), and more recently, the flareup between Honduras and El Salvador, among others. To differing degrees these conflicts were limited to largely symbolic military engagements lacking decisive encounters or results. The implicit self-restraint of the contestants was due, next to insufficiency and rapid attrition of resources, to the initiating party's immediate or principal objective: to contain internal disaffection or release accumulated frustrations, focused on external claims or events, by a militant display which would renew the government's popular mandate. The object is consequently *not* to eliminate internal difficulties in depth by a major military effort with material results. The commensurately limited external objective is merely to publicize a territorial, or other, claim—thus Pakistan's to Kashmir or Morocco's to historically Sheriffian portions of Algeria—and to legitimize it by a national deed in the absence of effective international or allied support. The related procedural objective is to interrupt prescription that might otherwise run against the claim, while compelling negotiations toward an at least partial satisfaction.

Outside restraints reinforce self-restraint in confining cathartic conflict to a very limited objective; their efficacy is likewise due largely to indigenous resource poverty. Resource exiguity increases as one moves from Asia via the Middle East to Africa; and the restraint potential of dependence on outside supplies was heightened whenever the claimants precipitating cathartic wars were weaker in mobilized or readily mobilizeable strength than the possessors—thus Somalia was weaker than Ethiopia, Morocco than Algeria, and Pakistan than India. The potential outside supplier could be, moreover, politically embarrassing as well as unreliable—e.g., the Soviet Union for Somalia, China for Pakistan—or reluctant to choose, as when both Morocco and Algeria depended primarily on French matériel, and both India and Pakistan on American and British, before they turned eastward to diversify supplies or virtually displace the original suppliers. This dampened the conflict automatically when the bigger powers followed competitive supply of arms in peacetime with concerted or parallel denial of replacements in wartime; actual or threatened cessation of deliveries was a more telling appeal to reason than the calls for cease-fire issuing from the U.N. or regional organizations such as the OAU.

Contrasting with stylized military maneuverings in a cathartic interstate conflict is the catastrophic enactment of internal strife. Such strife can take the form of an uncontrolled release of communal or socio-economically fuelled passions, constituting a riot (such as those between Hindus and Moslems following partition on the Indian sub-continent) or a rural jacquerie (more at home in Latin America), and invite or attend repression (such as that of East Bengali insurgents by the West Pakistani army prior to the second Indo-Pakistani war). Or else, such releases of pent-up sentiment can be in part manipulated by incumbent or insurgent elites in a civil war such as those of the Congo, Nigeria, and Yemen. The principal purpose is then not to demonstrate the existence of a state or a government's right to keep trying to govern, as in cathartic interstate conflicts, but (more along the lines set by the catalytic purpose) to dominate and, if impossible, to destroy the rival group; and it is not to arrest prescription against claims but to win the power to proscribe rivals at will and to avoid being proscribed oneself. Civil conflicts are thus commonly enacted not by way of contrived stalemates in a short engagement, but more typically by self-generating polarization of groups in a lengthy or intermittent conflict. They are reliably moderated neither by the paucity of resources, given the adequacy of even primitive instruments of destruction, nor by the pressures of great-power restraint, given the insufficient importance or too complex character of the stakes in such strife.

Outside restraint has been forthcoming where racial features (as in Katanga and the Congo generally) involving whites engendered humanitarian concern; and it may occur where the power-political implications of different outcomes of the civil strife are sufficiently extensive to arouse diplomatic concern, as in East Bengal. But intervention to apply restraint is paradoxically least likely where it risks offending the incumbents in an actually or potentially key country, such as Nigeria; potential significance merges then with utter insignificance (such as Burundi's) in insuring free hand for the stronger party. Although intra-state conflict with a spontaneous or manipulated cathartic function is different in key aspects from the corresponding interstate one, it will tend to be likewise inconclusive—with exceptions, as in Nigeria and Zanzibar, where capitulation or expulsion-extermination of the defeated party, respectively, produced a decision. The reason for inconclusiveness is that the capacity for biological regeneration of the decimated weaker groups will do duty for the attrition of material capabilities of both adversaries in the inter-state war.

In both intra- and inter-state conflicts with wholly or partially cathartic functions, then, the main interest from the systemic viewpoint lies in what follows upon them: what options the particular conflict revealed to be practically unavailable and what logjams, produced by the putative prior existence of options or by unspent authentic emotion, it had loosened and thus set afloat toward new configurations. Such clarification is the deliberate object of the party initiating a catalytic conflict. The party initiating a conventional military action for a cathartic purpose will tend to be weaker than the internal forces it wishes temporarily to assuage; the party initiating a conventional military action for a catalytic purpose is by contrast typically stronger (while in depth possibly more vulnerable) than the party which had set in train events and paramilitary operations which precipitated the conflict situation. The rule can be applied to Ethiopia, conventionally reacting against infiltrator-supporting Somalia, as well as to Algeria moving overtly against Moroccan inroads, to Israel squashing Egyptian initiatives in two wars, and to India escalating against a Pakistan forcefully backing tribesmen in Kashmir prior to the first war and trying to deal forcibly with rebellious East Bengalis prior to the second.

Beginning as a response, catalyzing military action will be more deliberate in the second round of a protracted conflict. Thus, in the first round in 1965, India too was largely propelled by the need for catharsis following her humiliating defeat by China; in the 1971 second round she deliberately waged a war to reshape the distribution of forces in South Asia so as to remove the Pakistani distraction and permit a concentrated deployment of India's increased conventional military strength against an internally reconsolidated and nuclearized China at a time when she was still being squeezed from the North by India's Soviet ally. Until India joined their ranks, China and Israel were the sole third-world protagonists of catalytic warfare. China's earlier thrust against India in the north and northeast aimed to clarify, and by so doing restructure, the relationship of forces of attraction and destruction between the two Asian developmental models. Israel's second and third thrusts against the Arab states was intended both to convince them of Israel's *de facto* superiority in the Middle Eastern balance of indigenous forces and to further enhance the superiority. All these raids (China's, Israel's, and India's) had the psychological objective, as distinct from need, to punish and humble the target states, with the outside possibility of forcing them into defeatist submission; whatever cathartic elements underlay them were due to propagandistically created war-psychoses and security fears in the aggressor countries. The specific diplomatic objective was to gain and hold solid territorial assets (in the Ladekh area by China, in Sinai and elsewhere by Israel, in "liberated" East Bengal and in a West Pakistan open to invasion by India), valuable both in themselves and for eventual bargaining over final territorial demarcation or diplomatic dispositions.

In the Nigerian civil war, it was the intrinsically weaker Biafra that aimed an initial military drive at reshaping the balance of power through the disintegration of the inherently more vulnerable rump-Nigeria into its component parts; this would have isolated the dominant north from the west and the midwest and from the sea. Disintegration along ethnic lines has been the common danger for relatively stronger Ethiopia (and Kenya) and India, and, consequently, the strategic objective of the adversaries. Israel's vulnerability has resided in her Palestinian subjects and the conflict-relevant difference in origins and opinions among the Jews themselves. Both Indo-Pakistani and Arab-Israeli relations have been, moreover, exacerbated by an original partition which, rejected as valid or binding by at least one side, exposed a contrived relationship of forces to the convergence of upsetting passions and revisionist programs (on India's part no less, if less spectacularly, than on the Arabs'). The catalyzing party being at once stronger and potentially more vulnerable, will typically employ superior military means in an offensive strategy for the "defensive" or at least pre-emptive immediate purpose of decisively subduing the weaker, but more resilient, adversary, either once again or once for all; in a catastrophic military-political context, a total defeat of one is required to guarantee the territorial integrity and internal cohesion of the other. Only where but the first, and possibly only, round is involved will an Ethiopia or Algeria resort to a mere token conventional-military counterthrust with the limited objective of demonstrating the impossibility of a facile forcible change in the status quo, which, if tolerated, would create a noxious precedent for a multi-ethnic party (Ethiopia) or for a party exposed to more than one claimant (Algeria). Such a conflict's enactment will, therefore, be determined more by the cathartic impetus of the claimant (Somalia and Morocco, respectively) than by the catalytic purpose of the defender, pending more intense hostilities if the claim persists and the balance of forces shifts further in the defendant's favor.

As for the weaker target of a massive catalytic thrust, he may in effect invite such thrust by prior activities. One possible purpose is to demonstrate to the public the vanity of an increasingly unreal ambition—for parity in Pakistan's case and for Israel's extermination in Egypt's—which blocks avenues to constructive internal efforts; another to convince other ethnic groups, as in West Pakistan, of the regime's unwillingness to yield autonomy or secession to any pressure but that arising from conventional military defeat. If the Pakistani are suspect of actually inviting military defeat to avoid losing to East Bengali guerrillas, Nasser's military-political posturing courted such defeat to avoid losing ground to Syrian radicals and actually, if unwittingly, prepared the ground for the Palestinian guerrillas. The differences between preponderantly cathartic and preponderantly catalytic functions and corresponding enactments of successive active spells in protracted wars show the "rounds" to be no mere repetitions or cyclical recurrences, but to propel systemic evolution and betoken it. Ideally, they gradually replace or at least complement emotional hostility with traditions-formative antagonisms capable of imparting continuity to "national" foreign policies and some coherence to regional systems.

The tendency to move from cathartic to catalytic purposes in protracted conflicts has been paralleled by a trend to conventional warfare where conflict remained active at all. Following the decline of subversive strategies in inter-state conflicts, as applied by a Nkrumah or Sukarno, non-communist sub-conventional warfare survived mainly, and not too efficaciously, in the Black Africans' contests with the white-dominated powers in Southern Africa and in yet smaller-scale actions in the Persian Gulf area. The counter-guerrilla, largely conventional, reactions to such efforts have been increasingly effective; success has not remained confined to the British-led resistance to Indonesian piracy and terrorism in the confrontation with Malaysia, and Ethiopia's conventional riposte was as effective against Somali infiltrators as Israel's and Jordan's was against the Palestinian "freedom fighters." More generally in the Middle East, lower forms of conflict enactment, including the propaganda war of nerves conducted from Cairo, designed to create rather than release emotion, tended to provoke effective conventional responses rather than provide an effective substitute for effective conventional military capability. Where such capability was lacking, warfare between states has been on the wane —as in Africa since the mid-1960s—and conflict tended to occur within states only, as in Nigeria, perhaps denoting a constant sum of conflict-readiness overall. By and large, despite some amateurish attempts in the third world to go beyond alternations to actual combinations of internal and external, conventional and sub-conventional, warfare, as well as of stand-off and subduance strategies, such syntheses remained the secret of especially Asian communists. As distinct from the China civil war, however, where the "synthesis" was apparently brought to a pitch of perfection, U.S. conventional intervention in Vietnam has by and large succeeded in deranging the "scientific" orchestration of the component elements by Asian communists and may have contributed to the formula's long-term decline.

The overall trend toward conventional modes of military enactment has increased the importance of matériel inputs by the great powers —their reinforcements as a counterpart to restraints—a fact of which the Soviet Union in particular has not been unaware. Taken by themselves, armies in the third world have tended to be small and inward-oriented. But they could be rapidly expanded in numbers—e.g., by the Federal Government in Nigeria and by Indonesia in the confrontation period—though not correspondingly improved in efficiency: the performance of government units against Biafra or of Egyptian regulars in Yemen against comparable adversaries was not impressive (much as the latter are rehabilitated by partial analogy with the U.S. in Vietnam). The inadequacy of internal resources apart from manpower generates high tolerance for quantitative imbalance between third world parties. This favors the defensive and the weaker side but also increases the importance of qualitative great-power inputs. Thus the Nigerian civil was was "decided" more directly by the British-backed maritime blockade of Biafra by the north than by the disparity in overland forces which, too, was largely the result of unequal reinforcements from the outside.

Matching the vertical factor of indigenous tolerance for high power-differentials and the dynamic one of the multiplier effect of great-power inputs, is the horizontal or static one of the low ceiling imposed upon third-world conflicts by the incidence of great-power restraint in the later stages of interstate conflicts. The result has been a rather high threshold in the third world for open conventional military conflict as either unpromising or unpredictable in terms of pre-war calculations and conditions, and a correspondingly high incidence (next to civil strife) of "concert." Such concert, conceived as superficial harmony, is but a facile alternative to conflict, however, in the absence of an adequate basis for a real concert of powers in a balance of forces imposing diplomatic, non-war modalities on reciprocal containment and compensation; in the best of cases real concert arises but rarely from a temporary state of multiple and diversified conflict relationships. Related to the deficiency of these relationships in the contemporary third world has been the very limited interlock between parallel conflicts via steady and efficacious alignments which would aggregate a regional balance of power and reconcile ongoing enactment of protracted conflicts with intermittent failings of individual contestants. Isolated exceptions from the rule have included Sudan's offensive cooperation with Somalia prior to the former's accommodation with Ethiopia, and the defense alignment of Ethiopia and Kenya against Somalia matching the latter's offensive one with Egypt against Ethiopia. But there has been no Indo-Afghan alliance against Pakistan, nor a Pakistan–Burma–Ceylon alignment against India, that would match the Indo-Soviet alignment against the Sino-Pakistani connection, while only verbal support was extended by Pakistan to Moslem Arabs against Israel in 1967 and by the former to Pakistan in 1971.

Such deficiencies denote a slow-moving development in the *political* modes of enacting conflicts. In that domain, a more pronounced parallel to conventionalized military modes has been the trend toward "pragmatic" forms of political conflict management. The characteristic tendency is to move repeatedly in successive phases of development from armed ideological propagation to pragmatic promotion of interests, and from pretensions to arbitrate issues of doctrinal orthodoxy to the more prosaic concern with the adjustment of such interests. In the contemporary third world, corresponding differences can be discerned in the respective political modes of a Nasser and a Sadat, a Sukarno and a Suharto, a Nehru and Mme Ghandi, while ideological agnosticism in relations with the third world spreads from the Soviet Union to China and ideologically formulated feuding is increasingly confined to inter-radical conflicts and to such key but non-governmental actors as the Palestinians or such marginal, inexperienced or irresponsible regimes, as the South Yemeni and Syrian. While promising parallels can be drawn in this respect between developments in the contemporary third world and earlier ones in Europe, the former's handicaps cannot be discounted. Apart from the all-pervasive impact on the third world of the industrial powers, the third world has also suffered from a relative paucity of political means for conflict enactment, power aggregation, and conflict resolution. Early Europe possessed them in her dynastic component permitting familial and marital alliances, aggregations, and (until the arrival of nationalism) moderation of conflict. The third world has forfeited a near-equivalent in the ideological affinities among its founding "dynasts" as the bases for fragile alignments and unions; and it has by and large rejected the recourse to up-to-date mechanisms such as political self-determination on the grass-roots level. As a result, and not least for resolution or avoidance of conflicts, the third world has come to depend on the none-too-promising expedient of differently motivated and functional regional organizations.

The Resolution of Conflicts. As a key presumptive repository of devolution of responsibility for order and security, regionalism is, however ambiguously, part of the long-term implications of the Nixon Doctrine. Regionalism plays a role in (attempts at) the resolution or avoidance of conflict among third-world countries. But, more importantly, the prospects for the third world are at least as dependent on the ways of resolving such conflicts in narrower frameworks and by more traditional means. By its close connection with the enactment of conflicts, their resolution profoundly affects evolution of state systems even if the variously coercive procedural modalities for settling conflicts change but little over time.

The most conclusive ways of resolving conflicts have traditionally been through changes in the structure of power and interests, attended by more conspicuous negotiations or institutional elaborations. The most common structural transformations have been, next to the outright suppression of one party by military decision, the dispersion of a conflict and its supersession. Structural dispersion entails the addition of at least a third party to the original conflicting parties unable decisively to coerce one another; it promotes resolution by permitting compensations for partial successes and failures incurred by the parties, and it typically induces competitive initiatives in the direction of peace as part of a race for the advantage accruing from priority. Whereas the most striking recent example of such dispersion is in the great-power arena, in China's integration into the Soviet-American conflict relationship, there has also been the addition of the Philippines' claims to the conflict between Indonesia and Malaysia and Bangla Desh's disgruntlements to the Indo-Pakistani rivalry. Least subject to deliberate manipulation, but because of this the most common and effective modality of conflict resolution, is the supersession of one conflict by another, which may but need not grow out of the preceding configuration of power, interests and concerns. Whereas many variants of possible supersession can be envisaged in relation to the conflicts in South Asia, the Middle East, and Africa, a relatively accomplished concrete example is the long-inactive but formally unresolved conflict between Morocco and Algeria. This conflict over the territorial implications of French decolonization has been provisionally supplanted by the locally somewhat artificial antagonism toward Israel and the more real contention with Spain over final decolonization in the Sahara.

Being most conclusive, structural modes of resolving conflicts also tend to be most productive of system evolution. By contrast, inconclusive ways of "resolving" conflict will tend to produce stagnation or retrogression for system, actor, or both. A productive resolution is more likely to flow from a militarily decisive outcome or, at least, a sustained if stalemated prior military action, than from token contests or merely verbal or otherwise simulated contentions. This corresponds to the fact that as the evolution of a state system begins in earnest, and the balance of power consequently assumes a discernible shape, conflicts are resolved less by internal weakening or disintegration of contestants and more by the fact or real possibility of an effective military impact of one upon another—less by dissolution and more by defeat. Such a development is indeed the precondition of systematic statecraft as a series of self-conscious adjustments to not wholly accidental or largely uncontrollable events, wrought in part at least by the deliberate application of power between as well as within "states." Few resolutions of conflict are clearly unproductive or productive in themselves; instead they are more or less likely to set in train events that do or do not foster the internal consolidation of actors, clarification of practically available options and roles, and provisional crystallization of power relationships—in short, political development in its internal and external dimensions.

Thus military defeat, which is the most conclusive form of conflict resolution, will be productive to the extent that it removes a distracting diversion from the contest between more effectively equal parties. To be distinguished from forcible suppression is the submission by a weaker party following token resistance or internal collapse, neither of which sufficiently tested, and thus qualified, the victor for a more strenuous intra- or inter-regional contest. Nor can such submission create either a moral basis for the defeated party's subsequent appeasement by the victor or else a politico-military basis for such party's secondary, but still effective, role in the new alignments attending the conflict's supersession. For instance, the resolution of the Indo-Pakistani conflict by negotiation or third-party mediation will be more or less conclusive and productive according to whether Pakistan's defeat by India in the second round will be finally viewed as irreversible. The appeasement will in turn depend on whether the defeat can be regarded as both decisive and honorable, thereby habilitating Pakistan for a respected, if secondary, role in the ensuing configuration of conflict and cooperation in South and West Asia.

If conclusiveness is served by a decisive military outcome and productive resolution may depend on tempering the weaker party's defeat by appeasement, the impression is one of irreconcilable opposites. Their manipulation can be initiated while the combat lasts, by sparing the weaker party the humiliation of military collapse by means which logically extend to a simulation of stalemate; after defeat, procedural magnanimity (e.g., on the issue of Pakistani "war criminals") need be supplemented by substantial compensation for defeat by the satisfaction of needs and claims compatible with the new balance of power and the successor conflict. In the Arab-Israeli conflict, the undisguisedly decisive Israeli victories have not insured a conclusive resolution; they may have impeded a productive one because the very nature of the Arab-Israeli balance makes it impossible for the total victories to be final. Hence, no material compensation which Israel might offer, in the form of economic advantage or even the return of most occupied territories and the establishment of a Palestinian buffer-state, is likely to appease the sensitivities of the Arabs until they have stood off Israel in a military contest. Conversely, it would take the compensation of an irrevocable acceptance of Israel—by a combination of formal recognition and irreversible economic interpenetration—to appease Israel's security fears after such a military stalemate, which would represent a defeat for her previous strategy of militarily humiliating the Arabs into resignation.

The stalemate which exists between the Arabs and Israel is an asymmetrical one—in their respective capabilities, opposing mobilized Israeli to presumably potential Arab superiority; and in terms of outcomes, to the extent that Israel's territorial expansion after each round makes her more secure in conventional military terms and more vulnerable in terms of declining international (or American) support and a rising quota of Arab subjects or infiltrators. Such a stalemate differs from the more common one between parties with relatively equal and symmetric capabilities producing either an extended draw or an alternation of inconclusive victories. This type of stalemate is the more likely one to promote a conclusive resolution of conflict as the conflict is superseded by one between at least partially different parties over more up-to-date stakes promising more decisive military outcomes. In such a case, the question whether the conclusive resolution is also productive will depend on the nature of the resulting new alignments rather than on the victor's readiness or scope for appeasement. Realignment is for supersession what reordering of power ranking is for suppression in marking a phase and denoting the system's flexibility. Stalemates and realignments spanning a small number of major protracted conflicts did much to promote the evolution of the European state system; they have been so far absent from the third world, with the possible partial exception involving China and India.

Similar criteria can be applied to civil conflicts. Thus the suppression of Biafra can be a productive resolution if the wartime cooperation between the Northern Hausas and the lesser tribes is complemented by an effective appeasement of the defeated Ibos in the newly multi-tribal framework, permitting tribal identification to expand to compatibility with Nigerian "nationhood." Conversely, the alternation of ineffectual revolt, repression, and submission on the part of the majority Bahutu and the minority Watusi tribes in Burundi, producing a parallel alternation of tribal violence and its subsidence, are not apt to produce either a conclusive or nation-productive resolution in the absence of a neutral, military or dynastic, third-party balancer or moderator. Retrogression to pre-imperial patterns of chronic tribal violence is more likely where lagging economic and political development make it difficult or impossible for tribal conflict to be superseded by intra- or inter-country conflicts over tribally neutral stakes within a favorable, because dovetailing and overall equilibrium-promoting, distribution of pre-eminent control over military force and politico-economic power among the several tribal groups. Nigeria paid with a civil war for a chance to recast the previously unworkable assortments; in the Iraqi majority's strife with the Kurds, the more international variety of supersession may have promoted an at least temporary conflict resolution as inter-state conflict and contest with Western oil companies was gathering momentum in the Red Sea and Persian Gulf areas.

If even partially valid, the preceding considerations have readily discernible implications for the policy attitude toward conflict and military aid of a great power interested in promoting the evolution of regional systems in the third world as a way either to reduce its involvement, without creating vacua of power and responsibility that might invite in other great powers, or also to expand the stake of at least the viable third-world countries in the overall international system. For such implications to become more firmly established and ready for explicit statement, it is necessary first to evaluate regional organization for political and economic cooperation as procedures for conclusive, and thus productive, resolution of conflict, as distinct from its avoidance.

In principle, regional organizations of an essentially political kind can help settle conflicts among members; they can help transfer these outside, and thus institutionally facilitate the supersession of inter-member conflicts; and they can profoundly transform the enactment of conflicts in ways tantamount to their suspension or even settlement. Have third-world organizations materially contributed to the definitive settlement, or abandonment, of contentious issues? So far, such key regional organizations as the OAU and the OAS were less efficacious in disposing of conflicts between members than in serving as a forum for legitimizing U.S. initiatives in Latin America and as a framework for third-party mediation in Africa. Whereas the Organization of American States was most useful, if decreasingly so, as a device for saving the face of proud Latin American regimes fearful of an exported "revolution," the Organization of African Unity's prime role was to save the face of not sufficiently powerful contestants facing attrition or exhaustion. When it came to enforcement, the OAS disguised American military action in, say, Santo Domingo as much as the OAU camouflaged the British intervention against military revolts in East Africa. Without U.S. backing, there was no OAS enforcement against even the pocket-sized war between Honduras and El Salvador; and the absence of all-out British military backing made the OAU inefficacious against South Rhodesia and, *a fortiori*, against Portugal and South Africa.

As an independent agent of conflict resolution, the OAS failed to play a significant role in military skirmishes such as those, in recent years, between Chile and Bolivia and between Peru and Ecuador, for instance; both before and after the cleavage between radicals and moderates had subsided, the OAU played only a secondary role as a forum for mediation helping suspend the Morocco-Algerian and Somalia-Ethiopian conflicts. It had an even lesser, because less unified, role in the civil wars in the Congo and in Nigeria. With respect to these, the principles of African unity and of the intangibility of African frontiers were counteracted by special concerns in enlarging one's particular influence (in the Congo case), or in correcting a potential imbalance of power (by curtailing Nigeria) on the part of African states, either directly by participating in the U.N. action in the Congo or indirectly by extending diplomatic recognition and other forms of support to Biafra. No attention was officially given most recently to such less conspicuous civil strife as that dividing Burundi, while the organization's principal role in the perhaps final disposition of the Morocco-Algerian conflict, by planned economic integration in the controversial sector, was one of after-event celebration. Just as much conspicuous action in Latin America was taken outside the OAS by sub-regional organizations (the Central American Common Market, venturing even into the field of "denuclearization" among members), so more restricted organizations such as the African and Malagasy Union (UAM) rivaled the OAU for feasible tasks. Finally, real and lasting resolution of conflict was more apt to be achieved in the yet more restricted setting of direct negotiations between parties—as between Mali and Mauretania over borders, or between Morocco and Mauretania over the latter's existence. OAU's limitation in this respect was not unlike that of the U.N. when it vainly sought to promote the resolution of the Arab-Israeli conflict (by the Jarring mission) in the absence of such negotiations and the prior conditions for a fruitful resolution. Similarly, the promise for an Indo-Pakistani peace settlement following the second round lay more in direct negotiations than in third-party officiousness along the Tashkent lines.

To compensate for inefficacy in settling conflict, regional organizations can help promote their resolution by transferring contentiousness to relations with outsiders. Thus, the OAU could help put a damper on inter-Black African conflicts by effectively managing the military-economic conflicts with residual white colonialism in Southern Africa (by way of its "African Liberation Committee"). So far, apart from fluctuating financial and other indirect contributions of members, there has been little progress toward integrated military, or any other efforts, to that end. In Africa, determined action against the white regimes had been until recently favored mainly by the not wholly representative radicals, for their particular reasons; a comparable zeal for an effective military-security organization in Asia was displayed by equally unrepresentative and specially interested countries such as South Korea and Taiwan. Neither the Asian Pacific Council, however, nor the "PATO" scheme (patterned on NATO) got anywhere near the stage where they could definitively submerge inter-country conflicts in an effective resistance effort aimed at China. Instead, the continuing latency of conflicts between the lesser countries was due mainly to the mere sense of threat from China and consequent dependence on U.S. backing for facing it. Only the five-power defense arrangement, intended to replace British presence and including Australia, New Zealand, and Britain next to the mutually disaffected Malaysia and Singapore, had perhaps such a conflict-reconciling effect between the two Asian parties.

Finally, regional organization can help resolve acute conflicts by transforming them into a competitively enacted regional "concert." In a real-world concert, diplomatic (and other non-military) reciprocal countervailing replaces a militantly enacted stalemate while being based on the presumption of its existence. One example is the veteran organization of the Arab League, which also implements, ineffectually, the transference and the settlement functions. A more recent attempt at transforming inter-member conflicts into concert is supplied by ASEAN; the organization includes, next to diplomatically ambitious Thailand and the territorially revisionist Philippines, post-Sukarno Indonesia as the key member to be contained diplomatically and compensated for restraint in terminating the confrontation with yet another member, Malaysia. In its present purpose ASEAN succeeds the pre-Suharto ASA (Association for Southeast Asia). It represents a more marked change still from Sukarno's Maphilindo, which did comprise Indonesia, but as a patent aspirant to a hegemonial role to be used against Malaysia. Most recently, the Federation of Arab Emirates in the Persian Gulf has been designed to moderate both territorial and leadership conflicts among members, contain a potentially strongest member (Bahrain), and protect one another against left-wing subversion fed from South Yemen. The federation thus illustrates in potentiality the extension of the transformation to the transference function and the bearing of both on the resolution of conflicts among members by negotiation or other formal modalities of settlement. One reason for the functional merger is that, whereas such organizations serve for concertation, they also serve, as did diplomatic representation at its start in Renaissance Italy, for mutual surveillance and consequent protection of members against one another's perfidy.

In favorable circumstances, the potential of regional organizations for transference and transformation of conflict relations among members can promote regional system formation in the third world. That means, however, that "concert" must remain competitive and transference foster intra-regional integration of effort. A truly significant contribution by regional organization to both conclusive resolution of conflict and regional (or inter-regional) system formation requires that it move beyond concerting toward integrating a new collective actor susceptible of withstanding an otherwise unmanageable power or combination within or without a region. Nothing of the kind has so far occurred in the third world, if only because such a collective actor is less likely to be egalitarian than hierarchical; it most probably has to cluster around a leading core-member maintaining his ascendancy by continuing power of attraction or capacity to impose his will in critical circumstances. If this is, extremely put, a prerequisite to regional organizations' productively contributing to both conflict resolution and system evolution, this is not necessarily in conformity with the motives which commonly induce members, and especially the lesser ones, to enter regional organizations.

Intrinsically great and virtually unbridgeable, the divergence in the

motives of the lesser and the larger states has been attenuated by only
one of the possible purposes behind membership in regional organization: to reintegrate a defeated or thwarted bidder for hegemony
into regional politics by way of a "concert," and into regional economics by coordinating development. Thus Indonesia's re-entry into
moderate Southeast Asian politics bailed her out of the liabilities of
the earlier policy associated with Maphilindo and the Organization of
Emerging Forces; and ex-imperial Japan has been slowly moving
toward participation in regional organization either inspired for that
purpose in large part by others, thus ASPAC, or envisioned by a succession of Japanese Prime or Foreign Ministers in the form of a mul-
tilaterialized co-prosperity sphere in Asia. Similarly, the African
moderates sought to make the Common African and Malagasy Organization (OCAM) attractive to politically defeated and economically depleted radical seekers of ascendancy, such as Guinea and
Mali; and one initial purpose of the OAU was to re-integrate into an
all-African framework members of assertive organizations, such as the
Casablanca Group, overtaken by events. In due course, there may
arise a comparably motivated organization for the Middle East,
centered politically on concert and economically on the Jordan River
valley, just as a regional organism to develop the Mekong River valley can come to facilitate the political integration of a not wholly
triumphant North Vietnam into the Southeast Asian regional fold.
Surely in Africa and possibly elsewhere, third-world organizational
efforts appear most useful as a method for fitting into a conventionally
evolving international system political forces which had challenged
that system's foundations and lost.

It follows that regional organizations which either reintegrate a
thwarted aspirant to local hegemony and convert him into a king pin
in an effective regional concert or can effect far-reaching integration
are the most, or the only, suitable ones for support by a great power
(like the United States) with a long-range stake in orderly development and regional system formation. By the same token, no such support on these grounds seems indicated for political regional organizations which anticipate the crystallization of regional systems and fail
to advance it, as well as for economically slanted regional organizations which are at variance with regional system formation insofar as
they pretend to eliminate inter-state conflict as a supposed obstacle
to development. The conclusion is confirmed by the failure of all so
far existing regional organizations for economic cooperation in the
third world to get anywhere near integrating a new collective actor;
and it is not decisively weakened by the fact that, instead of signif-

icantly aiding in resolving or avoiding conflicts, some of them at least have helped exacerbate conflicts without materially or visibly equipping parties to them for effectively enacting and conclusively resolving such conflicts by other means.

In this perspective one may view with some equanimity the failures of ambitious or premature schemes of regional economic cooperation in Africa and Latin America in particular to overcome problems such as unevenness and disparity among members. Indeed, they have tended to aggravate at least temporarily the very disparities they were supposed to relieve in common-market arrangements. Even more perhaps than in the generalized power-political perspective, the real or potential core-powers repelled rather than attracted cooperative efforts by economically still less endowed or advanced less-developed countries. The not wholly unfounded fear in the less privileged countries was that industrial integration and intra-regional free trade would work in favor of associates having a more favorable starting position and thus further intensify the initial maldistribution of trade and industry as well as the imbalance in costs and advantages of economic cooperation. The pervasive problem affected East Africa as well as (if not as much as?) Southern Africa and extended even to Central America's association of relatively equal small countries. Within countries, the conflict pitted devotees of gradual reforms against those who would block reform as either foreclosing or merely prefacing more basic revolution, while it set apart those who held most of political power from those who needed economic development or change most; in the circumstances, the wielders of military force became the ever more frequent arbiters between views and groups. Next to resource unevenness and divergences in bias, lack of complementarity in assets and potentials has been reflected in contrary pulls by extra-regional markets or suppliers from industrial parts of the world, both the U.S. and Western Europe with respect to Africa and Latin America and increasingly Japan in Asia and elsewhere. Due to these and related problems, such as the tendency to imbalance of payments and country unilateralism, some organizations (including the massively funded Alliance for Progress) went into decline verging on demise; others, including the auspiciously begun CACM, fell prey to arrested development once the accomplishment of easy targets raised the question of political and institutional prerequisites for tackling the hard ones. As part of the disenchantment, accusations against the imperialism of the developed industrial countries were increasingly matched by recriminations against the exploitation or expediential practices of more fortunate developing countries, regardless of their economies being liberal or managed, such as Argentina, South Africa, and India on the middle-power plane, and Guatemala (or El Salvador), Kenya or Ivory Coast, and possibly Thailand or Singapore, on the small-power plane.

In the wake of relative or absolute failures encountered by relatively vast frameworks of economic cooperation and development— including the initially not unpromising Conseil de l'Entente in Africa and the Latin American Free Trade Area—attention has increasingly turned to more narrowly based, including bilateral, projects often linked to a major river basin, be it the Mekong, Nile, Senegal, Jordan, or Ganges. This paralleled and may have had some direct rapport with the simultaneous deflation of economic-development strategies from grandiose industrialization to preliminary rural development and labor-intensive smaller-scale manufacturing as the most promising efforts. Apart from being none-too-efficacious in promoting their immediate purpose of integration, larger-scale economic organisms have also failed to be demonstrably helpful in resolving or avoiding conflict. As a matter of fact, they have tended to generate both socioeconomically and "tribally" (including nationally) defined conflicts within countries and between them, insofar as they stimulated the interplay between socio-economic "mobilization" and the political instinct for "monopolizing" gains for one group or country interest in conditions of unbalanced growth or endowment. If there was little relation between regional organization and the conflicts revolving around economically privileged Katanga and Biafra, there was some in the contest between the leading members of the West African Conseil de l'Entente (Ivory Coast and Senegal) over economic sway in less endowed countries (Guinea and Mali), and still more in the "Football War" between newly interdependent members of CACM, El Salvador and Honduras.

Thus also in economic contexts, the practical questions for the development of third-world countries into national or regional communities or systems revolve around conflict and its resolution. If there is to be some internal conflict, the choice is between one due to mobilization by economic development or conflict attending stagnation. The first compensates inflammation of both traditional and novel rivalries by its potential for eventually engendering stabler and more productive structures; the latter's tendency will be to mark a lasting retrogression to traditional parties and forms of conflict antedating European colonialism. The potentially productive effect of inter-state conflict on system formation and individual politico-economic development is most in evidence whenever conflict creates for the elites an imperative need for, or also removes through defeat even more than victory mass-psychological impediments to, purposefully fostered material strengthening. Conflict thus helps development in the long run even if disrupting it immediately. Moreover, if inter-state conflict will, sooner or later, be resolved or will recede, the choice is between conclusive resolution, however painful and destructive it may immediately be for the bested party, and inconclusive festering or fading of a conflict. Both intra-country stagnation and the failure to resolve inter-country conflict conclusively will tend to depress the level of conflicts to a form of inter-group strife which fosters the formation of national actors and regional systems only by long and convulsive detours, if at all. In a world where nothing stands still, such a situation will mean a retreat to the pre-colonial era, lacking both imperial balancers and stabilizeable indigenous balances of power and marked instead by a patternless waxing and waning of parties to apparently senseless violence which, in actuality, isolated elites apply with clinical detachment to the sole purpose of self-preservation through self-aggrandizement in a static universe.

With respect to the major industrial powers, the practical issue corresponding to economic development as a deliberate strategy is that of devolution of political responsibility; the issue most closely related to stagnation and retrogression in third-world countries is that of their consequent greater liability to reapportionment in spheres of influence. As regards devolution, all the shortcomings implicit in regional economic or political organization combine in pointing toward individual countries with middle-power potential as the more promising objects of such devolution of primary regional responsibilities. This, in turn, will have unavoidable consequences for, one, the allocation of military assistance so as to promote outcomes that are not only conclusive but also test the capacity for a larger role, and, two, for the constraints which profitably can or should be imposed on intra-regional conflicts focusing on such middle powers as initiators of expansion and targets of local resistance or counter-expansion.

In the more or less remote future, therefore, competitive regional system formation will again have to take precedence over "cooperative" regional organization in cases of their incompatibility. Such a reversal will parallel that in economic development insofar as the industrial cart is being replaced behind the rural horse; as a result, political development will really have begun to draw effectively on its international dimension. After an enervating period of more or less imposed imitation of the industrial world, the undeveloped world will have begun to grow through its own turmoil and trial. It will have learned that materially based "power" to evolve must be projected outward as well as husbanded internally—but also that conflict, to be productive, must be reserved for finite ends more reliably prompted by contact than by concept and more effectively pursued through catalytic than cathartic purposes.[2]

The Great and the Middle Powers:
Minimum Order and Managed Evolution

The prospect that middle powers rather than regional organizations are the more likely recipients of devolution enhances both the overlaps and the possible contradictions between the system-evolutionary process in the third world and the requirements and implications of the balance of power among the great powers. Related to the latter is the "balance" between reapportionment among the great powers and their co-responsibility for elementary order in the third world, both of which are subject to constraints not only from their uncertain dispositions but also from the extension of great-power relations to the lesser powers and forces in that world. While the present evolutionary stage of the greater powers, notably if their ranks are taken to include China, differs, the shared trait distinguishing them from smaller third-world countries and regions is that their basic capabilities and attitudes evolve near-automatically along similar lines. Their fundamental foreign-policy dispositions relate more coherently to a more broadly based material development than is the case with the less-developed lesser states; and they evolve in the direction of ultimate convergence in a relatively "conservative" concern with minimum order—however limited the "minimum" order may be to a stake in ultimate control over the wherewithal of disorder and however interspersed with conflict. This pattern of greater-power evolution has successively affected the ex-isolationist U.S. and the ex-revolutionary Soviet Union and now apparently begins to affect China; it derives from the inescapable pressures for accountable, even if not always responsible, action implicit in the impossibility to withdraw into passivity or impunity in relation to commensurate powers.

Reapportionment and Co-responsibility. The new phase of international relations heralded by the Nixon Doctrine follows upon and incorporates the relative failure of attempts by both the U.S. and the U.S.S.R. to be the principal or sole authority for a congenial variety

[2] For a fuller discussion of this section's subject matter, see the author's *States in Evolution: Changing Societies and Traditional Systems in World Politics* (Baltimore: The Johns Hopkins University Press, forthcoming).

of order in the third world. The parallels and even convergences in the experience and evolution of the two superpowers in the third world have been a necessary, if not sufficient, prelude to any subsequent parallelism or convergence in action. In barest summary, the point of relative convergence, as a possible basis for co-responsibility, has been reached by way of three phases partially overlapping in time. The first phase was one of doctrinaire hostility to European colonialism, evidenced by both Roosevelt and Stalin, as a more or less conscious means to remove structures of political power and economic relations obstructive of a new global order under American, Soviet, or American-Soviet auspices. The second phase was one of a relatively non-selective globalism, unfolding in the cold-war contest and covering the Truman-to-Johnson and the Khrushchev incumbencies and spanning, broadly, the period from Korea to Vietnam for the U.S. and the period following Korea up to Cuba for Soviet Russia. The third and last phase covered by the Nixon and the Brezhnev doctrines and policies, has been marked by greater reserve, but no less resolution—of the U.S., to limit its descent from pre-eminence, and of the Soviet Union, to reject other limits on ascent but parity, if any. The setting which permits reversion to wartime essays at an American-Soviet duopoly is one in which a shared exposure to foreign-policy problems may count for more than the measure of convergence in internal conditions and problems due to Soviet industrialization, while being underpinned by it. It is a setting freed from the uncomfortable presence of a third power, the British Empire, while the re-emergence of the latest incarnation of the Chinese empire as a near-conventional, if yet largely non-industrial, player slants relations between the two superpowers (and the three great powers) toward a choice between re-intensified competition and conditional and limited accord.

Larger great-power cooperation became a practical prospect at a turning point in post-war conflicts over expansion, which retraced in the main the dynamic of the original, European colonization of the outside world. Both eras of conflict were shaped by contests between pre-established defenders of a monopoly of access or control and challenging interlopers, exposing the latent tension between token (or "paper") appropriation or partition and their more effective forms. In the contemporary context, the initially token U.S. appropriation of the emerging third world through a species of apostolic succession to Europe's colonial empire, and the largely "paper" partition of the third world attempted by the Khrushchev offensives, were converted into a staggered process of more effective reapportionment by two categories of events. One was military and consisted in overt conflicts, ranging from the World War II struggle with Japan and over China to the Korean and Indo-Pakistani and Vietnam wars in Asia, and represented by the Arab-Israeli and inter-Arab conflicts in the Middle East and, incipiently, Persian Gulf areas. The other was political and consisted in the rise of communist China to the role of a practically significant third-party precipitant of more effective appropriation of positions in the third world by (and thus its reapportionment among) the great powers, if only as a preliminary to their eventual concertation. China's role here is analogous to Imperial Germany's role in the transition from token to effective partition of Africa and to a lesser degree of China before World War I. Thus, the recent re-emergence of modern China as a great power in Asia within a rigidly antagonistic context precipitated both the U.S. intervention in South Vietnam and the efforts by the Soviets to consolidate their position in Hanoi and beyond. Unilateral self-assertion by each of the three great powers was deemed necessary to optimize their respective positions for the purposes of both confrontation and any possible future accommodation on a basis approximating "balance." By contrast, if a comparable crisis recurred in a more relaxed three-power setting reflecting acceptance of the provisional results of the reapportionment process, the great powers could agree on a coordinated stance of aloofness or restraint, if only because the prospect of the relatively less immediately concerned or forward powers (e.g., the U.S. and U.S.S.R.) drawing closer together into a common front against the local activist (China) would discourage the latter from seeking one-sided advantage by massive support to the source of disturbance for fear of being isolated or outflanked in respect to more sensitive issues with higher security priority.

In the European past and the global present, reapportionment as a process is subject to several tendencies which operated unequally for the powers; it stimulated and (when accepted by all either as "inevitable" or "self-defeating") constrained their antagonisms in peripheral areas. One such tendency is toward preclusiveness. It has promoted expansion as a necessary precaution against a threat—mainly Soviet-inspired for the U.S. and China-wrought for the Soviet Union —even while belief declined in the profitability of new acquisitions, in terms of either the balance of trade or of power, which alone fuels a purely predatory expansion. Another tendency is toward the pursuit of permanence. It reflects the rise in the importance of prestige stakes which parallels the more overt involvement of the "state", as distinct from unofficial agents or private interests, and the deferral to an unpredictable future of the value of economic assets. The quest for permanence depresses tolerance for eviction from a position by indigenous or other forces, be it (in contemporary conditions) of the Soviet Union from Egypt or India or of the U.S. from Vietnam, in the absence of wider considerations or contrary pressures. A third tendency is toward the proliferation of increasing numbers of potentially relevant major powers, either as precipitants of effective appropriation or as substitutes preferred to the chief competitor as beneficiaries of eviction—thus in a devolutionary process. Yet another and related tendency is toward more or less reluctantly conceded parity between the major contestants in capability, status, and vulnerability as amphibious, land and naval, world powers with equivalent areas of "special" influence or interests.

The sum of these tendencies—toward preclusiveness, permanence, plurality, and parity—in turn increases certain probabilities. One is the probability, mainly in the short run, of direct (if constrained) confrontations over particular local issues between the major contestants replacing rivalry via lesser-state proxies or protagonists; the longer-range probability or at least enhanced prospect is for conventional negotiations and concert, involving two or more major powers, as a means of avoiding such confrontations as potentially disruptive of wider interests. Ideally, such "concert" would depend for efficacy on prior conditions. One is the segmentation of the third world's political geography into spheres and subjects of special interests, reciprocal abstention, and co-responsibility. Another is the standardization of the two or several major powers as qualitatively identical, not only nuclear but also both continental and maritime powers, susceptible of a shared definition of security and status. This implies in the contemporary setting a process of homogeneization as between the U.S. and the U.S.S.R. (and China) requiring the "maritimization" in both capability and outlook of the previously mainly continental powers. The final condition is that of a degree of separation of economic issues and interests from political and security issues; in the present setting this might be expressed in a shift from (bilateral) foreign aid to foreign trade as the principal vehicle for economic transactions between the developed and the developing countries.

Transformations tending toward such segmentation, symmetry, and politico-economic separation would reinforce parallel pressures for great-power accommodation and concertation. Such pressures are implicit in the interplay and interpenetration of the industrial and pre-industrial forces in the international system, notably for the U.S. and the Soviet Union; and, for all three great powers, they are implicit in absorbing domestic problems, in revolutionary military-technological

or also socio-economic imponderables, and in the dovetailing of evo-
lutively muted degrees of greater and lesser international conservatism (to be distinguished from the extreme reaction-revolution di-
chotomy). Jointly the transformations and pressures might conduce,
in part via a reapportionment of dominant influence which, while being "permanent" in any one power's intention, would be none the less
only temporary, to major-power co-responsibility for third-world order as part of a pluri-stage process of decolonization and regional
systems formation. Just as the latter, as a positive value, depends on
more problematic conflict, the "positive" value of great-power co-responsibility is problematically related to the more controversial factor
of reapportionment; it may consequently be futile to desire one without accepting some forms of the latter.

It is within such a framework or perspective that the late intensifi-
cation of Soviet involvement in the third world, following a period of
relative retrenchment after Cuba, should be viewed, along with the
trends toward more conventional modes of China's actions in the
third world following the domestic and vicariously external radicalism attendant on the Great Cultural Revolution. The tendency to reciprocal preclusion made both communist great powers favors established third-world governments as pathways to more immediate if not
necessarily more solid successes in withholding positions from one
another or taking them away from the United States; the tendency
has been manifest even in so recently "revolutionary" an area as the
Red Sea-Persian Gulf area, in favor of the incumbent governments in
the Sudan, Ethiopia, and even the South Arabian emirs to the disadvantage of secessionist (Eritrean) forces and revolutionary elements
previously supported by one or both communist powers. The tendency to favor established governments was only reinforced by past
frustrations the two powers, and not least the Soviet, incurred when
supporting indigenous revolutionary or subversive forces in Africa (in
the Congo, Mali, Guinea) and when maneuvering between the "Soviet" and the "Chinese" factions in especially the Asian communist
parties. The resulting shift was toward support for the Federal Nigerian Government and the Congress Government of India, respectively. The communist powers' change in emphasis had a parallel in
American reluctance to involve U.S. power and prestige overtly on
the side of conservative forces in, say, Chile against the "popular-
front" government following disappointments incurred in prior involvements against Castroite leftism and for reactionary or merely
mildly reformist governments in Latin America and elsewhere. If
Lagos matched and complemented Tashkent for Soviet Russia, San-

tiago paralleled the but tepid support for Islamabad (Pakistan) on the part of the U.S.

Among the communist powers, the pressures for "defensive" pre-emption were strengthened when they prompted involvements susceptible of containing or encircling the "socialist" rival. With respect to the U.S., the dictates of preclusion coincided for the Soviet Union with those of parity (as a multi-regional land-sea world power); the corresponding "parity" from China's viewpoint was to become for the U.S. a partner-antagonist equivalent with the Soviet Union as the precondition of the nuclear age's approximation of balance-of-power diplomacy among the three major powers. The requirements of more than nominal parity were in turn inseparable from the objective of relative permanence of gains. This militated, on the Soviet side, against indiscriminate support for a wide range of transient clientèle (favored in the Khrushchev era), as well as against token support for choice recipients, such as that illustrated by Tashkent in regard to India or by the (politically unproductive) commercial sale of arms to Lagos (in the early Brezhnev era). The consequence was a growing tendency for the Soviet Union to invest the still limited Soviet capacity for massive support in a small number of third-world countries with a substantial middle-power potential, such as the U.A.R. and India, and, secondarily, Iran or Indonesia; among the small countries, attention was increasingly confined to those such as Madagascar disposing of key naval facilities and assets. The still weaker China's only possible pathway to "permanence" of gains was apparent moderation of means and ends in relations with third-world governments and, as regards Taiwan, the United States. In order to maximize returns on limited resources, the Soviet Union also tried to back what appeared to be the stronger and likely-to-win side—with no assurance of guessing more correctly at the "conventional" potential of a party than previously at the "revolutionary" one. The paying gamble on India against Pakistan and Lagos against Biafra was offset by the wrong guess about Somalia relative to Ethiopia and, at least in the short run, the Arabs relative to Israel. Soviet support for potentially strong and, at least in appearance or long-range potentiality, relatively stronger parties, and their apparent abandonment of the presumption that the more revolutionary side is by definition the stronger or more likely to prevail, has contributed to the third-world trends from cathartic to catalytic and from sub-conventional to conventional conflicts. This trend in turn fed back into the bias favoring "conventional" diplomacy by the communist great powers themselves. That bias entailed the effacement of any possible earlier preference to intervene in "domestic" as against "interstate" conflicts and issues, complementing perhaps the newly stressed American reluctance to get involved in the former. In any event, the difference between "domestic" and "international" could be confused in the predominantly conventional context almost as much as in the revolutionary-subversive setting. Thus the re-escalation of superpower involvement in the Middle East in the aftermath of the 1967 war paralleled the reversion of that conflict to its character as a civil war between Jewish Zionists and anti-Zionist Palestinian forces, following the pre-1967 deflection of the conflict into one between Israel and the Arab states. The deeper Soviet involvement in the second Indo-Pakistani war was likewise attended by civil-war features well in excess of those evident in 1965.

Independently derived dispositions of the great powers to intervene, how much, in what kind of conflicts, and for what objective, have been conditioned by the dynamic of great-power intervention and counter-intervention. This has limited their freedom of choice in any individual instance and the degree of predictably practicable "concert." If both Soviet and Chinese interventions were at origin counter-interventions, in part, to a prior American presence or involvement, the sequence has tended to be reversed more recently. Thus the U.S. counter-intervened in the Middle East following the Soviet resupply of the Arabs; and, albeit on a limited diplomatic and naval plane, it did likewise in South Asia following the massive Soviet military and diplomatic support for India. The pattern of reciprocal stimulation, reflecting the interplay between the objectives of preclusion and parity if nothing else, was neatly illustrated in the Nigerian civil war. An initial Soviet sale of arms there to the Federal Government rendered impossible a great-power co-abstention as an alternative to co-responsible humanitarian or other interference and compelled countervailing British supplies for the same recipient; this in turn inspired belated French efforts to counterbalance Britain and English-speaking Africanism by aiding Biafra.

Soviet involvements and American counter-involvements have been directly related to whatever reapportionment of "spheres of influence" has been underway in the third world. The relation has been less direct, but still critical, to any present or future co-responsibility of the two powers, without qualitatively differing as regards China, as long as she was the bona fide third party in a great-power trio. The relation between unilateral intervention and co-responsibility is one of immediate conflict where an unbalancing material input by one great power sets off pressures for counter-involvement with an attendant increase in immediate rivalry; the relation becomes one of "fit" when unilateral or competitive .intervention has equilibrated the great powers' stakes in regional order. The practical expression of any fit between parallel or even conflicting interventions and co-responsibility has, moreover, been fostered in the third world by one particular feature of its conflicts: the greater than common ambiguity concerning the identity of the "aggressor." The ambiguity reflects the difference between precipitation of a conflict, not uncommonly by a relatively weaker revisionist party, and its actual initiation by the relatively stronger, if often internally more vulnerable, party prone to resist revisionism dynamically (i.e., expansively) in the name of the status quo. The resulting normative uncertainty has the practical-political counterpart in the facility with which the great powers, even if initially supporting opposite belligerents, can agree on measures of restraint; these will be taken, as they by and large were in the later stages of the Arab-Israeli war in 1967 and the Indo-Pakistani conflict in 1971, at a point where the compounds of risks and advantages of the belligerents in the continuance or escalation of a conflict intersect with those of the respective great-power patrons. Of however residual a significance, even in regard to action the great powers took within the U.N., the normative ambiguity meshes in with policy pragmatism or even opportunism. They jointly facilitate transactions for "minimum" order among great powers which face one another with a mix of competition and cooperation while facing the stronger emerging countries as their part-clients and part-competitors in the third world.

Dispositions and Devolution. Minimum order need mean no more than a relatively stable framework of circumscribed competition among and within both greater and lesser powers. The greater powers can administer such order in the third world by loosely "managing" an essentially autonomous evolution of regional orders. The dovetailing activities of greater and lesser powers occur in a global setting in which a tendency to structural dispersion into triangular relations for diplomatic purposes within an incipiently and unevenly multipolar pattern is circumscribed by the continuing primacy of the relations between the U.S. and the Soviet Union on both the nuclear and the diplomatic levels. This key "horizontal" relationship is affected not only by the rise (aided by American elevation) of China to active participation in triangular world politics and, as an influential background factor, by the possibility or even prospect that Japan (or even a "united" Western Europe) might rise to such a standing; it is also affected, and partially regulated, by "vertical" interplay—the tendency of a wider range of third-world middle powers to react to individual strategies of the great powers toward one another and toward key third-world countries and regions.

Such interplays will take different shapes in the different principal land areas. They differ even more in relation to the maritime spaces along the Mediterranean–Red Sea–Persian Gulf–Indian Ocean–China Sea axis, increasingly important in third-world affairs. The multiplicity of possible, but all secondary or minor, "third" maritime powers contrasts with the emerging bipolarity in naval power between a relatively receding U.S. and ascending Soviet Union. The process of change raises again the age-old issues of parity and preeminence between powers so far essentially continental (the U.S.S.R.) and maritime (the U.S.A.), as efforts at mere countervailing assume the appearance of encirclement efforts, initially of the Soviet Union by the United States and now by the Soviet Union of China and some at least of America's allies, if not the U.S. itself. The absence of an equivalent third naval power from the two-power contention over a new equilibrium in the distribution of assets and access occurs in conditions when China is navally weak, relatively potent naval powers such as Japan and some Western European countries have but geographically limited or largely but economic interests, and the naval capacity of an India or Indonesia is strictly local. The essential naval bipolarity simplifies somewhat the land-sea power relationships, while making the competition between the two superpowers somewhat more symmetrical. Thus standardized, American-Soviet competition can decline overall while having locally explosive manifestations at the same time.

The relative simplicity and symmetry are, however, offset, in lieu of a third competing naval power, by the internally somewhat contradictory duality in the critical attitudes of the superpowers. One concerns the divergence of criteria applied to the naval capability of one another: if the requirements of nuclear-strategic stability may be promoted, at least in the longer run, by relatively equal diffusion of naval capabilities (and, consequently, seaborne deterrents), more conventional, power-political and economic, interests and considerations continue to create a stake in naval-power monopoly or clear superiority. The other possible divergence concerns attitudes to the smaller states. They are objects of competitive wooing in their capacity as potential hosts for naval forces of the big seapowers; at the same time the latter fairly share the execration of such smaller states as pretenders to rights and resources on and under wide maritime zones adjoining their coasts which actually or potentially inhibit both the strategic and the economic interests of the superpowers. To the extent that such divergencies "depolarize" the dichotomies normally implicit in land-sea power relationships, they may partially substitute for the (provisionally?) absent third major naval power in the "triangular" pattern of world politics.

Within these equations of capacities and concerns on land and sea, prospects for a joint maintenance of minimum order by the great powers in areas to which they have comparable degree of access will depend on, first, their more or less hostile dispositions reflecting changing capabilities at least in part; and, second, their interactions with notably the middle powers and *their* dispositions. The "basic" hostility between the U.S. and either of the communist powers may be held to be on the whole systemic in character, symbolic in enactment, and occasionally cathartic more than catalytic in its immediate public purpose. By contrast, the conflict between the Soviet Union and China is territorial (or symbiotic?) in basic origin, due to physical contiguity, potentially catastrophic in enactment, and more fundamentally catalytic in purpose than cathartic, despite its passional ideological and even racist connotations. The Sino-Soviet conflict should, consequently, impede Sino-Soviet concertation in most (ideologically relatively neutral) situations more than the conflict between the U.S. and either the Soviet Union or China inhibits American-Soviet or American-Chinese concertation. This might provisionally reduce "joint" order-maintenance to two sets of more or less parallel and interrelated "concerts" between the United States and the Soviet Union and the United States and China in areas where China shares access with the two superpowers. Apart from such fundamental hostilities, basic dispositions toward sharing responsibility for minimum order will change with the growth of capabilities and thus the stake a power acquires in relatively orderly change, next to such dispositions being shaped by experiences with alternative basic policy orientations. So far, the real degree of Soviet-American convergence in this respect has been but partially matched in China's evolution. Basic to that evolution, next to China's conflict with Soviet Russia, has been the capability dimension. China's capability has become sufficiently great to reduce her qualitative identity with key third-world countries and thus her peculiar attractiveness for them; but it has remained so far sufficiently limited to reduce the possibility of effectively exploiting any residual attractiveness while creating a keen interest in material inputs from the West and Japan (as a replacement for earlier Soviet inputs).

All this has not removed all uncertainty regarding China's disposition to even partial and occasional participation in a great-power "concert" in the immediate future. Appraisals have fluctuated along with her actual attitudes in discerning either revolutionary or conservative goals and methods; aggressive or defensive dispositions and capabilities; self-reliance or dependence—self-reliance for China as well as for outside revolutionary forces, and dependence on the Soviet Union, in a perspective rooted in the Korean war, or on the United States in the inner-Asian and nuclear perspectives. Assessments of longer-range trends have not been made easier, moreover, by disagreements as to the present or likely future effect on China's foreign policy of either Maoist doctrines or Middle-Kingdom traditions; nor has it been very useful to agree that China's foreign policy has been largely a response to the domestic scene, itself marked by controversial and changing requirements and configurations of power. On balance, presumptions rooted in the history of the state system rather than of China herself have favored her becoming a third great power in good standing in due course, albeit on certain conditions only: that she could be correctly perceived as committed to "world revolution" by self-reliant means only; as aggressive for the sole purpose of securing consensual agreements on her borders, including Taiwan; as progressively "westernized" in both the language and the practices of foreign policy, if not otherwise, by dint of confining anti-Westernism to but verbal assaults; and as progressively globalized in outlook if not for some time in power both by her having been contained within a narrow regional orbit and by her efforts to evade that containment—in brief, that she could be seen as having overcompensated in tone for denials, deficiencies, and her merely defensive military capabilities rather than being intrinsically over-weening not only in ideological and cultural pretension but also in effectively envisaged foreign-policy purpose.

The different degrees or kinds of hostility among the great powers and the ranges within which their basic dispositions can be expected to fluctuate will crucially affect the practical prospects of joint minimum-order maintenance; so will the reactions by middle powers in particular to great-power actions and alignments and their consequent regulative impact on the great-power level. Apart from specific situations and structures, such reactions will reflect the basic dispositions of the several middle powers, significant in themselves and also because they in turn engender corresponding responses by the great powers. As they rise in political capacity in the wake of economic development or reconstruction, middle powers may seek a positive role or just autonomy, active interdependence with great powers or merely independence from them. The more concrete role in turn can be that of a rival of the greater states for power, or that of a repository of at least some of the responsibilities previously detained or exercised by the latter. As residuary legatees of the great powers, middle powers can succeed to either greater-power expansionism or to "imperial" order-maintenance; if they act as proxies for greater powers, they can do so in conflict (as when still-competing Pakistan substituted for China against India) or in the settlement of conflict (as perhaps one day an Iran or Turkey might act as peacemaker for the U.S. or also the Soviet Union in the Middle East). Most probably, the middle powers will be something in between, as conditions and issues change.

Always Janus-faced in their position between both greater and still smaller powers at all times, most actual or potential middle powers also suffer from a split political personality, either as they alternately seek greater individual roles and responsibility and recoil from its burdens and liabilities, or as they waver between mere regional leadership and regional "imperialism" with obvious consequences for the attitudes of, and toward, both the greater and the still lesser powers. Insofar as powers tend to react primarily upward rather than downward, it is appropriate to classify middle powers by their attitudes to the great powers rather than to the still lesser powers; moreover, the first attitude will tend to imply the second. It may, therefore, be provisionally useful in the presently highly fluid stage in middle-power capabilities and attitudes to differentiate between loyalist and rebellious middle powers, while providing for an intermediate group.

With the possible exception of Egypt in the late Nasser period, the Soviet Union has lacked loyalist middle powers. Its chances lie with those rebelling against the United States or qualifying their loyalism toward the United States by a desire for diversifying attachments, which tend to place them in the intermediate category. Japan has been the most important middle power, with ready capacity for great- or even super-power status and role, initiating a movement away from loyalism to an intermediate posture. Such a transition would complement the present Japanese "political" neutrality between the Soviet Union and China with that between the U.S. and the two communist great powers; and it would require putting additional teeth *and bite* into her present "armed" abstinence from regional and most of global politics. In its present neutral stance, Japan has carefully managed an economic rapprochement with the Soviet Union, bearing on general cooperation and the possibility of a specific one in regard to the development of Siberia, and a related diplomatic rapprochement, bearing on the revision of the post-World War II territorial settlement in Japan's favor; in intention at least the rapprochement is to be just sufficient to create a situation of diplomatic strength from which to embrace China on a basis of equality without being so far-reaching as to make Japan suspect of participating in efforts to contain China and thus finally alienate her. Only by making herself acceptable in principle to all three Asian great powers, and indissolubly aligned with (or irreparably alienated from) none, would Japan become fully qualified to enact the role of the "fourth" Asian great power opening the way to an ever-widening range of possible ad hoc alignments and counter-alignments among them. Until such time the more or less remote *prospect* of such a contingency, and uncertainty regarding its precise form, will actually weigh upon the relations of the existing great-power triangle in Asia more than any present Japanese actions.

The so far chiefly economic concerns of Japan have been of a kind with those of the other ex-imperial industrial middle powers in Europe. They have been only slowly gathering power-political implications which might propel Japan toward an active devolutionary or expansionist role in Asia. Most significant has been the growing economic involvement with Taiwan and South Korea, as sub-contracting manufacturers of labor-intensive products, and with Australia, as the major supplier of mineral raw-materials. Along with Japan's dependence on Middle East oil and consequent interest in Indonesia and Singapore as guardians of the Strait of Malacca, these entail vital interest in the political disposition and military security of these areas and of Japan's access to them. Should such regional concerns, which increasingly qualify Japan's overall economic orientation toward the industrial West and especially the Western Hemisphere, ever jell into Japan's assuming active responsibility in critical parts of the Western Pacific area, the overtly avowed target is unlikely to be an ambivalently viewed China. No more is the preferred partner likely to be an unequivocally depreciated India. By contrast, cooperation with Indonesia might legitimize Japan's at first devolutionary role in Asian eyes and cooperation with Australia in Western. Conversely, and so far, American involvement in Japan has been useful and perhaps necessary to reinforce U.S. credentials as a full-fledged party in the Asian balance of power and to assuage small-state fears (such as South Korea's) of a unilateral Japan; it may continue to be necessary in the future to "disperse" an otherwise irresoluble conflict among the two or three autochthnous Asiatic powers (Japan, China, and perhaps the Soviet Union).

If an "Asian" emphasis prevails in reactivated Japan's foreign policy, her role would tend more toward a hierarchical posture reflecting

Japanese superiority feelings unreceptive to even a pretense of equality of lesser states; this might or might not match, mesh in, or come into collision with, possibly similarly biased policies of a reascendant "Celestial Empire" of China—with implications for American, Soviet, and possibly Soviet-American or Sino-Soviet-American reactions. If a "western" emphasis prevails, Japan will cultivate with greater assiduity the institutional disguises of anti-egalitarian impulses congenial to the Western ways of politics among nations. In either event, just as China's ascension to sustained and sustainable global, and possibly also regional, role depends on a further erosion of revolutionary exaltation under the pressure of conventional security fears, Japan's assumption of an active and constructive regional role will have to be preceded by a further erosion of any remaining war-guilt mentality with the aid of a settled conviction of her essential peaceableness. This will imply a rehabilitation or at least reinterpretation of the wartime co-prosperity schemes as an antecedent to their modified reactivation. It is equally possible, however, that, like many a narrow-based (and not least off-shore insular) one-time expansionist in the past, Japan (matching an England-inspired Western Europe) will remain content with her current transition from imperium to emporium in the protective and lucrative crevices of a balance among the more massively based superstates, themselves anxious and able to do no more than extract maximum possible economic compensation as a fee for their apparently inescapable politico-military exertions.

Japan is the prototypical loyalist lately somewhat alienated by American policies and incipiently attracted by possibilities for emancipation implicit in a changing world-power configuration and rising national material power. The loyalist category has also included Great Britain in Europe (in contrast with rebellious France and, on a lower plane, Yugoslavia).[3] While not situated in Europe, all the other loyalists are, perhaps not accidentally and certainly disturbingly, in some way at least "European"—be it Brazil, South Africa, or Australia (and, to the extent of her conditional loyalism, Israel). South Africa shares with Brazil doctrinal anti-communism, albeit stressed in her case for foreign-policy reasons (to gain Western, and specifically American, sympathy and support); and she shares with Australia a "white" racial policy, albeit in her case more radical and only in the early stages of moderation. Such regionally atypical internal orientations, comprising in Brazil's case her Portuguese background, diminish eligi-

[3] See my discussion of middle powers in Robert E. Osgood et al, *America and the World: From the Truman Doctrine to Vietnam* (Baltimore: The Johns Hopkins University Press, 1970), pp. 409–17.

bility for a leading regional role; they might consequently channel its pursuit into an expansionist direction which would be difficult to sanction by the greatest Western power in its current dispositions. All the above-named loyalists, and Turkey as the one perhaps most advanced on the road to diversification or defection, have additional traits in common. They combine key strategic importance, avowed or not, for Western defense in notably its maritime (and consequently nuclear-strategic) dimension—be it in the Indian Ocean, South Atlantic, or Eastern Mediterranean; until recently, this importance insured to all of them except South Africa a reciprocally firm, if not total, American commitment to their defense. They are all, except currently Turkey, economically stable or fast-developing. None is, however, anxious to assume a primary role in regional defense as successor to either the British or the American empires, much as they have been willing to contribute to the American imperial-security effort in a measure sufficient to ensure a privileged standing and claim on reciprocity.

In this as in most other respects the loyalists differ from the rebellious middle powers, India and Egypt and North Vietnam. These do, of course, react or respond to great power actions and are even on occasion opportunistically "loyal" to a great power—currently the Soviet Union; their basic posture is, however, one of resentment of great-power ascendancy. None of them is economically stable and politically or economically attractive to still lesser states in their respective regions; the two non-communist middle powers are moreover internally unstable or vulnerable. All three, including India, are presently more concerned with national power and expansion than with regional order or security; they are anxious to replace receding Western empires, in more or less concealed competition with advancing Soviet and Chinese ones, but only as regards domination and not, or not yet, with respect to responsibilities and performance. The rebellious middle powers are even less the objects of a reliable great-power commitment to their security and survival (as middle powers) than are the loyalists. If isolated actions of support by the great powers are actuated by tactical expedience or transient situational compulsion, including ideological in the Soviet–North Vietnamese relations, the middle-power responses are correspondingly opportunistic and fickle.

While the rebels would replace empires, several of the middle powers in the intermediate category can also look back upon an imperial or otherwise impressive past of their own. This fact may account for a degree of relative moderation or maturity. It is more immediately significant for Iran than for Turkey (supposing the latter has already effectively moved into the intermediate category); and it is more recently significant for Indonesia, as an ex-rebellious middle power, than for Japan, if not necessarily lastingly so. In Israel, memories of a biblical past reinforce live rebellious-expansionist instincts against the loyalist manifestations of the instinct of self-preservation; the latter instinct may, however, also lead to replacing or undergirding loyalty to the U.S. with unilateral nuclear capability. Only Israel and Iran assert overtly at present with some militancy a historically and strategically founded territorial revisionism; Turkey and Indonesia are currently satisfied with a more discreet regional role. This is by definition a motley group in all other respects. The intermediate middle powers lean, however, in different degrees toward economic and political stability, while sharing more or less latent threats to it. With the possible exception of Turkey, they are to different degrees ambiguously suspended between an expansionist tendency and a preference for regional consolidation. A similar profile can be drawn for Algeria and is apt to be that of a reconsolidated Nigeria. As "nations," both lack an imperial past of their own, but in other respects they belong to this residual category of neither committedly loyalist nor compulsively rebellious middle powers.

The middle powers have come to occupy a critical position at the point of intersection between "mechanical" countervailing among the great powers for reapportionment or co-responsibility, and the "organic" evolution of lesser third-world states toward nation-statehood and regional systems. Loyalist middle-power dispositions will inhibit moves toward great-power concert insofar as they represent alternatives to it—unless the distribution of "loyalties" equilibrates the positions among the great powers while intensifying problems with less favorably disposed other third-world powers. Conversely, rebellious dispositions on the part of middle powers will tend to promote co-responsibility at least in the longer run, as they decrease stabilizable advantages from unilateral great-power policies and end by threatening the primacy in status and function of all great powers.

Independently of particular middle-power dispositions, in structural terms only, vertical interactions between great and middle powers will tend to distract the great powers from concentration on the requirements and possible advantages of concert. Thus India's reaction to the Sino-American rapprochement took the form of efforts to liquidate once and for all the Pakistani threat; her consequent dependence on Soviet aid and support has created the possibility of one-sided gains for the Soviets which, if they exceed "parity" or "balance" with the concerned great powers in the area, will dampen Soviet disposition to undertake co-responsibility for "minimum" order on the Indian subcontinent. By contrast, great-power readiness to incur the costs of concert is enhanced by the difficulty effectively and permanently to re-clientize major third-world powers, which in turn constitute the sole worthwhile targets and stakes for unilateral effort. The difficulty grows with the multiplicity of evolved middle powers systematically linked to one another or attentive to the others' experiences. In such conditions, the adverse response of at least some of them to great-power attempts to reapportion third-world areas by way of all-out visible support, as a substitute for covert subversion, will tend to regulate indirectly great-power conduct in the direction of limiting unilateral goals. A precondition to such regulation being effective is, of course, that more than one great power continues to be involved in third-world regional politics so that adversely reacting lesser powers continue to dispose of alternative backing. Thus the simultaneity of Soviet involvement in Egypt and India (or Iraq), in local conflicts, militated against any Soviet attempt to cling to or expand positions of influence in Egypt for fear of jeopardizing the more important stakes in India (or Iraq); and continued American involvement in the Middle East was no less important for the prospects of any Egyptian attempt to react adversely to Soviet efforts: to gain too many Arab friends (and attenuate Israeli antipathies) in the Middle East while not going far enough in substantiating either Sadat's tactical threats of offensive military action or his more real dependence on all-out defensive support against all comers in yet another round of warfare.

Great powers can treat and have reasons to treat individual middle powers as regional rivals, and be led to help still lesser states to contain them under the pretense of restraining, unilaterally or cooperatively, all third-world conflict; or they can regard them as regional allies in contests with other great powers and proceed to reinforce them competitively, possibly as a means to reapportionment by way of re-clientization; and finally, they can proceed either unilaterally or jointly progressively to devolve regional responsibilities to apparently constructively disposed middle powers. The prospects for devolution of responsibilities more or less freely consented by the great powers and permanently exercised by the middle ones will be greater where some of the latter have mutually cooperative relations—thus, in the future, a self-confining Japan and Indonesia or Australia in Asia, or Israel and Iran in the Middle East. Conversely, a conflict between middle powers, say between Iran and an Egypt-Iraqi combine, or between Indonesia and Australia, will tend to create a more ready basis for great-power intervention tending toward competitive reapportionment of the critical areas or toward attempts at establishing an overseeing co-responsibility. Thus motivated great-power responses may be at variance with the requirements of regional system evolution, however. The less capacity and will the great powers have to interfere with intra-state violence, the more imperative will be a deliberate and informed management of inter-state conflict. But any rigidities implicit in particular conflicts of interests either among the great powers themselves or between these and ascendant middle powers will inhibit attempts, even if forthcoming, to reconcile the containment of unproductive violence with the condonement of conflicts susceptible of identifying viable middle powers and thus conducing to the evolution of regional systems. In the process it will be of secondary interest only whether any resulting conflict between the different immediate and longer-range purposes is either reflected in or due to ill-adjusted restraints on conflict or ill-advised material reinforcements of individual parties to conflict by the great powers, acting jointly or individually.

Conclusion: Toward a Foreign-Policy Equilibrium?

The attenuation of conflicts in policy perspectives, between those focusing on the greater and unequally industrial powers and those directed to the lesser and less-developed powers, is a problem for all states of all categories; but it is more immediately the prerogative of the U.S. as the still greatest and also a newly self-limiting power. While the Nixon Doctrine and its elaborations in official pronouncements have juxtaposed the two policy perspectives treating them as complementary, actual policy actions and attitudes have on occasion pointed in the direction of one-sided or at least not fully integrated purpose.

On the surface, there are obvious points of correspondence between the concerns expressed in the Nixon Doctrine and the preceding analysis. The stress on continued American material aid to third-world countries, in compensation for reduced political intervention, addresses itself to the needs of politico-military balance and politico-economic development as alternatives preferred to anarchy and stagnation or retrogression. A discreet sympathy for economic regionalism and a more explicit acceptance of a circumspect American disengagement from even key areas point in the direction of devolution. Less clearly, but by necessary implication, the admission of something like reapportionment of the areas of special great power interests or even influence, however circumscribed, is a corollary to the Nixon Doctrine's commitment to rearranging relations with the communist great powers in the direction of co-responsibility for peace and order in the third world. And finally, and perhaps most ambiguously because of the different definitions one may apply to "system," support for the extension of the international system to third-world regions is overtly expressed in the call for an international system in which even the lesser powers would have a stake. More importantly perhaps, the support is implicit in the features of the doctrine which point toward an American stake in equalizing the basic survival chances of third-world countries by pledging aid against nuclear blackmail and overwhelming conventional military assaults across recognized international frontiers. Nor is it implausible to regard that support as implied, however unwittingly, in the doctrine's desiderata concerning great-power relations.

More basically still, the analysis is in accord with the Nixon Doctrine where it is opposed to any sweeping American withdrawal from the world's grey areas as incompatible with either great-power co-responsibility or management, however indirect, of system-evolution in the third world. The doctrine and its elaborations are, however, also at variance with the analysis where they pretend to seek a self-sufficient and perhaps self-justifying basis for great-power concert in unqualified opposition to the incidence of armed conflict in the third world. In principle, this would elevate the great-power dimension of the doctrine well above the lesser-state policy strand; if implemented, the imbalance in doctrinal formulations would insure incapacity to implement effectively either of the two strands of the grand "new" policy. In actuality, of course, the one-sided approach has reflected the supposed requirements not so much of a global process as of a particular problem: pacification in Vietnam with the aid of restructured relations with the communist great powers. This fact alone commands one to examine the question of coherence between the stated ends of the doctrine and the adopted or envisaged means, as well as the compatibility between the two kinds of ends (with respect to great and lesser powers) by way of illustrating problem areas rather than by imputing errors of judgment or insight to the conductors of policy.

The fundamental, if not sole, problem on the great-power level bears on the issue of reapportionment. The contrast, as intimated in Nixon Administration's key pronouncements, is between the self-restraint to be exhibited by all great powers as a token of commitment to co-responsibility and the penetration by communist great powers into new areas of influence, less by disguised subversion than by way of conspicuous military assistance to contentious less-developed countries. So far, administration critique has been directed mainly at the Soviet Union; the problem is apt to arise also in connection with China, however, when tactful wooing of Peking again yields to worries about China's real goals and intentions. The key problem raised by this attitude of the Nixon Administration has been this: Can a policy of co-responsibility be implemented without the communist powers first involving themselves in the third-world region to be a stage for it? If the answer is, as it must be, negative, the truly difficult next question is: What is the legitimate extent, and what are the legitimate means, of such involvement? As regards the means, experts can and do differ on the question whether the administration's strictures have exaggerated the irresponsibility and scope of Soviet military assistance in embattled third-world areas (perhaps as a relatively harmless device to appeal to China's current concern with Soviet "social imperialism" and to obliquely discourage Soviet military aid to North Vietnam); moreover, quite apart from subjective assessments, it is possible to argue that an economically weaker great power is compelled to rely chiefly on military and diplomatic instruments for matching or offsetting the more massive economic resources of a competitor if it is to "cooperate" with him at a later stage.

As regards the legitimate extent of Soviet penetration, its delimitation has been rendered exceptionally difficult by two factors: one is the apparent reluctance of the Nixon Administration sensibly to reduce American involvement and influence in key world areas (Western Europe and Japan) at this point and for immediate negotiating reasons by either disengagement or devolution; this raises the issue of "balance" and may intensify compensatory Soviet and Chinese drives. The other is the addition of the naval to the territorial dimension; this gives rise to the intractable quandary as to what constitutes "parity" between a maritimized continental state, with the advantage of land mass and central position, and an offshore continental island, like the U.S., with excentric lines and a fading command of the sea. The latter difficulty is not lessened by introducing a massive land power, China, as a third element into the equation; nor is the problem solved by relying for offsets against possible overall imbalance or localized disequilibria on the ideal consequences of a "standardization" or "symmetrization" in the capabilities and thus outlooks of the two naval-continental (plus nuclear) superpowers. The quandry enhances the importance of a practically less elusive issue: What is apt to be the possible, as contrasted with legitimate, extent of effective Soviet, or Chinese, penetration, in view of the relatively autonomous forces and consequent local reactions in the critical third-world areas such as the Middle East and the Persian Gulf area, and South and Southeast Asia? It may be that, in anything like the "foreseeable" future, the possible scope can be safely adjudged to be equally safely confined within limits fully consistent with a balance of power (in the sense of both influence and access) among the great powers, within key regions as well as inter-regionally. If so, the Nixon Administration has been either alarmist for propaganda reasons, to preserve summitry from the charge of insufficient vigilance; or it has been doctrinally inconsistent when trying to have the cake of co-responsibility while keeping all the goodies of exclusive or preponderant U.S. influence. Being probably both, the administration may also have been unintentionally cooperative with Soviet penetration by way of its attitudes and policies on the second, lesser-power level.

Reinforcement of lesser by great powers by military aid is central to the lesser-power level, instead of being merely incidental to the issue of self-restraint on the part of the great powers themselves. It bears on two related aspects of system evolution: maintenance of military balance between third-world states, as a factor in the enactment and resolution of conflicts, and responses to the self-assertion of (potential) middle powers resulting from military imbalance. In principle, the Nixon Doctrine is committed to maintaining military balances, as a key means to stability and a substitute for direct American intervention. In the three key conflicts of concern to the administration, actual policies have differed, however; nor would a consistent policy necessarily have promoted the doctrine's larger objectives. The administration upheld the military balance in Vietnam integrally and unequivocally with the aid of Vietnamization and American air support. Military supplies to Israel have been rationalized in terms of military balance, without being necessarily governed by that criterion, in view of the distracting factor of direct Soviet military involvement on the side of the Arabs as a safeguard against a (for them) disastrous fourth round, and the fluctuating American policy toward the Arabs inversely reflecting U.S. policy toward Israel and mirroring the ups and downs of hopes and strategies for peaceably liquidating the third round. And, finally, the Nixon Administration patently did not seek to reinforce Pakistan militarily, into something closer to military balance prior to the 1971 second round with India, whose military superiority had been vastly increased by Soviet supplies in the period following India's earlier clashes with China and Pakistan.

In any deeper sense, the issue is not one of an abstract rule of balance, but of the relation of military stalemate, or of a decisive military outcome resulting from the military superiority of one side, to more or less conclusive conflict resolution and its bearing on the constitution of viable actors in evolving regional systems. The administration's fostering of military stalemate in Vietnam has been but the foreground of efforts to engineer a preponderant political pressure by the communist great powers toward securing a peace settlement. To the extent that the most conclusive and productive conflict resolution deriving from a protracted military stalemate is the conflict's supersession by one henceforth more pertinent, the best hope for a long-term resolution of the Vietnam conflict in the period following military cease-fire and a likewise formal agreement on procedural rules for ongoing political competition has resided in a regrouping of "nationalist" forces in the country around opposition to "alien" dictation from the great powers, if such coalescence is no longer practicable against an "imperialist" north. Such resolution should be acceptable to the U.S. from the viewpoint of consequent reapportionment of influence in Southeast Asia in that it would give no single great power an immediate diplomatic advantage while leaving the U.S. free to bring its pervasive economic advantage to bear on longer-term developments. This would justify in the event what has been, under the circumstances, an assertive administration policy in and in regard to Indochina.

In the meantime, much will depend upon the second Nixon Administration's capacity to replace military Vietnamization in Southeast Asia with a diplomatic strategy for Indosinifying the framework for the conflict's more lasting resolution. The pursuit of such strategy would carry on the gradual and largely unintended transformation of the Vietnam war from a chemical compound of "negative" anti-Communism, anti-colonialism (of European vintage), and anti-neutralism (Asian-style) into a catalyst of transition to more positive and limited American objectives in the third world. For the pursuit to be effective, the neatly equipoised assumptions and assertions constituting the Nixon Doctrine will have to be converted into a strategy assorting controls of peace-observance in the field with a new concept for Indochina implementing a firm choice between the quite possibly alternative risks of regional sway approximating hegemony from the North and subversion entailing holocaust in the South.

By contrast, the asymmetrical stalemate in the Middle East (characterized by divergences in kinds of strength mobilizeable by the two sides in different time spans and, consequently, by a series of in-

conclusively "decisive" Israeli military victories), in part at least due
to ambiguous American policies in the area, has failed either to produce or promise worthwhile political results so far. This has raised the
question whether an American policy looking toward a "simulated
stalemate" or one fostering clear preponderance by one side might
not fare better. Simulated military stalemate presupposes American
pressure on Israel to limit the employment of her present *de facto*
military superiority, in both truce-time and in a next round, and to
abstain from utilizing that superiority for continued occupation and
gradual absorption of the conquered Arab territories. Conversely, the
U.S. might further enhance Israel's military preponderance while actively neutralizing the Soviets as a means to a fully, and for practical
purposes finally, decisive military outcome favorable to Israel. Such
an outcome requires, next to yet another Arab defeat, also an irre-
futable demonstration of Soviet military inferiority or, more probably,
irresolution in relation to the United States in the Middle East. The
first approach, compelling a partial Israeli retreat, would open the
way to possibly more fruitful realignments involving both the greater
and the lesser, and the more "radical" and "moderate," powers in the
region; the second would endow Israel with regional hegemony in
the wake of a Soviet-American confrontation. Both of these methods
of conflict resolution would in their different ways conduce to regional system formation: the first by promoting flexibility of alignments and possibilities of accommodation among ostensibly more
"equal" local parties; the second by permitting the U.S. to shift progressively to a more systematic support for a sobered and sustained
Arab resistance to Israel's ascendancy by means of long-range material and other self-strengthening (perhaps focused in a moderated
Egypt's sub-hegemony among adjoining Arabs). Even the first approach, moreover, would not enhance Soviet prospects of penetration
or reapportionment (by extending it to Israel) beyond its present
state of promising uncertainty, which fairly reflects American ambiguity. In other parts of the Middle East, the U.S. may go on favoring
military and other balances and stalemates between the key local
states; or it might seek to recover Iran by actively promoting its military and political preponderance in relation to Iraq and Saudi Arabia
in the triangular conflict in the Persian Gulf area. Such favoritism
might incite the Soviet Union either to escalate its wooing of Iran or
else counteract the U.S. via support for Iraq in ways that might further
offend Egypt's pretensions to a "special relationship" with the Soviet Union and thus leadership in the Arab world—a development interesting in itself and in its potentially productive effect on an Arab-
Israeli settlement.

The spectrum comprising American assertiveness in Southeast Asia and ambiguity in the Middle East has been completed by the American absence from any major part in the second Indo-Pakistani war in South Asia. Such abstention is not formally consistent with the doctrine's favor for military equilibrium between contentious lesser powers and its disfavor for trans-frontier aggression. The formal inconsistency would be of little moment, however, if a perceptible link could be established between the administration policy and any one of the two larger objectives of the doctrine. This is not easy to do, except by way of the hypothesis that the Nixon Administration actually favored India's decisive military success as an offset to the impending decline in American containment pressure on China while going through the motion of a token support for Pakistan that would be sufficient to create the fiction of "fighting" on the same side as China on the eve of the Peking summit while being insufficient either to provoke a clash with the Soviet Union or offend India "irreparably." The American diplomatic representations and naval demonstrations in favor of Pakistan were too symbolic tokens of sympathy to make up for the substantial prior reduction of effective military aid to Pakistan and to decisively supplement the more provocative than productive support of the Yahya Khan regime. The consequent impression of American absence from the confrontation is not adequately confuted by administration claims to have saved West Pakistan itself from dismemberment and to have redirected the Soviet Union, if only after India had secured her principal military objectives, from all-out support to virtually "co-responsible" efforts, paralleling the administration's, to restrain her. Such ex post facto claims need not be wholly rejected insofar as they illustrate the "handle" on local crises materializing from a direct Soviet involvement. But they may be discounted insofar as they somewhat too neatly echo administration assertions attending an earlier naval-diplomatic intervention in favor of the King of Jordan against Syria and represent a somewhat too miraculously cheap method for acquiring a controlling impact on events.

In the war's aftermath, the critical question for South Asia has been whether India's military victory had been sufficiently decisive to engender a conclusive resolution of the long-standing conflict. Insofar as such resolution was to occur by way of Pakistan's submission to India's hegemony on the subcontinent, both facilitated and moderated by the Indo-Pakistani conflict's being superseded by one permitting a lesser degree of their hostility or even a measure of cooperation, the Soviet postwar pre-eminence in the area can be a serious impediment to such resolution; if this proves to be the case, it would be the most serious charge against the prior administration policy which had fostered that pre-eminence by both "abandoning" Pakistan and "alienating" India (not least by publicly attributing to her extreme designs also in West Pakistan). Soviet pre-eminence would inhibit supersession of the Indo-Pakistani conflict insofar as it allowed Pakistan to look forward in post-war tractation to a re-equilibrating diplomatic move by the moderating Tashkent power closer to the Pakistani viewpoint; such a maneuver is open to the Soviet Union as long as India is impeded from a too sudden or far-reaching compensating move back to the U.S. by war-bred resentment compounding the material ties to the Soviets incurred in the pre-war period. Alternatively, Soviet pre-eminence is apt to inhibit Pakistan from cooperation with India for any purpose insofar as, under Soviet auspices, such cooperation would currently acquire a too crude bias against China, Pakistan's well-wisher if not supporter in the past war. By contrast a firmly balancing American policy might have contributed to a course and outcome of the war closer to a politico-military stalemate, to be eventually superseded by a common Indo-Pakistani front against the encroachments of all the great powers in the Indian Ocean area. Or else, finally, actual American support for India during the war would have weakened Soviet diplomatic leverage on India without materially enhancing that on Pakistan. An indiscreet Soviet "balancing" would have failed to win Pakistan over from China if not the U.S. while alienating an India rendered, by her military ascendancy, more than ever valuable to the Soviets as a counterpoise to China in the local balance of power in South Asia. In addition to flexibility, American neutrality or outright sympathy would have enhanced India's sensitivity and salience as the background power in the great-power triangle in Asia unbiased between the two superpowers and even, following the ego-salving military success against her China-substitute, with regard to China.

As events unfolded, in both South Asia and largely also in the Middle East, the administration has chiefly depended on the self-regulating shifts and consequently regulatory effects upward of rival local forces, adversely reacting to any one power's pre-eminence in any one country or region, for limiting the consequences of any one great power's failures as a counterpart to confining the other power's realistic ambitions and stable gains. An impossibility to win much has had the reassuring obverse of an impossibility to lose wholly; beyond some steadiness of nerve and domestic leeway it takes little skill, however, and still less elaborate doctrine to be such a felicitous condition's beneficiary.

By and large, the administration has displayed little manifest mastery of the implications of military assistance for either the formation of regional systems or the third world's segmentation into spheres of preponderant great-power influence. This is no damning charge considering the enormity of any deliberate effort to adjust particular problem-solving in third-world conflicts to both pressing immediate objectives (such as Vietnam pacification and reconciliation with China) and hypothetical requirements of a long-term evolutionary process, while keeping an eye on the side-effects of a policy for reapportionment and co-responsibility. It may simplify the task to attend to the effect of alternative policies on potential third-world middle powers as the surfacing focus of the different objectives and preoccupations. The vital middle seems to have been more keenly perceived from Moscow than from a Washington dividing its concerns between the Vietnam battleground and the great-power summits. The issue is nonetheless of critical importance for American foreign policy under the Nixon Doctrine in what it sets forth and, even more, in what it implies. As long as the U.S. could be basically inspired by the norms proper to a globally pre-eminent world power, singlehandedly upholding order in the several regions, the American attitude to potential regional imperialists had to be dogmatically negative. Middle-power self-assertion beyond a readily discernible definite point threatened to inhibit or bar outright U.S. access to still lesser states in a region, while creating a problem for the credibility and any wider appeal of American opposition to Communist-tinged expansionism.[4]

In the modified perspectives of the Nixon Doctrine, however, such dogmatic opposition is no longer either required or consistent with a revised fundamental concern. That concern is to devolve at least routine responsibility to indigenous regional powers and to contain, with the aid of such powers' reactions, the scope of reapportionment favorable to communist great powers while inducing these to share in a collective exercise of ultimate great-power responsibility for minimum order compatible with, and in due course sustained by, the crystallization of regional and inter-regional systems. In the new perspective, it may well be a key part of policy under the Nixon Doctrine actively to foster the rise of pivotal middle powers, if necessary at a cost to still lesser powers, in order to reinforce the level just below that of the great powers and without being excessively preoccupied

[4] This has been the principal thesis in my *War and Order* (Baltimore: The Johns Hopkins University Press, 1968). The issue of reciprocal access in relation to spheres of influence has been treated in *Imperial America* (Baltimore: The Johns Hopkins University Press, 1967), chapter 3.

with the truly small states, whose contribution to international stability and regional system formation can initially be but secondary. This would mean in practice that, in the next phase, rather than stimulate and sustain lesser-power resistance to potential middle powers and estop these from asserting themselves, American foreign policy would give the middle powers relatively free rein to prove themselves (or not) as foci of intra- and inter-regional (or sub-regional) balances of indigenous power. Only at a later stage could the still lesser (surviving?) states be reinforced either by inter-regionally competing middle powers against one another or by the great powers themselves, seeking to moderate or manipulate the middle-power level as part of definitively integrating intra- and inter-regional balances of power into the central or global international system. Somewhere along the line, regional organization might then come into its own at last, either as a framework of regional integration around ascendant middle powers or else as a framework for reintegrating at least partially thwarted regional aspirants to hegemony into a regional "concert." In this manner, the currently pervasive incompatibility between regional organization and system formation would give way to complementarity on terms acceptable at least partially to both the smaller and the bigger third-world countries, if only because these terms would represent the unavoidable outcome of largely or basically autonomous or indigenous processes. If such policy is still consistent with placing some obstacles in the path of "regional imperialists," if only to test their capacity to combine effective self-assertion with appeasement of weaker parties, realistic methods of managing system evolution do not require opposing the ascent of strong states in the name of regional peace, inter-nation equity, or great-power responsibility to guarantee either.

In this respect, the Nixon Administration has not had a compelling record either. Its ambivalence is most excusable in relation to the prospect of a unified Indochina under Hanoi's direction. It remains to consider, however, whether expansionism originating from Hanoi would not present an Indonesia-centered grouping and, by extension, Australia, with a more manageable and thus bracing threat or rival than could be a much too overwhelming China. Internal pressures and counterpressures within the United States have impeded clinically detached policies in the Middle East and Africa no less than in Asia. This helps explain a long-standing incapacity of American foreign policy to decide between Israel and the Arab states, much as a choice might be preferable to an unevenly implemented "evenhandedness." The related question of Iran has remained in the background

from which it might be propelled not only by continuing Soviet penetration into the Persian Gulf–Indian Ocean area but also, possibly,
by Pakistan's concurrent reorientation toward Western Asia in a recoil from the cost of a definitive settlement with India. A refusal to
choose between Iran and Saudi Arabia (or Iraq), if rivalry in the
area turns into overt conflict, would but reproduce and generalize the
Middle Eastern impasse. More critical still might in the longer run be
the inter-regional rapport between an expanding Israel and South Africa. Seeds of conflict between the two may be sown by Israel's policy of courting Black Africans all the way down to South Africa, in
order to counteract the Arabs' own "southern strategy" in Moslem Africa and, incidentally, to obscure the conspicuous parallels between
the supremacist tendencies and predicaments of both "white" wing
powers. The administration has been, to say the least, ambivalent
about, it not hostile to, a responsible strategic role for South Africa in
her maritime orbit, on the grounds of racial policy; the American reserve has only exceeded that cultivated toward Japan's role in regional security, intertwined with Japan's economic policies.

Administration attitudes toward Israel, South Africa, and Japan,
have had too delicate domestic ramifications in the United States to
be either easily reversible or their official rationales wholly convincing.
American ambivalence has had its price in diminished loyalties,
while American ambiguity enhanced the compensatory rebelliousness
of Egypt's post-Nasser regime, in search of a target—Israel if possible,
first the Soviet Union, and then again the U.S. if necessary. Despite
the obvious desire and need of an internally fragile post-Nasser regime to move out of exclusive dependence on the Soviet Union, it was
(long) as unable to move closer to the U.S. as the latter was unwilling either to pressure or promote Israel. In the process, inability (to
seek rapprochement with the U.S.) was represented as unwillingness
by the Egyptians, while the American side inclined to represent its
unwillingness (to exert pressure on Israel) as innate inability. Finally,
the policy of invidious goal-attribution without adequate means-
equalization employed toward India and Pakistan, while comprehen-
sible on all kinds of grounds, has not displayed any keen sensitivity
to India's alternative of either surviving as an expanding regional
great power or disintegrating into a congeries of sub-national parti-
cles in fact or form. Nor has the American policy seemed any more
sensitively attuned to the conditions in which India might be propelled, however unwillingly, into a productive regional role temporarily substituting for Japan's role and eventually aiding in circum-
scribing that role.

If the policy toward India in any degree reflected a doctrinal distaste for military aggression by lesser powers, the vulnerability of an internationally humiliated India to internal sectional and communal strife antecedent to disintegration illustrates well the risks of undifferentiated restraint on the use of interstate force in the third world. The problem concerns the third and last level of analysis and policy, interaction of all third-world states with the greater industrial powers. On that level it is questionable coordination to promote economic development with one hand, that directing "programs," while ignoring the potentially positive effect of conflict on economic development and promoting a depression of conflict to the domestic political scene with the other hand, that guiding diplomatic strategies insensitive to evolutionary "process." Nor is it any more adequate to proceed as if affirmation and action in favor of peaceable cooperation among third-world less-developed countries is the logical counterpart of, or the best practical shortcut to, consolidating a concert on the great-power level. It will not do, on moral grounds, to try vetoing conflicts among less-developed countries and thus, if the hypothesis has any validity, help depress conflict inward, because such conflicts risk provoking competitive interventions by great powers which generate internal conflict in the United States if not elsewhere. Nor will it do on moral or political grounds to invite the lesser powers to have a stake in the international system as long as they are debarred from the most efficacious motor force behind creating their part of it for and among themselves.

If the perspective of the industrial countries is at once nuclear and social, the orientation of the pre-industrial ones is still either sub-conventional or, increasingly perhaps, conventional in both war and politics while still keyed to the constitution of "states" as a precondition to the development of integrated and welfare-oriented "societies." As long as the gap or distance continues undiminished, the relation of the industrial and pre-industrial countries cannot go far beyond mutually exploitative interdependence and a reciprocally unhealthy interpenetration, as the third world re-exports the riotous-revolutionary modes back into the industrial world, while the latter offers its unassimilable norms and material temptations to the "poor" countries and its nuclear model to the embattled "rich" third-world countries inhibited in their conventional self-assertion. Moreover, possible nuclear infusions merely dramatize the dangers implicit, as a counterpart to distortions inherent in sweeping restraints, in undiscriminating material-military reinforcement of third-world countries. Even conventional military inputs cannot but derange the "normal" or "optimum" phasing of political development and system formation when, exceeding the requirements of effective enactment of conflicts and their conclusive outcomes, they quantitatively and qualitatively surpass the third-world country's absorptive capacity for up-to-date conflict modes within a technologically and socially less-evolved overall internal environment. To "elevate" the modes and methods of technologically enacting conflict above the natural level of the third world countries may be more significantly damaging to world stability than any hypothetical threat of intervention or counter-intervention producing the "escalation" of conflicts to the great-power level.

In the face of such fundamental problems, the Nixon Administration has chosen so far to follow the historically charted classic road of summitry (as a complement, perhaps, to its restoration-type domestic policies?). Such grand diplomacy, involving the great powers, can be viewed as creating the necessary preconditions for eventually "managing" (with the aid of a proper mix of restraint and reinforcement as well as self-restraint) the process of third-world development within the margin of choice engendered by partial accommodation among the great. That accommodation would extend to the third world the diplomatic flexibility achieved in the 1960s in Europe largely by Gaullist diplomacy and do so, again, by way of a diplomatic detente with China as a propellent toward a privileged entente or cooperation with the Soviet Union—the concern with China *per se* being merely enhanced relative to France's by the global scope of American diplomacy. Summitry could, however, degenerate into a substantively meaningless diplomatic "program" in and for itself, responding mainly to domestic and economic interests of the parties, and substituting for failures to manage effectively the larger process via such specific problems as the conflicts underway in the Middle East and South and Southeast Asia. A closely related failing would be to suppose that the short- (or first-) term predisposition of the Nixon Administration policy or strategy (as distinct from the Nixon Doctrine) to bracket the third world (outside Vietnam) out of the compass of prime concern could be indefinitely continued. It is not necessary to invoke widespread third-world "chaos" as the unacceptable price of such neglect; it may be neither unacceptable in itself nor assuredly forthcoming. Within the terms of the great-power level of the Nixon Administration doctrine *and* strategy itself, the proclivity to treat the third world arena as separable from the great-power arena or as the object of a merely negative concern (stressing non-entanglement of any one great power, and notably the U.S., in third-world conflicts and the "decoupling" of these from great-power relations) raises the question as to what political forces and issues would feed the mills and constitute the stakes of the diplomatic maneuvers and the diplomatic equilibrium between the two superpowers or, a fortiori, among the three "world powers." It is unlikely that the nuclear equations and an intra-European equilibrium would permanently suffice even between the U.S. and the Soviet Union (let alone between them and China) following the disappearance of the Vietnamese focus of great-power strategies—or, even if they sufficed, that they could long be shielded from the dangers of overconcentration (and overburdening) if isolated for great-power concern. It is no less unlikely that a merely negative or abstract concern to "decouple" or moderate third-world conflicts, without reference to the concrete implications of individual conflicts for regional balances of power (or systems) and middle-power aims and attitudes, would suffice to foster a sense of a "negative community of interests" on the nuclear model among the greater states sufficiently strong to undergird a *modus vivendi* in relation to the third world or more generally.

Consequently, the "logical implications" of the Nixon Doctrine, as discussed in this essay, even if going well beyond presently pursued minimalist administration strategy toward the third world, are only a short-term (and possibly but one-term) anticipation—just as the pious affirmations in the doctrine's official statements, which supply the text for such exegesis, are but short-term deferrals of concern with ways and means. That which is so far legitimately seen as only implied, can well become readily visible as a compelling practical problem in the not too remote future, unless super- or great-power summitry is really to subside into a self-sufficient program rather than being organically linked to a process, or degenerate into a public circus rather than debouching onto a modicum of "concert" as properly understood by foreign-policy initiates. Following the provisional appeasement of the nuclear arms-race's potential to engender either valid anxiety or theatrical *coups* and the demonstration of the European states' capacity to withstand superpower patronage, the third world may emerge as the key residual raw-material for crystallizing rudimentary elements of such concert. To speak of "concert" and "co-responsibility" is again a but provisional overstatement if one admits that, to be consolidated, a *modus vivendi* must gain a more stable basis in a shared *modus operandi* in fairly concrete circumstances over fairly specific stakes. Hence the need to integrate a bothersome but indispensable third world into a "new" American global policy before the void created by the "liquidation" of the Vietnam war has evolved into a dangerous vacuum of purpose underneath the diplomatic conference tables of the great.

More concrete and openly avowed programs than great-power summitry, subsumable under the doctrine, have comprised mainly the re-examination and revision of techniques and organizational frameworks for assistance to economic development. Their importance lies in the bearing of economic development on the generation and stakes of conflict, as well as on the compensation which economic assistance may represent for any outside limitation on the generation and enactment of conflict. A bias in favor of a multilateral approach to economic assistance, at least in principle, has tentatively extended to the economic field the likewise philosophical bias in favor of cooperation as against confrontation in the politico-military field. But the Executive's difficulty in securing Congressional backing for any major aid program and its own ambiguous approach to the trade side of economic promotion of both the actually developing and the poorest third world countries, as evidenced in the Third UNCTAD Conference in Santiago de Chile, have either thwarted or belied the administration's programmatic assertions.[5] The gap between theory and practice in this area may reflect the not atypical economic difficulties, and consequently self-regarding militancy or selfishness, of an imperial power in decline relative to former dependents or inferiors. In any event, the U.S. has been for at least the moment unable and unwilling to support economic development of third-world countries by either massive multilateral aid or multilaterally preferential trade; to more than theoretically opt for economic regionalism against a security-oriented one and more than tentatively favor bilateral vs. regional security and economic arrangements between third-world countries in some or most instances. This being so, the U.S. is all the less in a position to assert normative political principles or implement prudential policies which may, on the basis of historical experience and perhaps also common sense, inhibit the spontaneous self-assertion of native forces and relatively autonomous processes toward effective statehood and system in the third world.

Imperial order is systematically managed, and international systems evolve. The in-between of system evolution for the third world, managed in the sense only of being circumscribed and wherever possible promoted with the limited means and within the fluctuating limits implicit in a severally constrained cooperation among great powers, may yet be within the practical reach of an American foreign policy. It has been so far only implied in the Nixon Doctrine and has not been coherently pursued by the Nixon Administration.

[5] See chapter 8 of this volume, "Economic Policy and Development," by Benjamin Rowland.

It has been the object of this essay to place the Nixon Doctrine in the perspective of both different time dimensions and differently delimited structures. This conception of one's task corresponds to the basic object of the first Nixon Administration: to outline an outlook on world affairs; to set in train the fundamental preconditions of a "new" policy, notably with respect to the communist great powers; to appease if not resolve critical problems and conflicts in Asia and the Middle East; and to prepare and propose programs such as those for economic-development and military aid that would constitute usable instruments of a positive if prosaic policy. The undergirding hope and expectation has been that a two-term tenure would provide a chance, and the reconstructed two-power relationship with the Soviet Union the possibility, for producing material evidence of the doctrine's practical viability, not least in the third world.

In the circumstances, it would have been premature and even preposterous to attempt a definitive appraisal of results and achievements on the basis of a detailed examination of the not too-many salient events and incidents in the third world over the past four years. On the other hand, it has been not too adventurous to indicate briefly some of the critical points of intersection between the doctrine (and related policies) and a more elaborate framework of analysis. Such efforts are of more than momentary interest, insofar as the Nixon Doctrine as a precipitate of past administrations' policies or policy preferences—to be distinguished from ways in which the latter were actually proclaimed, normatively extrapolated, or exacerbated by circumstances—is likely to survive in essential points the Nixon Administration, if under a different name, as long as the basic givens which shaped it, and which themselves are provisional culminations of long-term developments rather than haphazard contingencies, remain what they are.

Such a view is too tame to satisfy those who prefer to consider the Nixon Doctrine as a temporary distraction placed in the path of a truly new long-range policy by political reaction itself subservient to the compulsions of an obsolete economic system. A basically new policy, one gathers, would abandon traditional interests for a harmony uniting a selfless, rejuvenated America with the third world's teeming millions, no later than some time between the American bicentennial and the second A.D. millennium. While favorable to all kinds of participation, such a policy would in practice mean definitively renouncing any remaining prospect for population growth-control as the first order of business of an updated concert among the trustees of mankind's long-term interests. Yet a reorientation of controls imposable by the industrial powers as the condition of any further aid or concern would profitably replace the so far prevalent obsessive concern with arms-control and conflict-limitation—cultivated by chancelleries groping for a least controversial common denominator among contentious nuclear powers and by individuals torn between diffuse anxieties and the desire to do some concrete good. Unless an early shift in the main thrust of controls occurs, however, any present savings in confined or repressed inter- or intra-state conflict in the third world (or in reduced arms expenditures) will in time pay the dividend of racially tainted hostility between the still-evolving developed and the proliferating but stagnant or retrogressive, unemployed and unemployable, parts of mankind.

These visions may represent too great a concession to a currently fashionable scare. They overlay, as a futuristic possibility, the alternatives for U.S. foreign policy rooted in the experiences of the past. One such alternative points to the consummation, after the present lull marked by the Nixon Doctrine, of America's imperial destiny Roman- and British-style; another to American foreign policy becoming the briefly sufficient cover-up for the most precipitate decay and decline on record after little more than two decades of American self-confidence as political nation and power. Realism can merge with resignation, however, to produce yet another and at once melancholy and reassuring possibility. In something like the Nixon Doctrine, the possibilities and the innermost capacities of the American people, smaller than some might have hoped, and the necessities of the American state, greater than others have since presumed to assert, may well have achieved an equilibrium which is more than a resting place for one administration.

Library of Congress Cataloging in Publication Data

Main entry under title.

Retreat from empire?

(America and the world, v. 2)
1. United States—Foreign relations—1969–   —
Addresses, essays, lectures.   I.   Osgood, Robert
Endicott.   II.   Series: America and the world
(Baltimore) v. 2.
E855.R47   1973   327.73   72-12359
ISBN 0-8018-1493-6
ISBN 0-8018-1499-5   (pbk)

new role of the president as the primary
maker of foreign policy and the decline
of congressional power.

Herbert S. Dinerstein turns to a consideration of the Soviet Union and
suggests that a re-evaluation of fundamental assumptions of Soviet foreign
policy is likely in the near future.
Laurence W. Martin looks at the specific
implications of military parity acknowledged in the recently concluded arms
limitation agreements. *Robert E. Osgood*
and *David P. Calleo,* respectively, ana-
lyze U.S. relations with Japan and
Europe. Professor Osgood is primarily
concerned with the political configurations now emerging; Professor Calleo
concentrates on evolving and changing
economic realities.

Benjamin M. Rowland considers problems of economic development and U.S.
policy toward the third world, concentrating on the case of Latin America.
George Liska examines the diminished
status of the third world in U.S. policy
calculations and speculates on the growth
of new regional orders among developing nations—an evolution he sees as a
major, perhaps most important, implication of the Nixon Doctrine.